Programs for the Gifted in Regular Classrooms

Critical Issues in

Gifted
Education

Programs for the Gifted
in Regular Classrooms

Edited by

C. June Maker

Assistant Editor

Diane Orzechowski-Harland

VOLUME III

Printed in the United States of America

Library of Congress Cataloging-in-Publication Data

Programs for the gifted in regular classrooms / editor, C. June Maker
  ; assistant editor, Diane Devi Orzechowski.
    p.   cm. — (Critical issues in gifted education ; v. 3)
  Includes bibliographical references.
  ISBN 0-89079-549-5
  1. Gifted children—Education—United States. I. Maker, C. June.
II. Orzechowski, Diane Devi. III. Series.
LC3993.9.P76 1992
370.95′3′0973—dc20   92-39
                                                  CIP

8700 Shoal Creek Boulevard
Austin, Texas 78758

1 2 3 4 5 6 7 8 9 10   97 96 95 94 93

To my family

Arnold Shartzer

Bernice Shartzer

Bonnie (Shartzer) Embrey

with love

CONTENTS

PREFACE

This book is the third volume in a series entitled *Critical Issues in Education of the Gifted.* The series was conceived and designed as an alternative to establishing a new journal because a book series could provide a forum for the consideration of issues in greater depth than could a journal.

The purpose of the series is to examine critically certain timely and controversial issues in the field of education of the gifted. This undertaking has as its goals the following:

- To rethink old issues
- To challenge the status quo
- To present conflicting opinions
- To generate a dialogue in print
- To analyze trends and directions
- To critique theory, practice, and research
- To provide not only a summary, but a true synthesis and transformation of ideas
- To develop awareness and understanding of new issues and new trends
- To provide new answers to old questions
- To ask new questions

The issues examined are related to all aspects of education of the gifted, and include, but are not limited to, program development, curricula, teaching strategies, the nature of giftedness and talent, staff selection and training, sociological perspectives, psychological development, counseling approaches, parent education, research, affective needs, and various subgroups of gifted or talented children.

In each volume, the central issue is examined from a multidisciplinary, multi-faceted point of view in an attempt to develop a comprehensive understanding of the various questions involved. Theories relating to the central issue, the research and evaluation data, and practical applications/educational implications are examined in each volume. The underlying philosophy is that comprehensive understanding requires that answers be given based on past experience and empirical data, but that unanswered questions and new perspectives accompany these answers.

Contributing authors are selected who represent a variety of disciplines and a variety of points of view, including theoreticians, researchers, and practitioners.

Most volumes in the series are designed by the series editor, with assistance in acquiring, reviewing, and editing from an advanced doctoral student. In some cases, a guest editor is responsible for these tasks.

The task of the editor is to reflect upon the different perspectives, identify areas of agreement among the authors, and call attention to other points of view not included in the articles. Finally, the editor's responsibility is to provide a synthesis of various perspectives and suggest possible new directions.

ACKNOWLEDGMENTS

To say "thank you" to all who have helped make this book possible is impossible! I will not attempt to do so, but I do wish to acknowledge the help of a few key people.

I wish to thank all of the contributors to this volume for their persistence, patience, and forgiveness. The birth of this book was much more time-consuming and difficult than any of us imagined at the beginning.

Mary Kord, my secretary and friend, has typed correspondence, kept mailing lists current, and accomplished miracles on the word processor. Without her help, I would not be able to produce manuscripts.

To Jim Gilmer and Trisha Fox-Moore, I am grateful for helping me grow in the faith, forgiveness, and peace that enabled me to let go of my problems and think clearly again.

Tomas Harland was a friend throughout the process, listening to my problems, offering wise suggestions, and, most of all, believing in me.

Chris McLean brought the sunshine into my cloudy skies, and encouraged me to finish the project.

Finally, and most importantly, Diane Orzechowski-Harland, my assistant editor, has been my friend and helper throughout the process. I appreciated her willingness to be a "gofer," her development of superior editing skills, her intelligence, her tenacity, her support, and her patience. Most of all, though, I thank Diane for her forgiveness, love, and friendship.

PURPOSE AND ORGANIZATION OF THE VOLUME

PURPOSE

The purpose of this volume is to examine critical issues related to the education of gifted students in regular classroom settings. Both theoretical and practical concerns are addressed, and solutions suggested. These concerns include those in schools in which other program models for serving gifted students already exist, as well as concerns of those whose primary (or only) service delivery model is the regular classroom.

STRUCTURE

The volume is separated into six parts. The first addresses the purpose(s) for providing services to accommodate the needs of gifted students in regular classrooms. The second part, directed toward program coordinators and administrators, is designed to address schoolwide management concerns. Next, ways to differentiate the curriculum are presented and discussed. A fourth part includes issues and solutions related to classroom management. Authors in Part V address issues related to the provision of out-of-school experiences that extend the learning of gifted students beyond the classroom and regular curriculum. Following is an outline of the organization of the book and the contributors:

I. Purpose
   A. Lead article (''general'' educator)
   B. Critique (educator of gifted students)

II. Schoolwide Management and Programs
   A. Teacher Assistance Teams
      1. Lead article (model developer)
      2. Critique (educator of the gifted)
   B. Advocate Liaison Program
      1. Lead article (model developer)
      2. Critique (educator of the gifted or regular school administrator)
   C. Demonstration Teaching
      1. Lead article (model developer)
      2. Critique (educator of the gifted or regular school administrator)

III. Curriculum Differentiation
   A. Content
      1. Lead article (educator of the gifted)
      2. Critique (educator of the gifted)
   B. Process
      1. Lead article (educator of the gifted)
      2. Critique (educator of the gifted)
   C. Products
      1. Lead article (educator of the gifted)
      2. Critique (educator of the gifted)
   D. Learning Environment
      1. Lead article (educator of the gifted)
      2. Critique (educator of the gifted)

IV. Classroom Management Systems and Techniques
   A. General Management Techniques
      1. Lead article (expert in classroom management and/or regular classroom teacher)
      2. Critique (expert in education of the gifted and/or regular classroom teacher)
   B. Individualization
      1. Lead article (expert in individualizing instruction and/or regular classroom teacher)
      2. Critique (expert in education of the gifted and/or regular classroom teacher)
   C. Learning Centers
      1. Lead article (expert in use of learning centers and/or regular classroom teacher)
      2. Critique (expert in education of the gifted and/or regular classroom teacher)

V. Programs and Models for Extending Learning Beyond the Classroom
   A. Mentorships
      1. Lead article (expert in education of the gifted and/or expert–practitioner in mentorship program)

    2. Critique (expert in education of the gifted and/or counselor)
  B. Internships
    1. Lead article (expert in education of the gifted and/or expert–practitioner in internship program)
    2. Critique (expert in education of the gifted and/or regular classroom teacher)
  C. Independent Study
    1. Lead article (expert in education of the gifted and/or expert–practitioner in program using independent study)
    2. Critique (expert in education of the gifted and/or regular classroom teacher)

VI. Gifted Students in the Regular Classroom: What Practices Are Defensible and Feasible? (summary and conclusion by the editor)

KEY AND GUIDING QUESTIONS

The key questions and guiding questions the authors in each section were asked to address are listed below. These questions were provided to give direction to authors and an overview of the general structure of the volume.

  I. Purpose

  Key Question
  Why should we educate gifted students in the regular classroom?

  Guiding Questions
  What are the advantages and disadvantages for the gifted student, other students, the teacher, and the on-site administrator?

  What cognitive and affective needs do gifted students have in a regular classroom situation?

  How are these needs met in the regular classroom setting?

  How might education of gifted students in a regular classroom situation impact the education of other students?

  How does removing gifted students from the regular classroom impact the education of other students?

  II. Schoolwide Management and Programs

  Key Question
  What problems and solutions do program developers and administrators have in their attempt to accommodate the needs of gifted students in regular classrooms?

Guiding Questions
A. What are teacher assistance teams (TATs)?

How can TATs be used to provide support services for gifted students?

What are the necessary elements of TATs?

What are some examples of successful uses of the TAT model?

What are the advantages and disadvantages of TATs?

B. What are advocate liaisons?

How can advocate liaisons be used to provide support services for gifted students?

What are the necessary elements of an advocate liaison model?

What are some examples of successful uses of the advocate liaison model?

What are the advantages and disadvantages of the advocate liaison model?

C. What is demonstration teaching?

How can demonstration teaching be used to support or provide services for gifted students?

What are the necessary elements of a demonstration teaching model?

What are some examples of successful uses of a demonstration teaching model?

What are the advantages and disadvantages of a demonstration teaching model?

III. Curriculum Differentiation

Key Questions
What techniques appropriate for gifted students can be used to benefit all children?

What techniques appropriate for gifted students should not be used with or would not be appropriate for all students?

Guiding Questions for Each Subsection
A. What is differentiated content for gifted learners?

How can/should the content taught in a regular class setting be differentiated to provide a more challenging and appropriate learning experience for gifted students?

    B. What are differentiated processes for gifted learners?

    How can/should the processes taught in a regular classroom setting be differentiated to provide a more challenging and appropriate learning experience for gifted students?

    C. What are differentiated products for gifted learners?

    How can/should the products developed by students in a regular classroom setting be differentiated to provide a more challenging and appropriate learning experience for gifted students?

    D. What is a differentiated learning environment for gifted learners?

    How can/should the environment of a regular classroom be differentiated to provide a more challenging and appropriate learning experience for gifted students?

IV. Classroom Management Systems and Techniques

Key Questions
How can regular classroom teachers manage their classrooms to enable them to meet the needs of children with a variety of talents and abilities when they have 25 to 30 children in their classes?

How should the success of these management techniques and procedures be determined?

Guiding Questions for Each Subsection
    A. What general management techniques can teachers use in a regular classroom situation to enable them to meet the needs of gifted students in their classrooms?

    What are some examples of successful use of general management techniques?

    B. What techniques can teachers employ to enable them to individualize the curriculum in ways that will benefit gifted students?

    What are some examples of individualized curricula and/or classrooms that have been successful in meeting the needs of gifted students?

    C. How can teachers develop learning centers for use in a regular classroom setting that are related to the curriculum and will be challenging and appropriate for gifted students?

    What are some examples of learning centers that have been used successfully with gifted students?

V. Programs and Models for Extending Learning Beyond the Classroom

Key Questions
What kinds of programs can be used to extend the learning of gifted students beyond the regular classroom setting?

What caveats can be given to those who attempt to develop these programs?

Guiding Questions for Each Subsection
A. What are mentorships?

How can mentorships be used to extend the learning of gifted students?

What are the necessary elements of a mentorship program?

What are some examples of successful mentorship programs?

B. What are internships?

How can internships be used to extend the learning of gifted students?

What are the necessary elements of an internship program?

What are some examples of successful internship programs?

C. What is independent study?

How can independent study be used to extend the learning of gifted students?

What are the necessary elements of an independent study program?

How much teacher involvement and monitoring is necessary?

VI. Volume Conclusion

Key Question
How can the necessary elements of a defensible program be addressed by and incorporated into a regular classroom delivery system?

Other Possible Questions to Consider
How can regular classroom teachers challenge gifted students appropriately but also be fair to a classroom of children with a wide range of abilities?

How can gifted students be motivated to go beyond what other students are expected to do in a regular classroom situation?

How can administrators be certain that regular classroom teachers are meeting the needs of gifted students?

What training does the regular classroom teacher need to meet the needs of gifted students?

What support services could be made available to assist the regular classroom teacher in meeting the needs of gifted students?

PART I

PURPOSE

Two authors, with divergent perspectives and experiential bases, were asked to respond to one key question: Why should we educate gifted children in the regular classroom? Thomas R. McDaniel provided his answer based on his perspective as a "regular" educator, now serving as dean of a college of education. James J. Gallagher responded to McDaniel based on his perspective as a "special" educator at many levels of education, and now a psychologist, researcher, and policy analyst. Gallagher, in addition, cannot avoid responding from his point of view as a parent of gifted children. Both authors also were asked to consider a series of guiding questions as they made their responses. A complete list of these questions can be found in the introduction to the volume, but two examples follow: "What are the advantages and disadvantages [of educating gifted children in the regular classroom] for the gifted student, other students, the teacher, and the on-site administrator?" "How does removing gifted students from the regular classroom impact the education of other students?"

As McDaniel states in Chapter 1, he argues for his position ("Gifted students should, to the maximum degree possible, be taught in the regular classroom") at the philosophical level, rather than addressing some of the practical concerns that would have been addressed had he responded to the guiding questions posed. Gallagher, in his response, reminds readers that, although a discussion in a volume such as this can remain at the philosophical level, teachers and administrators cannot afford to do so. They *must* consider the practical realities of the regular classroom environment in making decisions about the key question posed in this section. The essential difference I see between the two chapters is that, in response to my question "Why should we educate gifted children in the regular classroom?" McDaniel focuses on "should we?" whereas Gallagher focuses on "can we?"

1

McDaniel presents a cogent and important discussion of a philosophical issue that every educator, and especially those involved in education of the gifted, should consider carefully and thoroughly: "How can we achieve both excellence and equity in the public school?" The dynamic tension between the two relatively equal values of "excellence" and "equity" has influenced education in this country throughout history. As might be imagined and as McDaniel states, the question has never been answered fully. I believe it never will! McDaniel discusses the ideas and perspectives of influential educators and political leaders, as well as important events, throughout major periods of this country's history.

Education of the gifted is especially vulnerable to the outcomes (both clear and ambivalent) of the excellence–equity debate. The different provisions made to assist gifted people in achieving the highest levels of excellence of which they are capable, often are viewed as being inequitable because these provisions are not made for everyone (even though everyone may not need, or even desire, such services).

An important part of McDaniel's chapter is the "Lessons of the Past for the Future"; here he moves from reporting and summarizing to presenting his own views. While I am identifying my personal viewpoint, I might as well make clear my personal reactions to these ideas. I do not disagree strongly with the three major points he makes: (a) In a democratic society education itself should be democratic; (b) in the United States education must respond to the political and economic needs of the nation; and (c) public education ultimately is responsible for meeting the needs of all students in our society. I do, however, disagree with some of the ways McDaniel supports and applies these principles.

I believe that McDaniel and the readers of this book would profit from an examination of the words "isolate" and "separate," two words that McDaniel uses in his justification/explanation of the need to have a "democratic" educational system. McDaniel states, "When we isolate gifted and talented children from the mainstream—by separate schools, tracks, courses, grouping—we run the risk of contributing to an elitism that does not reflect a true democracy" (p. 15). I would like to make three major points regarding this statement. First, one cannot make the assumption that all special provisions that McDaniel lists (e.g., special schools, tracks, courses, grouping) contribute to the "isolation" of gifted students, or that they result in an attitude of elitism among gifted students. Second, one cannot assume that keeping gifted students in the regular classroom all the time does not contribute to their "isolation."

I do not disagree that some programs can and do contribute to isolation and to the development of elitist attitudes. For instance, tracking was used in the past as a way to provide for differing needs of students. Unfortunately, students were placed in these "tracks" based on limited, incomplete, or inappropriate information; placements were not reevaluated or reassessed frequently; minorities and students from poor families constituted a major portion of the lower tracks, whereas students from higher socioeconomic status and from white families constituted a major portion of the higher tracks; and no differentiation was made for abilities in different subjects (e.g., a student could not be in a high track in social studies and a low track in math, but was in a high or low track in everything). Tracking, as thus used, did contribute to separation, isolation, and elitism. In addition, it contributed to frustration, since very few people have equally high or low abilities in all areas of intelligence. Some special class arrangements also contribute to such attitudes, especially if administrators respond to pressure from "high-status" families to place their children in special classes even when these children do not qualify for the program.

However, not all special arrangements or groupings have these negative results. When differing abilities are recognized, for example, and students are labeled "gifted in math," "gifted in languages," and "gifted in drama," rather than some of these students being placed into a single group of "the gifted," the perceptions of and about these students are different. Grouping arrangements are much more similar to the natural groupings in our society if students are given opportunities to interact with those who have similar interests and abilities for some portion of their school days. We know from both experience and research that all individuals, including gifted children, gravitate toward those of similar abilities and interests. Gifted children, for instance, tend to develop friendships and close ties with older children, other gifted children, and adults rather than with their age-mates. These associations seem to result from similarities in interests and developmental levels.

Should gifted students be forced to limit their daily interactions to those involving a majority of individuals who cannot understand and/or are uninterested in what they are saying, with *no* opportunity to interact with a small group of students with similar interests or abilities because we are afraid they will develop elitist attitudes? Gallagher calls attention to the domains of general education in which abilities, talents, and interests form the basis for grouping arrangements, and asks why the intellectual domain should be treated differently from the others (e.g., music, athletics, drama).

The third point I would like to make about McDaniel's statement ("When we isolate gifted and talented children from the mainstream—by separate schools, tracks, courses, grouping—we run the risk of contributing to an elitism that does not reflect a true democracy") is that both "isolation" and "elitism" can result from *not* having special grouping arrangements. Many individuals become isolated and feel estranged from their peer groups and from society for a variety of reasons, which could include either that they have been separated or that they have been kept together with the group! In other words, gifted students can become isolated from their age-mates as a result of their participation in a special program or they can become isolated from their age-mates as a result of not participating in such a program. Gifted students, and adults as well, often try and fail on a daily basis to make themselves heard and understood by the general population. Another interesting observation made by teachers and parents is that some gifted students who remain in regular classroom settings develop elitist attitudes because they never encounter anyone who knows more or learns faster than they do. Their initial encounters with other gifted students often result in lowered self-concepts as these students realize they are not "the best" in everything. After a while, however, this initial devastating realization changes to a more realistic perception of themselves as being individuals with differing patterns of strengths and weaknesses, and a more realistic perception of others as well.

I believe parents, teachers, and administrators are more influential in the development of isolation and elitism in students than are the grouping arrangements themselves. Many authors in this volume have offered positive suggestions for educators, so I will not repeat them. I will simply encourage parents and educators both to use the label "gifted in _____" rather than "gifted" to refer to students and to their own children who have special abilities and talents. Completely different attitudes are implied and fostered by the use of these similar labels.

In general, the arguments presented in Chapter 1 seem to imply that our past failure to provide excellence for all students (including the gifted) is a clear indication that we will not be able to do so in the future unless we focus on the regular classroom as the major service delivery system. An interesting observation I cannot avoid noting is that Gallagher, in Chapter 2, uses a similar argument to support a different point of view. Gallagher asks, "Can the over 1 million elementary school teachers, given the resources and their environmental setting, provide an exciting and stimulating environment for gifted students who are often three, four, or five grades beyond their age-mates? If they can do it, why have they not been doing it . . . ?" (p. 20). He continues the discussion by pointing to our past failures as one of the reasons why special grouping arrangements and provisions became necessary to meet the needs of gifted and talented students. Gallagher agrees with McDaniel when he states that we need to learn from the past to improve the future, but wonders if we can agree on what the past lessons are.

McDaniel concludes his chapter by returning to the basic thesis of his chapter: Gifted students should, to the maximum degree possible, be taught in the regular classroom. He does not say, however, what "to the maximum degree possible" means in actual practice, but leaves that monumental task to Gallagher and the authors who follow. I suspect that Gallagher and McDaniel agree that more needs to be done to meet the needs of the gifted in the regular classroom than currently is being done. They would, perhaps, disagree on what is the maximum degree possible in the regular classroom.

Other authors in this book seem to agree that gifted students should have their needs met in the regular classroom to the maximum degree possible, and I suspect they also would disagree on what is this maximum degree. McDaniel is correct in stating that those authors whose chapters follow his have addressed many practical concerns related to his major thesis. The overwhelming consensus, however, seems to be that the regular classroom is an important setting in which to meet the needs of gifted students, but that it should not, cannot, and must not be the *only* setting in which appropriate services are provided. I invite you to ponder the questions raised by the two excellent chapters in this section, and to keep in mind the issues they raise as you explore the practical ideas and program approaches presented by a wide variety of authors.

I would like to end this discussion with a thought that seems impossible to dislodge from my mind. As I read both chapters, and considered what lessons the past might have for now and the future, I kept returning to the major concern expressed by critics of programs for the gifted: elitism. Educators, politicians, parents, and "the public" seem to be opposed to the development of an "intellectual elite" that, they fear, will rise to power because its members have received special benefits in the form of educational provisions that are exciting, motivating, and at an appropriately challenging intellectual level. My question for you to consider is this: *To what extent has our resistance to the development of an "aristocracy of talents and virtues" "without regard to wealth, birth, or other accidental conditions," as Thomas Jefferson advocated, been a major factor in our democracy being controlled by another, potentially more dangerous elite: the rich and powerful?* I do not know the answer to this or the following question: What percentage of our former or current political leaders attended public elementary or secondary schools, colleges, or universities; and what percentage attended private schools, colleges, and universities, where they were given special educational advantages simply because their families could afford to pay for them? How many other leaders had these same advantages because of status, friendships, and other factors we group under the heading of ''power''?

Education of the Gifted and the Excellence–Equity Debate: Lessons from History

Thomas R. McDaniel

We sail a changeful sea through halcyon days and storm. Our stability is but balance . . . (Robert Bridges, 1930, p.1)

Gifted students should, to the maximum degree possible, be taught in the regular classroom. As a "regular" educator interested in the history and philosophy of the public school, I will explain and defend this position as a guiding principle for educational policy in our time. I hope to present a coherent and compelling argument for my philosophical position, rather than deal with many of the practical concerns related to the general topic of this volume. I leave it to Gallagher and other contributors both to identify the omissions and failures of logic herein and to provide specificity and detail to this critical issue in the education of gifted students.

Why should we educate gifted students in the regular classroom? Historical, philosophical, social, psychological, and educational bases provide the reasons. These bases, of course, are interrelated in complex and intricate ways. Many major contributors to U.S. educational philosophy and policy have dealt with the never fully answered question: How can we achieve both excellence and equity in the public school? In some way or another, each of these major educators has dealt explicitly or implicitly with the larger question of excellence and equity and the more specific question of the relationship of the public school to gifted students. Ours is not the first generation to wrestle with questions of educational purpose and the problems of mainstreaming the gifted.

A final prefatory note: The reader will have observed my qualifier "to the maximum degree possible," and I offer no apology for that. Believing that the regular classroom should provide for all the educational needs of the gifted is as foolish as believing it should provide for none. I urge policymakers and curriculum designers to advance the notion that education of gifted students should become increasingly the province of the regular classroom.

FROM JEFFERSON TO MANN

In U.S. education, the public school has been the handmaiden of democracy, a way of life (as well as a way of governing) that depends upon an educated citizenry and a commitment to recognizing the equality of all men—and women. This philosophy does not imply that all people have equal gifts, but it does suggest that a democratic society requires a shared commitment to equality of opportunity, at least, and to equality of dignity in the community of man.

Thomas Jefferson argued for a public school in Virginia. In his 1779 Bill for the More General Diffusion of Knowledge, he proposed universal education in his state. In this proposal—too radical to succeed in his time—he called for 3 years of free education for free children, boys and girls, to impart basic skills and enough knowledge of history to ward off tyrants and other enemies of democracy. Of special interest to this discussion is his conviction that leaders in a democracy must be the most gifted individuals in a community and that they exist in all socioeconomic levels.

Jefferson espoused some elitist and aristocratic ideas, but he advocated a public school system that would identify and educate an "aristocracy of talents and virtues" (Lee, 1961, p. 7). In his 1779 bill, he argued that

> those persons who nature endowed with genius and virtue should be rendered by liberal education worthy to receive and able to guard the sacred deposit of the rights and liberties of their fellow citizens, and that they should be called to that charge without regard to wealth, birth, or other accidental condition. (Lee, 1961, p. 84)

He would ask each elementary school to identify one gifted student—"twenty of the best geniuses will be raked from the rubbish annually" (Lee, 1961, p. 91), he said—to send on to the grammar schools at public expense. Each grammar school would then send, on full scholarship, 10 "of the best learning and most hopeful geniuses" (Lee, 1961, p. 92) to The College of William and Mary. The Jeffersonian ideal of a free public education system, both to strengthen the common education of all citizens and to identify and nurture the gifted, has influenced educational policy in the United States for over 200 years.

Horace Mann was successful in refining and extending the free public school concept in the more urban and homogeneous population of Massachusetts in the 1830s and 1840s. He argued that universal education would be the "great equalizer of the conditions of men—the balance wheel of the social machinery" (Cremin, 1957, p. 87). As Cremin (1957) noted, Mann's "effort was to fashion a new American character out of a maze of conflicting cultural conditions. And his tool was the common school" (p. 8). He fought against aristocracy, especially that found in European governments and educational institutions. In his 1848 annual report to the Massachusetts Board of Education, he said,

According to the European theory, men are divided into classes—some to toil and earn, others to seize and enjoy. According to the Massachusetts theory, all are to have an equal chance. . . . The latter tends to equality of condition; the former to the grossest inequalities. (Cremin, 1957, p. 84)

For both Jefferson and Mann, the essential purpose of public education was to promote democratic values in the new republic, to eliminate artificial aristocracies in society, and to build social harmony by way of a public school system. The gifted would rise to the top, and should be challenged to assume leadership roles in school and society, but the need for coherence, unity—*e pluribus unum*—took precedence over the needs of the individual.

EARLY 20TH CENTURY REFORMS

By the beginning of the 20th century, evidence was accumulating that the great changes in society brought on by industrialization, immigration, and urbanization were not being matched by the school system, which was, unfortunately, increasingly stagnant, rigid, and narrow. Progressive reformers, led by John Dewey, called for reforms that would make public schools more democratic and more scientific. Dewey's ideas are consistent with, and an extension of, Mann's. Cremin (1961) drew this comparison:

Like Mann, Dewey recognized that education is a matter of individual growth and development; but like Mann too, his emphasis was ever on the social, the common, the public aspects of experience. Ultimately Dewey believed that democracy would be achieved only as schooling was popularized in character as well as clientele. (p. 126)

Perhaps Dewey's most important idea was that a democratic society required a public school that is itself thoroughly and truly democratic (Dewey, 1916).

To make the public school more democratic, Dewey proposed that practical studies be viewed "as instrumentalities through which the school itself shall be made a genuine form of active community life, instead of a place set apart in which to learn lessons" (Dworkin, 1959, p. 39). He eschewed ability grouping as unnatural and artificial and complained that barriers between students ran against the spirit of the "embryonic community" that a school, at its best, should be. In his child-centered, experience-based, activity-oriented school, children would learn social responsibility and social competence by real-life problem solving in a heterogeneous classroom. He believed that every public school should have an intermingling of youth of different races, religions, cultures, *and* abilities to create a broad community to which each child must learn to adjust. In the adjusting and the interacting, intelligence is released, said Dewey, for intelligence is activated only in a social, problem-solving experience (Dewey, 1938, pp. 62–63).

The point we should consider in Dewey's progressive philosophy is his insistence that schools not merely preach democracy, but manifest it in form and substance. If gifted and talented children are separated from their classmates of lesser ability, he held, we run the risk of creating aristocratic stratification within the school community. Stratification, Dewey implied in many of his works, is inimical to democracy. As Perkinson (1976) concluded, Dewey was convinced that "democracy differs from all other forms of association because it is more ethical; it allows for the greatest amount of participation in determining the common good" (p. 202). If we accept any measure of Dewey's conception of the connection between a democratic school and a democratic society, we will be cautious about intraschool arrangements that take gifted students out of the "regular" classroom.

THE POST-SPUTNIK ERA

In the post-Sputnik era, an era much like our own, many educators called for major reforms in public education. The antiprogressive reactionaries of the 1940s and 1950s—Arthur Bestor, Mortimer Smith, Alfred Lynd, Hyman Rickover, and others—laid a groundwork of criticism of the egalitarian social philosophy of Dewey and his followers. When the Russians launched the first space satellite in 1957, Americans began looking in earnest for ways to make public schools more academic, more competitive, and more concerned with the identification and development of the gifted.

This was the age of curriculum reform. Jerome Bruner (1959), in his book *The Process of Education,* introduced, or at least popularized, the work of Piaget in this country. Study committees sprang up everywhere as college professors and school leaders worked out the new curricula in math, sciences, and social studies. The new curricula emphasized "discovery learning" and academic subject matter. The academically talented student became a new object of concern for policymakers.

James B. Conant was a policymaker extraordinaire. In *The American High School Today* (1959), he outlined a series of 21 recommendations to strengthen that unique U.S. invention, the "comprehensive high school." Philosophically a Jeffersonian—among his many books is *Thomas Jefferson and the Development of American Public Education* (1962)—Conant, a former Harvard president, argued always for academic excellence. He complained that "thousands of high schools do not even offer the kind of instruction which challenges the academically talented students" (1960, p. 58).

What Conant proposed, and many educators bought, was a reorganization of schools into large, consolidated, comprehensive high schools that would become, as he liked to say, "instruments of democracy." But, like Jefferson, he felt the tension between excellence and equity and tried to have both. On the side of equity—the democratic impulse in his philosophy—he proposed that elementary and secondary schools provide a general education as a preparation for citizenship. In addition, the consolidated high schools would have, under one roof, programs for all the children of a community. Homerooms should be organized as "significant social units in the school" to develop "an understanding between students of different levels of academic ability and vocational goals" (1959, p. 74). Furthermore, all students would take a course in social studies in the senior year in which they would be grouped heterogeneously. This course should develop "mutual respect and understanding between different types of students" (1959, p. 75).

On the side of excellence, Conant proposed subject-by-subject grouping according to ability, a minimum elective program for the academically talented, special arrangements for the highly gifted, an annual academic inventory of the gifted, and academic honors lists. He held rather traditional notions of curriculum and of the gifted, recommending the following programs for gifted high school students:

> Four years of mathematics, four years of one foreign language, three years of science, in addition to the required four years of English and three years of social studies; a total of eighteen courses with homework to be taken in four years. This program will require at least fifteen hours of homework each week. (1959, p. 57)

Conant's widely adopted recommendations put new emphasis on the gifted and tended to separate them from the regular classroom. The consolidated high school was large enough to provide a range of advanced courses suitable only for the academically talented. The school, he said, should do even more for the "highly gifted," those students of high ability who constitute on a national basis about 3% of the student population. He would have a tutor assigned to this group who would keep in close touch with these individual students enrolled in challenging courses, help them develop their special interests, and encourage them to enroll in advanced placement classes in the senior year.

Can the comprehensive high school provide equity and excellence? Conant frequently called this tension a "false antithesis"; yet he could find in his national search only eight schools that met his criteria for a good comprehensive high school, a school that would (a) provide a good general education for all the citizens of a democracy, (b) provide elective programs for the majority who want useful skills, and (c) educate the gifted. In *The American High School Today*, Conant argued against tracking the gifted, but for grouping them homogeneously subject by subject. His special tutors for the "highly gifted" were forerunners of resource teachers, guidance counselors for the gifted, and special teachers of the gifted—not in the high school alone, but more frequently now in elementary schools. Conant's real interest was in excellence and in the academically talented student who would, like Jefferson's geniuses "culled from the rubbish," go to prestigious colleges and ultimately help the United States regain its superior position in world affairs. His unanticipated legacy would usher the nation into a new wave of democratic reforms of educational policy and practice in the turbulent 1960s.

As educators in the post-Sputnik era scurried to prepare U.S. youth for the space race—to produce more scientists, engineers, leaders, thinkers—emphasis in program and policy shifted toward excellence. Special schools for the sciences and for the arts flourished, and public schools deemphasized vocational and general education in favor of more academic, specialized preparation in traditional subjects. Grouping and tracking became widely accepted practices, and the emergence of stronger research in psychological testing led to greater emphasis on (and acceptance of) individual differences in human intelligence and to the use of standardized tests of ability and achievement. The pioneering work of Binet, Simon, Terman, Guilford, Pegnato and Birch, and Getzels and Jackson laid a foundation for identifying and educating gifted and talented learners that was now supporting new programming for the gifted. Conant himself argued vigorously for the expanded use of aptitude tests (especially those prepared by the Educational Testing Service) in screening and placing students and identifying that most important national resource, the highly gifted child.

THE NEOPROGRESSIVES IN THE 1960s

The solutions and successes of one era became the problem for the next. A neglect, part real and part imagined, of the social goals of education combined with a social malaise to raise anew the question of educational purpose and practice in U.S. public schools. Urban blight, unrest among blacks, the emergence of a youth culture (or counterculture) on college campuses, and dissatisfaction with the Johnson administration's support of the Vietnam War combined to create major social problems in the mid-1960s. Riots in the cities and protests on campus led to criticism of a public school system that was viewed by many as part of the problem rather than part of the solution. Eloquent, and sometimes bombastic, books castigated the Conant conception of schools as sorting machines to identify and develop academically gifted students, separating them from mainstream into special courses and programs.

For example, in *Growing Up Absurd* (1960), Paul Goodman gave an early alarm that the large, bureaucratic, academically focused, homogeneously grouped public school was at risk. Here, said Goodman, the scholastically bright are bribed and forced to achieve, to succeed in the rat race and the space race, to become a super elite in a competitive society. This stratification and grouping replaces genuine community—in school and society—with an organized system that impedes human growth. About this system of schooling, Goodman said, "It is lacking in the opportunity to be useful. It thwarts aptitude and creates stupidity. It corrupts ingenuous patriotism. It corrupts the fine arts. It shackles science. . . . It has no community" (p. 12). This loss of community results in despair and cynicism for the bright and the not-so-bright alike who learn that in schools "life is inevitably routine, depersonalized, venally graded" (Goodman, 1960, p. 48).

In the excellence–equity debate, the "romantic critics" and "radical school reformers" of the 1960s came down on the side of equity. Attention shifted from the academically gifted to the socially deprived. A kind of child-centered neoprogressivism emerged in the open classroom movement as the whiz-kid era of Kennedy's New Frontier meritocracy gave way to the social activism and egalitarianism of Johnson's Great Society. The post-Sputnik drive for excellence produced scientists and engineers who would lead the United States, eventually, to victory in the race to put a man on the moon—but at a cost to community and democracy.

One can argue, also, that academic excellence in the 1960s was neglected, distorted, and misused. The political and economic needs of the nation seemed to run roughshod over the personal and developmental needs of the gifted student. Bright kids frequently were rushed into high-powered science programs and were pressured, or coddled, to be the best and the brightest for the sake of national security and national pride. In the process, we produced a glut of scientists. Furthermore, educators tended to embrace a narrow definition of giftedness, limiting it to intellectual prowess as detected by intelligence and aptitude tests. As Tannenbaum (1979) pointed out, during this era,

> little more than lip service was paid to the needs of a special breed of students not gifted academically but possessing exceptional talent in the arts, mechanics, and social leadership. Also, whatever work was done in measuring divergent productivity remained in the research laboratory. . . . Finally, the national talent hunt failed to penetrate socially disadvantaged minorities whose record of school achievement were well below national norms. (p. 14)

In the latter half of the decade, and into the 1970s, attention shifted away from "the national talent hunt" for academically excellent students and toward a new quest for equity in a public school system that was just beginning to implement a policy of desegregated schools in the wake of the 1954 *Brown v. Board of Education* decision. The criticisms by egalitarian reformers such as Goodman, Friedenberg (1965), and Holt (1964) soon led to more egalitarian practices in the school as advocated by Silberman (1970), Postman and Weingartner (1969), and Kohl (1969). The open classroom concept, which found its U.S. roots in progressive education and its contemporary models in the English infant schools, was tried in many public school systems across the nation.

The renewed interest in the disadvantaged, in social justice, and in "relevance" (a popular cry of the era) led to curricular reform, more flexible scheduling, and individualized learning approaches (e.g., centers, learning activity packages, and modules), and to greater emphasis on integrated studies and "hands-on" learning. This egalitarian interest no doubt diverted attention from the gifted and created suspicion of intelligence testing. To hold that a test should decree who would get special services and assistance on the road to success and high achievement while others are selected for the low-status positions in society seemed patently anti-democratic, even racist. This suspicion about testing echoed the complaint of Horace Mann concerning the European theory of class distinctions.

The era of the 1960s raised doubts about the importance of special education for gifted students, about identification of the gifted via standardized tests, and about grouping practices that seemed to result in a kind of *de facto* racial segregation. Classrooms for gifted students were (and continue to be) predominantly populated by white Anglo-Saxon students from middle and upper class homes. During this turbulent decade, reformers (and many of the most intellectually gifted students themselves) rejected the goals of academic excellence in favor of the social goals of education and a more humane, personally satisfying lifestyle, a life devoted to liberation from authoritarian structures and narrow academic experiences in schools. As Reimer put it in his classic *School Is Dead* (1971), the problem of the public school has been its tendency to maintain "a dominant hierarchy of privilege . . . with the opportunity for members of the currently privileged class to retain their status in the new meritocracy'' (p. 52).

THE PRESENT

In the last two decades, we have seen yet another swing of the pendulum from the equity espoused in the 1960s to the excellence movement of the 1980s. Within that swing, we have witnessed unrivaled advancements in research on, and programs for, the gifted. The U.S. Congress in 1970 mandated new attention to the gifted with its passage of Section 806, ''Provisions Related to Gifted and Talented Children,'' which was added to the existing Elementary and Secondary Education Amendments of 1969. Federal leadership through the Bureau of the Handicapped has been augmented by important court decisions. A Pennsylvania court in 1986 ruled that an 11-year-old gifted child was not being given appropriate educational services in his part-time educational program, which suggests that gifted children may now have legal rights to an education appropriate to their individual needs. The notion that social justice and equal opportunity must prevail within schools through racial integration and mainstreaming of the handicapped (as required by the 1975 Public Law 94-142) seems to be moving from the initial target groups to the gifted. In the present era, the gifted have joined other minorities in the educational mainstream.

Running against the movement for mainstreaming, however, is the contemporary effort to identify the gifted student so that funding and programming can be arranged. This effort often results in a myriad of services and classes for the gifted student away from the regular classroom. Feldhusen (1986) described the potentially negative effects of such identification and segregation of the gifted:

> If the identification processes are focused too strongly on finding *the* gifted child, labeling is likely to follow. Cornell (1983) has demonstrated positive and negative effects of labeling children as gifted. Palmer (1983) suggested that the major impact of labels is the attributions or expectations associated with the labels. Gifted youth often abhor labeling (American Association for Gifted Children, 1978), but parents and school personnel persist in labeling youth as gifted while deploring or fearing the growth of a sense of elitism among them. In developing programs for gifted youth there should be explicit policy consideration of labeling procedures and the control or limitations that should be imposed. (p. 239)

His analysis must give educators pause as they consider how best to serve gifted students in today's schools.

The so-called excellence movement of the 1980s has given impetus to this renewed concern for the education of the gifted. As in the post-Sputnik era, concerns for quality (rather than equality) of education emerged in the context of international competition. This time, the competition was economic and industrial in nature and it came from Japan. The challenge from abroad elicited new criticisms that schools were soft on academics, were caught up in vocationalism and values clarification, and were failing (once again) to produce high achievers and creative thinkers. The National Commission on Excellence in Education declared in its 1983 bellweather report that "a rising tide of mediocrity" in public education has made us "a nation at risk." The executive director of this commission later noted the nation is at risk "because competitors throughout the world are overtaking our once unchallenged lead in commerce, industry, science and technological innovation" (Goldberg & Harvey, 1983, p. 15).

In the international competition, U.S. schools seemed far behind the schools of other countries. Such statistics as these supported the commission's contention that our neglect of quality and standards for academic excellence threatened the very future of our democratic society:

- On 19 international assessments of student achievement U.S. students never ranked first or second and were last 7 times.
- Some 23 million American adults are functionally illiterate.
- From 1963 to 1980 a virtually unbroken decline characterized average scores on the Scholastic Aptitude Test (SAT).
- In the same time-frame there was a dramatic decline in the number of students who demonstrated superior achievement on the SAT.
- Between 1975 and 1980 the number of remedial mathematics courses offered in four-year public colleges increased by 72%. (Goldberg & Harvey, 1983, p. 15)

Criticism poured out in a flood of subsequent commission reports and educational tracts, and the message was always the same: Public education has failed to provide high standards for academic excellence, stringent requirements for graduation, and rigorous intellectual training for all of our youth—but particularly for the ablest.

The reform challenge from the excellence proponents sounds strikingly similar to those put forth by critics of progressive education from Arthur Bestor to James Conant. Some, like Gilbert Sewall (1983), pointed to the failures of the open school reformers:

Yet there was one fatal flaw. Few sixties- and seventies-style reformers were very interested in protecting and advancing high standards of scholarship or discipline. They lost sight of the school's communal, conserving obligations to sustain what is best in the civilization. Once in control of the education establishment, they let their salient interests in cultural pluralism, group compensation, and subject novelties render them blind to falling student outcomes. Through the seventies new ideas and initiatives that seemed to them wise, penetrating, shrewd, and politic struck more and more of their clients as muddled, silly, finally offensive. Gradually the liberal consensus's view came to seem implausible. (p. 166)

Others, like Ravitch (1984), argued that the excellence reforms of the 1980s actually have been a reaffirmation of a U.S. commitment to democratic values. She said,

Most of the national commission and task forces have recommended a basic required curriculum for all students—on grounds that the schools must educate everyone and that a democratic society needs a citizenry in which cultural and scientific literacy is highly developed. The goal of cultural and scientific literacy need not imply a monolithic curriculum, but it does imply a minimum foundation of required studies in the centrally important academic disciplines. Common requirements, however, have long been opposed by a substantial segment of the education profession, which harbors a deeply ingrained hostility toward such words as "standards," "subject matter" and even "excellence" (which is perceived as a code word for academic elitism). (p. 88)

In either case, the contemporary reforms place even greater emphasis on educating the gifted. The National Commission on Excellence in Education insisted that the pursuit of excellence and the pursuit of equity are not incompatible goals and that we cannot permit one to yield to the other "either in principle or in practice." Is that true for the education of gifted students as well? It is not true if gifted students are effectively eliminated from the mainstream by way of pull-out programs, magnet schools, tracking, and other stratifying techniques.

LESSONS OF THE PAST FOR THE FUTURE

Our 200 years of U.S. educational history provide some important lessons for us as we look at the future of special education for the gifted in the public school system. Furthermore, these lessons support the idea that we should, to the maximum degree possible, educate the gifted in the regular classroom.

1. *In a democratic society, education itself should be democratic.*

This lesson has been difficult to learn. In the early days of the republic, the restrictions on education for women, and even more so for blacks, were reflected in a less than democratic school system. Jefferson's ideal (which excluded slaves) for a free education of a few years duration has been extended gradually in length and scope to serve a diverse population in our time, but education itself has often suffered from authoritarianism and a rigid class system all its own. As Dewey and the romantic critics of the 1960s argued, an aristocratic and bureaucratic factory-model school provides meager nourishment for the democratic spirit. When we isolate gifted and talented children from the mainstream—by separate schools, tracks, courses, grouping—we run the risk of contributing to an elitism that does not reflect a true democracy.

2. *In the United States, education must respond to the political and economic needs of the nation.*

Sometimes this lesson points out both the faith we have in the power of education to serve society and the failure we assign to that function of public schools. In the Jeffersonian ideal, the country needed talented leaders to govern and intelligent citizens to exercise their vote. Mann, too, saw education as the way to produce a more moral and enlightened citizenry. He also saw the need to make education practical so as to produce well-trained workers for the industrializing society and to nurture industrial leaders. Dewey emphasized the social goals of education to heal the industrial revolution's fragmented democracy, but he was convinced that his "new education" would be able to solve all manner of scientific and social problems while contributing to the goal of vocation. For Conant and the excellence reformers of the 1980s, the production of highly trained specialists would keep the United States competitive in the international arena. At their best, all of these shapers of educational policy have seen the political and economic needs as a challenge to the *total* society. Gifted individuals are an important part of our society—but only a part. All citizens must be prepared to be productive workers and problem solvers in a heterogeneous workforce. Excellence is a goal for all students.

> 3. *Public education is ultimately responsible for meeting the needs of all students in our society.*

This lesson often is buried under the political rhetoric calling for either excellence or equity. It is embodied in the nature of democracy, of course, but tends to be lost in the carping criticism that schools are antidemocratic or anti-intellectual. In our country, reformers will *always* find public education neglecting excellence or equity. This will happen, in part, because schools always lag behind social change. Nevertheless, from Jefferson to the present, a strong conviction among shapers of educational policy has been that public schools exist to help each student realize his or her full potential, whatever that might be. In many ways, this proposition serves as the ballast for the educational ship as it leans toward either excellence or equity. Schools can serve democratic purposes or political–economic purposes; however, if they do not serve the purpose of talent development in all children, they will fall short of their promise. Education for the gifted in the last two decades has served an especially praiseworthy function in U.S. education by emphasizing this sometimes forgotten lesson. In no other era has so much attention been paid to the vast array of gifts and talents individuals might possess—and must develop. Who is to say in whom the gift may be found and, indeed, what the gift may be?

CONCLUSION

The rich and winding history of public education in the United States suggests that the three lessons discussed above can work as parameters for educational policy: We neglect their import at great peril to the body politic. Each alone is incomplete as a guide for sound educational policy; in reasonable tension, they will keep us from the shoals of educational extremism. In this respect, we should see our goal as meeting the social, political–economic, and individual needs of the gifted and the nation in a balanced and integrated fashion. Such an approach will provide maximum benefits for individuals *and* for our democracy. The task is not easy, but it is ours.

The task is difficult for many reasons. The "public" to be served by public education in the 1980s is far more diverse than the one envisioned by Jefferson, Mann, and Dewey. A heterogeneous classroom today may include Asians, African-Americans, Hispanics, and other racial or cultural groups; youngsters who are learning disabled, mentally retarded, orthopedically impaired, and handicapped in other ways; and a wide variety of intellectual and achievement levels, including the gifted. The gifted students are not merely the brightest and the high achievers, but include the underachieving gifted, artistically talented, and outstanding leaders.

Furthermore, the demands on the regular classroom teacher to be more accountable, more skilled, and more productive already create extraordinary expectations and pressures. For education of the gifted to succeed in the regular classroom, much work must be done by regular teachers and teachers of the gifted to improve the conditions for learning and teaching in the regular classroom. Such improvements are possible; indeed, they are imperative. Educators of the gifted must concentrate on helping the regular teacher organize and differentiate instruction, individualize the curriculum, and manage behavior and interactions in ways that improve education for gifted children within a diverse, heterogeneous, multicultural classroom. Educators today can respond successfully to this challenge by bringing the considerable resources, research, and experience of educators of the gifted to bear on the regular classroom. In the future, education of the gifted will concern itself more and more with educating regular teachers at all levels and with providing those teachers the kind of staff development, resources, and administrative services required to make instruction of the gifted truly effective in the regular classroom. This is a most important responsibility, and opportunity, for education of the gifted today.

Thus, I argue for a concept of programming for the gifted in which this educational enterprise is located firmly within the regular classroom—to the maximum degree possible. What is that degree? In what specific ways can schools provide for the needs of the gifted in regular classroom settings? How can the splendid accomplishments of educators of the gifted, and of the students themselves, be capitalized on for the benefit of the total school population? My fellow contributors to this volume provide a host of perspectives, insights, and answers to questions like these.

REFERENCES

Bridges, R. (1930). *Testament of beauty.* New York: Oxford University Press.

Bruner, J. S. (1959). *The process of education.* New York: Vintage Books.

Conant, J. B. (1959). *The American high school today: A first report to interested citizens.* New York: McGraw-Hill.

Conant, J. B. (1960). *The child, the parent, and the state.* Cambridge: Harvard University Press.

Cremin, L. A. (1957). *The republic and the school: Horace Mann on the education of free men.* New York: Teachers College Press.

Cremin, L. A. (1961). *The transformation of the school: Progressivism in American education, 1876–1957.* New York: Random House.

Dewey, J. (1916). *Democracy and education.* New York: Macmillan.

Dewey, J. (1938). *Experience and education.* New York: Collier.

Dworkin, M. S. (1959). *Dewey on education: Selections.* New York: Teachers College Press.

Feldhusen, J. F. (1986). Policies and procedures for the development of defensible programs for the gifted. In C. J. Maker (Ed.), *Critical issues in gifted education: Vol. 1. Defensible programs for the gifted* (pp. 235–255). Austin, TX: PRO-ED.

Friedenberg, E. Z. (1965). *Coming of age in America.* New York: Random House.

Goldberg, M., & Harvey, J. (1983). A nation at risk: The report of the National Commission on Excellence in Education. *Phi Delta Kappan, 65,* 14–18.

Goodman, P. (1960). *Growing up absurd.* New York: Random House.

Holt, J. (1964). *How children fail.* New York: Pitman.

Kohl, H. R. (1969). *The open classroom: A practical guide to a new way of teaching.* New York: The New York Review.

Lee, G. C. (1961). *Crusade against ignorance: Thomas Jefferson on education.* New York: Teachers College Press.

Perkinson, H. J. (1976). *Two hundred years of American educational thought.* New York: Longman.

Postman, N., & Weingartner, C. (1969). *Teaching as a subversive activity.* New York: Delacorte Press.

Ravitch, D. (1984). The continuing crises: Fashions in education. *The American Scholar, 53,* 88.

Reimer, E. (1971). *School is dead.* New York: Doubleday.

Sewall, G. T. (1983). *Necessary lessons: Decline and renewal in American schools.* New York: Free Press.

Silberman, C. (1970). *Crisis in the classroom.* New York: Random House.

Tannenbaum, A. J. (1979). Pre-Sputnik to post-Watergate concern about the gifted. In H. A. Passow (Ed.), *The gifted and the talented: Their education and development* (pp. 5–27). The seventy-eighth yearbook of the National Society for the Study of Education. Chicago: University of Chicago Press.

2

Comments on McDaniel's "Education of the Gifted and the Excellence–Equity Debate"

James J. Gallagher

McDaniel has provided a good summary of the history of the education of the gifted over the past few decades, and we are indebted to him for a clear exposition on the tension between *excellence* and *equity,* because that is precisely the issue that has concerned educators throughout that era. It has been three decades since John Gardner (1961) wrote a small book titled *Can We Be Both Excellent and Equal?* It was the issue then, and it remains the issue now.

I believe the issue would be better met in McDaniel's chapter if he did not appear to be arguing against a phantom educator of the gifted. As one reads the chapter, one gets a composite portrait of this phantom educator. He or she is someone who cares only for intellectual stimulation of gifted children; he or she is willing to set adrift minorities and average students and cares little for their education; he or she is essentially undemocratic, and willing to see the public school system corroded and abandoned in his or her single-minded elitism. Perhaps McDaniel knows such an educator, but in my 30 years in this field, I have never met one of that description.

Instead, I have met a lot of people who are deeply concerned about the education of all schoolchildren and their needs, who are committed to fair treatment and equity for all, as well as to the development of excellence. If we have differences of opinion, these differences stem from a different perception of how best to achieve some common goals, rather than a difference in basic values themselves.

Incidentally, McDaniel passes up the opportunity to attack those who would really undermine the public school system of the United States. These people are those who are powerful and wealthy; who pass up the opportunity to place their children in the "democratic," urban school systems that McDaniel supports; and who, instead, place their sons and daughters in Exeter, or Groton, or Rosemont, or any of 50 private preparatory school settings that these parents prefer.

The key element of educating gifted students in the regular classroom is whether the regular classroom is a responsive environment. Can the over 1 million elementary school teachers, given the resources and their environmental setting, provide an exciting and stimulating environment for gifted students who are often three, four, or five grades beyond their age-mates? If they can do it, why have they not been doing it, when the overwhelming comment of these students is that their education is one cauldron of boredom (DeLisle, 1987)?

It is the manifest inability of the regular classroom teacher to provide for these youngsters that has stimulated the development of the resource rooms, magnet schools, special classes, and mentorships. Educational programs for the gifted are not part of a plot for the elite to take over the world, but rather a desperate attempt on the part of parents and caring educators to try and create a better learning environment for these students.

McDaniel reports rather dramatic statistics from the National Commission on Excellence in Education showing the sorry performance of U.S. students in international comparisons. Surprisingly, he also concludes that the regular classroom, without substantial modifications, could turn that dismal record around.

If we reflect for a moment on dimensions of the educational system other than the special provisions for gifted students, we find that there *is* a grouping on the basis of talent and interest in practically every domain. Does the athletic coach accept all students as they attempt to compete for excellence in a sport, or are only the very best and most competent taken? Does the music director of the school orchestra who wishes to compete in a state contest take the very best, trained instrumentalists or a random sample of the general student population? If the school wishes to present an exciting drama or musical, does the drama coach take those students who have special abilities and talents in drama or a heterogeneous collection of students? The answers to these questions are obvious, so why is it surprising that, whenever discussions of significant intellectual ideas and content are concerned, the educator would think of doing the same thing that is done in every other domain of the school?

McDaniel presents lessons of the past for the future, but the problem with drawing lessons from the past is that everyone seems to find different lessons there. I believe it was Hegel who supposedly said, "the only thing we learn from history, is that we don't learn from history." I would prefer to believe that there *are* lessons to be learned from history, even if we might disagree on what they are.

The first lesson in McDaniel's chapter is that "in a democratic society, education itself should be democratic." I must confess that I do not understand that statement. Democracy is a political concept, not an educational concept. Democracy is designed to diffuse power among the people so that those who govern do so by the consent of the governed. It is a strategy by which we frustrate powerful men and women whose ego needs may overcome their concern for the general public. I am inclined to think that what McDaniel has in mind is the concept of equal educational opportunity rather than that the students should elect their teachers and choose their own curriculum in true democratic fashion.

Finally, I would suggest that if, as McDaniel suggests in his concluding statements, improvements are possible in the regular classroom (and on this we agree), and that educators of the gifted must concentrate on helping the regular teachers organize and differentiate instruction, and improve education for gifted children within a diverse heterogeneous, multicultural classroom, then the best proof of this assumption is a demonstration.

If there can be a clear demonstration that the regular classroom is the proper place for gifted students, then these ideas need to be put into operational form so that clear benefits come not only to gifted students, but to all students in the classroom. Once this is proven, parents and educators will rush to adopt that particular procedure. Until demonstrations of the advantages of the regular classrooms are available in some widespread form, alternative strategies will be sought by parents and educators who are concerned about the individual child and the need for education to respond to the political and economic needs of the nation.

Alternative strategies may not remove gifted students from the public school entirely, but may remove them from their age-mates for a period of time, so that they can master more adequately complex systems of ideas that are beyond the capabilities of the average and below-average student. Such separation is more likely and desirable the older the student is because the gifted adolescent is farther apart in development from his or her age-mates than is the gifted preteen.

We need both excellence and equity in our educational future. The correct paths to simultaneously reach these goals still lie ahead of us.

REFERENCES

Delisle, J. (1987). *Gifted children speak out.* New York: Walker & Co.
Gardner, J. (1961). *Excellence.* New York: Harper & Row.

PART II

SCHOOLWIDE
MANAGEMENT AND
PROGRAMS

In this section, six writers discuss models for schoolwide management and programs designed to serve gifted students in regular classroom settings. James Chalfant and Margaret Van Dusen Pysh present a model developed for the purpose of providing peer assistance to regular classroom teachers. Although the model has been viewed mainly as a method for serving handicapped children, as Chalfant and Van Dusen Pysh show us, these teacher assistance teams (TATs) can be used very effectively in the provision of better instruction for gifted students. Barbara Moller, in her reaction to the lead chapter, agrees that TATs are valuable, and suggests expansion of the model to address schoolwide problems, problems common to many teachers, and problems identified by individuals other than regular classroom teachers (e.g., students, parents, and administrators).

Next, Sharon Hooker presents the advocate liaison, a program added to an existing pull-out and demonstration teaching approach to provide support and assistance to both regular and special classroom teachers. The main purpose of the program is to provide better services to gifted students in the regular classroom through the assistance of an advocate liaison at each school. Joyce VanTassel-Baska reacts to the author's presentation of the model, and calls for more clarity in its presentation. To assist local program developers to achieve this needed clarity, she presents a framework that can be used for program development at the local level to better serve the needs of gifted students.

Finally, Marilyn Rice describes a demonstration teaching model used in her district, and explains how it was developed. The stated purpose of this program is to provide services to gifted students in regular classroom settings, both as a supplement to a resource room (pull-out) program in Grades 4 through 6, and as the only program provided for students in Grades 1 through 3. A secondary purpose, or "hidden agenda," of the program is to provide staff development for regular classroom teachers. In a critique of Rice's presentation of the model, Janice Szabos describes a version of the demonstration teaching model used in her district. Although the implementations of the model seem similar in the two districts, the purposes seem somewhat different. In addition to its usefulness for staff development and direct services, Szabos views the model as a means for observing and identifying primary-age children who may be gifted so they can be served later and more appropriately in a special program.

KEY QUESTION AND ANSWERS

The key question presented to authors of this section was, "What problems and solutions do program developers and administrators have in their attempt to accommodate the needs of gifted students in regular classrooms?" All were asked also to address specific questions about the particular models they were describing: (a) What is the model? (b) How can it be used to provide support services for gifted students? (c) What are the necessary elements of the model? (d) What are some examples of successful uses of the model? and (e) What are the advantages and disadvantages of the model?

Because the specific questions regarding each model have been addressed in detail by the authors of individual chapters, I focus attention here on the key question for the section, and present my synthesis of the various perspectives. I do not attempt to identify the source of every idea, but recommend that readers consult individual chapters for further information. The key question has two parts: problems and solutions. Interestingly, more problems than solutions are presented, but many problems seem to be solved in some way by the solutions described.

Problems

In this presentation of problems, I have taken the liberty of being selective rather than exhaustive, and have not attempted to present problems in mutually exclusive categories. Instead, I have selected what seem to be the most important problems in educating gifted students in regular classroom settings, based on my own experience and the writing of authors in this section.

Setting Goals

One of the first problems faced is that of choosing and defining program goals. A related problem is deciding where these goals can best be met. For example, development of critical and creative thinking abilities might be incorporated more easily into the curriculum of the regular classroom than the development of independent learning skills. Students may need a special teacher to supervise independent projects and teach relevant skills to a group of children with interest in a similar topic.

Identifying Giftedness

Classroom teachers need to be assisted in the process of identification, and the process itself needs to be related directly to the program provided. The assessment process needs to include instruments and procedures that will enable educators to make decisions regarding appropriate placements, and to justify these placements to parents and other constituents. Classroom teachers need to improve their skills in observing children, and learn what behaviors are indicative of giftedness.

Improving Communication Between and Among Teachers

Teachers who are providing direct services to a particular child need to discuss and coordinate their goals and strategies. They need time and "vehicles" for meetings and discussions. In addition, teachers need to discuss common problems and pool their knowledge regarding solutions to the problems involved in challenging gifted children. If the primary or only delivery model is the regular classroom, this communication will be between those who have served the student in the past and the current teacher.

Improving Communication Between Teachers and Administrators

This problem is especially relevant for regular classroom teachers, who are seldom released from teaching duties to attend schoolwide or districtwide meetings. Often, they are unfamiliar with the goals of the program for the gifted and do not know what is happening in other schools, other classrooms, or a special program. Frequently, the teachers' understanding of what has happened in pull-out programs is based entirely on the comments of students who attend these programs. We all know how incomplete these descriptions can be!

Providing a Program for Each Child that Is Coherent, Connected, and Appropriate

The program or services provided for every gifted child need to be viewed from a particular point in time (across programs or services) and from a longitudinal perspective (across several years). When the student is served only in a regular classroom setting, articulation from year to year is the greatest concern; however, when a resource room (pull-out) program is provided, articulation is needed across programs as well as from year to year.

Assuring Consistency of Services to Students by Teachers with Varied Skills and Interests

Perhaps one of the most significant problems faced by principals, coordinators, and program developers is how to assure consistency across teachers when the program for gifted students is based in the regular classroom. Teacher education programs include little, if any, emphasis on providing for the gifted; and teachers have varying degrees of interest in acquiring additional skills. In addition, a wide range of attitudes regarding the types of programs needed by gifted students exist among teachers.

Serving a Wide Range of Levels and Types of Gifted Students in Each Classroom

Recognition of the range and types of giftedness by program developers and the community increases the complexity of programming. The regular classroom setting is viewed as the place to focus on the development of a wide variety of talents and abilities so that every student is challenged to develop his or her special abilities. Teachers must recognize these abilities and know how to develop them. If all gifted students are educated in the regular classroom, teachers also must be able to recognize and meet the needs of gifted underachievers, gifted students with handicaps or disabilities, minority and disadvantaged gifted students, students who are highly gifted, and students gifted in a variety of areas.

Balancing Individual and Group Needs of Both Gifted and Average Students

Given the practical realities of providing a curriculum for a diverse group of students, a classroom teacher cannot attend to every need of every student on an individual basis. Grouping according to needs and interests must occur for effective teaching, but individualized instruction also is necessary. In addition, teachers must attend to the differing social and emotional needs of their students, planning certain activities involving group interaction and others in which students work alone. Educators also must recognize that gifted students need opportunities to interact with intellectual peers as well as age-mates, and make provisions for meeting these needs.

Providing Adequate Resources

Often, if not always, resources are limited and a program must be developed within these constraints. Students need specialized materials, and teachers need materials and references to enable them to provide a challenging program. Personnel are needed to provide support for classroom teachers, and funding may not be available. Thus, existing personnel, already overworked and underpaid, may be the only ones available to operate the program. Time is another resource that is limited. Classroom teachers, who must plan for all the children in their classes, have limited time to make special provisions for gifted students. Resource teachers also may have a large number of children on their caseload, and cannot be expected to provide help to all regular classroom teachers in the schools they serve.

Defining Effective Curriculum, Roles of All Involved Success,
and Needed Changes

Another significant problem is how to define curriculum that is differentiated to meet the needs of a wide range of children, to decide which aspects of this curriculum are delivered through various parts of the program, and to assure that all aspects are related. Roles of all teachers involved need to be defined clearly. What will constitute student growth and satisfactory progress and what constitutes program success must be defined before they can be measured and evaluated. Developing such definitions prior to program initiation, or at least in the beginning, will be helpful, and is considered essential by some. Changes needed to achieve success also must be defined.

Monitoring and Evaluating Progress and Success

Systems and procedures must be established to document teaching strategies, student reactions to these strategies, teacher reactions to use of certain techniques, student growth, teacher growth, and any other indicators needed to describe and evaluate the program. Information must be accurate and collected in a way that is not seen as a threat to the classroom teacher.

Balancing School-Based, Classroom-Based, and
Central Administration–Based Management

What decisions are made by the principal? What decisions are made by the classroom teacher? What decisions are the responsibility of the central administration? How do we assure that these decisions do not conflict? All these questions must be considered in the day-to-day and long-term management of a program.

The Solutions

One way to present the solutions advocated by authors in this section is to discuss how each model addresses and solves each problem identified. However, this seems somewhat repetitious of the individual chapters. Szabos presents in her chapter a brief introduction to the effective schools literature, and lists norms of effective schools: experimentation, collegiality, tangible support, honest communication, and reaching out to the knowledge bases about teaching. These norms seem to be contained in each of the models discussed. Therefore, a useful organization seems to be to show (a) how these norms relate to the problems of educating gifted students in the regular classroom and (b) how each of them is or can be incorporated into the models (teacher assistance teams, advocate liaisons, demonstration teaching). A bird's-eye view of the following section is presented in Table II.1. In the table, the major problems identified by authors in this part are listed in Column 1. In Column 2 are the components of effective schools. Some components seem to relate to all

Table II.1 Relationship of Effective Schools' Norms to Problems and Models Related to Educating the Gifted in Regular Classrooms

Problems	Components of Effective Schools	Models
Setting goals Identifying giftedness	Experimentation	TAT AL DT
Improving communication between and among teachers Improving communication between teachers and administrators Providing a program for each child that is coherent, connected, and appropriate	Collegiality	TAT AL DT
Assuring consistency of services to students by teachers with varied skills and interests Serving a wide range of levels and types of gifted students in each classroom Balancing individual and group needs of both gifted and average students Providing adequate resources	Tangible support	TAT AL DT
Defining effective curriculum roles of all involved, success, and needed changes	Honest communication	TAT AL DT
Monitoring and evaluating progress and success Balancing school-based, classroom-based, and central administration–based management	Reaching out to knowledge bases about teaching	TAT AL DT

Note. TAT = teacher assistance team; AL = advocate liaison; DT = demonstration teaching.

problems, but I have attempted to show the most important relationships addressed by the chapter authors.

Experimentation

In the TAT model, teachers are given specific suggestions for working with children they identify as having problems. They experiment with these solutions, and can request assistance at any time from the team. The team adopts an attitude of experimentation in its operational procedures and in the solutions it proposes. The advocate liaison, a new concept, also can be experimental in nature, and it is used as a way to provide teachers with new ideas and strategies they can test with individual children. Demonstration teaching also can be used to encourage teachers to try new ways of teaching. Teachers are introduced to these new ways through direct demonstration, are given materials needed to try out these new approaches, and are assisted by those who conducted the demonstration. Demonstration teachers also are available to discuss the new approach, analyze its usefulness for particular children, and observe the classroom teacher as he or she tries a new strategy.

Collegiality

All models and all authors have addressed this component; it seems to be integral to the conception and success of the approaches. In the TAT model, for instance, group problem solving is accomplished by peers who are nonjudgmental, who have faced similar problems, and who wish to provide the best education possible for the students in their school. Peer coaching, observation in classrooms, follow-up discussions, and many other aspects of collegiality are inherent in the approach. An advocate liaison is a colleague who has volunteered to assist other teachers in the school in the development of appropriate programs. This colleague provides and/or secures materials, fosters discussions, teaches, and provides a communication link, as one who is familiar with teachers, parents, students, and the context of the school. In the demonstration teaching model, collegiality also is an important component. Lessons are presented in the teachers' classrooms, discussions of their usefulness are fostered, and an atmosphere of cooperation is engendered. Peer coaching, observation, and follow-up in a nonjudgmental atmosphere are involved in the successful use of this model. Collegiality can be fostered within a school, as well as between and among schools or between and among components of a program. For example, if teachers from a resource room program present demonstration lessons for and discuss them with regular classroom teachers from the schools served by their pullout programs, they increase collegiality across the various components of a program.

Tangible Support

Support for regular classroom teachers is provided as an integral part of all models presented. In the TAT model, teachers can request support in the form of problem solving regarding students they recognize as needing assistance. They are given specific solutions, as well as examples of ways to monitor and measure progress. Team members provide follow-up support until problems are resolved. Tangible support from the advocate liaison program is in the form of specific ideas for challenging students, as well as specialized materials that can be used with gifted students. The advocate liaison is familiar with the resources available through the central administration of the program, and can secure support for the efforts of classroom teachers that they might not otherwise know about or be able to find. With the demonstration teaching model, classroom teachers receive many forms of tangible support: (a) well-planned examples of curriculum and teaching strategies useful in regular classroom settings, (b) follow-up materials useful with all children in the classroom, (c) a peer–expert with whom to discuss observations of teaching strategies and student participation, and (d) a peer–expert who returns to the classroom throughout the year.

Honest Communication

This factor in effective schools is not inherent in the models, but is necessary to their successful use—or the successful use and implementation of any educational innovation. All models presented have as one of their goals or benefits the enhancement of communication. If this communication is honest, it will be more effective. Use of the TAT includes requests from teachers for assistance with problem children, a clear description of the teacher's perception of the student's assets and liabilities, and a description of techniques used with the student. This information is read by team members, and they request additional information or clarification when needed. One member of the team observes in the classroom prior to problem-solving sessions. All these strategies are designed to produce clear and accurate communication regarding the student and his or her behavior in the classroom environment. A major goal of the advocate model is improved communication between central administration (e.g., the coordinators of the program for the gifted) and classroom teachers. Because advocate liaisons attend meetings in which they learn about goals, philosophy, curriculum, and resources of/for the program for the gifted, they can communicate these on a daily basis to teachers who need and desire such information. Because the demonstration teacher shows classroom teachers how to use a particular strategy, communication is direct—through observation. The teacher can see how a technique works, and can observe student participation rather than relying upon someone else's description of how a particular teaching strategy might work. The demonstration teacher and classroom teacher can discuss a student's behavior based on a common experience of observing him or her. Identification of giftedness is thereby facilitated through honest, clear, direct communication. The demonstration teaching model also facilitates honest, clear, direct communication from classroom teachers to the program coordinators, as demonstration teachers can become familiar with the realities of the classrooms and schools they serve.

Reaching Out to Knowledge Bases About Teaching

All models discussed provide a vehicle for teachers to reach out and increase their knowledge about the teaching–learning process. Those who are providing services— TAT members, advocate liaisons, demonstration teachers—as well as those who are receiving services are increasing their knowledge and understanding. TAT members encounter many and varied problems for which they must develop practical solutions; advocate liaisons must learn about many classrooms, many students, a districtwide program for gifted students, and available resources; and demonstration teachers must understand what they are modeling at a much higher level (or in greater depth) than they would have to if they were using it rather than teaching it. When inservice training is provided in conjunction with the models, learning is enhanced.

Relationship of Effective Schools Components to Problems of Educating Gifted Students in Regular Classrooms

Experimentation, the first effective school component, seems especially important in solving problems of serving students with unique needs. Teachers need to be encouraged to try new methods for (a) serving the unique needs of gifted students, (b) grouping students, (c) balancing individual and group needs, and (d) monitoring and evaluating progress. Experimentation, coupled with *tangible support* in the form of human, material, and creative assistance to assure success, can result in positive experiences and a desire to experiment again. Teachers are willing to try new approaches when they know follow-up is available and nonjudgmental advice will be forthcoming. *Collegiality* must be fostered to facilitate the setting of common goals and the balancing of management concerns from schools, classrooms, and the central administration. When an atmosphere of cooperation and mutual support is present, services to a particular student can be provided by several individuals in a coherent and connected manner. *Honest communication* is necessary in the solving of any problem faced by program developers. However, it is particularly important in the setting of goals, identification of giftedness, monitoring and evaluation of progress, and communication between and among those who are providing services or developing programs. Finally, *reaching out to knowledge bases about teaching* is essential if educators are to improve their programs for students and solve the problems they face. With the emergence of new technology and new methods for challenging gifted students, educators need to adapt old approaches and develop and apply new ones. Education of gifted children is a relatively new field of special education, and little research has been conducted in the past, so our knowledge base as a field is new, and has not been included in teacher education programs until recently.

CONCLUSION

Four approaches to serving gifted students in regular classroom settings are provided in this section. My introduction has been focused toward providing an answer to the key question of the section: What problems and solutions do program developers and administrators have in their attempt to accommodate the needs of gifted students in regular classrooms? In my answer, I have summarized and synthesized information about the models, and have shown how certain components of effective schools interact to provide ways to solve important problems.

No educational remedy or model can, in and of itself, provide solutions to problems. The models must be implemented appropriately, adapted for individual settings, and evaluated to determine their effectiveness. The models described in this section have been successful in certain settings, and deserve attention and experimentation in others.

3

Teacher Assistance Teams: Implications for the Gifted

James C. Chalfant
Margaret Van Dusen Pysh

The goal for U.S. education is to provide an effective educational environment in which the individual needs of all students can be met and their unique capabilities developed to the highest possible levels. Currently, however, many students (10% to 20%) in our public schools are failing to reach their full potential because of behavioral, social–emotional, learning, and/or language problems that impede their progress (Will, 1986). Students having difficulty in school can include those typically labeled gifted, normal, or disabled.

The Individuals with Disabilities Education Act (IDEA) (formerly the Education of All Handicapped Children Act) has mandated support for special education programs, with legal safeguards for students who are disabled. Many schools do not have organized programs, however, to support normal or gifted and talented students who are having difficulty in school (Karnes & Johnson, 1991; Whitmore & Maker, 1985).

Gifted and talented students present a unique challenge to their teachers. Many gifted students are advanced far beyond their classroom peers in knowledge and skill level, whereas other gifted and talented students may achieve well below their estimated intellectual potential because of poor work habits or social–emotional problems.

When gifted or talented students lose interest or become bored, they may develop poor work habits or become disruptive (Kirk & Gallagher, 1989). Gifted students may interrupt or correct their classmates and teacher, or may mock their peers. These behaviors do not win friends. When gifted children are teased because they are "different," they feel that others do not understand them or like them. Gifted children, like all children, want to be accepted and liked, but when they feel alienated and are isolated from their peer group, they may develop low self-esteem. Classroom teachers often find it difficult to provide these students with an education that meets their individual academic and social needs, challenges their capabilities, and helps them to reach their true potential. The most predominant model for helping gifted students in need is the pull-out program at the elementary level (Vaughn, Feldhusen, & Asher, 1991) and advanced classes, honors classes, or independent study at the high school level (Clark, 1988). Thus, gifted students are in the regular classroom most of the time.

In this chapter, we present a model that may be used at all grade levels and in a variety of settings to support classroom teachers who are trying to individualize instruction for gifted students, or for any student whose needs are not being met in school. The teacher assistance team (TAT) is designed to provide prompt accessible support to teachers upon request. The system has proven successful in assisting teachers in designing strategies for helping students with special needs within the framework of the regular classroom (Chalfant & Pysh, 1989; Gilmer, 1985; Hayek, 1987; Ortiz & Wilkinson, 1991).

THE TEACHER ASSISTANCE TEAM CONCEPT

The teacher assistance team is a building-level problem-solving unit. A TAT usually consists of a core of three elected teachers, who assist other teachers in (a) analyzing and better understanding why students are experiencing learning and behavior problems in the classroom; (b) generating specific goals for teachers and students; (c) brainstorming practical strategies that the teachers can use to meet more effectively the needs of individual students; (d) developing procedures to measure student progress; and (e) providing follow-up support while the teachers implement recommended strategies. This model is based on five assumptions (Chalfant, Pysh, & Moultrie, 1979):

1. Enormous knowledge and talent exists among classroom teachers.
2. Regular classroom teachers can and do help many students with learning and behavior problems.
3. Teachers learn best by doing.
4. Classroom teachers, with some assistance, can help more students with learning and behavioral problems.
5. Teachers can resolve many more problems by working together than by working alone.

The TAT model provides a forum in which teachers can meet together and engage in a positive, productive, problem-solving process. Teachers may request assistance from a TAT team to help them analyze and better understand classroom problems and create practical solutions for the classroom. A teacher might request assistance in teaching an individual student or a group of students, generating strategies for dealing with an entire class, modifying the curriculum, preparing for a parent conference, or counseling a student. The TAT serves as a teacher support group and exists to help teachers cope with a wide range of situations and students.

TATs should not be confused with the multidisciplinary teams composed of the psychologist, social worker, guidance counselor, school nurse, special teacher, regular teacher, and others, which are mandated by law and are responsible for implementing special education referral and placement processes required by IDEA. In contrast, the TAT functions as a day-to-day collegial consultation unit for teachers within a particular school. Any staff member can be invited to participate on the TAT as needed. No required legal or procedural guidelines exist, and each school faculty can develop the operational procedures that will fit its needs.

The basic TAT concept is simple and easily understood, but the actual implementation and maintenance of a TAT requires administrative support and a fairly high degree of staff commitment. The building staff will need to become knowledgeable and proficient in group problem-solving techniques.

TEAM OPERATING PROCEDURES

The teachers in each building should develop for their TAT the operating procedures they feel would be appropriate and effective in their school. Figure 3.1 illustrates the key points to be considered. The text that follows is numbered to correspond to the appropriate stages of Figure 3.1. To illustrate each of these points, a case study of a gifted adolescent boy, age 16, is presented.[1]

I. Teacher Contacts Teacher Assistance Team

The first consideration is to establish a procedure for accessing the TAT. For example, Ms. Mueller was an English teacher in a large high school in Arizona. In her class was Eric, a 16-year-old gifted male student, who was failing her English class. In fact, Eric was failing all but one of his classes. The only class Eric was not failing was drama, in which he consistently did ''A'' work. Ms. Mueller worked with Eric in class and also tried to help him after school. She encouraged him, counseled him, and talked with his parents with no apparent results. His performance on written assignments and tests grew steadily worse. After Ms. Mueller exhausted her own ideas and strategies for helping Eric, she contacted the TAT by completing a request for assistance form. Her responses on the form are presented in Figure 3.2. She gave the completed form to the TAT leader.

Request for assistance forms should be designed so that they can be completed easily in 10 to 15 minutes. The forms should include at least these four important questions (Chalfant et al., 1979):

1. Describe what you would like the student to do that he or she does not presently do.

---

[1]The authors thank the TAT members from Rockford, Illinois, and Riverton, Illinois, for their assistance in developing the case study of Eric. Thanks to the Rockford TAT of Robert Beebe, Julie Buchmann, Eloise Dettmer, Ruth Wrate, and Sara Ingrassia, and to the Riverton TAT of Sara Schlichting, Amy Smith, Marilyn Robertson, Jeff Koger, Jim Gardner, and Pam Roesler.

THE TEACHER ASSISTANCE TEAM OPERATING PROCEDURE

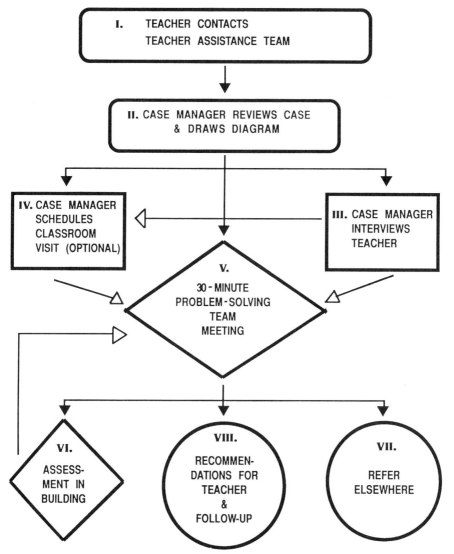

Figure 3.1 The Teacher Assistance Team Operating Procedure.

2. Describe what you have done to help the student cope with his or her problems.
3. Describe what the student does (assets) and what the student does not do (deficits).
4. Provide relevant background information.

Request for Assistance Form

Student's Name   Eric M.

Age   16

Grade   Junior

Teacher's Name   Ms. Mueller

Please complete the following four questions to assist us in working with your concerns.

1. Describe what you would like the student to do that he or she does not presently do.

   Listen to instructions, explanations, and discussions

   Be organized

   Set realistic work goals and accomplish them

   Use class time wisely

   Complete written composition assignments

   Feel better about English class and participate more

2. Describe what you have done to help the student cope with his or her problems.

   Talked to him about personal things to let him know I value him as a person despite his unsatisfactory achievement in English.

   Encouraged him to do all assignments and ask me for help at any time.

   Sent progress reports to parents.

   Talked to him about the relationship between written language studied in English class and oral language which is so important to actors and the theater.

3. Describe what the student does (assets) and what the student does not do (deficits).

Assets	Deficits
Excellent and enthusiastic reader (one of the few who didn't scream over The Scarlet Letter*).*	*Very bright but failing all classes* *Grades 1st & 2nd quarters:*
Highly intelligent—IQ 135	*English D E* *ROTC D E*
Excellent actor; National Thespians; Earned a lead part in junior class play	*Algebra E E* *Gov't C – D*
Physically attractive; articulate	*Attitudes and efforts in courses rated poor or very poor*
Recognizes he doesn't work hard on assignments he dislikes	*Angry about changing state, community, and high school*
Not disruptive	*Often reads when he should listen, partici-pate, or work*
Grade in drama—A; attitude and effort in drama is excellent	*No friends, poor social skills, not socially close to anyone*
	Doesn't use class time to work on assign-ments or use teacher as a resource
	Lies to himself and teacher about what he is going to accomplish
	Very disorganized

4. Please provide relevant background information.

   High intellectual potential—IQ 135

   Transferred to Arizona from Illinois in September

   Good to average grades in previous high school

Figure 3.2 Form for Requesting Assistance from the Teacher Assistance Team.

II. Case Manager Reviews Case and Draws Diagram

The TAT leader alerts other team members that a request for assistance has been received. Each TAT member reads and analyzes the request independently and lists any specific questions he or she has concerning the information. One team member is appointed as case manager to review the case, analyze the student's problems, and draw a problem interaction diagram (PID) (see Figure 3.3). Drawing a visual

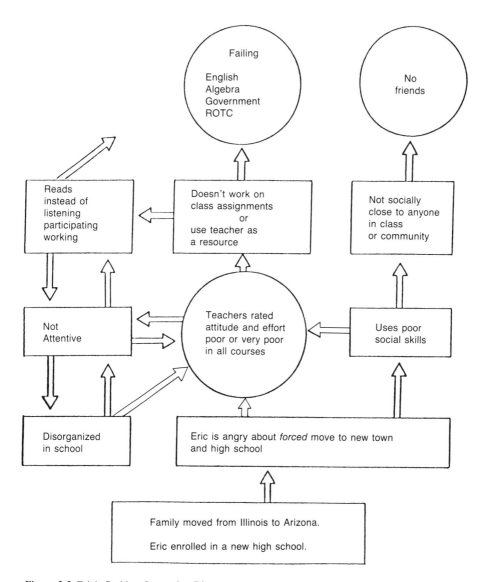

Figure 3.3 Eric's Problem Interaction Diagram.

graphic representation of a student's problem in the classroom can be a useful procedure for identifying the problem areas of concern, showing their interrelationships,
and providing a visual conceptualization of what a student's problem might be. The
diagram is used to help the TAT and the teacher reach a consensus about the nature
of the student's problem and to make decisions about how intervention should be
accomplished.

III. Case Manager Interviews Teacher to Request Specific Information

The case manager visits with Ms. Mueller briefly to interview her, ask questions that TAT members have raised, and share the proposed diagram of the case.
Many TATs have found that interviews and/or observations are helpful strategies
for clarifying specific issues with the requesting teacher and saving time in the TAT
meeting. These interviews and observations take place after the request for assistance
is received and before the TAT meeting. Interviewing and/or observing are particularly delicate processes because, understandably, teachers often fear that TAT members may be making judgments about them or about the quality of their teaching.
Therefore, diplomacy and an atmosphere of support and safety are critical. Team
members can use several methods to reduce teacher anxiety and concern during the
interview process (Chalfant & Pysh, 1987):

1. Only one TAT member should conduct the interview, and must make clear
to the teacher that the purpose of the interview is to clarify information and help
the TAT members better understand the situation from the teacher's perspective.
The situation must be psychologically "safe" and perceived as mutual.

2. Keep questions to the point. Ask only questions that are truly necessary to
clarify the issues about which the teacher is concerned.

3. Do not judge the teacher in any way. The purpose of the interview is not
to determine whether the teacher has done "the right thing," but to increase the
accuracy of TAT members' understanding of the situation. The teacher should be
treated as "the expert" with respect to the student in question. The interviewer is
there to learn from the teacher.

4. Control the rate at which questions are asked, keep voice tone supportive,
and monitor facial and bodily expressions and actively listen. People often infer
approval or disapproval from tone and posture, regardless of the words that are
spoken.

IV. Case Manager Schedules Classroom Visit

After receiving permission from Ms. Mueller, the TAT case manager who
conducted the interview may visit the classroom to observe Eric. A visit to the
classroom can provide additional insights to the problem. Such a visit should be
made *only* with the teacher's permission, and the student must not be singled out
in any way.

V. Schedule and Conduct the 30-Minute Problem-Solving Team Meeting

The TAT leader schedules a 30-minute problem-solving meeting at a mutually agreeable time for Ms. Mueller and the team. A six-stage procedure is used to conduct the meeting so that all necessary steps are completed within 30 minutes.

1. *Reach a Consensus* (5 minutes): The TAT leader or the case manager (a) calls the TAT to order, summarizes the problem(s) briefly by presenting the PID and Ms. Mueller's changes, if any; (b) reviews the answers to the questions raised previously by the TAT members; and (c) ensures that the TAT members and the teacher have a common understanding of the problem(s) to be addressed.

2. *Establish Goals* (3 minutes): Ms. Mueller is asked to select a specific goal or goals for which she would like assistance. She selects three goals: (a) that Eric improve his attitude and effort in completing his assignments, (b) that he become more organized in his work, and (c) that he make some friends. These objectives are recorded on the TAT recommendation form (see Figure 3.4).

In some cases, TAT members may need to help the teacher state the goal or goals in more precise behavioral language. For example, if Ms. Mueller stated, "I want Eric to improve his self-concept," the TAT might ask her to describe how she believed Eric's behavior would have to change to show an improvement in his self-concept. For example, if Eric constantly makes derogatory statements about himself, improvement in self-concept might be shown by his saying more positive things about himself. It is most effective to limit the initial selection of goals to one or two highly specific, behaviorally precise goals.

3. *Brainstorm Suggestions* (10 minutes): The TAT leader reviews the strategies Ms. Mueller has already used (Question 2 on the request for assistance form). The TAT and Ms. Mueller then engage in a creative brainstorming process and generate as many suggestions for the chosen goal as possible within a 10-minute time period. One TAT member records each suggestion. Some teams use blackboards, overhead projectors, or butcher paper so everyone can follow the brainstorm list. In 10 minutes, from 10 to 30 suggestions can be generated if lengthy explanations, discussions, and debates about strategies are prohibited during the brainstorming process (see Figure 3.4).

4. *Teacher Selects Suggestions for Use* (2 minutes): After the brainstorming process is completed, Ms. Mueller is asked to select and indicate on the list those suggestions that she feels comfortable in implementing.

5. *Team Refines Suggestions and Designs a System for Measuring Student Progress* (8 minutes): Many of the suggestions that were generated do not require additional explanation or amplification. Ms. Mueller knows how to implement them as they are written. On one suggestion, however, Ms. Mueller requests amplification. The team assists Ms. Mueller to develop a contract system to help Eric complete his compositions and special assignments. Other teacher-selected suggestions are discussed to identify and resolve potential barriers to implementation, such as materials or permissions needed.

The TAT then helps Ms. Mueller design practical classroom techniques for measuring Eric's progress on the selected goals (see Figure 3.4). An objective method

| NAME OF CHILD | AGE | GRADE LEVEL | NAME OF TEACHER |
| Eric M. | 16 | Junior | J. Mueller |

| | | DATE | |
| | | Instruction Begun | Objective Achieved |

GOAL(S)	BRAINSTORM SUGGESTIONS	MEASUREMENT PROCEDURES	Instruction Begun	Objective Achieved
1. To improve attitude and effort in completing written assignments and composition in English	A. Ask him to write a composition about the fall play B. Throw out ideas and suggestions to encourage writing C. Have him dictate into a cassette, then play back and write from that; turn in cassette and composition D. Team write contract with him for assignment composition E. Teacher write contract with him for a specific assignment F. Use card to record + and – for on-task performance G. Have a written assignment done in student pairs H. Have him teach a lesson from a lesson plan he wrote I. Have him give an oral book report	A. For each English assignment in composition, the teacher and Eric record the following data: • Composition turned in on time? Yes ____ No ____ • Percentage completed ____ • Grade for *completed* portions • Actual grade for assignments B. Check number of times Eric uses teacher as a resource C. Record time on task when engaged in classwork	11/04	05/01

(Continued)

Figure 3.4 TAT Recommendations.

GOAL(S)	BRAINSTORM SUGGESTIONS	MEASUREMENT PROCEDURES	DATE	
			Instruction Begun	Objective Achieved
1. (continued)	J. Use play scripts as assignment to motivate him K. Work with and be responsible for less articulate or younger students L. Oral book review with a partner			
2. To become organized in his work	A. Set up colored folder system for each assignment and class B. Repeat assignments to teacher verbally to be sure they were understood C. Eric makes checklist for things to be done—checks it with teacher for accuracy before beginning assignment D. Compare checklist with another student	A. Have Eric check items to be done on checklist each day and turn in to teacher	12/08	
3. To improve social skills and make new friends	A. Have Eric work with less academically capable but more socially adept student B. Assist drama teacher with freshman play	A. Observe Eric's relationships over time in terms of talking, working, or seeking out others; keep a log on indicators of change	01/15	

(Continued)

Figure 3.4 (Continued).

GOAL(S)	BRAINSTORM SUGGESTIONS	MEASUREMENT PROCEDURES	DATE	
			Instruction Begun	Objective Achieved
3. *(continued)*	C. Earn reward for whole class based on work completion			
	D. Pair with various other students on activities			
	E. Serve as director in class play; act out written or reading assignments			
	F. Have counselor or homeroom teacher talk with Eric and/or his parents about their move, loss of friends, discomfort of starting over, efforts that need to be made			
	G. Use Eric's intelligence to help him gain insight to his feelings and how to change things for himself socially and academically			
	H. Join the drama club			

Figure 3.4 *(Continued).*

for measuring student progress is important, because intermittent progress can be difficult to perceive. Students do not suddenly improve. Progress is often inconsistent or slow, and successes are usually interspersed with failures. In time, however, the number of successful responses increase and the unsuccessful responses decrease if the interventions are successful.

Measuring student improvement often reinforces the teacher's efforts. Measurement procedures can be informal and simple, such as counts of the frequency of certain behaviors, percentages of appropriate and inappropriate behaviors, amount of time on task, logs, and a collection of samples of written assignments and tests. Giving the teacher a measurement schedule and specifying what might be measured and when it could be measured is helpful. A common procedure is for the teacher to measure behavior before intervention begins (to provide a baseline), and then measure it at specified intervals several times per week after intervention begins. For example, before beginning the intervention strategies generated by the TAT, Ms. Mueller could record the number of times Eric completed his English compositions and maintain a log describing his efforts and behavior during these assignments for a week. When Ms. Mueller obtains a baseline, she talks with Eric about his problems in composition. Eric then signs a contract with Ms. Mueller, who follows the measurement procedures described in Figure 3.4 for Objective 1.

6. *Follow-Up* (2 minutes): A follow-up team meeting with Ms. Mueller is scheduled within 2 to 6 weeks after the first TAT meeting to determine whether the recommended strategies are achieving the teacher's goals. The case manager contacts Ms. Mueller informally at least once each week to find out how things are going. Systematic follow-up is essential in helping teachers implement and readjust recommended stategies.

VI. Team Assessment

The TAT may need to clarify questions that have arisen about a particular student or classroom situation during the team meeting. The TAT may help the teacher plan informal classroom assessment procedures to answer such questions. In Eric's case, for example, the team asks Ms. Mueller to observe and record how much time he spends on a task before he stops, how often certain tasks are attempted, or which tasks are attempted more frequently than others.

VII. Refer Elsewhere for Evaluation

In certain situations, a TAT may decide to refer a teacher or a student for help. Eric and his family, for example, might be referred for counseling to help Eric better understand the reasons for the family move and the consequent impact of the move on all members of the family, and to discuss ways that Eric and the family can try to cope with the change in their lives. If the teacher or the TAT members believe a student may be disabled, they should immediately begin the special education referral process. A teacher always retains the right and has the responsibility of referring any suspected disabled student to the appropriate special education system immediately.

VIII. Recommendations for Teachers and Follow-Up

The suggestions developed during the brainstorming session are copied during or immediately after the meeting and given to Ms. Mueller. The original suggestions, the PID, and the request for assistance are placed in a folder, labeled, and filed for future reference. To assure confidentiality, TATs may wish to delete student names and merely keep case records by teacher name and/or case number.

EFFECTIVENESS OF TAT

Data have been gathered on the effectiveness of TATs in urban, suburban, and rural schools. Fifteen teams in Illinois, Nebraska, and Arizona generated recommendations for 200 students with learning and behavior problems (Chalfant & Pysh, 1981). The learning potential of 116 students was normal or above. The TATs successfully resolved the problems of 103 students, an 89% success rate. Teams earned a 100% success rate in assisting the classroom teachers of 30 disabled students who were being mainstreamed in regular classrooms. The TATs were not successful, however, in resolving the problems of 54 students who were thought by their teachers to be ''normal.'' These students were referred via the TAT process to special education for testing, and all were found to be eligible for special education services. Thus, the TATs identified 54 unidentified disabled students.

In a study of teams in Illinois, Maine, Maryland, and Nebraska, Gilmer (1985) found that teams successfully resolved the problems of 72% of the students served. Team success was measured by examining three criteria: (a) the degree to which written objectives for the student were achieved or nearly achieved, (b) the degree to which the TAT and the teacher both agreed that the student and the teacher were coping satisfactorily in the classroom, and (c) whether the team had withdrawn all support for at least 6 weeks. Data demonstrated that a building-level TAT model can be effective in helping teachers with normal, gifted, or disabled students (Chalfant & Pysh, 1989). A need exists, however, to gather data on the specific effectiveness of this model with larger numbers of gifted children with different kinds of problems. The model may be effective with certain problems of the gifted and not with others.

CHARACTERISTICS OF SUCCESSFUL TEAMS

Schools using teacher assistance teams that have proven to be successful over a long period of time seem to have six common characteristics:

1. Teachers within a building recognize that students are having difficulty, and that their needs are not being met. These teachers genuinely want to receive help in learning to work more effectively with students, rather than blaming the student or assuming the student belongs elsewhere and is someone else's responsibility.

2. Teachers are willing to ask for assistance. Although many teachers express a desire for assistance, they may not be comfortable asking for it. Some teachers are afraid of being viewed as incompetent by their fellow teachers or their principal. Whether teachers are willing to admit they have a problem in their classroom depends on the kind and degree of "safety" created by the TAT members and the principal. To paraphrase a principal in Ohio, "In my building, I will view teachers who use this process as caring more about students, as going above and beyond what's required, and as more competent than others."

3. Teachers believe that other teachers possess creativity and knowledge that can be helpful to them. Some teachers believe only an "expert" could help them, not their peers.

4. Teachers try new alternatives that might be foreign to their usual teaching style.

5. The principal, and preferably also the superintendent and board of education, provide support to the TATs. Administrators must make the TAT an accepted part of the system, provide options by restructuring TAT members' schedules or responsibilities to allow TATs to meet, and identifying ways to reinforce teachers who give their time to serve on and use these teams.

6. TATs should receive at least 6 hours of training in how to analyze classroom problems, engage in group problem-solving activities, operate effective and efficient meetings, measure student progress, and establish a TAT in a school.

ESTABLISHING A TEAM IN YOUR SCHOOL

If a building-level TAT is to be established and maintained, it must be part of the "system." This means that teams must have administrative support from the superintendent, the principal, and the school staff. The purpose of a TAT and the way it differs from the special education process must be clarified and understood.

The first step for beginning a TAT in a school district is to orient the administration. Administrative support, particularly by the principal, is critical to TAT success. The principal must believe in the ability of his or her staff to serve as resources for one another and provide the external support to make the TAT succeed. This includes finding a place and time for the TAT to meet. Teams normally meet before school, during the lunch hour, or after school, and require a room (preferably with a round table) that can be scheduled at the same time(s) each week. Administrators can encourage staff members to use the TAT by praising them and giving their participation recognition in faculty meetings, and by taking time to thank them informally for their interest in "going above and beyond the call of duty."

Some building principals provide "adjusted time" for team members who serve on TATs. This can be done in several ways. TAT members can be relieved of other duties for serving on the team, such as playground duty, hallway duty, bus duty, or curriculum committee duty. Team members may be given preference to attend conventions, letters of commendation can be placed in their files, and points may be given for salary increases or recertification experience and training.

The second step in establishing a TAT is to orient the building staff to the concept. At this stage, the principal needs to be the key figure in providing the proper perspective on this program. His or her explanation of this concept and how it will benefit the staff and fit into the school's structure is the central factor in faculty acceptance. A principal's willingness and overt desire to "empower" teachers to assist one another will set the stage for staff acceptance. This can be done by conducting an orientation on TATs for the staff, providing reading materials, showing videotapes, or having a team from another school demonstrate how the process works.

The third step in implementation is to prepare the TAT or the whole staff by training them in the procedures necessary for establishing and running an effective problem-solving group. Training should include hands-on experience and feedback on each aspect of the model: how to fill out the four questions on the request for assistance form, how to analyze student information and draw case diagrams, how to interview teachers and observe students, how to run efficient and effective 30-minute problem-solving meetings, and how to follow up on cases.

We believe a 6-hour inservice training program is required to teach these basic skills and procedures for organizing a team, being familiar with the group dynamics and the group problem-solving process, and learning the management techniques for conducting effective and efficient meetings. If your school has a Future Problem-Solving Team or an Odyssey of the Mind program, the coaches of these teams would be able to provide insights into group problem solving, as well as supply references or resources (Alvino, 1991; Micklus, 1984).

The fourth step in developing a TAT program is to provide technical assistance and follow-up to teams to help them cope successfully with the problems that inevitably arise in attempting to place a new program in an established system in a school. Buildings with teams begin requesting specific content areas for inservice programs. Typical inservice training sought by teams after they have been operating from 6 months to a year includes sessions on clarifying teacher information, methods for refining operating procedures for the team, additional information on group dynamics and communication skills, and classroom strategies for behavior management, self-concept, work habits, and individualizing academic instruction in the regular classroom.

The fifth step in implementation is to evaluate the performance of the TATs with respect to teacher satisfaction, student achievement of goals, and cost-effectiveness. For example, a questionnaire can be constructed asking teachers to describe what they found helpful about the teams, problems they encountered, and recommendations they would like to make. A 5-point Likert scale could be used to accompany the recorded progress of the student on instructional or behavioral objectives. Cost-effectiveness could be studied by comparing (a) data on special education referrals and their accompanying diagnostic costs before the teams were organized with (b) these same data after the teams have been operating for 1 or 2 years.

ADVANTAGES OF TAT

TATs provide an alternative for assisting teachers in individualizing instruction for gifted, average, and disabled students. Teams can help teachers increase their skill and comfort levels in dealing with students who have unique needs and provide a credible, immediate source of suggestions for teachers who request assistance. The TAT suggestions are realistic and feasible ones that have been tried by peers, and often can be generalized to other students. One of the greatest advantages of a TAT is creating a building environment where staff concern for students can result in a positive, constructive, problem-solving process of benefit to both students and teachers.

Administrators find TATs helpful because they create a buildingwide forum for sharing teacher competencies that often remain hidden in individual classrooms (Morrow, 1987). Communication and respect for other members of the staff are improved, and staff time is used more effectively and productively. Individual teacher and building morale can be enhanced through the opportunity to share concerns and resolve them together. Teachers trying to meet the needs of ''special'' students feel much less ''alone'' and frustrated.

Teachers use their wide array of teaching skills and curriculum knowledge when faced with students who have unique needs. Gifted students and others, however, can present challenges that are particularly frustrating, and sometimes teachers feel overwhelmed. Teachers often find they can better cope and more effectively individualize for students with unique needs by helping each other analyze student problems, gain new perspectives, and generate alternative strategies for use in the classroom. A TAT provides a positive and creative way for school staffs to share their abilities and skills and assist each other in helping children who are disabled, average, or gifted.

REFERENCES

Alvino, J. (1991). *Future Problem Solving Program.* Available from J. Alvino, 315 W. Huron, Ste. 140B, Ann Arbor, MI 48103-4203.

Chalfant, J., & Pysh, M. (1981, November). *Teacher assistance teams: A model for within-building problem solving.*

Chalfant, J. C., & Pysh, M. V. (1987). *Teacher assistance team workshops materials.* Unpublished materials presented at Association for Children with Learning Disabilities, San Antonio, TX.

Chalfant, J. C., & Pysh, M. V. (1989). Teacher assistance teams: Five descriptive studies on 96 teams. *Remedial and Special Education, 10*(6), 49–58.

Chalfant, J., Pysh, M., & Moultrie, R. (1979). Teacher assistance teams: A model for within-building problem solving. *Learning Disability Quarterly, 2,* 85–96.

Clark, B. (1988). *Growing up gifted* (3rd. ed.). Columbus, OH: Merrill.

Gilmer, J. (1985). *Factors related to the success and failure of teacher assistance teams in elementary schools.* Unpublished doctoral dissertation, University of Arizona, Tucson.

Hayek, R. A. (1987). The teacher assistance team: A pre-referral support system. *Focus on Exceptional Children, 20*(1), 1–7.

Karnes, M. B., & Johnson, L. J. (1991). Gifted handicapped. In N. Colangelo & G. A. Davis (Eds.), *Handbook of gifted education* (pp. 428–437). Boston: Allyn & Bacon.

Kirk, S. A., & Gallagher, J. J. (1989). *Educating exceptional children.* Boston: Houghton Mifflin.

Micklus, C. S. (1984). *Oddyssey of the mind: Problems to develop creativity.* Glassboro, NJ: Creative Competitions.

Morrow, G. (1987). *The compassionate school.* Englewood Cliffs, NJ: Prentice-Hall.

Ortiz, A. A., & Wilkinson, C. Y. (1991). Assessment and intervention model for the bilingual exceptional student. *Teacher Education and Special Education, 14*(1), 35–42.

Vaughn, V. L., Feldhusen, J. F., & Asher, J. W. (1991). Meta-analysis and review of research on pull-out programs in gifted education. *Gifted Child Quarterly, 35*(2), 92–98.

Whitmore, J. R., & Maker, C. J. (1985). *Intellectual giftedness in disabled persons.* Austin, TX: PRO-ED.

Will, M. (1986). *Educating students with learning problems: A shared responsibility.* Washington, DC: U.S. Department of Education, Office of Special Education and Rehabilitation Services.

4

Critique of the Teacher Assistance Teams Chapter by Chalfant and Van Dusen Pysh

Barbara W. Moller

The teacher assistance team (TAT) described in the previous chapter by Chalfant and Van Dusen Pysh provides a model for school-based intervention to assist teachers who recognize academic, behavioral, or sociological adjustment problems in learners. By using available resources at a school site, this model may increase teacher effectiveness through a support system of collegial problem solving. The model contributes to the professionalization of education by formalizing a system of assistance from peer teachers. Because this model is based on a teacher request process, it should be particularly helpful to faculties with many inexperienced teachers. As a nonevaluative option for seeking and receiving assistance, master teachers are encouraged to assume leadership roles, providing individual problem solving in a supportive atmosphere.

REFERRALS TO THE TAT

Chalfant and Van Dusen Pysh recommend that operating procedures for the team be developed by the teachers in each building, and key points are included to illustrate this process. The suggested four-question form enables classroom teachers to describe expectations, the nature of the problem, assets and deficits, and relevant background information. Although adoption of this form may be an efficient way to initiate the team, personnel at some schools may benefit from a more open-ended approach to defining existing problems and developing the process to address their concerns.

The entire faculty may participate in a formative session in which one staff member facilitates the identification of problems at the particular site. The discussion of recurring problems should illustrate the need for a TAT and also may delineate areas in which schoolwide inservice or resources would be beneficial. Using this strategy to initiate the process encourages teachers to assess their own needs and the available options to address identified problems.

An open-ended consideration of needs for assistance by the TAT may produce ideas that will enhance the model presented by Chalfant and Van Dusen Pysh. For example, novice teachers may request feedback on their effectiveness with various types of learners. Few schools have an established system for requesting such assistance; typically, the only source of feedback is the administrator who reviews a teacher's performance to determine employment status. Under such circumstances, teachers are seldom comfortable discussing their effectiveness with problem learners. Creating a forum for colleagues to provide feedback and classroom assistance may encourage teachers who are uncertain of their own effectiveness with individual students to seek another professional opinion. When visiting classrooms, the TAT might offer encouragement and reinforcement, as well as identifying problems that require further investigation.

Staff requests for feedback are only one indicator of a need for assistance. Site administrators may identify areas of concern through schoolwide data on student performance. For example, an analysis of achievement scores and teacher grading may indicate students who are not performing near expectancy level. Discrepancies, such as scores in the superior range of standardized tests achieved by students who receive average or below-average grades, also should be investigated.

By requesting administrative input on achievement, teachers who serve large numbers of students may become aware of individual learners' special needs. The TAT provides a vehicle to investigate why achievement may not meet expectations and offers options to address identified problems. This intervention may remediate individual learning discrepancies with no negative consequences for the classroom teacher who serves these students.

Administrators also receive indications of achievement problems from discipline referrals and parent conferences. A busy administrator may have limited opportunities to communicate a pattern of unsatisfactory adjustment to all teachers who serve a particular child; consequently, some immediate problems may be remedied without requesting further professional intervention. The TAT provides an option in such instances to investigate individual adjustment difficulties and plan appropriate educational modifications.

Students are another source of referrals to the TAT. Although a formal system of student requests for teacher assistance might be difficult to implement without creating the appearance of a complaint form, students who are experiencing difficulty adjusting to classrooms, peers, or academic demands might be offered the opportunity to seek assistance from an impartial team of professionals. The provisions for assistance might begin with a classroom visit, followed by a team meeting to suggest strategies to be implemented by the student, the teacher, parents, or other support personnel.

MEMBERSHIP AND SCHOOLWIDE RESOURCES

The TAT is described by Chalfant and Van Dusen Pysh as a core of three elected teachers. They add that any staff member may be invited to participate on the TAT as needed. Election by peers probably will assure that team members will be respected and trusted by the majority of the faculty. The flexibility to involve other staff members, however, may be critical to providing a balanced perspective in dealing with complex problems and offering expertise and insightful solutions.

To achieve this balance, a newly elected TAT should survey the resources represented by the team, other faculty members, and supportive services. These resources then may be matched to needs identified through referrals. As the team responds to requests for assistance, efforts should be made to include members who represent different ethnic groups, both sexes, and expertise in various academic disciplines.

By incorporating a broad perspective, solutions offered to individual classroom teachers may have schoolwide implications. For example, if providing appropriate curriculum for students who learn rapidly is requested by one teacher, the TAT might make the solution available to other instructors who serve advanced learners. If an initial solution was to modify instructional strategies or the learning environment in one classroom, the TAT may discover that this problem merits schoolwide consideration. Assistance might be provided to every teacher working with advanced learners, or the TAT might work with the administration to design and implement an enrichment program that would serve students from the entire school.

As effective solutions are implemented, a vehicle should be developed to make these available to other faculty members and to explore needs for further training. Inservice training may sensitize teachers to the special needs of students with unusual learning abilities and styles and illustrate options for matching teaching strategies to these students' needs. Workshops may include demonstrations, participatory experiences, and an exchange of best practices. Teachers may find that some needs may best be addressed on a schoolwide basis, such as planning together to exchange materials or cross-grouping to provide appropriate instructional challenges.

The collegial support nurtured by a TAT may provide a means for teachers to share ideas, materials, and resources throughout a school. Communication often is difficult in large schools, particularly if the faculty has experienced considerable turnover. In such cases, the challenges of meeting all requests for teacher assistance may be served by a team that identifies the strengths of each faculty member and arranges partnerships of complementary abilities. Administrative assistance may be involved when a change in course content, level of instruction, or class schedule would remedy problems that are difficult to solve in individual classrooms.

TRAINING FOR TATs

TATs provide the greatest benefit to gifted learners when team members possess a thorough understanding of above-average learners and the ways in which special services meet their needs. Chalfant and Van Dusen Pysh describe the effectiveness of TATs in referring students to be evaluated for special education services. Training in special learning needs will provide the expertise required for the team to assist with referrals to child study teams and to suggest classroom strategies that stimulate abilities and remediate disabilities.

Experienced observers may assist with identification of gifted students, particularly when a team member knowledgeable in characteristics of giftedness spends time with teachers who have limited experience with the complex behaviors associated with exceptional ability. For example, a student who completes assignments rapidly and asks numerous divergent questions may be perceived as being off task and creating a distraction to classroom learning. The trained observer, however, may recognize this behavior as indicating a need for additional stimulation and suggest appropriate modifications to the learning environment.

As programs for the gifted are developed in which educators respond to a wide range of instructional needs, identification of gifted learners should involve classroom observers sensitive to special learning requirements, such as those of the culturally different learner, the gifted student with learning disabilities, and the individual with unusual abilities in one area, such as mathematics, and average or below aptitude in another, such as language. Observers who understand these special needs may increase referrals and assist with culturally balanced identification without requiring intensive training for the total staff in this area.

CONCLUSION

In summary, a TAT may have a positive impact on the identification of gifted students and may enhance the regular classroom teachers' abilities to provide appropriate instruction for high-achieving students. This assistance, however, should not substitute for special services for the gifted. As the TAT increases the general educator's awareness of gifted students' needs, referrals to special programs may be increased and appropriate instructional modifications may be extended into classrooms where teachers seek assistance in adjusting strategies for these exceptional learners.

A Program Option
for Advanced Learners

Sharon K. Hooker

This chapter chronicles the birth and development of a program for gifted students. Professionals in an elementary program for gifted students recognized that special needs of advanced learners in their school system were being benignly neglected. These professionals also recognized that these able children had academic, social, and creative needs requiring special nurturing and programming.

The objective of the program for the gifted and talented when the program began was to expand service delivery to a group of advanced learners who would be instructed full time by their homeroom teacher, but whose progress would be accelerated and challenged, particularly in their demonstrated area(s) of strength. A member of the staff at each school, designated as an advocate–liaison, would assist classroom teachers in differentiating curriculum and in helping advanced learners and gifted learners build on their areas of strength. This component of the program was implemented in addition to existing pull-out resource rooms (Grades 2 through 6) and a teacher–consultant model (kindergarten and first grade).

IDENTIFICATION AND SERVICE DELIVERY MODELS

The state of Arizona requires that all children whose test results are two standard deviations above the norm on a state-approved intelligence test be served by the local school district. In the mandate, special education for gifted pupils is defined as expanding academic curriculum offerings as may be required to provide an educational program commensurate with the academic abilities and potential of the gifted pupils.

Located in a metropolitan city in the southwest, the school district under discussion enrolls about 11,000 students. District policy requires that the net be cast wider in the identification process than the state mandate requires, because research has shown that half the children scoring at the seventh stanine on a group intelligence test would actually score at the ninth stanine if an individual intelligence test were administered (Pegnato & Birch, 1959). A higher cutoff would result in many

53

gifted students being missed (Clark, 1979). No educators can afford to screen out 50% of our most able children because of imprecision in our instruments, and which children are in which half is not clear!

Tests administered in group settings are unlikely to identify underachieving gifted children or those with special talents who are also poor in reading. For such students, for a learning disabled gifted student, or for a bilingual student, an individual intelligence test is the test of choice (of course, bilingual psychologists administer the test to a bilingual child). *All* those referred for testing should be given individual intelligence tests, because of their reputation as being more reliable than the group tests, but cost is prohibitive. The district's philosophy reflects a commitment to provide appropriate educational opportunities and experiences for children of varying abilities, to ascertain individual needs and interests, and to provide for these to the highest degree possible. Children who have special abilities and potential far beyond that of their peers should be educated in a differentiated manner, with programming and instructional methods adapted to their unique needs.

Children are screened for inclusion in the program for gifted and talented using the following criteria: They must be referred by a parent, teacher, or by a ninth stanine score on the standardized achievement test (math or reading) given each year, and they must score in the seventh, eighth, or ninth stanine on a group intelligence test. In addition, a student scoring in the seventh or eighth stanine needs supporting subjective data from two teachers who have known the child well. A student scoring in the ninth stanine does not *require* supporting subjective data for inclusion in the program because of the state mandate; however, subjective information is generally secured, because it gives a more complete profile and will help in planning to meet that individual's needs. Information is solicited from teachers about a child's learning characteristics, motivation, and creativity. Achievement test scores are included in the screening process on all first- through sixth-grade students, with data being quantified and weighted on a Baldwin Identification Matrix (Baldwin, 1978).

No single instrument is a sufficient basis upon which to assess the multifaceted nature of giftedness. Diverse kinds of instruments and approaches are needed to find diverse kinds of exceptional ability. Both informal and formal procedures are necessary to avoid bias and to include all gifted students in need of special programming (Richert, 1982).

The program has two models used to deliver service to the most talented students. In one, an itinerant teacher meets with kindergarten and first-grade students at their home school and provides curriculum and resources for follow-up by the children and their teachers. The teacher–consultant model is implemented wherein a certified teacher with training in education of the gifted models various learning processes in the kindergarten and first-grade classrooms by demonstrating special lessons. In this model, *both* the students and the classroom teachers profit from the lesson.

If the identified child has made satisfactory progress in his or her regular classroom learning, as evidenced by the first-grade standardized achievement measures, and if motivation to learn has been observed in the sessions with the teacher of the gifted, the child is placed in the pull-out program for gifted and talented, the second model. If an identified gifted child has not demonstrated above-average achievement, or if he or she has not exhibited curiosity and motivation to learn in the enrichment program, he or she can be placed on the advanced learner strand. The students in this strand are then closely monitored by the homeroom teacher and an advocate–liaison at the elementary school. The advocate–liaison's role at the elementary school is to promote the interest of the gifted and advanced learner. The identification file for each advanced learner will be reviewed yearly by the program's teaching staff with the goal of matching services to the student's needs.

Historical data were accumulated, whereby the relative success of each student who had been in the program was compared with the respective profile developed for identification. Cutoff points were determined to establish entry levels where success in the program would be predictable (as much as anyone's success can ever be predicted). Four cutoff points for entry into the program were established: one for entry into the kindergarten and first-grade teacher–consultant model; one for entry into the pull-out, enrichment program for Grades 2 through 6; slightly lower cutoff points for advanced learners in kindergarten and first grade; and lower cutoff points for advanced learners in Grades 2 through 6.

Children in Grades 2 through 6 who are involved in the pull-out, enrichment program are bussed weekly from their homes or schools to attend a full day of special classes. The bussing provision exemplifies the district's commitment to program equity and equal access for all.

Underrepresentation of gifted students from minority groups is a concern among educators. The ethnic composition of the district in 1987 was 63% Hispanic, 30% Anglo, 3% black, 3% Native American, and .5% Oriental and Asian. The program's ethnic composition has always been very near to that of the district, a condition that results, in part, from multiple index screening and identification, rather than reliance on only one test score. Responsiveness of the program staff to teacher and parent input into the screening process is a second cause for the close match between district and program populations in ethnic percentages: If a teacher or parent has reason to believe that the stanine score on a group intelligence test underrepresents a child's true ability, the staff retests, using a different instrument. If a youngster has been given two group intelligence tests and still is referred to the program at another grade level by another professional, a staff member refers that child for an individual test to be administered by a psychologist. Subjective data are updated if the screening committee (comprising program teachers and the director/teacher) believes that teacher attitude or bias, the passage of time, or family crisis may have colored the initial reporting. Third, extraordinary efforts are made to secure permission to test all children referred for screening, from multiple mailing attempts and telephone requests to home visits by principals or program staff members.

PROGRAM RATIONALE

The rationale for special education for gifted students advanced by Barbara Clark (1979) is subscribed to by this school district:

1. Giftedness arises from an interactive process that involves challenging innate abilities with a stimulating environment. To retain their giftedness and to ensure personal and academic development, gifted children must participate in appropriate programs.

2. *Each* person has the right to learn at the most appropriate level for his or her abilities.

3. When people are restricted in development, they become bored and frustrated. Physical and psychological pain results from being thwarted and diminished as a person.

4. Society gains from the highest development of all its members. That which actualizes the individual benefits the society.

5. Gifted youngsters need to be with others who are like themselves, so that their ideas and interests are not perceived as odd and different.

One's self-concept is formed in part on the basis of how other persons see him or her; if people like you, you like yourself. A second way a self-concept is formed is through basic self-acceptance and involves a belief that one is intrinsically worthy. A third way, conditional self-acceptance, is to derive conclusions about self-worth based on external standards and expectations. If one meets the expectations set by others, then he or she is of value. A fourth way is self-evaluation, and involves one's estimate of how well one's attributes compare with those of others. A real-to-ideal comparison allows one to judge how his or her real self compares with the ideal self, that is, the correspondence between what the person is and what the person thinks he or she should be (Johnson, 1986). Grouping gifted youngsters for at least part of their instruction allows a more accurate perspective of who they are.

6. Gains are significant when the needs of the gifted are considered in designing the educational program. These students show gains in achievement, sense of competence, efficiency in a work environment, problem-solving skills, and the ability to see different perspectives.

7. This population of individuals contributes disproportionately in all areas of human endeavor. Society benefits from the products of an innovative, highly functioning gifted individual.

PROGRAM GOALS

Goals for the gifted and talented programming in kindergarten through sixth grade include the following:

1. Each student will develop an intrinsic motivation for excellence and individual responsibility.
2. Each student will accept and develop his or her gifts and increase personal challenges.
3. Each student will develop a positive self-concept.
4. Each student will develop attitudes and skills necessary to interact acceptably and comfortably with others.

5. Each student will develop competencies at a high cognitive level.
6. Each student will develop independent, intuitive, discriminating, critical, and creative learning strategies.
7. Each student will develop competencies in complex, abstract, and divergent thinking.

The advanced learners generally were succeeding in the school system. The district wanted to nurture their competencies and talents, to enhance their critical and creative thinking skills, and to sustain their love of learning. Gifted students also frequently need acceleration within content areas. This is most appropriately accomplished within the home school setting by out-of-level placements (e.g., mathematics, reading) and individualized pacing. Other kinds of curriculum modifications for the gifted learner were also suggested by the advocate–liaisons and the program staff. These modifications are discussed in the curriculum differentiation section.

ADVOCACY IN THE ADVANCED LEARNER PROGRAM STRAND

The teacher–director of the program met with elementary principals to discuss the efficacy of the new strand and underscored the fact that they were *already* responsible for meeting the academic, social, and personal needs of these bright children. The intent of the advanced learner strand was to help them meet their obligation by offering assistance, training, and resources.

Job responsibilities and competencies for the advocate–liaisons were posted to advertise these nonpaid positions. The district was seeking energetic people who had (a) knowledge of the nature and needs of advanced learners and/or willingness to learn the same, (b) knowledge of affective/psychological needs of gifted children and/or willingness to learn the same, (c) knowledge of approaches to extension and enrichment of subject areas, (d) skill in individualized teaching techniques, (e) skill in facilitating independent research and study skills, (f) skill in individual counseling of advanced learners, (g) the ability to work effectively with other teachers, and (h) an interest in and enthusiasm for working with advanced learners.

The district also posted the job description. The advocate–liaisons' responsibilities would include the following: (a) become acquainted with the students identified as advanced learners, (b) facilitate appropriate student placement within the disciplines, (c) encourage and assist teachers in securing appropriate instructional materials for the advanced learner, (d) stimulate interest and concern for the able learner, (e) work cooperatively with other personnel in evaluating the program, (f) assist in identification of students for the program, (g) facilitate open communication with classroom teachers and program teachers, (h) document delivery of student services and progress throughout the school year, and (i) in some cases work with students. The list of competencies indicated we were clearly looking for an executive.

How could already overloaded professionals see their way clear to do more? Who would volunteer their time? At some schools, there would be an advocate–liaison for both primary and intermediate grades. At every campus, however, there were volunteers. Some individuals considered the position as a personal growth experience. Others were pursuing their interest in giftedness. Still others believed the position would be of merit for their career ladder portfolios. Each gave time and energy to make the fledgling strand of the program work for children. Without these volunteers and their desire to make a difference in their schools, the advanced learner program would have been only a dream.

Teachers, librarians, and specialists volunteered to serve as advocate–liaisons in response to the postings, and the advanced learner strand was launched. Each year, the teachers in the program offered to the advocate–liaisons in-service training on characteristics and concomitant problems and needs of gifted students, screening and identification, and curricular modifications. Because gifted youngsters spent the majority of their time in their homerooms, our intent was to affect the teaching within those homerooms. Advocates left the training sessions with articles, handbooks, a philosophy, and the knowledge that their work lay ahead.

To prepare the advocates for their resource positions, the staff of the program for the gifted also furnished the advocates with handbooks for parents, a resource book on curriculum differentiation for the gifted child in the regular classroom, and articles on creativity and emotional needs of the gifted. The program staff continued to send articles on a variety of topics to remind all teachers of kindergarten through sixth-grade classes of the needs of their most able students, to focus on strategies that would work with their most capable, and to highlight the resource teachers' roles. Even though 1986 had been declared the "Year of the Gifted Child" in Arizona, the district's goal was to create an *ongoing* concern and a high level of awareness for this neglected minority. The district did not want concern about better education for this population to be a fleeting interest.

DISTRICTWIDE RESOURCE LIBRARY

Money was budgeted for establishing a lending library to support this outreach program; the funding for the lending library was $1,500 the first year of the advanced learner strand and $2,500 the second year. The advocate–liaisons and the teachers in the program for the gifted cooperatively selected the resource materials, relying upon informal methods of surveying teachers' needs the first year and a more formal, written survey the second year. Teachers were requested to state the content and skill areas for which enrichment materials were most needed, and their responses were useful in the selection process.

A catalog listing the enrichment materials available to all kindergarten through sixth-grade teachers was organized around specific content areas and thinking skills, with an emphasis on integrating the two. The program personnel purchased materials in the content areas of reading, language arts, mathematics, social studies, and sciences; in the creative and critical thinking skills; and in methods and skills of research. Materials were cataloged and readied for sending to classrooms; some resources were laminated, and everything was prepared for districtwide delivery in suitable containers. Catalogs were sent to every elementary teacher, and requisition forms were made available at each school.

To order enrichment materials for classroom use, teachers could place a telephone request with the program secretary, send a requisition form through school mail, or ask an advocate–liaison for assistance in securing books, posters, activities, manipulatives, cards, games, puzzles, or units to suit their purposes. Within a day of the order, materials would be in the hands of children and teachers, ready for use.

The enrichment materials available for loan were intended to help teachers plan for their most able students, whether or not they were identified as gifted or advanced learners. The district also believed, however, that grouping the bright children for portions of their instruction would facilitate their constructive socialization, achievement, and psychological health.

GROUPING (AND REGROUPING)

Classroom teachers could group their brightest students for part of their day; advocate–liaisons who were school librarians had a special opportunity to group children according to interests. In schools where the advocate–liaison was a librarian, opportunities were available for the advanced learner both inside the classroom and inside the library.

Grouping children for cooperative learning experiences has been found to promote positive interaction patterns, feelings of psychological acceptance and psychological success, liking for other students and the instructor, and expectations of rewarding future interactions with collaborators. Cooperative learning experiences promote the use of higher reasoning strategies and greater critical thinking competencies and contributes to more positive attitudes toward both the subject area and the instructional experience. Because cooperativeness is positively related to a number of indices of psychological health, schools should be organized to promote those tendencies (Johnson & Johnson, 1987). Therefore, the district promotes cooperative learning strategies as ways to teach advanced learners.

During the screening and identification in the fall of the first year, some students who were part of the pull-out program were reassigned to the advanced learner strand because their performance had not been satisfactory; lack of motivation to participate was the only reason that children's placement was changed. Ten children were affected. Parents were advised of the need for a change in placement.

In the fall of the second year, when testing was completed, some students' placement changed in the other direction, from the advanced learner strand to the primary or intermediate pull-out program. Their records showed increased achievement and the updated matrices qualified them for pull-out (where entrance standards were higher). The placements of 7 primary children and 5 intermediate-level children changed. Parents were invited to attend an educational program in which the purposes of the program for the gifted and talented were explained and written permission to place their children in the pull-out program was secured.

CURRICULUM DIFFERENTIATION

Because the advanced learner strand is in its infancy, only 1 year's curriculum modifications are currently available. As people witness the successes of colleagues, opportunities made available to the advanced learners and gifted learners within the home school setting probably will increase in diversity and in number.

In the area of reading, students were engaged in reporting on trade books and presenting their books as a project or television production; other students made audiotapes to enable younger children to read along at learning centers. Professionals involved children in reading selections from the Junior Great Books Program and in discussions focused on higher level reasoning, values, and creative thinking. Children read in particular genres, such as folktales, and analyzed the styles of authors, noted similarities between various folktales, and engaged in critical thinking and in dramatization of the genre. Some advanced learners analyzed book illustrations and produced their own, focusing on the impact of images. Many children were accelerated in their reading instruction. For enrichment, some students read and reported events from the newspaper; some conducted independent research on the country of the newspaper article; and others read in depth about a person or an issue selected from an article.

In language arts, students were engaged in similar activities, with some advanced learners writing about authors, researching a country (the book's setting) or a time period, or otherwise extending a literary experience. Students conducted interviews and incorporated them into class newspapers or yearbooks. They wrote in various modes: legends, folktales, various kinds of poetry, plays, articles, stories, letters, newspaper reports, and summaries. Advanced learners participated in radio broadcasts, role-playing experiences, plays and dramatizations, their schoolwide and districtwide spelling bee, and a districtwide Young Authors' Conference. Students learned about and tried mime, pursued listening activities on their own, investigated two-way versus one-way communication, submitted their best writing for publication, and learned and practiced canons of speaking to an audience.

Independent study allows students to pursue an area of interest or talent and can be a rewarding enterprise; some advanced learners conducted library research, using note-taking and study skills, self-pacing, and high-level reasoning. Some teachers substituted comprehension activities in science and social studies with projects requiring analysis, synthesis, and evaluation. Some students conducted science experiments, made science projects to teach others, and participated in science fairs; others conducted surveys and produced slide photography; and some applied their mapping skills and developed social studies units and centers for use by classmates. Some advanced learners instructed the whole class, using their own lesson plans.

In the area of mathematics, the most common modification was acceleration and out-of-level placement in the curriculum. Some teachers provided enrichment activities, manipulatives, and tutoring opportunities. Some asked their students to write original story problems. Other teachers allowed their advanced learner(s) to teach the class a skill in math.

Teachers enhanced critical thinking with simulations (e.g., the Stock Market game), centers focusing on reasoning and logic, critical thinking activities, and games such as Chess. Some students were involved in planning for school-related functions.

Teachers spent less time in the area of creative thinking than on critical thinking. The director intends to advocate strongly for more divergent thinking. A few teachers reported using guided imagery and other imagination activities; others reported creative follow-up to literature and some limited integration of creative thinking into the content areas.

Computer-assisted instruction and word processing were alternatives available at many schools. One advocate–liaison even established a computer club.

RECORD KEEPING

During the first year of the advanced learner strand, advocate–liaisons and the teachers in the program for gifted students met as a whole to compare successes, concerns, and curriculum differentiation in use at various schools. A monthly log helped structure the facilitative function for each advocate–liaison, so the person would be viewed always as one of a helping professional. This record-keeping function was intended to spur conversation and creative thinking between professionals about curriculum differentiation for the advanced learners and their gifted peers.

LOOSE ENDS

What remains to be done? What are our concerns? Across this district, and perhaps the nation, teachers feel shortchanged in three significant ways: time to plan adequately, a salary commensurate with training and contribution to society, and sagging public opinion for the teaching profession. One deficiency in the advanced learner model is related to two of the three teacher concerns: Advocate–liaisons *should* be compensated for this extracurricular responsibility, for it is beyond the scope of their own contracts and cuts into the other precious resource, time. The dedication of educators is evidenced by their willingness to volunteer to give more time and energy when they are already feeling sorely stretched. The third area of concern, diminished status, is probably reflective of a general malaise and lack of confidence in all public servants and officials.

The teachers in the program recognize that more frequent one-to-one communication with classroom teachers would be desirable, particularly with those teachers with whom we "share" a gifted child. The communication problem is aggravated when the teacher of the gifted is responsible not only for developing curriculum and teaching approximately 70 to 75 children, but having ongoing involvement in the districtwide screening and identification process and with the advanced learner strand. The primary and intermediate pull-out classes draw their populations from 11 elementary schools in this district, so the problem of busy schedules for all teachers concerned is compounded by geographic distance.

In an effort to meet the need of meaningful communication, letters outlining curriculum are sent to teachers of students in the pull-out program, and, at the end of the semester, a behavioral report card is sent to each child's classroom teacher. The card provides sections for reporting performance habits; capacity to work independently; critical thinking skills; creative problem-solving abilities; self-concept development, values, and interpersonal skills; research and communication skills; and quality of production.

Classroom teachers need additional inservice training on characteristics of the gifted learner and on curriculum differentiation. The staff members of the program for the gifted recognize this need and are planning one or more districtwide, after-school inservice training workshops. Teachers will still need time to plan for implementing new strategies. Unfortunately, the time for teachers to internalize new information and to integrate it into their own curriculum is still at issue. Teachers, strapped for time, need help in differentiating curriculum. Otherwise, the excuse for not providing special services—"They'll make it on their own"—could become a comfortable one. Gifted and advanced learners deserve an appropriate education.

CONCLUSION

The advanced learner model is a conceivable one for any school district. It requires more creative resources than financial resources, although funding for a lending library and stipends for advocate–liaisons is a minimal level of support. This model is *a second layer* of service and not the only one. It represents one of a number of modifications of regular school programs to adapt instruction to children who deviate from the average.

Nothing is new under the sun. Still, creative energy is necessary for such a program to succeed. Creative persons are very diverse in backgrounds, but they have in common an attitude of optimism (Kirk & Gallagher, 1979). In this program, both creative energy and high expectations for children fuel our efforts.

REFERENCES

Baldwin, A. (1978). Educational planning for the gifted. In A. Baldwin, G. Gear, & L. Lucito (Eds.), *Educational planning for the gifted: Overcoming cultural, geographic and socioeconomic barriers* (pp. 1–17). Reston, VA: Council for Exceptional Children.

Clark, B. (1979). *Growing up gifted.* Columbus, OH: Merrill.

Johnson, D. (1986). *Reaching out.* Englewood Cliffs, NJ: Prentice-Hall.

Johnson, D. W., & Johnson, R. (1987). *Learning together and alone.* Englewood Cliffs, NJ: Prentice-Hall.

Kirk, S., & Gallagher, J. (1979). *Educating exceptional children* (3rd ed.). Boston: Houghton Mifflin.

Pegnato, C., & Birch, J. (1959). Locating gifted children in junior high schools: A comparison of methods. *Exceptional Children, 26,* 303–304.

Richert, E. (1982). *National report on identification.* Sewell, NJ: Educational Improvement Center–South.

6

A Reaction to Local Program Development as a Disjointed Enterprise

Joyce VanTassel-Baska

The advanced learner model using an advocate liaison teacher as described in the previous chapter by Hooker offers an interesting perspective on meeting the needs of gifted learners in core curriculum areas, where a pull-out program is the predominant service delivery for the gifted program. Many writers have argued strongly for attention to the needs of high-ability learners in content areas (Maker, 1982; Passow, 1986; VanTassel-Baska, 1986b; VanTassel-Baska et al., 1988). In elementary self-contained programs for the gifted, such needs are addressed as a natural aspect of the programming model (VanTassel-Baska, Willis, & Meyers, 1989). In many secondary programs, content areas become the organizers for special classes, the predominant form of programming at that level (Gallagher, 1985). Moreover, the success of the talent search model nationwide has contributed important research evidence that suggests major benefits to gifted learners accruing from study of advanced content (Benbow & Stanley, 1983; Sawyer, 1986; VanTassel-Baska, 1986a).

In spirit, the program case study outlined by Hooker attempts to address the issue of advanced content learning for the gifted through the creative use of a specialist. However, what beneficial effects accrue to gifted learners who are capable of advancement appear to be differential and diffused. The role of the advocate liaison as defined signals a need for assistance in many areas of the program, yet only two aspects of the job description relate directly or indirectly to differential intervention for gifted children. Thus, the strategy could be perceived as a way to increase personnel in the gifted program whose major responsibility is ''cleaning up messes'' brought about by a faulty conception of programming in the first place.

The reading of Hooker's chapter on the use of a teacher-cadre labeled ''advocate liaisons'' raises several questions and issues. The first issue is the program definition within which such a cadre appears to be operating. As a reader of the manuscript,

I find that the program differentiation is unclear. The pull-out program is described to be for bright, motivated, and high-achieving students; the advanced learner program is described to be for bright, unmotivated, and moderate to low achievers. A strange assumption is being made here: that you do not have to be well motivated or a high achiever to be accelerated in content, but you do have to exhibit those qualities to do pull-out project work. Regardless of this conflictual reasoning, Hooker also is unclear about which learners receive service from the advocate liaison and why—both groups of identified gifted learners or only the group not served by the pull-out experience?

A second issue to be examined is the schemata used for program development. Sketchy findings are reported from the first year of using the advocate liaison model, but what was being examined is unclear. Apparently, no evaluation data were collected consistently. We do not know, for example, how many students from each designated group of gifted learners benefited from the Junior Great Books Program, from independent study, or from book production. Nor do we know the nature, extent, and quality of their work. We also do not know the objectives of either program model or the extent to which they were realized in the first year. The description of the program includes heavy emphasis on delineating the process by which it was enacted rather than the substance of student interventions that the model brought about. Thus, the reader is left wondering what guided the program development effort other than general philosophical tenets deeply held.

A third issue for consideration relates to the role of the advocate–liaison. The description reads as if these persons were hired without a sense of role definition or an idea regarding how curriculum might proceed for identified groups of learners. By implication, the whole concept rested on what individual teachers might be able to do without direction or a framework to guide them. Such a notion counters everything we know about systematic interventions for gifted learners. The assumption that gifted programs can be institutionalized with volunteers and spotty interventions seems naive and simplistic.

A last issue related to Hooker's chapter that needs to be considered deals with identification. Several important aspects of the identification process were difficult to discern. If, as Hooker described, teachers of the gifted conducted activities with primary children to look for exceptional ability, why were children not assigned to the program based on contextual performance rather than prior test scores? Additionally, the purpose for using a diversity of identification instruments, and what relationship they bore to the planned programs, remains unclear. Moreover, how was the weighting of criteria determined, and how did it affect the overall placement decisions?

These issues are crucial to understanding clearly the program described in Hooker's chapter. In the absence of such clarity, it seems appropriate to diverge from further commentary on the chapter, and to share a perspective on a reasonable approach to local program development that takes into account (a) the need to describe accurately desired program outcomes, (b) the need to consider the role of teachers in the process, and (c) the need to monitor carefully the program's implementation.

THE CONCEPT OF A PROGRAM FRAMEWORK

One important way of proceeding with program development involves an examination of desired outcomes for students at the end of a specified period of time deemed appropriate for observing change. The curriculum framework concept also affords a way to look at programs for the gifted across grade levels and content disciplines, linking the outcome statements to curriculum differentiation models and strategies. In this way, the resultant framework is representative of all aspects of the program.

The program model used as the basis for the framework (see Figure 6.1) uses the following terminology that may be useful to define:

1. *Cognitive end-product goals* are outcomes gifted students should achieve as a result of spending *X* number of years in special programs.
2. *Cognitive process goals* are representative processes that teachers of the gifted must employ to help gifted learners achieve their goals.
3. *Affective end-product goals* are outcomes in the affective area that gifted learners should take away from their program experiences.
4. *Affective process goals* are representative processes that teachers must incorporate into classroom activities to help gifted students achieve their worthy ends in affective areas.
5. *Instructional process goals* are those instructional techniques that must be practiced by teachers with regularity to reinforce the direction of student growth patterns.

The model then represents a clear delineation of desirable outcomes from programs for the gifted influenced by both curriculum and instructional input resulting in program implementation. This model provides us with the most expansive view of curriculum for the gifted because it can encompass Grades K through 12 in all potential areas of inquiry.

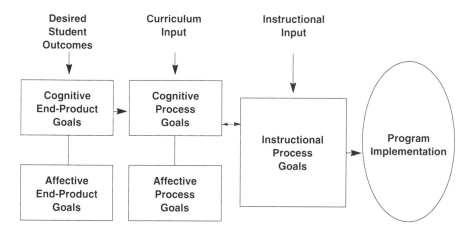

Figure 6.1 Program-Level Framework for Planning and Articulation.

The following example of the application of this framework to a program for gifted learners serves as a real example of how the framework might be employed in a local district program. The expectation levels cited in the example represent an attempt to differentiate outcomes for gifted learners from what would be acceptable for more typical learners and to examine outcome issues from a broad perspective. For example, scoring a 4 on an advanced placement exam may be appropriate for gifted students in high school, but not at other levels. Obviously, individual school districts need to tailor the model to their own time specification needs, grade levels, and areas of program intervention. Nonetheless, it presents a comprehensive view of program development implications that should be agreed upon *before,* not after, a program has been put in place.

EXAMPLE OF FRAMEWORK APPLICATION

Cognitive End-Product Goals

Content Skills and Concepts

By the end of the program, the student will

1. Achieve 90% mastery of new material in appropriate content areas (including reading/language arts/English, mathematics, social studies, and sciences).
2. Master 90% of the core curricular areas in half the time allotted to average learners.
3. Achieve an average score on advanced placement tests of 3 on a scale of 5 in relevant areas.

Process Skills/Product Development

By the end of the program, the student will

1. Achieve an average of 4.0 on a 5.0-point teacher checklist designed to measure process skill application.
2. Receive a good to superior rating on a product completed for relevant areas.
3. Perform at a level at least 1.5 standard deviations above the mean using regular norms or comparable gifted norms on a test measuring specific thinking skills.
4. Score a combined level of 1100 on the Scholastic Aptitude Test as a college-bound senior.

Concept Development

By the end of the program, the student will

1. Achieve an average of 3.5 out of 5.0 points on, for example, a science project, oral report, or written essay that integrates a concept within a domain of inquiry (alternative media, such as films, music, videos, art, might be used).

2. Achieve an average of 3.5 out of 5.0 points on a written essay which integrates a concept across domains of inquiry (alternative media such as films, music, art, videos might be used).

Affective End-Product Goals

By the end of the program, the student will

1. Demonstrate effective social interactions by receiving a minimum of 80% score on an observation form.
2. Demonstrate understanding and application of coping strategies through the use of journal writing or oral interview that reflects a good to superior level.
3. Develop a plan that specifies future academic and career goals.
4. Demonstrate 85% proficiency in the acquisition of independent learning habits on a performance checklist.

Cognitive Process Goals

During the program, the teacher will

1. Conduct diagnostic testing at regular intervals to determine curricular placement in appropriate content areas (including reading, language arts, English, mathematics, social studies and science, art, music).
2. Reorganize text materials across units to accommodate conceptual level of students in appropriate content areas (including language arts, mathematics, social studies, science, art, music).

Process/Product Skill Development

During the program, the teacher will

1. Use activities that teach inference, deductive reasoning, inductive reasoning, analogies, and evaluation of arguments in appropriate content areas.
2. Use activities that teach ideational fluency, flexibility, and elaboration in appropriate content areas.
3. Use activities that teach fact finding, problem finding and defining, idea generation and alternative solution finding, evaluating among solutions, and developing a plan of action in appropriate content areas.
4. Use activities that teach skills in defining a problem, gathering data, developing hypotheses, observing/experimenting/recording data, analyzing data, generating conclusions, and drawing implications in appropriate content areas.
5. Use activities that teach skills in oral communication in appropriate content areas.

6. Use activities that teach skills in prewriting, developing a thesis, providing supportive evidence, handling transitions, generating conclusions, editing, revising, and rewriting in appropriate content areas.

Concept Development

During the program, the teacher will

1. Present ideas, issues, and themes within the knowledge domains of science, mathematics, literature, art, music, history, and philosophy.
2. Demonstrate how key ideas, issues, and themes in one area (see list above) relate to other knowledge areas.

Affective Process Goals

During the program, the teacher will

1. Use activities that develop the social skills of (a) establishing and maintaining positive relationships with peers and (b) working cooperatively with others.
2. Use activities that develop the coping skills of (a) dealing with oversensitivity to what others say and do, (b) developing tolerance, (c) dealing with the problems of perfectionism, (d) developing relaxation techniques, and (e) coping with feelings of inferiority and inadequacy.
3. Use activities that optimize the good learning habits of studying, achieving, and being actively engaged in the learning experience.

Instructional Process Goals[1]

During the program, the teacher will

1. Conduct group discussions.
2. Select questions that stimulate higher level thinking.
3. Use varied teaching strategies effectively.
4. Use critical thinking skills in appropriate contexts.
5. Encourage independent thinking and open inquiry.
6. Understand and encourage student ideas and student-directed work.
7. Demonstrate understanding of the educational implications of giftedness.
8. Use creative thinking techniques.
9. Use problem-solving techniques.
10. Synthesize student assessment data and curriculum content effectively.

---

[1]Adaptation of the Martinson–Weiner scale (Martinson, 1974) has been made to link these goals to an assessment tool.

CLASSROOM LEARNER LEVEL FRAMEWORK

Although establishing student and teacher goals at a program level is necessary and worthwhile, equally useful is viewing the program development process at another level. This level is the individual classroom, where student goals become translated into learning objectives, and teachers' curriculum and instructional processes become translated into specific activities and daily instructional processes. Moreover, both monitoring and evaluation of the program must be done at this level (see Figure 6.2).

Without the use of such frameworks, what works and what does not work in programming for the gifted and why evaluation results emerge as they do will continue to be difficult to understand. However, until program planners at the local levels are willing to consider systematic approaches to studying the efficacy of what they do, we, as a field, will continue to flounder, being excited by novelty rather than proven effectiveness.

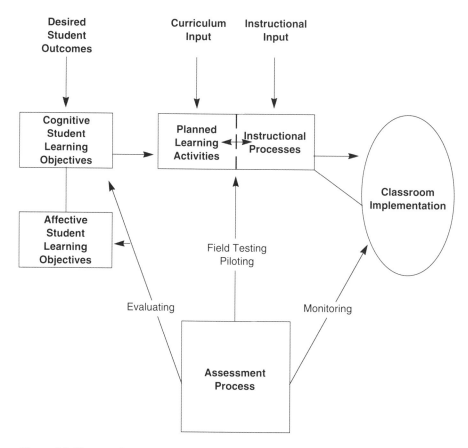

Figure 6.2 Classroom/Learner Level Framework for Planning, Implementation, and Assessment.

REFERENCES

Benbow, C. P. & Stanley, J. C. (1983). *Academic precocity, its aspects and nurturance.* Baltimore, MD: Johns Hopkins Press.

Gallagher, J. J. (1985). *Teaching the gifted child* (3rd ed.). Boston: Allyn & Bacon.

Maker, C. J. (1982). *Curriculum development for the gifted.* Austin, TX: PRO-ED.

Martinson, R. (1974). *Martinson–Weiner rating scale of behaviors in teachers of the gifted: A guide toward better teaching for the gifted.* Ventura, CA: Ventura County Superintendent of Schools Office.

Passow, A. H. (1986). Curriculum for the gifted and talented at the secondary level. *Gifted Child Quarterly, 30,* 186–191.

Sawyer, R. (1986). Intellectual challenges and emotional support of the precocious child. *Journal of Counseling and Development, 64,* 593–597.

VanTassel-Baska, J. (1986a). The case for acceleration. In J. Maker (Ed.), *Critical issues in gifted education: Vol. I. Defensible programs for the gifted* (pp. 179–196). Austin, TX: PRO-ED.

VanTassel-Baska, J. (1986b). Effective curriculum and instructional models for talented students. *Gifted Child Quarterly, 30,* 164–169.

VanTasssel-Baska, J., Feldhusen, J., Seeley, K., Wheatley, G., Silverman, L., & Foster, W. (1988). *Comprehensive curriculum for gifted learners.* Boston: Allyn & Bacon.

VanTassel-Baska, J., Willis, G., & Meyers, D. (1989). Evaluation of a full-time self-contained class for gifted students. *Gifted Child Quarterly, 33,* 7–10.

7

The Use of the Demonstration Teaching Model in Education of the Gifted

Marilyn A. Rice

The demonstration teaching model can be a vital component of a districtwide program for gifted students. It can serve as a complement to a pull-out program; a beginning step in the development of a districtwide, comprehensive program; or a worthwhile addition to a program based on continuous progress or nongraded design.

Basically, a program for gifted students should be individualized. The content and pace should be altered to meet the needs of the gifted. Opportunities are incorporated that require students to think and process information, the ultimate goal being to help students learn how to learn.

WHAT IS DEMONSTRATION TEACHING?

According to Putnam (1985), a demonstration teaching model involves ''teaching demonstrations by teacher educators as a primary mode of illustrating how to apply theory in practice'' (p. 36). Putnam's work, however, refers to teacher training at the university level, and the types of demonstrations referred to involve working with videotaped and live demonstrations with varying sizes of groups and content.

Demonstration teaching also may be used at the elementary and secondary levels. Teacher educators or specialized demonstration teachers can present lessons in classrooms with the regular classroom teacher observing. A written lesson plan should be given to the classroom teacher for a reference. Follow-up activities, such as centers and suggestions for extension of the ideas, also should be included so both teacher and students are able to apply what they have learned. For example, if the demonstration lesson was on the working of logic problems, a set of logic problems printed on cardstock, laminated, and perhaps fastened with a metal ring might be left for the students to work during their free time. A sheet with a written explanation of how to work logic problems as well as an extension activity, such as having the students write their own logic problems, should also be provided.

An additional aid or support for demonstration lessons could be inservice training where the classroom teachers would be able to learn about varying kinds of logic problems. During the inservice training, the teachers might write lessons that illustrate various uses of logic in math or science. They might also make a center where the students can learn to write logic problems that could be given to classmates to work.

USE OF DEMONSTRATION TEACHING IN SUPPORTING AND PROVIDING SERVICES FOR GIFTED STUDENTS

Demonstration teaching can be an effective support and provider of services for gifted students. It can serve as a bridge between what occurs in the regular classroom and in the pull-out program for the gifted. Demonstration teachers can teach in regular classrooms using techniques employed in the classroom for gifted students so the regular teacher can connect theory and practice.

As a result, those who are recognized as gifted students, as well as other able students not selected for the program for the gifted, may benefit from these strategies throughout the week. These strategies include the teaching of higher level thinking, which has been found to improve basic skills in low achievers (G. Garcia, personal communication, December 1987; Winocur, 1985). They also include heuristic teaching, also known as the discovery method. During heuristic teaching, the teacher serves as a guide and, through appropriate questioning and experiences, enables the students to discover the main ideas of the lesson themselves. Lessons can be heuristic by degree. The teacher can communicate some concepts and develop them, but can let the students discover others in the same lesson. For example, in a lesson on "fads," the teacher can define the term, but let students discover how once a fad is used by the population in general, it is no longer a fad. Another benefit of the model is that, while the demonstration teacher is teaching, the classroom teacher is able to observe his or her students and pay special attention to learning patterns that he or she might not have seen otherwise. This has led to more accuracy in determining candidates for programs for the gifted in Richardson, Texas.

The demonstration teaching program is enriching and enjoyable for all students. It provides nonthreatening, stimulating learning activities through lessons and centers that remain in the classrooms after each lesson, enabling all students to benefit from and enjoy teaching strategies generally limited to the gifted.

NECESSARY ELEMENTS OF A DEMONSTRATION TEACHING MODEL

Effective Curriculum

The curriculum needs to be designed and taught with the idea of effectiveness and economy in mind. In other words, the greatest return possible must be achieved through a minimum of teacher and student time expended. To aid economy and transfer, the curriculum should be organized around high-level generalizations, patterns, and/or the "structure of a subject" as suggested by Bruner (1960, p. 6). High-level generalizations are statements connecting concepts. A concept is somewhat abstract, and it usually deals with a class or category. For example, through playing with the cats of several families in the neighborhood, a child may develop the concept in his or her mind of "cat." Then upon seeing a cat in another situation at the home of a relative, the child will recognize that animal as also a cat. A generalization about cats that could be applied in a new situation would include information such as "Cats have four legs." The concepts that are connected are "cats" and "legs."

Generalizations possess varying degrees of abstractness. A high-level generalization shows relationships between concepts on an abstract level. As such, there are many situations in which they can be applied. Such a generalization might be, "In a democracy, persons must bargain, negotiate, and compromise to reach consensus."

Also helpful is the teaching of a consensus model of all the processes used in education of gifted students. In Richardson Independent School District (ISD), the consensus model employed is referred to as High-Tech Thinking. I developed this model, which serves as a "hook," according to T. Epley (personal communication, August 1987). As a hook, it aids students to learn other thinking models and to transfer their thinking to their nonacademic lives. In Table 7.1, I summarize commonly used thinking skills models and demonstrate how each has components that may be characterized as input, process, and output. In Table 7.2, I describe the objectives of High-Tech Thinking for students and distinguish high-tech from assembly line thinking processes.

The content of the curriculum should extend or build upon what the students already know. Teachers often have ideas regarding what they would like to see extended. Children also come to school with a large amount of information. These sources—the student and teachers—should be considered by curriculum designers.

Opportunity should be provided for development of higher level thinking skills. This can be achieved through the use of open-ended questions (i.e., questions that do not have a single correct answer), such as, "What are characteristics of a desert?" "What desert animal would you like to have as a pet? Why?" "What are all the ways you can think of to get the answer 6?" "What are at least two ways you can use a Venn diagram?"

Activities also can be open ended. These are activities for which there is no single right solution. An example of such an activity would be to design a flag that would be appropriate to fly over a colony on the planet Mars.

An important point is that the open-ended questions and activities be designed so they lead toward the understanding of a high-level generalization around which the unit of study is built. This gives the study structure. It prevents the attitude that "anything goes" regarding the responses of the students. An example of such a lesson design is a lesson on salt written for a primary grade level. The main high-level generalization might be, "The events that occur today are related to events of the past." An open-ended activity might be for a group of students to act out the Roman soldiers receiving payment for their work in money that would be used to buy salt.

Table 7.1 High-Tech Thinking: Summary of Models of Thinking Skills Used in Education of the Gifted

Model	Input	Process	Output
Bloom's Taxonomy (Bloom, 1956)	Knowledge	Comprehension Application Analysis Synthesis Evaluation	Synthesis Evaluation
Problem solving (Parnes, 1977)	Mess Fact finding	Problem finding Idea finding Solution finding	Solution finding
		Acceptance Finding	
Scientific method	Observe	Question Infer Hypothesize (invention) Compare	Conclusion Prediction
Creative thinking	Gather information Brainstorm	Brainstorm Incubate Insight (Aha)	Insight Evaluate
Renzulli (Renzulli, 1977)	Type I Exploratory	Type II Process or group training	Type III Independent study
Piaget (Piaget & Inhelder, 1969)	Assimilation	Accommodation	Adaptation
Structure of Intellect (Meeker, 1969)	Cognition	Divergent Convergent Memory	Convergent Evaluation
Research	Gather information	Prioritize Organize Synthesize	Synthesize Report
Taba (Taba, 1966)	Observation Recall Reading	Guided discussion	Concepts Generalizations Application of information Values

This exchange led to the word *salary*, which comes from the Latin word *salarium*, meaning "money used to buy salt." As skill in designing the curriculum increases, teachers may categorize the questions and activities as to how they fit with one of the thinking models, such as Bloom's (1956) Taxonomy or critical thinking.

The two lessons in Appendix 7.A, which were designed to teach students the elements of High-Tech Thinking, exemplify these necessary elements. The main

---

Table 7.2 High-Tech Thinking

Objectives
1. Students will know the meanings of the three basic components of thinking: input, process, output.
2. Students will identify how/when they use input, process, and output in their everyday lives.
3. Students will discover that, to improve the quality of their thinking, they need to have quality input and to spend time at the processing stage.
4. Students will label the three basic processes—input, process, and output—in the complex models used in education of the gifted, such as Bloom's (1956) Taxonomy, Parnes's (1977) Creative Problem Solving, and the scientific method.

Glossary
High-tech thinking—Emphasizes the importance of quality input and processing of information in arriving at quality output or valid conclusions. Involves analyzing, synthesizing, and evaluating input.
  Nonexamples of high-tech thinking: The repetition of learned responses, such as is done when reviewing math facts or repeating memorized definitions.
  Examples of high-tech thinking: Painting a picture, playing a sport, debating, solving any type of problem where the answers or solutions are not readily apparent or where there is no single right answer.
Assembly line thinking—Involves little need for the participant to do much information processing; thus, does not require the gathering of quality input.
  Nonexamples of assembly line thinking: Items listed as examples of high-tech thinking.
  Examples of assembly line thinking: Items listed under nonexamples of high-tech thinking.

---

high-level generalization the lessons illustrate is, ''One can learn better how to learn (i.e., to have better quality output) by having better quality input and staying in the input and process phases when learning something new.'' This generalization applies in all areas of students' lives.

In the demonstration lessons (Appendix 7.A), much effort is spent on building on or extending what the students already know. The comparison of the mind's activity with that of a computer builds upon the knowledge that children have regarding computers. The students' base of understanding also is extended by the examples that are given to illustrate the concepts of input, process, and output, such as painting a picture or baking a cake. Use is made of the student's store of information and experiences throughout by using open-ended questions and activities. For example, students are asked, ''Which is most important in your opinion: input or process? Why?'' They are asked to build upon their existing knowledge when they are requested to distinguish the input, process, and output of a math lesson, a board game, or other activities.

An example of an open-ended activity is the presentation of simple materials, such as three or four squares of colored paper and a sheet of manila paper with the open-ended instructions, ''Create a design.'' An example of an open-ended question that leads toward a high-level generalization is, "Which design did you like best, the first one or the second one? Why?"

The use of the consensus model as a hook that aids in learning other models is in the "extension/transfer" section of the lesson. Even though the students have never worked with the three models, Bloom's Taxonomy, Parnes's (1977) Creative Problem Solving, and the scientific method, they will be able to classify the steps as to which are input, process, and output quite accurately. Because of this design, the concepts and generalizations developed are very meaningful. This result makes the return, or understanding developed relative to time and effort, very effective.

Planning Time

Lessons with centers and follow-up activities need to be developed. The time to do this should be built into the schedule throughout the year.

At the beginning of the year, time needs to be allowed for scheduling. The demonstration teachers should meet with the principals of each school where they are scheduled to teach. A schedule needs to be obtained from the principals for each classroom teacher so the demonstration teaching can be done at a time convenient for each classroom. The purposes of the program should be explained to the principals, who need to be reminded to tell the teachers to remain in the room during the lessons to observe student reactions. The teachers can learn about their students when observing their reactions to process teaching. By asking students their reasoning, the instructor is able to determine the quality of a student's intelligence in a way that is not possible in other situations.

All demonstration teachers then should go to each classroom teacher in whose room they will be teaching and introduce themselves. They must remove the idea that they are any threat to the classroom teachers. One way is to ask for feedback and help. They also need to remind the classroom teacher to focus on the classroom students' reactions to the lessons. The fact that the demonstration teachers serve partly as teacher trainers remains a hidden agenda.

Lessons should be scheduled during the reading, language arts, math, science, or social studies periods. Although the demonstration lessons will not necessarily correspond to those subjects, the processes used should meet the essential elements that those subjects cover and thus can be substituted. The demonstration teacher should avoid scheduling lessons during a teacher's off-period, such as physical education, music, art, or recess, as this arouses great resentment and resistance in both teachers and students.

After the lesson is developed, schedules are made by the demonstration teachers, and a copy for each school should be sent to that school. Never should the demonstration teacher give anyone a copy of his or her entire teaching schedule.

Each classroom teacher should receive a copy of the time and dates of lessons in his or her classroom. These should be delivered personally, but they can be sent by interschool mail.

Because the lessons cannot be scheduled until the demonstration teacher has all the teachers' individual schedules, the lessons cannot start at the beginning of the fall term. This time is used for visiting principals and teachers. It also allows the demonstration teachers time to develop the material to be used in the program. The materials must be developed by the teachers, as they are not available on the market.

Presentations

A period of time approximately 20 to 40 minutes in length, depending upon the age of the students, should be set aside for the lessons on a regular basis. The classroom teacher must remain in the classroom and be attentive during the demonstration lesson.

The presentation should be organized around some form of effective lesson design. Compared with a traditional lesson, a lesson that encourages thinking provides more opportunity for the students to talk. For example, the students may discuss and state the purpose of the lesson rather than having the teacher do so, as in a more traditional skill development lesson.

A wide variety of learning styles should be accommodated when lessons are designed. Visual learners, especially, should be considered. Colorful, creative posters and transparencies are particularly effective.

A Consensus Model: High-Tech Thinking

After working with various phases of education programming for gifted and talented students, I developed a consensus model of several thinking process models and called it High-Tech Thinking (Rice, 1987, pp. 142–148). Teachers and students understand the model easily because they can begin immediately to transfer it to all their learning experiences, whether they involve solving problems, making decisions, or learning other thinking processes. The model is used in the intermediate-level program for gifted students in Grades 4, 5, and 6. Two of the three lessons used to introduce and teach it in the Realizing Excellence in Academic Cognition Heuristically (REACH) Program (the gifted and talented program in Richardson ISD, which is based on the resource room model) are included in Appendix 7.A. The model currently is being used in Richardson's demonstration teaching program for fourth grade, which is called Outreach. Ruth Lawrence, former coordinator of the REACH Program, suggests that High-Tech Thinking be used to provide the scope and sequence for demonstration teaching programs.

The High-Tech Thinking Model was developed around nine models for high-level thinking skills that commonly form the basis for curriculum development in most programs for the gifted (see Table 7.1). After reading much curriculum based on these models, I concluded that the models had similar characteristics that could be related to a computer. A similar model, synthesized in 1945, comprised other thinking process models (Smith & Tyler, 1945, cited in Costa, 1985). Costa described this idea as "a simple yet dynamic model of human intellectual functioning which could serve as a basis for curriculum and instruction" (p. 62). This is exactly what has been done in Richardson.

Teachers

The teachers chosen to do the demonstration teaching are a key to a successful program, once administrative support is established. Ruth Lawrence, the former coordinator of REACH, stated that the teachers chosen need to have healthy egos and to be "a bit of a ham." She lists the following other characteristics these teachers need:

1. Thorough training in strategies for teaching the gifted
2. Warmth and good people skills (i.e., ability to talk *with*, not *at*, students and to be sensitive to students and other teachers)
3. Good common sense, as well as intelligence
4. Enjoyment of teaching and development of teaching materials
5. Attractive looking, if possible (demonstration teachers should be more dressed up than the classroom teacher is required to be)

USE OF THE DEMONSTRATION TEACHING MODEL IN A PRIMARY PROGRAM FOR THE GIFTED

The Cognitive and Thinking Skills (CATS) program was a demonstration teaching model that was part of the REACH program in Richardson, Texas, until the 1991–1992 school year when a primary program for the gifted was mandated by the state of Texas. CATS was chosen as one of six exemplary programs in the state by the Texas Education Agency. As a result, a booklet has been printed (Texas Education Agency, 1988) and distributed along with a videotape that explains the program and offers suggestions for ways school districts may set up their own program.

Through the spring of 1991, the CATS program consisted of five teachers who taught lessons periodically in all the primary classrooms of the 35 elementary schools across the district. Twenty to 40 minutes were allotted for lessons, depending upon the grade level. The lessons were delivered weekly in the third grade and once every 6 weeks in the first and second grades.

The CATS lessons were designed to develop higher level thinking and creativity. Supplementary materials, such as learning centers and suggestions for extension, were developed to leave in classrooms after lessons were presented.

The CATS program came into existence in 1980. Two years earlier, a very successful resource room program called REACH had been initiated in Grades 4, 5, and 6. Parent pressure was then brought to bear upon the administrators to provide for gifted students in Grades 1, 2, and 3. A major difficulty to be faced was that of identifying gifted children of primary age.

The demonstration teaching model eliminated that problem in that it did not require students to be identified. It also was very economical in cost and time as it did not require an additional classroom. Another plus was that it contributed to teacher training for the regular classroom teacher without adding extra time at work.

The program was especially appealing to top-level administrators because of the low cost factor, as well as the parent enthusiasm for higher level thinking skills for their students. Principals were anxious to offer the program because no additional workload was involved.

CATS was a new application of the demonstration teaching model and was designed by the coordinator of the program, Ruth Lawrence. She decided that the teachers should operate out of a central office location so they would be accepted as experts by the classroom teacher. Originally, only one teacher was involved. She developed curriculum, prepared centers based on curriculum, and taught classes in every third-grade classroom in the district. Third-grade classrooms numbered 113 at the time. During the second year (1981–1982), three teachers were in the program. They taught in each third-grade class every other week. In 1982–1983, five teachers were involved, who taught in all third-grade classes every week. They also taught in second-grade classes once every 6 weeks. In the fall of 1983, first-grade classes were added to the program. The five teachers visited the first-grade classes twice during the 1984–1985 school year. From 1986 to 1991, four to five teachers worked in the program. During the 1991–1992 school year, the state of Texas mandated that gifted students in all grade levels need to be identified and served. As a result, the demonstration teachers developed and taught curricula in a primary resource room program during the 1991–1992 school year. Because of the demand from both teachers and principals, however, the CATS program is still being implemented. The demonstration teachers lead workshops for teachers in the regular classroom to teach lessons, model techniques, and distribute materials developed in the CATS program.

Although various thinking and academic skills were developed in the CATS program, nine skills received special emphasis. The curriculum was developed to emphasize attribute finding, classification, problem solving (as developed by Parnes, 1977), logical thinking, creative thinking, qualification skills, scientific method, analysis, and communication.

Attribute finding is the identification of characteristics of objects and the attachment of labels or names to identify those characteristics. An example of an attribute activity is sorting objects according to texture, relative size, or color. In the CATS program, this activity was done with varying shapes on a flannel board. The children were asked to group the shapes that had common attributes.

Classification skills are related to attribute finding in that common qualities are singled out in objects. The objects are grouped according to those qualities. For example, after listing all the foods they like to eat, students might group them according to common attributes and give the grouping a label (e.g., they might list various foods and then classify them as to their color). In a CATS lesson on animals, students list many types of animals. Then the teacher asks, "Which of these animals go together because they are alike in some way?" The teacher writes a symbol beside those animals the children list as similar; then a child gives the grouping a label or title. The children may note that the animals may be classified under more than one title or label.

Creative Problem Solving is a five-step process developed by Parnes (1977). The first step is to acknowledge that there is a mess. The next step is fact finding, which entails the gathering of all the information available concerning the mess. The problem-finding step follows, in which the participant determines the "real problem." Then, the problem is stated in a positive manner. The letters for "In What Ways Might We"—IWWMW—serve to remind the participant as to how this might be done. An example of a problem statement is, "In what ways might we make our school playground a safer place to be?" The next step is idea finding, where the students diverge and brainstorm all the possible ideas they can to solve the problem. For solution finding, the best five or so ideas are selected and judged according to student-generated criteria, such as ease of implementation and cost. After the best solution is identified, the acceptance-finding step is implemented. In Parnes's model, this step involves finding ways to get the ideas accepted and includes repetition of all the former steps. In the CATS program, students were given problems or messes (as described by Parnes) on cards. Then they were taught to work through these problems using this model.

Logical thinking involves thinking in a step-by-step manner through reasoning, and often uses the process of elimination, to achieve a reasonable answer. Students may work formal logic problems, in which they are given two or three sets of variables and the task is to figure out the answers through the use of a grid or matrix. Logical thinking also may be developed through math activities.

Creative thinking, as done by the CATS teachers, encourages fluency, flexibility, and originality. It usually involves brainstorming. Creative thinking lessons are those taught to the first graders at the beginning of the year.

Qualification skills involve finding out how things are alike and different. In the CATS program, forced relationships are emphasized. The students are shown pictures of unlike objects, such as a book and a chair, and are asked, "How is a book like a chair?" They also are asked, "How are they different?"

The scientific method as developed by the CATS teachers involves stating a hypothesis, gathering information, experimenting, analyzing results, and forming a conclusion. Tasks are provided using this process with science content.

Analysis involves breaking both structures and operations into parts, and identifying order and connections where they exist. An analysis lesson taught by CATS teachers might involve the use of a chair in the teaching of Bloom's Taxonomy. For example, after teaching students about the levels of Bloom's Taxonomy, the demonstration teacher might refer to a chair and ask students, "What level of Bloom's Taxonomy am I thinking of when I ask you to list the parts of this chair?" (analysis). "What level am I referring to when I ask you to design a new chair?" (synthesis).

Communication is the skill the students use when they are asked to describe clearly their thinking or reasoning so that others understand it easily. This skill is promoted throughout the CATS lessons as students are asked continually to express themselves, either in expanding on an idea or in giving a reason for their decisions.

Advantages of Demonstration Teaching Model

Comments of the teachers show that they look forward to the visits by the CATS teachers. They do not resent the time allotted for the lessons, and they wish for more opportunity than they have to be with the demonstration teachers. The students also look forward to this time. On the CATS evaluations at the end of the year, the teachers repeatedly make such comments as, "Our students look forward to each CATS lesson" and "The class so enjoyed the CATS lessons this year!"

The chief advantage of the demonstration model is that the principle of modeling is employed. Scott Peck, in his best seller *The Road Less Traveled* (1978), stressed the effectiveness of modeling as a learning technique. He mentioned that children primarily learn self-discipline and other important behaviors through their parents' example or modeling.

There are many other reasons why modeling is a worthwhile, effective effort. When classroom teachers observe demonstration lessons, the situation is completely nonthreatening so they are able to be more open to learning. By making a point to meet with each classroom teacher individually early in the year before beginning the demonstration lessons, the CATS teachers foster the nonthreatening atmosphere and lay the groundwork for a mutually supportive relationship. The CATS teachers offer to help in any way possible and welcome any ideas or suggestions from the classroom teachers. Together, they discuss and evaluate the students and their reactions. At no time are the classroom teachers placed in a position where they might be judged.

Because the lessons take place in the teachers' own classrooms with their students, the lessons give the classroom teachers a unique opportunity to observe their own students responding to various strategies implemented by the demonstration teachers. Frequently, this leads to insights regarding the students' abilities. This has led to the nomination and placement in gifted programs of students who would otherwise have been overlooked.

The consistent, regular contact over a year's time gives the classroom teachers time to absorb and try out the ideas presented in demonstration lessons. That the classroom teachers actually try out ideas is verified by such comments as "she has brought many innovative ideas with her, which not only enhanced the CATS lessons but benefited me in other areas." Another comment was, "I also benefited from the higher level of thinking aspects."

The overall positive attitude of the classroom teachers was expressed in such comments as, "I am so pleased Richardson ISD offers such a top notch program. It does an excellent job of encouraging students to develop and use their higher level thinking skills. Please continue and expand the CATS program!"

The program is extremely cost-effective when the cost in time and money is compared with the benefit. The lessons take place during the regular schoolday; therefore, no release time is needed. The model requires no additional workload for the regular classroom teacher. In fact, it decreases the workload while increasing the teacher's skills. This combination of factors cannot be faulted.

The idea is powerful in a district, such as Richardson ISD, that also has a pull-out resource room program. The use of demonstration lessons makes special education for gifted learners seem less elitist or mysterious to the classroom teacher. The model also facilitates more of a congruence between the regular homeroom and the special education classroom, thereby making both places able to deal with gifted children more effectively.

In general, the demonstration teaching model fosters very positive public relations. In 1977, at the Fifth National Leadership Training Institute on the Gifted and Talented at Columbia University, J. Curry stated that dissatisfied classroom teachers can undermine a program for gifted students. Based on teacher comments, the teacher support at Richardson ISD for CATS and for programs for the gifted in general has been increased greatly.

The program, as a whole, becomes more vital if opportunities are provided for regular classroom teachers to attend workshops. Thus, the teachers can continue to learn about what they have observed in the CATS lessons and apply their new understanding in their own situations.

Disadvantages of the Demonstration Teaching Model

The main disadvantage of the demonstration teaching model is that components can be left out easily or expectations can be inappropriate. As a result, it can easily be misjudged as ineffective. Two elements that are important to its success are the careful development of the lessons and the attentiveness of the classroom teacher. To expect the demonstration teaching model to *be* the gifted program is inappropriate. It should merely be considered complementary to one that is more focused on the needs of the gifted.

The effectiveness of demonstrations is lowered if the lessons do not lead to an understanding of high-level generalizations or patterns. The lessons are of more limited value in such cases because the ability to transfer what is learned to new situations is lacking. Transfer, or being able to use the information learned in other situations, is especially important in this model because the lesson times are so limited.

A key to the effectiveness of the program is the attentiveness of the classroom teacher. He or she must not consider the time of the lesson as a break time. The teachers must be notified by someone in authority, such as the principal, that they must remain in their classrooms during the demonstration lessons and refrain from using the time to grade papers or write lesson plans.

Demonstration teaching can provide a powerfully effective boost for or link between gifted students, special programs, and the remainder of the educational system. It should not be considered a complete answer or the only opportunity offered to the gifted to meet their special needs. Another program thrust is needed to meet other needs of the students, including helping them (a) to exercise their ability to process complex and often ambiguous information, (b) to form abstract generalizations, and (c) to set their own goals and follow them through. Especially important is that gifted students learn how to learn and extend themselves so that they move beyond being consumers of knowledge and become producers. Gifted students, however, also need exposure to other gifted students and special strategies used in the demonstration teaching model.

The demonstration lesson must be, by its nature, teacher directed; consequently, the students have little opportunity to explore individually, set their own goals, and follow through. Also, the demonstration teachers must aim the impact and complexity of lessons toward the class as a whole; therefore, the gifted students are not as continually challenged as they are in settings where the abilities fall in a higher and more narrow range.

USE OF THE DEMONSTRATION TEACHING MODEL IN AN INTERMEDIATE-LEVEL PROGRAM FOR THE GIFTED

While the CATS program served Grades K through 3, the fourth-grade students in Richardson schools were served by a demonstration teaching model referred to as "Outreach." It was set up in a manner similar to CATS; however, the demonstration lesson teachers also were the resource room teachers who regularly served the intermediate grade level gifted students 4 days each week in a pull-out program. They prepared lessons and centers for five or six lessons through the year and taught them in regular classrooms on Fridays. These lessons were based on higher level thinking skills, but more emphasis was given to critical thinking skills in Outreach than in the CATS program.

UNANTICIPATED PROBLEMS AND THEIR SOLUTIONS

A common problem in the demonstration teaching programs is the lack of attentiveness of the classroom teachers. They might rather use the time to work on lesson plans, grade papers, or find an excuse to be absent from the room. This problem can best be handled by clear instructions from the principal.

Another situation that occurred at Richardson ISD was that the demonstration teacher was applauded spontaneously by students. So that the classroom teacher would not perceive this as an affront, she purposely was involved in the next two lessons so that she, too, might receive applause.

The storage of materials is also a challenge, especially in larger districts. A list of the parts of each center should be made and distributed so teachers can check to see which parts, if any, need replacing and give the list to the demonstration teacher for handling. If there is no central place to store the materials, each classroom teacher can place the centers in brown paper bags, mark them, and place them in storage in the individual school library. The demonstration teacher may then pick them up at the beginning of the next fall term to redistribute.

CONCLUSION

Overall, the demonstration teaching model can enhance the learning of the gifted child in the regular classroom as the teacher learns new teaching strategies and applies what he or she learns. Encouraging and challenging students to think and guiding them to be independent learners in the manner commonly done in programs for the gifted is beneficial for all students. According to Wayne Craigen (1987), Irving Sato aptly stated that differentiated curriculum for the gifted is different in degree, not in kind. Therefore, the work done in regular classrooms using the demonstration teaching model may well serve to upgrade the educational experiences for all students.

Appendix 7.A

Two High-Tech Thinking Lessons
(based on Madeline Hunter's Lesson Design—see Table 7.3)

LESSON 1—HIGH-TECH THINKING:
ON LINE TO HIGHER LEVEL THINKING

Materials Needed

Props, which vary depending upon the demonstration

Transparencies of mainframe computer titled "Learning How to Learn Through High-Tech Thinking" (Figures 7.1 and 7.3)

Transparency of "Thinking: Discover Relationships" (Figure 7.2)

Pens for writing on overhead

A piece of paper for each class member with simple mark on it, for example,   or

Focus

 I. State, "Metacognition means thinking about thinking. When we do this, we can use our brain more effectively. Today, we will learn to think about our thinking and talk about our thinking. We will be on track toward learning to improve our minds."

 II. Hold up props. Say, "I could take these tubes of paint, brushes, and paper which are very similar to the ones used by Renoir over a hundred years ago and I still wouldn't have a masterpiece. Why?"

   You may do the same with the ingredients of a cake, the parts of a model, a seed, or clothing. Have fun with it!

   Ask, "What would be different in my painting a picture or in Renoir's doing so?" (Ability, objects to paint, supplies.)

   "This leads us into what might be called 'High-Tech Thinking.'"

   Ask the children, "What do you think 'high-tech' means?" (Computers, high technology.)

Continue, "What kind of thinking is appropriate in a time of 'high technology'?" (Know computers. Learn new things.) You might probe, "Is it possible that you may have to figure out answers that have never been known before? Why?" (New discoveries are made all the time.) "We can call finding new answers 'problem solving.'"

Say, "When we learn how our mind works, we can use it more effectively. Suppose you had a new elaborate computer in your classroom and no one knew how to use it. Would it be very helpful?" (No.) "Understanding your mind helps you to use it more effectively."

Instruction

I. *Providing Information.* Say, "Your mind is really like a computer when it handles information."

Ask, "What is the information that is put into the computer called?" (Input.) "What is it called when it comes out?" (Output.) "When the computer is working out the information, what is it called?" (Process.) "Like a computer, your mind experiences input, process, and output." Teacher may point out that the figure on transparency (Figure 7.1) is not a refrigerator, a stove, or a video game but an old-fashioned computer from the late sixties.

A. Talk through transparency (Figure 7.1). Say, "How does your mind gather input?" (Looking, listening, tasting, smelling, touching.) "Do you already have some things inside you that would be input?" (Past knowledge, feelings, imagination.) "It's not easy to look or to listen. These tasks require life-long learning. An art instructor once said that an artist should be able to see twenty shades of green in the leaves of a tree. Depending on what is being listened for, listening skills vary. For example, you would listen to step-by-step instructions regarding how to fix a bicycle differently from listening to your friend describe his or her vacation."

B. Say, "Process is simple. It can often be described as discovering relationships of one thing to another." (May show transparency of Figure 7.2.)
  1. Say, "Relationships may be thought of as vertical or horizontal."
     a. Ask, "Cause–effect would be which?" (Horizontal.) Say, "Think of an event like wearing a sweater to school one day. Now think backwards. What had to happen before you put it on?" (The weather became colder.) "That may be called the cause. Now what do you predict will happen because you wore your sweater?" (I will be warm and comfortable.) "That would be a prediction or an effect." The teacher may point to symbols depicting this one.
     b. Say, "The next process could be called vertical. It is what might happen when a very young person sees a number of cats. He or she has an idea of what 'catness' is. The next time the person sees some small

Learning How to Learn Through

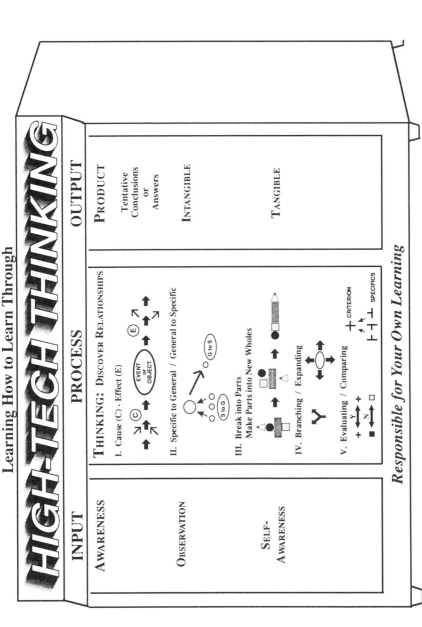

Figure 7.1 High-Tech Thinking Model Partially Filled in. (Transparency for Lessons 1 and 2.)

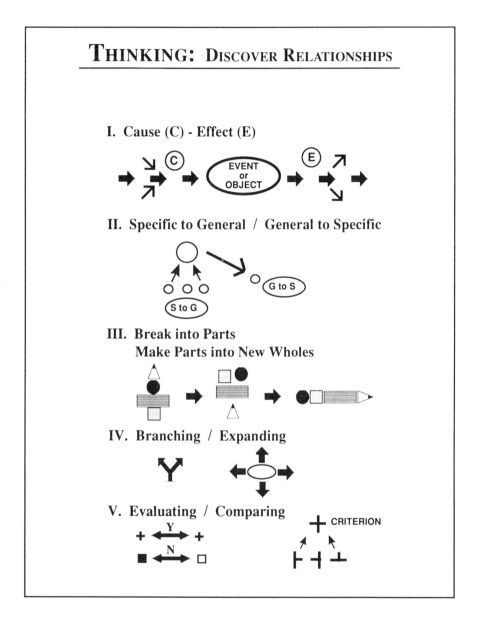

Figure 7.2 High-Tech Thinking Model: Processes. (To be used, if needed, during lessons.)

animal, he or she will be able to determine which small animal meets the criteria of 'catness' and is, indeed, a cat.''

2. Say, ''Another way to recognize relationships is to break a whole into parts. When might you do this?'' (Break a toy, an engine, a story, a paragraph, a word.) ''Sometimes these parts can be combined to form new wholes. When does this happen?'' (Leggos™ to build a new structure, words to write a new story, etc.) ''What is another name for this process?'' (Creativity, synthesis, combining.)

3. Say, ''The next relationship occurs when one new idea leads to another which may lead to another. What might be other names for this section?'' (Divergent thinking or brainstorming.) ''This too might aid persons in moving from parts to new wholes. For example, if you were trying to figure out all the ways you could decorate a birthday cake, you might put the parts together into a whole and make a new design. What other examples come to your mind?'' (A new design for a bicycle, computer, etc.)

Using overhead (Figure 7.3), ask, ''What is the input when a picture is painted?'' (Brush, paint, canvas, what is being observed, artist's talent.) Write down student's responses on transparency. ''What is the process?'' (Putting the paint on the canvas. Thinking. Imagining.) Ask, ''Which is more important, input or process?'' (Both are important.) ''What is used by computer programmers that tells what happens if input is not correct?'' (GIGO.) ''What does it mean?'' (Garbage in, garbage out.)

II. *Checking for Understanding.* ''What are examples of activities in your classroom where there is input, process, and output?'' (Reading class, math lesson, centers.) Write answers on overhead. Ask students to explain their answers.

Guided Practice

I. Hand out a paper to each student with a simple design, such as a squiggle or a square that fills the page. Every sheet has the same design.

II. Say, ''Look at the design in various ways until you can see it as an object. Make a picture so that the line is an important part of the picture. You will have only 5 minutes. You may not be finished when I stop you. If not, stop before you are finished. You may finish later.''

III. After 5 minutes, stop the students. Ask them to metacognize or think about their thinking. Ask, ''What was the input of the assignment I gave you?'' (Instructions, square, squiggle, pencil or colored markers, student's imagination, talent, and experience.) ''What was the process that occurred?'' (Looking at paper in different ways. Drawing. Thinking. Imagining.) ''What was the output?'' (Picture.) Write students' replies on transparency of computer that has blank panels (Figure 7.3).

Learning How to Learn Through

HIGH-TECH THINKING

INPUT	PROCESS	OUTPUT

Responsible for Your Own Learning

Figure 7.3 High-Tech Thinking Model with Main Headings. (Transparency and worksheet for Lesson 2.)

Closure

"What can you do that will enable you to use your mind more effectively?" (Metacognize.)

"What object is similar to your mind in the way it handles information?" (Computer.)

"What are the three ways a computer deals with information?" (Gathers input, processes it so that there is output.)

"What is GIGO?" (Garbage in, garbage out.) "What does it mean?" (When input is not good, output will not be good.)

"Through the day, think about how and when you gather information, and how you process information so that you have output." (Answers will vary. They may include playing baseball, discovering the meaning of new words through context clues, getting homework assignments, etc.)

LESSON 2 – HIGH-TECH THINKING: ON LINE TO HIGHER LEVEL THINKING

Materials Needed

Transparency of computer model (Figure 7.1)
Clear transparency
Vis-à-Vis
Toothpicks
9 × 12 inch manila paper
Squares of three different colors of paper about 3 × 3 inch square per group of students
Glue sticks; markers; pencils
Copies of computer model sheet (Figures 7.1 and 7.3)

Focus

  I. What is "high-tech thinking"?

 II. What mechanism is often compared to the mind in the way it handles information?

III. Describe the steps it uses in handling information. (Give labels and describe in own words.)

Instruction

  I. *Check for Understanding.* Say, "Give some examples of when you do high-tech thinking." (Playing soccer, planning a party, etc.) "Give some examples

of assembly line thinking.'' (Answering math facts.) ''Sometimes these may
be termed 'factory thinking.' Why?'' (In a factory, raw materials are processed
into products in a repetitious way. Math facts, when they have been memorized, appear also to be processed repetitiously.) The teacher may wish to write
responses on overhead, such as,

High-Tech Thinking

Examples	Nonexamples

II. When an overhead projector is turned on, objects placed on it will create a
shadow on the screen. The following demonstration is done this way.

    A. Ask, ''What's the lowest number of toothpicks you need to build one
square?'' (Four.) ''Two squares?'' (Seven.) Show on overhead.

    B. ''What pattern do you see?'' (After the first square, you add two or three
toothpicks because they share sides. As the number of squares increase,
the number of toothpicks increase by two or three.) This may be written
on the board or on a transparency:

Toothpicks	Squares
4	1
7	2
10	3
12	4

    C. Have the students reflect on the thinking they have just done. Ask them
to metacognize, or think about their thinking, and write on a sheet of paper
that has three columns on it labeled input, process, and output (Figure 7.3).
Help them to find words like *compare, relationship,* and *patterns* for their
thinking processes.

III. Say, ''Some questions have no single *right* answer but are important to ask
because they help us to think more deeply. For example, which part of thinking
(input, process, or output) do you think is the most important? Why do you
think so?'' Note that the purpose of the question is to force the students to recognize that both good input and process are extremely important.

Guided Practice

  I. Divide students into groups of three. Give each group a copy of the computer
model sheet (Figure 7.3), a 9 × 12 inch sheet of manila paper, a glue stick
(see below), and three or four squares of colored paper. Say, ''You have each
been given identical materials. You have 5 minutes to create a design. You may
fold the squares but do not cut or tear them.'' At this time, the teacher may
tell them to refrain from using the glue or may simply not hand it to the students until later.

II. As they work, the teacher should check on the plans of the groups. When the groups have crystalized their thinking about what to make and are ready to paste the squares down on paper, ask the students to stop what they are doing. Say, "Now take your squares off the sheet of manila paper and start planning again."

III. Give the students a short time to replan and glue their project. Ask, "How do you feel about being asked to change your plans?" (Mad. Disappointed.) "Which design did you like the best, the first one or the second one. Why?" Tell them, "Research shows that when people stay in the input and process phases longer, their products are higher in quality than when those phases are short." (Parnes, 1977, for example, cautions that closure should not be reached too quickly.)

IV. Hand each group a chart with the computer model (Figure 7.3) and input, process, and output on it. Say, "Fill in your chart with what was your thinking. You may use the transparency to remind you of words to use. When you finish, you may share your thinking or metacognition with the group. Be sure to tell when you thought what. For example, you might say something like, 'We thought like process number three when you told us to stop and change our design. We had to break up the parts of our old design and create a new one.' "

Extension/Transfer

Show transparencies on overhead of Parnes's (1977) Creative Problem Solving Model, Bloom's (1956) Taxonomy, scientific method, and other models if you like. Whether the students have seen them before is unimportant. Ask, "Based on our lesson about input, process, and output, which of these labels would be input, process, or output?" The students may conclude that some of the steps can be both. This would be accurate.

Closure

I. Have the students place the objects they have created in a place where they can be seen by everyone. Say, "Observe these objects carefully and give a sentence that tells about *all* of them. Everyone used the same four objects but created very different products." Encourage many responses. Students may write them on paper before sharing. Then they may share their most original responses.

II. Discuss with your group what is the input, process, and output of a math lesson, the logic center, game center, and so on. Say, "In order to improve the chances of your having better output (more right answers, better grades) what might you do in terms of input and process?" (Stay in those parts longer. Be more aware during input. Do not give up if in the process phase.)

Table 7.3 Five-Step Lesson Plan Cycle

1. *Focus*
   a. Task
   b. Objective
   c. Purpose
   d. Transfer

2. *Instruction*
   a. *Provide information*
      - Definition
      - Critical attribute
      - Examples
      - Explanation
      - Model
   b. *Check for understanding*
      - Key questions
      - Student's own words
      - Examples/nonexamples
      - Generate
      - Active participation

3. *Guided practice*
   a. Activity
   b. Overt response
   c. Monitoring
   d. Check for understanding
   e. Knowledge of results

4. *Independent practice*
   a. Final assessment
   b. Perform behavior alone
   c. Additional practice
   d. Knowledge of results

5. *Closure*

Note. These lessons employ the Five-Step Lesson Plan Cycle based on Madeline Hunter's Lesson Design and disseminated by the Regional Service Centers in Texas (Hunter & Russell, 1977).

REFERENCES

Bloom, B. S. (Ed.). (1956). *Taxonomy of educational objective: The classification of educational goals. Handbook I: Cognitive Domain.* New York: Longmans, Green.

Bruner, J. S. (1960). *The process of education.* Cambridge: Harvard University Press.

Costa, A. L. (1985). Teaching for intelligent behavior. In L. Winocur (Ed.), *Project impact training manual* (pp. 60–73). Huntington Beach, CA: Orange County Department of Education.

Craigen, W. (1987, November). Symposium conducted at a meeting of the Texas Association of Gifted and Talented, Dallas.

Hunter, M., & Russell, D. (1977, September). How can I plan more effective lessons? *Instructor,* pp. 74–75, 88–90.

Meeker, M. N. (1969). *The structure of intellect: Its interpretation and uses.* Columbus, OH: Merrill.

Parnes, S. J. (1977). Guiding creative action. *The GIfted Child Quarterly, 21,* 460–476.

Peck, S. (1978). *The road less traveled.* New York: Simon and Schuster.

Piaget, J., & Inhelder, B. (1969). *The psychology of the child.* New York: Basic Books.

Putnam, J. (1985). Perceived benefits and limitations of teacher education demonstration lessons. *Journal of Teacher Education, 36,* 36–41.

Renzulli, J. S. (1977). *The enrichment triad model: A guide for the gifted and talented.* Wethersfield, CT: Creative Learning Press.

Rice, M. A. (1987). Shortcuts to developing giftedness in children, the Reach Program, Texas, USA. *Gifted Education International, 4*(3), 142–148.

Taba, H. (1966). *Teaching strategies and cognitive functioning in elementary school children* (USOE Cooperative Research Project No. 2404). San Francisco: San Francisco State College.

Texas Education Agency. (1988). *The future is now: Gifted education for all. Creative and academic thinking skills Richardson Independent School District.* Austin, TX: Author.

Winocur, L. (1985). Script. In L. Winocur (Ed.), *Project impact: District site coordinator training manual* (p. 45). Huntington Beach, CA: Orange County Department of Education.

8

Demonstration Teaching:
Another View

Janice R. Szabos

In her chapter "The Use of the Demonstration Teaching Model in Education of the Gifted," Rice shares with the reader an idea that works. Her overview of the implementation of the model suggests an approach that has potential not only for direct instruction for gifted students, but also for staff development. Rarely does an educational model offer both. Such a promising model deserves a more elaborate discussion, however, than has been offered in the previous chapter.

Although modeling is not a new concept, the idea of demonstration teaching as part of a program for gifted students has not been explored to any great extent. References in the literature to this type of programming seem relatively nonexistent. To consider the efficacy of this model for educating gifted students requires that one address the purposes and the components of such a model. Rice has presented the reader with a bird's-eye view of the model, but neglects to examine it in detail and to provide a foundation for understanding its framework. Her rather superficial treatment seems to suggest that others should try this model because it works in the author's school district. I feel that the very solid foundations of the model must be brought forward for consideration, so that one can form a personal opinion about the theoretical merits of the model, rather than considering it merely from the standpoint of implementation.

Rice fails to address issues regarding the general purposes for providing a delivery system of special services for gifted students. The basis for satisfaction with the model seems to be that everyone is content with or feels good about the model. Even though feeling good about a program is a worthy goal, it certainly cannot be considered as a reason for adopting a model. Many teaching strategies may appeal to a large number of the people involved in a program, yet may not be effective in achieving the goals of the program.

DEMONSTRATION TEACHING MODEL: DEFINITION REVISITED

No educator can begin to analyze the demonstration teaching model without comprehending its essence. Rice has neglected to provide a foundation for the model by way of a definition. The one suggested in Rice's chapter—"teaching demonstrations by teacher educators as a primary mode of illustrating how to apply theory in practice" (Putnam, 1985, p. 36)—offers a weak description borrowed from work on teacher training at the university level. A definition of the demonstration teaching model in education for the gifted must be distinctive to its purpose of educating gifted students. To assist the reader in understanding the model and my analysis of Rice's chapter, I offer the following as a working definition.

The demonstration teaching model used in educating gifted students is a process model that provides classroom teachers with a framework for making adaptations to the learning environment for gifted students. The delivery of the model is primarily through demonstration lessons, generally conducted by a specialist in the education of gifted students. The model serves to heighten awareness of the needs of gifted learners, show examples of strategies useful in meeting those needs, and assist in the identification of gifted students. Essential components of the demonstration teaching model include (a) definition of goals, (b) theoretical background, (c) demonstration/observation, and (d) dialogue/analysis. The foundations for the demonstration teaching model lie within research studies and writings in several areas: education of the gifted, staff development, effective schools, and theories of learning.

Education of the Gifted

Most educators would agree to some common goals for developing an instructional climate conducive to the education of gifted students. A list of common goals would certainly include provision for (a) a challenging instructional environment, (b) support for social and emotional needs, (c) flexible approaches to learning, (d) active participation in problem solving, and (e) development of higher level thought processes.

The demonstration teaching model used in educating gifted students is supportive of these goals. The focus of the demonstration lessons can correspond to any one or a combination of goals. Rice suggests that the model is useful for providing "a bridge between what occurs in the regular classroom and in the pull-out program for the gifted. Even though this function is potentially important, again, Rice is shortsighted in her view of the use of the model. An examination of the roles carried out by various people when using the model can provide an in-depth view of the model's usefulness. The information in Table 8.1 suggests that a much stronger role is needed for the classroom teacher than Rice suggests in her chapter. I am particularly disturbed by Rice's comments on the attentiveness of the classroom teacher: "He or she must not consider the time of the lesson as a break time. The teachers must be notified by someone in authority, such as the principal, that they need to remain in their classrooms during the demonstration lessons." Fundamentally

Table 8.1 Roles in Gifted Education Programs

Person	Role
Administrator	Supports demonstration model
	Provides staff training time
	Arranges scheduling of specialist teacher
	Evaluates effectiveness of educational programs for gifted students
Gifted program specialist	Provides or arranges theoretical training in education of the gifted for classroom teachers
	Demonstrates lessons in the classroom
	Initiates follow-up dialogue and analysis of lessons
	Provides support materials following the lesson
	Establishes an ongoing relationship with teachers
	Evaluates effectiveness of educational program for gifted students
Classroom teacher	Participates in in-service training on education for gifted students
	Prepares for demonstration lessons
	Observes and analyzes demonstration lessons
	Discusses lessons in relation to needs of students
	Modifies classroom instruction to accommodate gifted students
	Evaluates effectiveness of educational program for gifted students

lacking in these comments is an understanding of the potential of the classroom teacher for instructional change. One exciting thing about the demonstration teaching model is that its use is supported by considerable writing and research in the areas of school improvement and staff development.

Staff Development

An important message for consideration of the demonstration teaching model as a vehicle for staff development is contained in a model call the RPTIM Model (Wood, McQuarrie, & Thompson, 1982). The authors of this five-stage model suggest that consideration be given to (a) readiness, (b) planning, (c) training, (d) implementation, and (e) maintenance. Each of these stages is compatible with, and, in fact, integral to the success of the demonstration teaching model. *Readiness* involves the establishment of a positive school climate, goal setting, and the identification of a local school plan. The *planning* stage provides the school staff with opportunities for assessing needs and resources, as well as for developing new outlooks and feelings toward the plan. In the third stage, *training* is provided to present key individuals with an understanding of the model and its function in the total school improvement plan. Participants receive the knowledge and skill training needed to implement the model. Stage four, *implementation,* involves direct modeling in classrooms. The final stage, *maintenance,* includes an ongoing system of training and support, including a continuing assessment of the model and its implementation. Each of these stages is crucial for educators to address in the implementation of the demonstration model; to bypass any one of them would jeopardize the effectiveness of the model. Rice emphasizes the implementation stage, but fails to address the other essential phases.

The demonstration teaching model offers many benefits to the classroom teacher. These benefits, however, cannot be realized unless the classroom teacher is receptive and motivated to participate actively in the process. Research in working with adult learners has shown that the concerns of teachers must be addressed and the teacher must be made to feel essential to the educational process. The first step toward achieving this goal is to provide teachers with theory and information to assist them in understanding the needs of gifted students. Once teachers are motivated to make special provisions for gifted students, they need assistance in learning strategies that will be useful in differentiating instruction. The demonstration component of the model is useful in showing the skills and strategies at work, and in offering a climate for dialogue about the demonstrations. When the concerns and problems of the classroom teachers are addressed specifically and consistently, teachers will become the most vital link for the differentiated education process for gifted students. The demonstration teaching model provides classroom teachers with an opportunity to experience collegiality, professional growth, and support for their efforts.

Effective Schools

Saphier and King (1985) have examined the culture of schools and defined 12 specific school norms that can interact effectively with the central values of the school. The demonstration teaching model offers a climate for a positive influence on several of these norms (Garmston, 1987) (e.g., experimentation, collegiality, tangible support, honest communication, and reaching out to the knowledge bases about teaching). In a critique of the effective schools research, Stedman (1987) suggested that extensive inservice training should be included in the effective school formula. He indicated that the most effective schools include practical on-the-job training, demonstration lessons, live and videotaped observations, and assistance with selections of materials and teaching techniques. In effective schools, training is an integral part of a collaborative educational environment that helps to support a community of teachers dedicated to self-improvement. In such a climate, the demonstration teaching model can be effective in making a difference for gifted students.

Theories of Learning

Research about the effects of modeling behavior in classrooms substantiates the fact that learners acquire much of their behavior, feelings, attitudes, and values through imitation and modeling (Joyce, Hersh, & McKibbin, 1983). A number of studies suggest that learners adopt new patterns of behavior or modify their own behavior on the basis of observation alone (Wilson, 1987). Although these studies might support Rice's presentation of the demonstration teaching model solely in relation to the actual demonstration lessons, they do not negate the fact that inservice training about the nature and needs of gifted students and dialogue about the demonstration lessons can enhance the learning and increase the likelihood of application by the regular classroom teacher. Rice describes this connection of prior knowledge about gifted learners with observations of model teaching when she refers to the connection of "theory and practice."

WHAT IS TO BE DEMONSTRATED?

Rice suggests a process model for use in the demonstration lessons. Although, in addition to this model, she does mention the use of "high-level generalizations, patterns, and/or the structure of a subject" as possibilities, these are neither described nor used in sample lessons.

Rice leaves the reader with little "feel" for what should be considered for demonstration purposes. The basis for the content of demonstration lessons can be determined in a number of ways. A district emphasis may suggest a specific model, such as the "High-Tech Thinking" model presented in the lead chapter. Other alternatives might be included in a defined scope and sequence for thinking skills, with demonstration lessons developed for each of grades K–12. Lessons in specific content areas with a variety of activities suitable for a range of student abilities, highlighting differentiation for the gifted, might also be considered. Another area for demonstration is the use of flexible groupings for the instruction of gifted learners. The specialist in educating gifted and talented students can show how to form interest groups, skills groups, cooperative groups, partners, or discussion groups to match the needs of selected gifted students. The Junior Great Books Program is an example of a literary discussion group format that provides training in critical questioning and student responses. The specialist may demonstrate how to manage classroom projects and activities in which some gifted students work together as partners or in small groups. Certain academic skills may be taught in more depth to some students while the majority of the class learns the same content without the additional elaboration. A demonstration of optional groupings provides the classroom teacher with a broader repertoire for differentiation.

One of the most effective ways to develop a collegial spirit as part of the demonstration teaching model is for the consultant/specialist to assist the classroom teacher in an area of instruction selected by the teacher. The modeling would then be particularly relevant to the individual needs of the teacher and his or her students. Consideration also should be given to using the demonstration teaching model to meet the social and emotional needs of gifted students. A consultant/specialist might demonstrate effective responses, dialogue, decision-making techniques, or problem-solving models to assist students in meeting their needs.

The decision about the content of the demonstrations always should be based on the goals of the educational program for gifted students. Professionals in the field of education for gifted students recognize that the regular classroom is the place where most gifted students spend the majority of their time while in school. Therefore, any model that provides promise for improving instruction in the regular classroom is applauded. Rice presents a model that would appear to be effective in the regular classroom and useful in a variety of settings. This flexibility of fit is an important factor for administrators to consider. I would emphasize that the model is appropriate for all grade levels, and is compatible with the peer teaching model (Garmston, 1987).

Emphasis on the importance of what happens for gifted students in the regular classroom is supported by the current trend toward school-based program management. This trend is a significant indicator of the value of the demonstration teaching model. Researchers reveal that district goals for gifted students are translated most effectively at the school level (Joyce et al., 1983). Local school administrators and teachers should work together to develop meaningful schoolwide objectives, program plans, and evaluation procedures that focus on the differentiated needs of their gifted students. The role of the central office becomes one of support for the efforts of the local schools. In this supporting role, the central office should provide assistance to schools in their quest for the best ways to provide services for gifted students. The search should be reflective and deliberative, and related to the school-based goals and objectives established for the program. School-based planning and evaluation provide a strong foundation for meaningful differentiation for gifted students.

ADVANTAGES OF THE DEMONSTRATION TEACHING MODEL

In the lead chapter, Rice suggests that the main advantage of the demonstration teaching model is the use of the principle of modeling. She also identifies the following advantages that the model provides:

- A nonthreatening atmosphere for the classroom teacher
- Opportunities for transfer of skills to other classroom activities
- A positive attitude among classroom teachers
- A cost-effective delivery system
- A decreased workload for the classroom teacher
- Congruence with other program services for the gifted

Rice's view of these advantages is shortsighted, however. Each of the suggested advantages may or may not be present in the delivery of the model. For example, the presence of a consultant/specialist may be threatening to a classroom teacher. The demeanor of the consultant, the perspective of the classroom teacher, and the extent of staff development efforts to motivate and prepare the teacher for the demonstration are crucial factors to the success of the model. When they are welcomed, demonstrations can provide the climate for a collaborative effort between classroom teacher and consultant/teacher. The demonstration should assist the classroom teacher in building sensitivity to the range of abilities possessed by the students, as well as the subtle and direct ways in which the environment can be mediated to provide a climate for the development of the students' abilities.

Rice's suggestion that the demonstrations offer classroom teachers opportunities to transfer observed skills to other classroom activities is clearly a goal of the model; however, this is a long-term goal. Teachers must have background knowledge of the skills and strategies to be observed, and must be able to delineate the elements of differentiated education for gifted students. In this sense, I do not view the model as one that decreases the workload for classroom teachers. Rather, it develops a climate for professional growth and satisfaction, a clearer view of education for gifted students, and partnership roles in that education. When positive conditions for the implementation of the model are present, effective and efficient use of school resources occurs to assist in achieving the goals of the program for gifted students. The following are major advantages of the demonstration teaching model from my perspective:

1. *Better instruction for all students.* Although the model can be used solely with identified groups of gifted learners, its most frequent use is in the regular classrooms, with all students. The demonstration lessons emphasize ways in which instruction, questioning, expectations, assignments, groupings, and other strategies can be adapted to meet a range of student needs. Because the classroom teacher has a rare opportunity to observe not only the demonstration teaching, but also the reactions of the students, the model provides a focus for the improvement of instruction.

2. *Differentiated instruction for gifted students.* Most classroom teachers are eager to meet the individual needs of students. However, because the gifted students appear more ready to "make it on their own," they often receive less consideration in the teachers' planning of lessons. The demonstration lesson helps the classroom teacher see a plan for addressing the strengths of gifted students. Richert and McGonnel (1983) suggested several areas of focus for such planning. Considering *criteria,* they outlined areas of student interest, ability, learning styles, decision-making and self-evaluation skills, critical and creative thinking skills, and product/problem-solving emphases. In the area of *strategies,* Richert and McGonnel suggested acceleration, substitution, enrichment, independent study, and learning centers. When considering activities as differentiated for gifted students, Richert and McGonnel suggested that they should meet four or more of the criteria outlined above, and should provide modifications in one or more of the six strategies. Such modifications as modeled through demonstration teaching provide the beginnings of appropriate differentiation for gifted students in the regular classroom.

3. *A staff development model for instructional change.* The demonstration teaching model builds professionalism by offering a climate for growth. The inservice training helps build an awareness of need and an information base. Regular demonstrations in the classroom offer a time for personal application, dialogue about learning modifications, and clarification of teaching strategies and management issues. The consultant/specialist can build a partnership with the classroom teacher so that the experience becomes a collaborative effort. When successful, the model leads the

classroom teacher to a leadership role in the collaboration, since that teacher has specific knowledge about the individual students and their needs.

DISADVANTAGES OF THE DEMONSTRATION TEACHING MODEL

A consideration of the disadvantages of the model must revolve around the elements of time. Rice emphasizes this point when she notes that the model should not be considered "a complete answer or the only opportunity offered to the gifted to meet their special needs." The demonstration model centers around educating teachers about the needs of gifted students. The content of this education is treated lightly in preservice programs for teachers, and many teachers feel threatened and inadequate in considering the teaching of gifted learners. Much time is needed to assist classroom teachers in achieving an adequate level of knowledge and expertise in educating gifted students. Although the demonstration teaching model can be very effective, it cannot be regarded as a model that provides direct services to gifted students to the extent they require.

Although demonstration teaching can be a part of an effective delivery model for educating gifted students, a more comprehensive approach to differentiation must be maintained. Teachers and administrators must be made aware that participation in demonstration teaching is not sufficient to meet the needs of gifted students. Although the model offers strong staff development, additional complementary program services are essential. A school-based plan for differentiation would include continued staff training through program specialists, teacher assistance teams, and/or building-level advocates to help teachers see the variety of ways in which they can address the needs of their gifted students.

Because the environment for demonstration teaching is typically the regular classroom, it does not foster efforts to assist teachers in providing time for gifted students to have some opportunities for experiences with intellectual peers. The confines of a regular classroom limit these opportunities; however, the teacher must be aware of this need and make provisions for it. This need was mentioned by Rice in her description of the gifted learner and the model.

Although Rice's treatment of the model can be criticized as being simplistic, she has attempted to present a supportive view of a most promising model. The ideas presented in her description of the Richardson ISD demonstration teaching program are encouraging to those who view the model as an excellent source for differentiated instruction for gifted students. The model includes the best of several theories of instruction to effect change for a specific purpose: the creation of a classroom climate conducive to instruction for gifted students. When all teachers in a school become proficient teachers of gifted students, a spirit of informed cooperation exists to support a commitment to meeting the students' needs.

THE DEMONSTRATION TEACHING MODEL IN ACTION

Fairfax (Virginia) County public school personnel have adopted a demonstration teaching model for their primary (Grades K through 3) program for gifted students.

The program developers view giftedness as an emerging characteristic in young children. The model offers options and opportunities for all students to explore their potential. A strong staff development component is provided through inservice, ongoing demonstration lessons, and resource personnel to help teachers analyze their teaching strategies according to principles for educating gifted students. In addition, a framework is provided for organizing and analyzing direct observations of children, as well as different ways of thinking about assessing student potential. The program strongly supports the personal, social, and cognitive growth of students who have been identified formally as gifted.

The K–3 program provides a focus for thinking about students' strengths, as well as teaching to accommodate gifted students. A series of lessons called "Response Lessons" is the primary vehicle for articulation of concepts about giftedness, teaching strategies for instruction, development of thinking skills, and formal and informal observations of students to evaluate their strength profiles. At each grade level, nine Response Lessons have been developed around a model of instruction called the SELF model (Table 8.2). Each lesson is related to the regular curriculum for a specific grade level. As indicated in Table 8.2, the SELF model is a framework for the Response Lessons. It facilitates the incorporation of experiences in critical and creative thinking into each lesson. Through these experiences, students are encouraged to reveal their present knowledge, consider alternative possibilities, make connections, and participate in problem solving. As a framework, the model is effective for helping teachers rewrite traditional lessons to include a stronger emphasis on teaching for thinking.

Table 8.2 The SELF Model

The four-stage SELF model provides students with opportunities to:

SENSE and develop an awareness of the content. This stage helps assure that all students have had experiences in the area to be discussed. It should give each child a baseline of knowledge from which to explore.

EXPLORE and think creatively about a content area. At this stage, students are encouraged to think of all the possibilities. Response activities involve students in creative, innovative, inventive, and imaginative thinking.

LINK and think critically about a content area. At this stage, students are encouraged to connect new concepts related to the content to ones they have developed already. To develop and reinforce new concepts, students are involved in activities to observe, compare, classify, relate, organize, and analyze.

FOCUS and solve a problem to their satisfaction, using analytical and decision-making skills. This stage offers activities that ask students to consider a situation, problem posed, question asked, or issue addressed, and to come up with their best solutions.

The SELF model is used in preliminary inservice training provided for all classroom teachers prior to beginning the demonstration lessons. The training emphasizes the characteristics of gifted learners, effective teaching strategies, and observation skills. Key personnel in the implementation of the demonstrations are the classroom teachers, reading teachers, and librarians, all of whom receive initial training; a resource teacher for gifted students who continues school-based training sessions, demonstration lessons, and consultations: and a liaison teacher who teaches at a primary grade level, but also represents the school. The liaison teachers receive additional training in education of the gifted through the central office, and serve as advocates for the program in their schools. Principals also receive training in the demonstration model, and facilitate the scheduling of demonstration lessons.

Each class receives four demonstration lessons from the resource teacher; the remaining five lessons are taught by the classroom teacher. During the lessons, the teacher looks for certain characteristics demonstrated by gifted children, so that a stronger awareness of their presence can be fostered. In Table 8.3, I present an overview of the SELF model, which is helpful for guiding observations of the lessons. The components of the model are specified, along with corresponding student tasks that are woven into each lesson to enhance student thinking. The last column in the table contains behaviors of gifted students that may be elicited during the lesson. A sample lesson to be taught in kindergarten is included in Table 8.4. Note that the Teacher Observations column also is included for each lesson plan so that the teacher modeling the lesson will be able to note student behaviors using the same language as the classroom teacher. Following the lesson, the classroom teacher and the resource teacher discuss the students, their responses, the delivery of the lesson, and follow-up activities that might be suitable for individual students. In addition, the teachers may begin to discuss specific students likely to be identified as gifted during the formal committee review process. When lessons have not been modeled by the resource teacher, the classroom teacher makes notations about the lesson and responses of students for later discussion with the resource teacher. At times, the resource teacher may be present when the classroom teacher is presenting a response lesson. Presence of the resource teacher is always at the request of the classroom teacher, and shows the beginnings of a peer coaching relationship.

The K–3 program for the gifted and talented also contains a component of direct intervention for identified students. This intervention, called Differentiated Services, provides an individual plan for meeting the specific needs of a child. Although the experiences provided through the demonstration lessons are valuable for the identified students, they are only one part of the child's differentiated program. Most of the Differentiated Services are provided within the regular classroom; therefore, the training the classroom teacher receives is invaluable in suggesting ways to accommodate the gifted learners.

The K–3 program for the gifted and talented in Fairfax County is in its second year, having been piloted at several schools last year. The program represents a major commitment of the school system to meeting the needs of young gifted students. Teachers, administrators, and community members have received the program with enthusiasm. The program has opened a lot of doors for communication about

Table 8.3 An Overview of the Response Lesson Model

Teaching Goals	Student Tasks		Teacher Observations
SENSE Help students to think about the lesson.	Observe Taste Touch Smell	Hear Feel Review	*Informed, Abstract* *Thinking* Intricate ideas Pondering Openness to puzzles Analysis Evaluation Connections Interpretations
EXPLORE Help students think about many possibili- ties, real and imaginary.	Imagine Change Elaborate Design Magnify Minify List	Substitute Combine Adapt Eliminate Reverse Rearrange Visualize	Broad information Concepts Generalizations Quick processing *Creative Thinking* Fluency Flexibility Originality Elaboration
LINK Help students make connections to the real world.	Compare Classify Organize Relate	Pattern Sequence Analyze	Seeking alternatives Sensing gaps Visualization Intuition Sensitivity Inventiveness Sensing problems Design of questions *Risk Taking* Guessing
FOCUS Help students consider a new solution to a specific problem.	Summarize Interpret Criticize Hypothesize	Decide Assess Solve	Self-confidence Less need for structure Comfort Decision making *Advanced Language* Vocabulary Oral expression Writing Reading Terminology Specificity Detail

Table 8.4 Response Lesson for Grade K

Unit Title: Working Together
Lesson Title: Vehicles

		Look For:
SENSE	*Help students begin to think about the lesson.*	*Informed, Abstract Thinking*
	Say, "How do students get to school?" (Give time for response.)	Intricate ideas
	"Are there any safety rules you must remember when you ride the bus, walk to school, and/or ride to school in a car?"	Pondering
		Openness to puzzles
	Show some vehicle pictures. Say, "Which one would you like to go to school in? Why?"	Analysis
		Evaluation
		Connections
		Interpretations
		Broad information
		Concepts
EXPLORE	*Help students think about many possibilities, real and imaginary.*	Generalizations
		Quick processing
	Say, "If you were *very* tiny, how could you get to school?"	*Creative Thinking*
		Fluency
		Flexibility
LINK	*Help students make connections to the real world.*	Originality
		Elaboration
	Say, "What can you think of that moves people?" (Elevator, car, truck, plane, skates)	Seeking alternatives
		Sensing gaps
		Visualization
		Intuition
	Say, "How can we move people from one place to another?" (Push, pull, roll, use wheels, special bike, use balloons, use the wind, swing them)	Sensitivity
		Inventiveness
		Sensing problems
		Design of questions
		Risk Taking
		Guessing
FOCUS	*Help students consider a new solution to a specific problem.*	Self-confidence
		Less need for structure
		Comfort
	Say, "Today you're not going to ride the school bus, your mother or father is not bringing you, and you're not walking. How are you going to get to school? Draw a new vehicle to get you to school."	Decision making
		Advanced Language
		Vocabulary
		Oral expression
	Optional sharing: Encourage students to share their drawings with the group and tell one rule about its use.	Writing
		Reading
		Terminology
	Materials: 12 × 18 inch drawing paper crayons	Specificity
		Detail

advanced learners, as well as about children who may not yet seem gifted, but whose behaviors indicate strengths in some specific areas. Teachers are benefiting from a staff development plan with a continuous, developmental focus. Most important, a dynamic view of giftedness is taken, which offers every child an opportunity for success while emphasizing the very real needs of gifted students.

REFERENCES

Garmston, R. (1987). How administrators support peer coaching. *Educational Leadership, 44*(5), 18–26.

Joyce, B., Hersch, R., & McKibbin, M. (1983). *The structure of school improvement* (pp. 138–142). New York: Longman.

Putnam, J. (1985). Perceived benefits and limitations of teacher education demonstration lessons. *Journal of Teacher Education, 36,* 36–41.

Richert, E., & McGonnel, R. (1983). *Curriculum in the regular classroom for gifted.* Sewell, NJ: Educational Improvement Center–South.

Saphier, J., & King, M. (1985). Good seeds grow in strong cultures. *Educational Leadership, 42*(6), 67.

Stedman, L. (1987). It's time we changed the effective schools formula. *Phi Delta Kappan, 69*(3), 215–224.

Wilson, J. (1987). Instructor modeling in teacher education classes. *Journal of Research and Development in Education, 20,* 77–81.

Wood, F., McQuarrie, F., & Thompson, S. (1982). Practitioners and professors agree on effective staff development practices. *Educational Leadership, 40,* 28–31.

PART III

CURRICULUM
DIFFERENTIATION

As I sat down to write this introduction, I realized I am stuck again with the same old question I have tried to answer many times (and, I might add, with varying degrees of success). This time, however, it is no one's fault but mine. I did this to myself. *I* posed the question, and now I must answer it. This question, in some form, has been asked by every educator and parent concerned with providing an appropriate education for gifted students. Two versions of the question are "Aren't the methods you advocate for gifted students good for *all* children?" and "What do you mean by a 'qualitatively different' curriculum for the gifted?"

My first major attempt to answer this question in writing was in *Curriculum Development for the Gifted* (Maker, 1982), in which I focused on defining a qualitatively different curriculum in the areas of content, process, product, and learning environment. Differentiation, I reasoned, needed to be designed to build upon and extend the characteristics that make the students different—both now and in the future. Based on a review of traits common to gifted students, I recommended principles to guide educators in curriculum design. This list of principles, however, included some that were important in the education of all children. I tended to respond to some critics who pointed out this fact by focusing on content as the area in most need of differentiation. I responded to others by stating that many of the differences in curriculum designed for different learners were differences in *degree,* not in *kind.* For example, gifted students need more emphasis on higher levels of thinking, more open-ended questions and activities, more independence.

The "degree" answer satisfied neither me nor my critics entirely, and I continued to search for a better way to respond. In Volume I of *Critical Issues in Gifted Education* (Maker, 1986), I stressed the problems of practicality, and reminded readers that, even though many educators recognize the value of certain teaching strategies for all children, these techniques simply are not being used. Although these methods would be good for all students, they are essential for the gifted; thus, if one must make a choice about how to spend valuable time and resources, this rationale would work. Well, this answer was not good enough for me, either, but when I received David Berliner's (1986) manuscript and thought about the value of catastrophe theory and its application to this problem, I became very excited.

According to catastrophe theory, several differences of "degree" add up to a difference in "kind." In other words, when several quantitative differences (e.g., in content, process, product, environment) are combined, they result in a different *type* of curriculum. A further application of this idea is to recommend that any one change in the curriculum, by itself, does not constitute the qualitatively different curriculum that gifted students need. An appropriate educational program for the gifted is one in which many possibilities for differentiation exist, and several are combined to fit the needs of individual students—resulting in a qualitatively different curriculum.

I still am not completely satisfied with my answers. I do not disagree with any of the answers I have provided in the past, but I am still searching for more and better ways to address an age-old problem. It is a key concept in this field.

The question is rephrased this time, however, and separated into two parts. Better questions usually result in better answers!

What techniques appropriate for gifted students can be used to benefit all children?

What techniques appropriate for gifted students should not be used with or would not be appropriate for all students?

Separating the problem into two questions gives the first clue to my answer. I *do* believe that not all methods we advocate for use with gifted students should be used with all students. One needs only to present an assignment or problem to a group of students and watch their faces to know that different learning experiences are needed for different students. When gifted students react with excitement and others react with frustration or fear, I know I have found an experience that fits into an answer to the second question. If I observe a group of faces—some bored, some mildly interested, some excited, some deadpan—and no clear pattern of reactions can be seen based on abilities, I know I have found an experience that fits an answer to the first question.

Perhaps most learning experiences fit into the first category: Most techniques appropriate for gifted students can be used to benefit other children. All techniques recommended for the gifted cannot, however, be used to benefit all students at all times. How, then, does one decide? I would like to propose both a simple and a complex answer. First, the simple answer: Any teacher interested in knowing whether a particular strategy will benefit all (or most) of the students in the class should try it and observe the results. When students are excited and challenged, when they enjoy participating in activities, when they demonstrate growth in important knowledge or skills, and when important goals are reached, experiences can be considered successful. If students are frustrated, fearful, bored, or unmotivated; if they find ways to avoid participating; if they fail to demonstrate growth in important areas; or if they fail to achieve the goals we set, learning experiences can be considered unsuccessful, and need to be changed.

Basically, at this point in my career, I am not ready to make definitive generalizations about which strategies advocated for the gifted will and will not be beneficial for students who are not gifted. Students, teachers, and situations are too different for any generalization to work.

Beyond this simple answer, I would like to propose another based on materials reviewed by one of the chapter authors in this section, and then review briefly the answers provided by all these authors. In her critique of Shirley Schiever's chapter on differentiating the learning environment for gifted students, Dorothy Sisk discusses Abraham Maslow's hierarchy of needs, and lists the special needs of gifted students at each level of the hierarchy. Maslow (1954) listed five categories of basic needs that should be considered in the design of educational programs. He stated that each lowest or most basic level must be met before the learner is capable of or motivated to meet the next highest needs. The categories of needs, from lowest to highest, are the following: *physical* (e.g., food, water, shelter, warmth), *security* (e.g., stability, protection, and freedom from fear, anxiety, chaos), *belonging* (e.g., love, affection), *self-esteem and competence* (e.g., desire for achievement, for feeling adequate, for mastery and competence), and *self-actualization* of higher abilities. Examination of Maslow's highest level of needs will help educators view decisions about differing instruction for gifted students. At this level, the student is concerned with fulfillment, a feeling that one has attained what is possible and desirable, given his or her abilities and interests. Students concerned with self-actualization have had their lower needs met, and are concerned with reaching to the highest levels of their capabilities—with finding and pushing their limits.

Although gifted students may have characteristics and needs that are somewhat different from other students at the lower levels of Maslow's hierarchy, the needs are basically the same, and can be met in ways similar to the satisfaction of needs of other learners. However, the needs of gifted learners diverge more clearly from others at the highest level. Because gifted students, by definition, possess a greater capacity for achievement and development of higher abilities, their needs are more different from the needs of other students at this level.

I am not suggesting that only gifted students who are becoming "self-actualized" have needs that are significantly or qualitatively different from the needs of other students. What I am suggesting, however, is that more differences between gifted and nongifted students can be observed (and must be met) at the self-actualization level than at the other levels of need. This idea forms the basis of my brief review of the ideas presented by authors in this section. It may offer a "filter" or "hook" for readers as they explore the excellent ideas presented for differentiating the curriculum for gifted learners in the regular classroom.

In his discussion of content appropriate for gifted students, Roger Shanley recommends the use of generalizations as a way to help select content for all students.

Thus, all students are provided opportunities to learn and to grapple with the same important ideas. The differences he suggests to accommodate different needs of the gifted are (a) developing an understanding of *more* of the important ideas and (b) using more complex, challenging reading materials to achieve an understanding of these important ideas (which implies developing the ideas in more depth and complexity). All students are provided similar learning experiences designed to develop their physical, security, belonging, and self-esteem and competence needs; however, differences are evident in the complexity of experiences designed to provide a challenge for gifted students to explore and use their highest abilities.

In her critique, Gloria Grotjan reminds Roger Shanley that he has not provided teachers with clear answers to questions regarding delivery of content. In other words, teachers must decide which students study which specific content, and these decisions must be defensible. Classroom teachers need guidance in making decisions, and they need to be involved when general curricular decisions are made. Student self-selection, according to Grotjan, may or may not be appropriate, and, if used, a vehicle for self-selection should be described.

Hilda Rosselli's chapter about process differentiation for the gifted contains many excellent suggestions for teachers to modify instruction in the regular classroom and to provide for a variety of needs. Much of her discussion is centered on the use of certain general principles for the benefit of students at all levels of ability in the classroom. Her suggestions seem to fit with my general thesis regarding Maslow's hierarchy. One example is the use of open-ended questions. She recommends use of open-ended questions as a way to invite students to enter a discussion (security) with a group of students in which a variety of ideas is acceptable (belonging), and students are challenged to use their information in new ways to achieve mastery and acquire needed skills (self-esteem and competence). She suggests that gifted students with leadership abilities be encouraged to lead discussions once they have learned the questioning sequence. This seems to be a quite different kind of experience, one that exemplifies the experiences needed to enable gifted students to "self-actualize" and develop their highest abilities. An important fact to note here, too, is that this experience is recommended for students with a particular kind of giftedness, not for all gifted students regardless of the types of abilities they possess.

Pacing, another principle for differentiating the process of instruction, is viewed by Rosselli as a vehicle for the teacher to accommodate the needs of slow-learning students for more time to learn skills and concepts, and to complete assignments while offering gifted students time to take a "detour" into related areas of interest. In this example, slower learning students may need to spend extra time mastering a skill because of their need for self-esteem and competence, whereas gifted students may be ready to explore higher abilities and develop interests in new, or more complex areas.

Diane Orzechowski-Harland, in her critique of Rosselli's chapter, focuses on the role of the teacher in choosing and implementing processes advocated for use with gifted students. She recognizes the complexity of the role, and focuses on three major issues: (a) the importance of understanding one's own thinking style preferences and their impact on curriculum development, (b) the challenge of selecting the most appropriate strategies to introduce and implement in a systematic way, and (c) becoming skilled in using strategies that are unfamiliar. Knowing one's personal style preferences helps teachers help students assess preferences, and assists teachers in meeting basic needs of all students (acceptance of personal styles, developing ways to build upon existing styles and preferences, and helping students explore new thinking styles), as well as know which students are not being challenged or extended within the existing curriculum. A variety of options is available to teachers, and they can choose models/techniques that benefit the whole class, as well as those needed for only a few students. Teachers must practice, receive feedback, and, ultimately, internalize these methods and models.

In their discussion of strategies for assisting students in the development of differentiated products through independent investigations, Sally Reis and Gina Schack (lead article) and Sandy Lethem (critique) recommend that all students be given opportunities to do investigations in areas of interest. They suggest many ways to assure that students' physical needs, needs for security (e.g., methods for collecting data; strategies for conducting research; step-by-step plans; clear, agreed-upon criteria for evaluation), belonging (e.g., acceptance of their interests and methods of investigation, feeling that the teacher is their friend and guide rather than judge), and self-esteem and competence (e.g., ways to define the limits of an investigation, decide which questions to answer, evaluate own progress, choose audiences and products) can be met during the course of an independent investigation. They also suggest a number of techniques designed to assist students in self-actualization.

The interview process described by Reis and Schack, for example, helps teachers to distinguish between those who have achieved a level of competence and skill with which they are satisfied and those who have a burning desire to investigate a certain topic and develop a product that is truly different. This interview process, I believe, can help teachers distinguish whether students are at the self-actualization level of motivation with regard to a particular interest area. Lethem's suggestions for giving managerial assistance to students rather than assuming managerial responsibilities seem to be a similar category according to Maslow's hierarchy. Students will learn many valuable "life skills" through managing their own projects. In addition, the step of identifying audiences and final products seems to be an important area for differentiation between gifted and nongifted, and between lower levels of needs and self-actualization.

Shirley Schiever's description of the learning environment for all children includes all the elements needed to meet children's needs for physical safety, security, belonging, self-esteem, and competence. In her description of ways to achieve psychological, emotional, and physical safety, for example, she recommends consistent discipline, or freedom within limits, and cautions teachers against unknowing putdowns and humiliation of children (security needs). She also discusses respect, appreciation of differences, and teaching how to resolve conflict (belonging needs) as a necessary part of psychological, emotional, and physical safety. Some of Schiever's recommendations for questioning strategies (e.g., acceptance without comment) are designed to establish safety and a sense of belonging to the group. When she describes how teachers can communicate their excitement about and value of what students are learning, she is describing the kind of environment students need for developing self-esteem and competence; and in many of the suggestions for developing a stimulating and challenging educational experience, self-esteem and competence needs (e.g., teaching concepts through hands-on experiences, integrating information from experiences through discussions) are addressed.

Schiever also provides many suggestions for classroom teachers to motivate and assist all students in moving toward self-actualization of abilities. Teachers who communicate their excitement about what they are teaching and learning show their students what self-actualizing is like, and when they develop an environment with stimulating and challenging educational experiences, teachers provide a way for students to explore and develop their higher abilities. Schiever recommends encouraging students to ''stretch'' by using the principles of questioning that she outlines. Particularly important in this context is open-endedness, questioning requiring processing of information, seeking variety and building on answers of others, and seeking clarification or extension.

In the last part of her chapter, Schiever describes elements of the environment in which differentiation for the gifted needs to occur. Each of the six dimensions (student-centeredness, independence, openness, acceptance, complexity, mobility) includes a focus on ways to help students, particularly those who are gifted, find ways to explore and develop their higher abilities.

Dorothy Sisk uses Maslow's hierarchy of needs in her critique of Schiever's chapter. She discusses the special needs gifted students have in each of the categories Maslow identifies, and suggests adding the development of complex and intense thinking (i.e., integrated thinking skills) as an important challenge for gifted students. She presents three generic thinking models (inquiry, problem solving, and decision making) that interact with questioning strategies. These also can be used to help gifted students challenge and develop their competence and higher level abilities. Sisk's environmental dimension of interdependence seems to be crucial for the development of higher abilities in students with leadership and interpersonal skills, and her dimension of encouraging creativity is an important aspect of self-actualization for the gifted, who have a strong desire to produce new knowledge and new products.

CONCLUSION

In answer to the question ''What techniques appropriate for gifted students can be used to benefit all children?'' I would answer ''most of them.'' Many differences exist among children, teachers, and situations; therefore, strategies need to be adapted, modified, and used in appropriate situations if they are to be of benefit to children. One way to view the selection and use of teaching strategies recommended for the gifted is to use Maslow's hierarchy of needs as a filter. In the chapters that follow, many techniques are presented and ways of adapting them for use in regular classroom settings are explained.

The question ''What techniques appropriate for gifted students should not be used with or would not be appropriate for all students?'' could be answered in at least two ways: (a) "those that require abilities or skills not possessed by students, thus resulting in frustration and/or feelings of incompetence," and (b) "those that challenge the highest abilities when children have not yet had lower level needs such as belonging and self-esteem and competence met." I have summarized some of the ideas presented by authors in this section. Many more are explained in depth by the authors.

REFERENCES

Berliner, D. (1986). Catastrophes and interactions: Comments on "The Mistaken Metaphor." In C. J. Maker, *Critical issues in gifted education: Defensible programs for the gifted.* Austin, TX: PRO-ED.

Maker, C. J. (1982). *Curriculum development for the gifted.* Austin, TX: PRO-ED.

Maker, C. J. (Ed.). (1986). *Critical issues in gifted education: Defensible programs for the gifted.* Austin, TX: PRO-ED.

Maslow, A. H. (1954). *Motivation and personality.* New York: Harper.

9

Becoming Content
(kən-tĕnt′, adj.)
with Content (kŏn′-tĕnt, n.)

Roger Shanley

Educators often struggle to develop suitable content for students ranging in ability levels and backgrounds. Especially challenging for teachers is the responsibility of providing appropriate content for the gifted student in a regular classroom. However, modifying regular curricular content may be of greater importance than modifications in process, product, or learning environment. I believe the sophistication of content (e.g., complexity and abstractness) affects the process, product, and learning environment in classrooms for gifted students. Imagine a chef trying to create a spectacular meal of Chateaubriand using inferior or lower quality meat. As he cooked, the process of preparing the meat would be affected because the steps necessary to complete the meal would be hindered by the weakness of the ingredients—the inability of the meat to become tender. The kitchen (learning environment) would be negatively affected because, in efforts to tenderize the meat, the chef might clutter the workplace. Also, the end product would be affected by the poor taste of the original meat. Similarly, a teacher would struggle far more to create a stimulating lesson based on Hilda Taba's (1966) Teaching Strategies using the content based on Paul Zindel's (1970) *The Effect of Gamma Rays on Man-in-the-Moon Marigolds* than from Harper Lee's (1960) *To Kill a Mockingbird*. I believe that, when students develop a product using these two works as examples, the depth of conceptual ingredients in Lee's work would enable students to develop complex products on subjects such as prejudice, caste system, or superstition. Finding such concepts in Zindel's work is far more difficult. Also, logical modification of learning environment for Lee's novel results in visits to courtrooms, for example, but Zindel's play does not yield itself as easily to such modification.

Based on the principle that curriculum for gifted students should be qualitatively different from the basic curriculum for all children (Maker, 1982), teachers should decide what characterizes a curriculum that is qualitatively different in content, and then select such characteristic content. Although ideas about qualitatively different curriculum vary, experts in the area of educating gifted students provide important considerations about the content found within qualitatively different programs for the gifted.

Two of the 10 propositions and corollaries proposed by Virgil Ward (1961; referred to in figures with Roman numerals) relate to appropriate content for gifted students:

> That the curriculum should consist of economically chosen experiences designed to promote the civic, social, and personal adequacy of the intellectually superior individual. (p. 102)
> That the instruction of the intellectually superior should include content pertaining to the foundations of civilization. (p. 170)

In his Enrichment Triad Model, Joseph Renzulli (1977) referred to "enrichment," and suggested that curriculum content for the gifted meet two specific criteria: Enrichment should (a) take into account the students' specific content interests, and (b) allow students the opportunity to pursue topic areas (where they have superior potential for performance) to unlimited levels of inquiry.

Sandra Kaplan (1974, p. 123) presented three "procedures for presenting learning opportunities," two of which are most applicable for content selection for programs for the gifted:

> *Exposure:* Students are exposed to experiences, materials, and information which is outside the bounds of the regular curriculum, does not match age/grade expectations, and introduces something new or unusual. (p. 123)
> *Extension:* Students are afforded opportunities to elaborate on the regular curriculum through additional allocation of working time, materials and experiences, and/or further self-initiated or related study. (p. 123)

James Gallagher (1975) made the point that, of the three aspects appropriate for modification in curriculum for the gifted (content of the program, method of presentation of content, and nature of the student's learning environment), content modifications should include greater emphasis on more complex and abstract concepts. Gallagher and colleagues (1966) developed a system of classifying content according to the following three levels of abstractness:

1. Data or topics in which the focus of the discussion is on things and facts rather than on more abstract ideas, and such topics should be able to be experienced through the senses.
2. Concepts or topics centering on ideas or classes of items and, although data may be part of the concepts, emphasis is placed on abstraction.
3. Generalizations or statements containing two or more concepts that are interrelated as part of a system or part of a larger generalization, and the topic of the generalization has broad applicability.

June Maker (1982) identified a number of similar modifications of the content found in programs for gifted students that provide both enrichment and acceleration. Like Gallagher, Maker encouraged content organization around key concepts to emphasize abstractness and complexity, explaining that the result facilitates economy in the learning process. In addition, Maker (1986) suggested that content for gifted students include "a systematic sampling of major branches of learning in addition to the study of creative people and methods of inquiry used in the various branches of knowledge studied" (p. 2).

Related to Gallagher's emphasis on abstractness and complexity and Maker's emphasis on economy and organization, Womack (1966) believed that the use of generalizations can enable teachers to select appropriate content for gifted students at each grade level. In his definition, generalizations are sentences with two or more concepts interrelated in a logical manner with the sentences' topics based on a large idea with broad applicability. Womack's approach, referred to in this article as *the top–down approach,* contains the following six steps for using generalizations to select and organize content for gifted students:

1. Compile an authoritative list of generalizations.
2. Choose from the list those generalizations that most likely can be discovered from the prescribed content of the course.
3. Arrange the chosen generalizations in a priority order of those that must be learned to those that may or may not be necessary for the particular course.
4. Decide which of the "must" generalizations the students can discover from a particular unit of study. The teacher now has a list of generalizations that students can discover unit by unit.
5. Decide which unit has generalizations that absolutely must be learned and which has generalizations that could be omitted if necessary.
6. Arrange the units with "absolutely must" generalizations in a sequence based on one of the usual criteria, such as chronology, expanding environments, or a topical approach.

Another approach for using generalizations for selecting qualitatively different content is based on Womack's approach. I developed and call this *the bottom–up approach*:

1. Determine units of content material most applicable for a particular grade level as suggested by the district or program objectives. Focus on units that contain many concepts.
2. Determine the most "concept-laden" units, considering the two criteria used by Bruner (1960) to make decisions about content: (a) When fully developed, is the concept worth being known by an adult? (b) Having known the concept as a child, does a person become a better adult?
3. Develop generalizations using combinations of two or more concepts, as well as indicating a relationship between the concepts. The result will be generalizations at one of Womack's four levels of generality and inclusiveness (Maker, 1982):
   a. Subgeneralizations are those that have limited rather than universal application, as in this example: "In fascist countries, the people are the servants of the state rather than served by the state" (p. 4).

  b. Normative generalizations express a value judgment and thus have only limited application, as in this example: "Democracy has survived only because of the role played by political parties" (p. 5).
  c. Methodological generalizations are principles or rules that describe a skill or technique for a field of study, as in this example: "Area geographical relations can be seen most readily by the use of map symbols and scales" (p. 5).
  d. Substantive generalizations are broad inclusive statements in complete grammatical sentence form which serve as a principle or rule (p. 1), as in this example: "A division of labor leads to increased productivity and a rising standard of living" (p. 8).
4. Determine other units or content in related or different disciplines that support, extend, or modify the generalizations developed in Step 3.
5. Determine the most "authoritative" or "substantive" generalizations by asking for verification of validity by professionals in the field of study examined in the generalization.
6. Group units and generalizations in the most logical manner to achieve the best affective and cognitive results, following patterns such as sequence, chronology, or cause and effect.

I believe the bottom–up approach can enable teachers of regular classes to provide qualitatively different content for gifted students in their classes. One benefit of the approach is that regular content can be the starting point for selection of content, and those materials or units possessing sufficient depth and number of related concepts are selected for all students in the class. With such material as a starting point, the teacher can then enrich and/or accelerate the content for the gifted student and assist the student in selecting additional content based on the suggestions for developing qualitatively different content by such authorities as Ward, Renzulli, Gallagher, Maker, Womack, and Kaplan.

My view of qualitatively different content for gifted students combines the content considerations from these authorities and includes an emphasis on relating materials from the past and present to enable students to work logically with important issues of the future, an important task for gifted students (Kaplan, 1986). Influenced by the view of Joyce VanTassel-Baska (1986) that programs for gifted students should be based on content areas such as sciences, mathematics, humanities, social sciences, and behavioral sciences, I will describe appropriate content for gifted students in a regular ninth-grade English classroom that blends the "regular" content of English with the "enriched" content of humanities. In addition, I recommend extensions of the content area material based on the characteristics of qualitatively different content recommended. I also make suggestions for modifying content areas other than English and at various age and grade levels.

Why begin with the regular curricular content? In the subject area of English, a wide range of prescribed content exists from school district to school district. However, I believe that most traditional English programs strive to enable students to become competent or proficient in the essential skills of reading, writing, speaking, listening, and thinking; therefore, content found within regular English programs that facilitates essential skill acquisition is worthy of use with gifted students as well. VanTassel-Baska (1986) believed that gifted students benefit from "compressed content" in traditional areas of learning to develop proficiency skills, resulting in greater growth in similar and "holistic" areas. Using compressed content material that the teacher has rearranged to accommodate the more rapid rate of learning in gifted students (Terman, 1925) is a good way to gain acceptance for differentiated education for gifted students. Teachers can explain that the "best" content is not being saved for gifted students. Instead, all students receive quality content. The difference between the regular and modified content results when gifted students and the teacher either accelerate or enrich the regular classroom content based on the students' unique characteristics or interests.

CONTENT EXAMPLE OF THE BOTTOM–UP APPROACH

A standard literary work used in ninth-grade English classes is *Romeo and Juliet* by William Shakespeare (1600/1959). Appropriate for the wide range of cognitive and affective levels found in freshmen, the play contains many related concepts from which gifted students can form generalizations. In addition, Shakespeare created a rich plot dealing with a number of problems that are still found relevant to today's adolescents. With careful planning, the teacher can provide appropriate content and experiences for all students. Figure 9.1 is an example of the bottom–up approach used with *Romeo and Juliet* and includes teacher–student activities during the unit.

In the regular curriculum, the teacher's emphasis usually is on the structure of the drama, the dialogue and stage directions, the uniqueness of Shakespearean language, the characterization, and the plot. Based on my experiences, I believe that students benefit more from listening to an audiotape as a large group at the beginning of the play than engaging in silent reading or reading parts in small groups. When difficult or important passages occur, the teacher can then elaborate. As the students become more familiar with the play, however, less teacher input is required and more student involvement results. Oral readings are successful, and students' comments and questions become more frequent as the plot "thickens." Most teachers discuss the setting of the play at the beginning to increase understanding of the action, whereas the middle of the play is an appropriate place to explain the characteristics of Shakespeare's time. The teacher can refer briefly to Queen Elizabeth and her lineage, England's social and economic traits, and drama's popularity as one of the only forms of entertainment for the people. When discussion becomes more frequent, the teacher can explain structural elements of act, scene, and line count to increase the accuracy and complexity of the student discussion. Often, teachers use objective tests with regular classes to determine knowledge of the play's main elements, but other evaluation methods also are appropriate.

Students' written versions of an updated scene shows the instructor a student's knowledge of the play's main elements, as well as allows for student creativity. For example, one student might choose to "update" the balcony scene by changing the

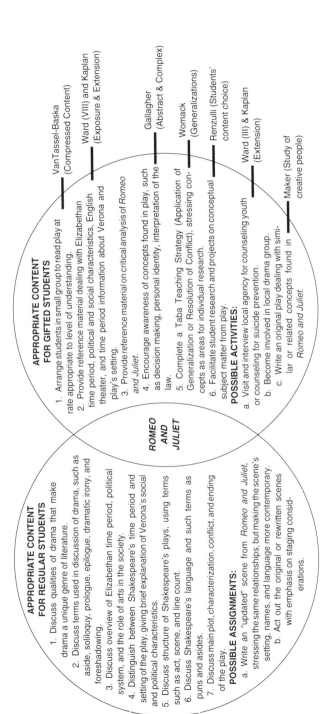

Generalizations for gifted students resulting from the bottom–up approach:

1. Interaction among individuals or groups frequently results in hostile encounters or struggles. Conflict is characteristic of growth and development in individuals and of civilization as a whole.

2. Man's development of human traits and his perception of himself as a particular personality derive from his group associations.

3. In all societies, the functions of socialization and acculturation are tasks of the family, and every society has developed rather complex, lengthy processes by which it prepares its youth for induction into society.

Figure 9.1 Visualization of Shanley's Bottom–Up Approach.

setting to the upper level of a mall. The male character, Rocky, is listening to Jannee proclaim her love for him, as well as lament the fact that his name separates them, for he is a skater and she is a schoolgirl. When the student updates the dialogue, yet remains consistent with the plot and meaning of the original script, the teacher can assess accurately the student's understanding of the original plot and conflict. For students bold enough, acting scenes from the original script or scenes created by classmates can add another dimension to the activity.

By ninth grade, many gifted students have read or viewed one or more plays by Shakespeare. Rather than bore them with explanations directed to the novice reader of Shakespeare, the teacher should enable such students to read at their own rate. Providing an audiotape is appropriate, but many gifted students prefer silent reading or small group oral reading. Using the Folger edition of Shakespeare's *Romeo and Juliet* (the one listed in the references) is recommended, for the notes in the edition can be the first of many resources for gifted students. When questions or concerns arise, the students can find answers in the reference section of the classroom. Note that these materials are not strictly for the gifted students in the class. Students following the format of the regular curriculum also are encouraged to do additional research. To generate thought about concepts and themes contained in the play, the teacher also can provide critical analyses of the play, encouraging the students to probe into specific yet abstract areas, such as the complex motives of Friar Laurence's actions and advice about moderation. If no prior lesson on the qualities of concepts has occurred, the teacher can discuss the concepts and work with students to identify examples, such as moderation, decision making, fate, personal identity, loyalty, hate, and love.

To promote self-direction (Treffinger, 1975), the teacher can lead a Hilda Taba Teaching Strategies (Schiever, 1991) discussion—the Application of Generalizations—beginning with focusing questions such as "What do you think would have happened if Romeo had not killed Tybalt?" or "What do you think would have happened if Romeo and Juliet had been allowed to marry without any interference?" The teacher also might use Taba's Resolution of Conflict Strategy to generate alternative solutions to the violent and destructive solution Romeo found in the play. Both strategies encourage the students to think about the concepts in the play and support their ideas with specific material from the play. Also, students discover relationships among concepts by participating in Taba Teaching Strategies. The teacher can use student interest in the related concepts to suggest research activities to be performed inside and outside the school environment.

Research and self-directed activities might include visits to local counseling agencies to discuss suicide prevention, addictive behavior, and decision making or problem solving. The content of students' inquiries on such visits fulfills many of the characteristics suggested by Renzulli (1977) in the Enrichment Triad Model because the students are looking for "real solutions" to "real problems." Another possible extension or "enrichment" activity would be visiting the local theater company and viewing a play. By seeing a live production and talking with the actors, students would be having contact with creative people, a content suggestion made by Maker (1982). Note that other content suggestions are matched with content application in Figure 9.1.

By focusing on concepts such as interaction, hostility, conflict, growth, self-perception, personality, group associations, socialization, acculturation, family, society, and induction into society found in a concept-laden work such as *Romeo and Juliet*, the teacher can create generalizations such as the three found in Figure 9.1. By thinking of other related works that contain similar concepts or that support, modify, or extend the generalizations, the teacher can provide qualitatively different content for gifted students in the regular classroom.

CONTENT EXAMPLE OF THE TOP–DOWN APPROACH

In his six-step approach, Womack (1966) suggested that a teacher provide appropriate content for gifted students in a regular class by using generalizations as the starting point of content selection. Following this method, the teacher might find that the content selected for the gifted students is different from the content selected for other students. Such different content results from the teacher's need to provide material for the gifted students with enough depth to allow for the extension, modification, or support of the "must" generalizations selected by the teacher in Step 4 of Womack's approach. If the teacher considers the concepts found in "must" generalizations when selecting content for the regular students, the content selected for the regular students will have a conceptual basis and will allow the teacher to hold group discussions about similar thematic or conceptual issues related to the different content with all students. Proceeding in such a manner will assure that the teacher follows the scope and sequence for the grade level for both the gifted and regular students; however, the teacher is provided the flexibility needed to allow for extension, enrichment, or acceleration of the content for the gifted students. If, for example, a teacher of English wanted to provide qualitatively different content for the gifted students in a regular class, Womack's approach would be practiced in the following method. After the teacher has compiled a list of authoritative generalizations at the start of the school year (Womack, Step 1), the teacher decides which generalizations could be taught by using the "prescribed" content of the course (Womack, Step 2). For example, the three generalizations used in the example of the bottom–up approach could be arranged according to the teacher's priority for the year's schedule (Womack, Step 3). The teacher then selects a unit of study appropriate for working with the "must" generalizations (Womack, Step 4), such as a freshman drama unit in which two plays are chosen—one for the interest and ability level of the regular students in the class and one for the interest and ability level of the gifted students in the class. *The Effect of Gamma Rays on Man-in-the-Moon Marigolds* by Paul Zindel (1970) is a highly readable play with relatively current subject matter and believable conflict among family members. From my experience, however, gifted students find the play slow and overly obvious. A play more challenging for the gifted students, but containing similar concepts and themes, is *Merchant of Venice* by Shakespeare (1600/1957). I believe regular students in the class would find Shakespeare's drama too complicated and miss the concepts simply because they are trying to follow the language and plot.

In *The Effect of Gamma Rays on Man-in-the-Moon Marigolds,* a matriarchal family includes two daughters with opposite personalities who develop methods of coping with their eccentric mother. Besides discussing with the regular students the standard elements of drama, the teacher can facilitate discussions about various concepts or current issues. Figure 9.2 is an illustration of procedures for using Zindel's and Shakespeare's plays in a regular classroom.

Students could examine the following topics: family structures (i.e., matriarchal, patriarchal, and extended), peer pressure and its effect on students' lives, stereotyping, gender roles, career options, and the role of the past and present on an individual's future. All these ideas are expressed in the plot of Zindel's play and can serve to stimulate discussion with students, as well as allow for interesting evaluation of student knowledge and response to the play. For example, students could rewrite the ending of the play based on the knowledge from the script. By evaluating the accuracy of understanding on which the student based the new ending, the teacher could determine the student's understanding of the play and the student's feelings about the characters. Another possibility is to ask the regular students to write in the voice or act in the manner of one of the characters set 20 years in the future. The students would be required to use the materials from the play on which to base their predictions about the chosen character. For example, to dramatize the mother's feeling of being haunted by her past, one student might depict her as continuously reliving the past, being unaware of the present, and ignorant or uncaring about the future. On the other hand, one student might depict Tillie, the youngest daughter and main character, as a successful scientist who keeps in contact with her mother but avoids intimacy because her confused past is not as motivating as her persent life or future aspirations.

Similar in basic conceptual material but far richer in complexity of plot and intricacy of conflict is *Merchant of Venice.* Shakespeare's play contains a fascinating patriarchal family structure, as portrayed in Shylock's domineering household. Examples of various bonds, ranging from friendship and love to legal prejudice against ethnicity and gender, complicated decision making, role reversals, role of fate or destiny, and interpretation of the law, are other topics woven into the plot. Such concepts, combined with the richness of language and imagery, give *Merchant of Venice* appropriate content from which the students can extend, modify, or support the three "must" generalizations the teacher used to choose the play.

The teacher can facilitate an understanding of the play by (a) allowing the gifted students to read it at their own rate, and (b) providing the students with a variety of reference materials, such as the notes found in the Folger edition of the play (the 1973 reprint of Shakespeare, 1957) and audiovisual material about Venice, the type of discrimination found in the time period, and usury practices and laws. As students examine various concepts of interest rates and borrowing, a modern form of usury, Kaplan's procedure of "exposure" is followed. Kaplan's approach of experience, materials, and information which is outside the normal area or the normal curriculum or does not match age or grade expectations as well as introducing new ideas, would be followed in such investigations. By examining the mathematical, political, and social implications of interest practices in banking and loan institu-

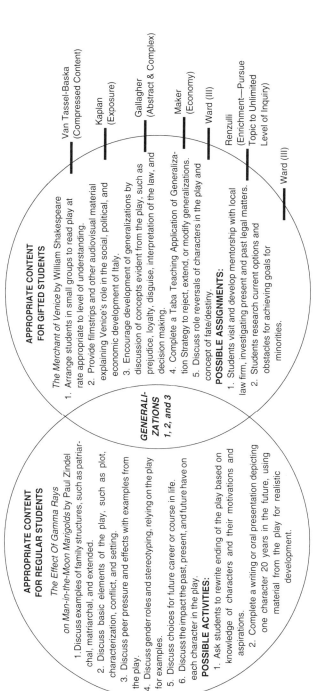

APPROPRIATE CONTENT FOR REGULAR STUDENTS

The Effect Of Gamma Rays on Man-in-the-Moon Marigolds by Paul Zindel

1. Discuss examples of family structures, such as patriarchal, matriarchal, and extended.
2. Discuss basic elements of the play, such as plot, characterization, conflict, and setting.
3. Discuss peer pressure and effects with examples from the play.
4. Discuss gender roles and stereotyping, relying on the play for examples.
5. Discuss choices for future career or course in life.
6. Discuss the impact the past, present, and future have on each character in the play.

POSSIBLE ACTIVITIES:

1. Ask students to rewrite ending of the play based on knowledge of characters and their motivations and aspirations.
2. Complete a writing or oral presentation depicting one character 20 years in the future, using material from the play for realistic development.

GENERALIZATIONS 1, 2, and 3

APPROPRIATE CONTENT FOR GIFTED STUDENTS

The Merchant of Venice by William Shakespeare

1. Arrange students in small groups to read play at rate appropriate to level of understanding.
2. Provide filmstrips and other audiovisual material explaining Venice's role in the social, political, and economic development of Italy.
3. Encourage development of generalizations by discussion of concepts evident from the play, such as prejudice, loyalty, disguise, interpretation of the law, and decision making.
4. Complete a Taba Teaching Application of Generalization Strategy to reject, extend, or modify generalizations.
5. Discuss role reversals of characters in the play and concept of fate/destiny.

POSSIBLE ASSIGNMENTS:

1. Students visit and develop mentorship with local law firm, investigating present and past legal matters.
2. Students research current options and obstacles for achieving goals for minorities.

Van Tassel-Baska (Compressed Content)
Kaplan (Exposure)
Gallagher (Abstract & Complex)
Maker (Economy)
Ward (III)
Renzulli (Enrichment—Pursue Topic to Unlimited Level of Inquiry)
Ward (III)

"Must" generalizations for gifted students:

1. Interaction among individuals or groups frequently results in hostile encounters or struggles. Conflict is characteristic of growth and development in individuals and of civilization as a whole.
2. Man's development of human traits and his perception of himself as a particular personality derive from his group associations.
3. In all societies, the functions of socialization and acculturation are tasks of the family, and every society has developed rather complex, lengthy processes by which it prepares its youth for induction into society.

Figure 9.2 Visualization of Womack's Top–Down Approach.

tions (as well as the failure of savings and loan institutions), students certainly would be outside the "normal" curriculum. Also, the teacher could lead an Application of Generalizations (Schiever, 1991) strategy so students could extend, modify, or support one of the three "must" generalizations, following the concept of "economy" suggested by Maker. While discussing play-related topics (e.g., role reversals, fate, gender and religious discrimination, obedience to parents, and decision making), students would be examining the concepts contained within all three "must" generalizations, and the teacher would be following Ward's suggestion by encouraging discussion about experiences "designed to promote civic, social, and personal adequacy of the intellectually superior individuals"(p. 11).

An activity focusing on the legal issues contained within the play, such as the "spirit of the law" and the "letter of the law," would broaden the scope of the study. A student might visit a local law firm to investigate changes that have occurred in certain laws and reasons for their change. The student might then develop a historical survey showing trends in legal interpretation and factors affecting such decisions. Such visits could be structured and systematic, meaning the experiences would be weekly, biweekly, or monthly, as well as arranged for a specific legal issue or concept, such as immigration law or bankruptcy. The teacher could develop a procedure for monitoring the visits, and an informal mentorship could be fostered with the hope that a more formal relationship might be arranged in later years, such as occurs with the Junior Achievement Program or The Professional Internship Program. The minimentorship approach would enable the teacher to follow Renzulli's suggestion about "enrichment" and allow the student to pursue a topic to as unlimited a level of inquiry as schedules and school restrictions would allow.

Another gifted student might examine the present level of difficulty faced by one or more minority groups due to prejudice. The student might visit the local Office of Civil Rights to gain greater insight into obstacles or conflicts faced by minorities in achieving goals. The role of family in goal achievement and peer pressure might be examined by interviewing successful local minority leaders. The student might examine patterns of prejudicial behavior toward the minority group over time and make predictions about the future based on past patterns. Also, the student might become involved in a long-term commitment to help with a certain cause; and the civic, social, and personal nature of the activity would follow the suggestion made by Ward in his third proposition.

Discussing Shakespeare's intent in developing the character of Shylock in *Merchant of Venice* is another activity that would broaden the students' understanding of the play. One interpretation might be that Shakespeare's depiction of Shylock and the treatment shown Shylock by the other characters in the play did not reflect his views of the Jewish faith or lifestyle, but was instead simply mirroring the views held by the people of the time. The discussion about the author's intent might encourage a student to examine the discipline of drama and creative writing. With the teacher's assistance, the student might be paired with a local writer or drama critic to understand better the creative writing process of the discipline of critiquing another's work. The student could investigate some of the types of inquiry and related concepts found within the field of creative writing or critical review. The investigations would follow Bruner's idea of the structure of the discipline (Bruner, 1960). Rather than simply writing a critique, the students would observe the process followed by professionals in the field, examining the inquiry itself, as well as the basic ideas of that discipline.

EXAMPLES AT VARIOUS LEVELS AND IN VARIOUS SUBJECT AREAS

The bottom–up approach used with middle school students in a social studies class is illustrated in Figure 9.3. The newspaper often is used by teachers for examining current events, and extension of enrichment based on the activities assigned to the regular students is provided. By including material from the Roman Empire and encouraging the gifted students to discover trends or patterns, a blend of past and present information can be used to make predictions about the future.

A middle school science class following the bottom–up approach is depicted in Figure 9.4. A unit dealing with ecosystems allows for important science content to be examined by both the regular and gifted students, and serves as a foundation for further research or projects. By directing student thought toward implications of the intrusion of an "alien" element into an ecosystem, the teacher can stimulate discussion about future trends in ecological issues.

Procedures to be used with all students in a regular classroom following the top–down approach in an elementary math unit are shown in Figure 9.5. Using the generalizations based on concepts about number systems, ratios, and proportions, the teacher can provide appropriate activities for all students in class. Also included for the gifted students is enrichment dealing with historical development of number systems and creative combinations, as well as uses of number systems in ratios and proportions.

Figure 9.6 contains the procedures for using the top–down approach with elementary students in an art unit. In the unit, the teacher uses concepts such as style preference and factors that influence public opinion or fate's effect on the artist to encourage individual awareness of style preference in art. Historical references to the factors that affected artists throughout time also are included. Activities such as the Hilda Taba Interpretation of Data Strategy seem appropriate based on the cause-and-effect nature of the unit.

ADDITIONAL CONSIDERATIONS

Cultural values and traditions should be considered when selecting content for all students. When gifted students are presented with qualitatively different content whose contextual reference relates to their culture, great benefits might result (Kaplan, 1986). For example, I believe Hispanic students would be most receptive to examination of concepts about family structure and traditional Hispanic values if the work were written by a Hispanic author about Hispanic families. Suggest ways to include culturally appropriate content in curriculum for gifted minority students.

Content Unit: Current Events Using the Newspaper

Content Procedures with Regular Students	Content Procedures with Gifted Students
1. Distinguish between sections in newspaper for separation of international, national, state, and local news.	1. Include gifted students in Activities 1–5 with other students in class.
2. Discuss objectivity and subjectivity as well as denotation and connotation in news reports.	2. Extend discussion of connotation, denotation, objectivity, and subjectivity by including examples of different news versions on historically important stories, such as the Kennedy assassinations, King assassination, recent stock market "scare," or U.S. and Soviet summit meetings.
3. Discuss presentation methods of photographs, headlines, captions, and cartoons or caricatures.	3. Provide reference material about Roman civilization, selecting sources that compress or highlight important leaders, events, and beliefs of the Roman Republic and Empire.
4. Examine the same news story reported by a variety of newspapers, such as two local papers, one larger metropolitan newspaper, and a religiously based newspaper.	4. Complete a Hilda Taba Application of Generalization Strategy with students on information supplied about Roman civilization's leaders, events, or beliefs.
5. Examine various stories on similar subject matter, such as economy, military, governmental, and legal issues.	5. Ask students to note similarities and differences in areas such as economy, military, government, and legal issues, encouraging students to gather information using concepts as the focus, such as interdependence, evolution of governmental styles, conflict and its resolution, and cultural evolution or dissolution.
6. Possible activities:	6. Possible activities:
a. Pair or group students based on interest in subject matter, requiring students to paraphrase and outline a week or more of news dealing with the subject.	a. Ask students to organize some representation of trends apparent in Roman civilization in areas of study, such as economy, military, or government. Encourage work with a variety of presentation styles, such as a visual flowchart and an audiotape explanation.
b. Ask students to write a letter to the editor on a subject from a news story or respond to an earlier letter to the editor, emphasizing facts gained from reading earlier news accounts.	
c. Ask paired or grouped students to "report" a news item from activities occurring in the class or the school, following ideas discussed on objectivity, subjectivity, denotation, and connotation.	

(Continued)

Figure 9.3 Visualization of Bottom–Up Approach with Middle School Students in Social Studies Class.

Content Procedures with Regular Students	Content Procedures with Gifted Students
	6. *(continued)*
	b. Based on trends apparent in Roman civilization, ask students to create a similar visualization for current events from the newspaper.
	c. Based on the consequences of the events in Roman time that caused the trend, ask students to make predictions about the long-range effects of current trends.
	d. Ask students to complete Activity 6b or 6c for regular students, using the information found in past and current trends for subject matter.

Possible "must" generalizations resulting from bottom–up approach in social studies/current events:
1. Governments are created for many purposes. Throughout history, the peoples of the world have experimented with a wide variety of governments.
2. Conflict, violent and nonviolent, has been a major factor throughout human history and in all cultures.
3. All people are interdependent. They must rely on others for essential ingredients, such as physical items, as well as interact with one another in relation to many cognitive and affective issues.

Figure 9.3 *(Continued).*

Content Unit: Ecosystems

Content Procedures with Regular Students	Content Procedures with Gifted Students

1. Discuss concept of ecosystem and different approaches for examination, such as habitat or environmental approach and communities approach.
  a. Discuss terms such as *limiting factor* and *symbiosis* in relation to habitat approach and *autecology* and *synecology* in relation to communities approach.
2. Discuss concepts of interdependence of living and nonliving things within the environment.
3. Examine various environments, such as fresh water, marine, terrestrial, and symbiotic.
4. Discuss the concept of biosphere and different sizes and types of biosphere and ecosystems.
5. Discuss examples of ecosystems and biospheres, such as Disney World in Florida, Environmental Research Lab in Arizona, and Biosphere II in Arizona.
6. Possible activities:
  a. Ask students to create visualizations of ecosystems of one of the four environments (fresh water, marine, terrestrial, or symbiotic), using pictures or drawings of living and nonliving elements.
  b. Ask students to give a "tour" of their ecosystem visualization in a "sales pitch" manner, stressing the specific important living and nonliving elements and the interdependence of the major ingredients of the ecosystem.
  c. Ask students to write an advertisement for the ecosystem, stressing the same ingredients stressed in Activity 6b.
	1. Include gifted students in Activities 1–5 with other students, emphasizing both open and closed ecosystems.
	2. Based on information from Activities 1–5, conduct a Hilda Taba Interpretation of Data Strategy dealing with the causes or effects of the presence or absence of various elements or items in the ecosystem.
	3. Discuss possible implications of introducing a new nonliving or living element into the ecosystem.
	4. Complete a Hilda Taba Application of Generalization Strategy dealing with introduction of a new, foreign element into a closed ecosystem.
	5. Possible activities:
	  a. Ask students to make contact with local experts of ecosystems, encouraging visits to local sites, such as Environmental Research Lab or Biosphere II.
	  b. Ask students to create a diorama illustration of an ecosystem in which more than one environment is visualized, such as marine and fresh-water scene with possible overlap of ecosystems.
	  c. Ask students to create a visualization for school or classroom as an ecosystem, stressing the concept of interdependence.
	    1. Ask students to include a description of effects on the school ecosystem if a new element were added, such as a monetary merit system for good grades or longer school schedule.

Possible "must" generalizations resulting from bottom–up approach in science class:
1. In a closed ecosystem, all living and nonliving things are interdependent with one another and their environment.
2. A living thing is a product of its heredity and environment.

Figure 9.4 Visualization of Bottom–Up Approach with Middle School Students in Science Class.

Content Unit: Number Systems/Ratios/Proportions

Content Procedures with Regular Students	Content Procedures with Gifted Students
1. Ask students to list 10 recent activities and select two in which they saw, heard, listened, touched, or felt many things, such as "I listened to four songs."	1. Include gifted students in Activities 1–5 with other students, emphasizing concepts of number systems and ratios/proportions with gifted students when possible.
2. Show students various ways to represent the numbers of their items, using Roman numerals, Arabic numbers, or fractions, and discuss possible reasons for using different number systems to represent items, such as "I ate one-half of the pizza."	2. Provide students with explanation of the historical significance of number system development and a different culture's reliance on its system instead of another system, such as the Roman's reliance on Roman numerals.
3. Using rulers, ask students to measure two distances and have them report results in both inches and centimeters. Discuss ratio of centimeters to inches.	3. Using the ruler and balance beam, ask students to make predictions of the ratio of length of a line to another object, such as a coin, or the weight of one object to another object's weight. Ask students for explanations and reasons for statements about ratios.
4. Using any other item for measurement, such as pencils or coins, ask students to determine ratios of the new item to the length measured, such as six inches = five quarters.	4. Provide information about additional number systems, such as binary systems, negative numbers, and decimals, and ask students to suggest everyday situations in which it would be useful to use such number systems.
5. Using a balance beam, illustrate ratio concept of weight using wood blocks and steel balls. For example, show that four wood blocks = one steel ball's weight.	5. Possible activities:
6. Possible activities:	a. Ask students to develop a brief story or "tall tale" in which a character encounters a series of times where different number systems are used, and the character is required to explain the number system to other characters in the situation. For example, the little girl from *ET* explains why there are Roman numerals on the afternoon cartoons because they were set in an earlier time.
a. Ask students to write explanations of two or more situations in which they might use two or more number systems in daily experience.	b. Provide students with a number of "mind-bender" activities, such as the problem of filling one size jug from a smaller size jug or predicting the next number in a series of numbers. Ask students to make their own problems based on those given to them.
b. Ask students to create a situation in which they might use the idea of ratio to explain the size or weight of an everyday object, such as "The size of the snake was the same as seven of my shoes."	

"Must" generalizations using the top-down approach:

1. Many specific number systems exist and can be used for everyday mathematical activities.
2. Measurement is the assignment of numbers to represent properties such as length, weight, ratios, and proportions.

Figure 9.5 Visualization of Top–Down Approach with Elementary Students in Math Class.

Content Unit: Influences on Taste in Art and Artists

Content Procedures with Regular Students	*Content Procedures with Gifted Students*
1. Show students a variety of paintings from different time periods and on different subjects.	1. Include gifted students in Activities 1–5 with other students.
2. Ask students to explain their reasons for liking one work and disliking another work.	2. Complete a Hilda Taba Application of Generalization Strategy, using such focusing questions as "What might have caused the artist to paint in this way?" or "What might have caused the artist to change his method of painting in this way?"
3. Briefly explain some geographical, racial, climatic, and historical factors existing when a certain artist painted certain pictures.	3. Provide students with a series of art from a specific time period and ask them what trends, patterns, or changes they notice from early to later in the time period.
4. Using their earlier responses, ask students to group their reasons for likes and dislikes of paintings using the types of factors mentioned by the teacher.	4. Provide students with examples of modern art. Ask students to predict what new patterns, trends, or changes will occur in art in the next 100 years. Ask students to give reasons for the public's preference in support for their statements.
5. Show students paintings by an artist before and after achieving fame and ask what differences are apparent and possible causes for the differences. Ask students what they predict the public must have been like during the artist's rise to fame.	5. Possible activities:
6. Possible activities:	a. Ask students to assume the role of an artist in a new time and place. Ask students to write about or sketch a painting the new artist would create. Also, obtain reasons from the students concerning factors that might cause such a painting.
a. Ask students to write down or sketch a scene they would like to create at the present time. Encourage explanation or depiction of specific details.	b. Assuming the role of the same painter from Activity 5a, ask students to write or sketch another painting after the painter has achieved fame. Obtain reasons from students regarding changes in style or subject, as well as possible other factors affecting the artist.
b. Ask students to write down or sketch the same scene and changes that would result if they had already become famous. Encourage explanation or depiction of specific details.	

"Must" generalizations using the top-down approach:
1. Style preference and the production of art are influenced by geographic, climatic, racial, and historical factors.
2. Fame, combined with changes in public taste, affects all artists.

Figure 9.6 Visualization of Top-Down Approach with Elementary Students in Art Unit.

One way to modify the unit shown in Figure 9.2 would be to assign culturally relevant readings to students from different ethnic groups. For example, instead of using *Merchant of Venice* with all gifted students, black students could discover similar concepts from the play *Raisin in the Sun* by Lorraine Hansberry (1958), and Hispanic students could discover similar concepts from *Bless Me, Ultima* by Rudolpho Anaya (1972).

Administrative considerations also should be mentioned. Communication among the teacher and administrators, parents, and community members is essential to allowing the extension or enrichment that results from providing qualitatively different content. Administrators must work with the teacher to provide flexible scheduling when outside visits are scheduled; parents must work with administrators and the teacher to ensure safe transportation and knowledge of enrichment activities; and community members must be willing to give of their time and expertise to stimulate the bright minds of tomorrow.

REFERENCES

Anaya, R. (1972). *Bless me Ultima.* Santa Fe: Tonatiuh-Quinto Sol International.

Bruner, J. S. (1960). *The process of education.* Cambridge: Harvard University Press.

Gallagher, J. J. (1975). *Teaching the gifted child* (2nd ed.). Boston: Allyn & Bacon.

Gallagher, J. J., Shaffer, F., Phillips, S., Addy, S., Rainer, M., & Nelson, T. (1966). *A system of topic classification.* Urbana: University of Illinois, Institute for Research on Exceptional Children.

Hansberry, L. (1958). *Raisin in the sun.* New York: New American Library.

Kaplan, S. N. (1974). *Providing programs for the gifted and talented: A handbook.* Ventura, CA: Office of the Ventura County Superintendent of Schools.

Kaplan, S. N. (1986). Qualitatively differentiated curricula. In C. J. Maker (Ed.), *Critical issues in gifted education: Defensible programs for the gifted* (pp. 121–134). Austin, TX: PRO-ED.

Lee, H. (1960). *To kill a mockingbird.* Philadelphia: Warner Books.

Maker, C. J. (1982). *Curriculum development for the gifted.* Austin, TX: PRO-ED.

Maker, C. J. (1986). *Frames of discovery: A process approach to identifying talent in special populations.* Unpublished manuscript, Division of Special Education and Rehabilitation University of Arizona, Tucson.

Renzulli, J. S. (1977). *The enrichment triad model: A guide for developing defensible programs for the gifted and talented.* Wethersfield, CT: Creative Learning Press.

Schiever, S. W. (1991). *A comprehensive approach to teaching thinking.* Boston: Allyn and Bacon.

Shakespeare, W. (1957). *Merchant of Venice* (Louis B. Wright & Virginia A. LaMar, Eds.). New York: Washington Square Press. (Original work published 1600)

Shakespeare, W. (1959). *Romeo and Juliet* (Louis B. Wright & Virginia A. LaMar, Eds.). New York: Washington Square Press. (Original work published 1597)

Taba, H. (1966). *Teaching strategies and cognitive functioning in elementary school children* (USOE Cooperative Research Project No. 2404). San Francisco: San Francisco State College.

Terman, L. M. (1925). *Genetic studies of genuis (Vol. 1): Mental and physical traits of a thousand gifted children.* Palo Alto: Stanford University Press.

Treffinger, D. J. (1975). Teaching for self-directed learning: A priority for the gifted and talented. *Gifted Child Quarterly, 19,* 46–59.

VanTassel-Baska, J. (1984). Appropriate curriculum for the gifted. In J. Feldhusen (Ed.), *Toward excellence in gifted education* (pp. 45–83). Denver: Love.

VanTassel-Baska, J. (1986). Effective curriculum and instructional models for talented students. *Gifted Child Quarterly, 30,* 164–169.

Ward, V. S. (1961). *Educating the gifted: An axiomatic approach.* Columbus, OH: Merrill.

Womack, J. G. (1966). *Discovering the structure of social studies.* New York: Benzinger Bros.

Zindel, P. (1970). *The effect of gamma rays on man-in-the-moon marigolds.* New York: Bantam Books.

10

"Becoming Content (kən-těnt´, adj.) with Content (kǒn´-těnt, n.)": A Critical Analysis

Gloria Grotjan

Roger Shanley presents a strong case to support the position that curriculum content should be differentiated for gifted learners within the regular classroom. His position is supported with extensive documentation from well-known experts in the field of education of the gifted, as well as others who have addressed differentiated content.

One of the most interesting aspects of this article is Shanley's bottom–up approach to the selection of subject matter and materials. Based on an inversion of Womack's (1966) method of using generalizations to select and organize the curriculum, Shanley's model begins the determination of content by examining an array of district or program objectives applicable to a particular grade level, then moves up through sequential steps to culminate in generalizations derived from those objectives.

Shanley develops examples using his own bottom–up and Womack's top–down approaches for both selecting and organizing differentiated curriculum for regular and gifted students in the same classroom. His examples span grade levels from elementary through ninth grade. He presents units for art, social studies, math, English, and science. Thus, Shanley has gone to great lengths to demonstrate the feasibility of the procedure across a wide span of subject matter and grade levels. On the whole, each unit appears structurally sound and provides an excellent introduction for those teachers who may be interested in exploring ways to differentiate content to meet the needs of their gifted students.

A major weakness with Shanley's chapter is the lack of references or sources from the regular educator's perspective. Use of this approach is based on a premise stated in the introductory paragraph: "Especially challenging for teachers is the responsibility of providing appropriate content for the gifted student in a regular classroom.'' Is that Shanley's opinion, or does the statement accurately reflect the attitude of regular classroom teachers? My opinion is that an additional clause would improve this opening statement. The modification would read, ''Especially challenging for teachers is the responsibility of providing appropriate content for the gifted student in a regular classroom *without compromising the quality of education provided for the majority of the learners.*''

Although educators of the gifted, steeped in the philosophies of the article's major references, may concur with the original statement, the issue is whether the teacher who will implement these activities agrees with that premise. What evidence, either from research or from practice, suggests that these content differentiations will benefit both regular and gifted students? What data indicate that these modifications can be made economically and efficiently? What leads one to believe that this approach, or combination of approaches, is so compelling as to ensure the broad base of support and cooperation between administrators, teachers, and community called for in the closing paragraph?

This technique has merit. As explained, it appears to be a means for providing appropriate content for the gifted child served in a regular classroom. However, unless the program is delivered by a trained educator of the gifted, the danger is that it would not/could not be put into practice. Three suggestions are offered for Shanley's chapter that would enable teachers to provide qualitatively different experiences for the gifted students while maintaining or improving instruction for regular students in the same classroom:

1. Broaden the empirical base for this model by using references from current mainstream educational literature. Possibly, modify the position statement as described earlier in this critique.
2. Involve regular educators in developing the examples to be used. Field testing would enhance the practicality of the sample units, as would step-by-step instructions for how to implement them.
3. Clarify how different assignments will be made, unless one assumes an automatic separation of gifted students into a group within each classroom. If that is the case, state it.

Professionals in education of the gifted agree that curriculum for gifted students should differ from the standard curriculum. (Rather, there is agreement to the extent that any group of professionals reaches consensus!) As we examine the issue of providing appropriate experiences for gifted learners, the task is not to convince the specialist, but the mainstream educator. The inclusion of current literature germane to professional general educators would lend credence to Shanley's proposal. If the crucial audience is curriculum committees and classroom teachers from the mainstream, a tactical advantage accrues when one uses references familiar to that audience. I believe the reader would relax and be more receptive if that bibliography included the likes of Goodlad and Holt, and Carnegie and Holmes interspersed with Gallagher, Maker, Renzulli, Terman, and Kaplan.

To present both sides of an issue is a basic tenet when proposing change. Besides the matters of fairness and audience ease, another advantage exists when using references from the main body of educational knowledge/philosophy. The task of convincing the audience becomes infinitely easier if a review of that literature produces support for the author's contention that sophistication is a key factor in affecting process, product, and learning environment, and if support is demonstrated for any of the specifics presented in the approaches. On the other hand, if that review unearths arguments against any aspect of the author's plan, it would seem prudent to deal with those issues by revising the model or, at the very least, offering a rebuttal in the initial presentation.

Suggestion 2, involving the general educators in the development of any model that teaches to both normal and gifted children, seems so basic as to require no further justification. If Suggestion 2 is followed, the resulting teacher input should also assist in Suggestion 3, defining the means for selecting the different groups. As it stands, this is a gray area, which weakens the model considerably.

The first example, a bottom–up approach to teaching *Romeo and Juliet,* leaves me uncertain as to how the teacher gets the two groups for different treatments. Is this an arbitrary assignment wherein Red Birds have the "regular content" and Blue Birds have the "gifted content"? Is the separation on the basis of some relevant pretest? Do the students self-select?

Even more problems can be identified with the second example, a top–down approach applied to a ninth-grade English class. Content decisions seem to be made solely according to Womack's model. That model, drawn from a social studies background, may not be directly applicable to English curriculum decisions. Certainly, choosing two such disparate pieces of literature purely on the basis of sociological generalizations (presented in Figure 9.2) may raise some questions with English curriculum committees. I do not think that mainstream English teachers were consulted.

If, somehow, a teacher got beyond that criticism, would the students be assigned to different plays only on the basis of their intellectual abilities? Although the author says the plays are to be chosen to match the interests and abilities of each group, the examples seem to preclude individual student interest as a criterion for selection.

The examples for science, art, social studies, and math are similar to one another in that the differentiation proceeds after a set of common experiences for both groups. Again, the author does not address how the teacher decides who shall participate in enrichment activities designed for regular students and those designed for gifted students.

Finally, I have a fourth suggestion for Shanley: Delete the last section of the chapter, "Additional Considerations." The paragraphs that illustrate further curriculum differentiation on the basis of cultural values and traditions appear to imply that ninth-grade Hispanic and black students would not be introduced to *The Merchant of Venice* and that white students would not study *Raisin in the Sun* or *Bless Me, Ultima.* In my opinion, such a suggestion raises far more questions than it answers for the issue at stake.

The final paragraph, in which the author makes sweeping requirements for teachers, administrators, and community, should be postponed until that constituency has been involved in the model. At that time, natural revisions are likely to be apparent.

For whatever reasons gifted children were "pulled out" of classrooms in the past, and whatever has been learned about gifted learners in those segregated settings, the success of an inclusionary program depends on the ability and willingness of those who will implement it. To propose a model for educating gifted students in a regular classroom with apparent disregard for the regular classroom teacher and the concerns of regular education's constituency is naive.

REFERENCE

Womack, J. G. (1966). *Discovering the structure of social studies.* New York: Benzinger Bros.

11

Process Differentiation for Gifted Learners in the Regular Classroom: Teaching to Everyone's Needs

Hilda Rosselli

The challenge of differentiating education for gifted learners within the regular classroom is addressed most easily by careful differentiation of the *way* students are taught. Process differentiation is not dependent on any costly equipment, administrative changes, additional allocations for personnel, or school board decisions. However, like other elements of differentiated education for gifted students (content, product, and environment), process differentiation *does* require teacher commitment. It also demands an acceptance of the belief that individuals learn in different ways and that certain characteristics of gifted students should influence how these students are taught.

Many regular classroom teachers may already use successfully the processes described in this chapter, but they may not understand why some students respond differently to certain approaches over others. Although the belief is inappropriate that only the gifted learners are benefiting from differentiated instruction, research on the psychology of gifted individuals helps us to see that students with above-average abilities have specific learning styles, preferences, and tendencies.

In this chapter, I review the elements of process differentiation that have influenced the education of gifted students and the appropriateness of their use in the regular classroom. I provide specific examples of strategies that teachers can incorporate into the daily classroom routine to help them differentiate the processes of teaching.

In 1979, when the Curriculum Council of the National/State Leadership Training Institute met to develop a set of principles that would differentiate curriculum experiences for gifted students, principles were defined that have guided the development of numerous subsequent gifted programs. These principles included the following:

- More elaborate, complex, and in-depth study of major ideas, problems, and themes that integrate knowledge with and across systems of thought
- Development and application of productive thinking skills to enable students to reconceptualize existing knowledge and/or generate new knowledge
- Exploration of constantly changing knowledge and information, and development of an attitude that knowledge is worth pursuing in an open world
- Promotion of self-initiated and self-directed learning and growth
- Development of self-understandings and the understanding of one's relationship to persons, societal institutions, nature, and culture

Kaplan (1979) further refined these processes to fall into three categories: basic skills, research skills, and thinking skills. *Basic skills* for gifted learners should be included if they have not already been mastered or if they need to be reinforced or extended. *Research skills* help the gifted learner to acquire, analyze, and share information that may not be included in the regular curriculum, but which is of interest or importance to him or her. The development of *advanced thinking skills* enables gifted learners to approach the curriculum content in ways compatible with their unique characteristics.

VanTassel-Baska (1985) described the development of process skills in students as "basics for the gifted," which would be incorporated into the students' study of all content areas, not developed separately as isolated skills. These "basics" include opportunities to practice critical thinking, creative thinking, problem solving, research, and decision making.

Maker (1982b) suggested that processes used in programs for gifted students should include the following:

1. Emphasis on higher levels of thinking
2. Open-endedness, both in the design of the activities and in the attitudes of the teacher implementing them
3. Development of inductive reasoning processes through discovery whenever possible
4. Requirements for students to explain their reasoning as well as provide conclusions
5. Permission for students to choose topics to study and methods to use to the extent that students develop self-directedness in their learning
6. Encouragement and permission to interact in group situations
7. A rapid pace commensurate with students' learning rates to avoid boredom

The Enrichment Triad Model (Renzulli, 1977) categorizes the training of thinking and development of research skills under Type II activities, which follow exploratory types of learning experiences (Type I) and precede in-depth student investigations. To give teachers of gifted students more guidance in determining which skills falling into Type II activities they should teach and when they should teach them, Renzulli and Reis (1985) developed a Taxonomy of Type II Enrichment Processes. Categories include cognitive and affective training; learning how to learn; using advanced research and reference materials; and developing written, oral, and visual communication techniques. The use of such a taxonomy was intended to help teachers conduct needs assessments, make decisions regarding program objectives, select appropriate curriculum materials, and establish a base from which to design evaluation instruments.

The relationship between content and process has been a topic of frequent discussion by educators. Renzulli (1977) described process as a means and not an end of instruction. Thus, the bond between high-level thinking and high-level content needs to be evident. Maker (1982a) wrote that teachers of the gifted must not ignore the big ideas in the academic disciplines or the concepts needed for further learning in pursuit of a "how to think" curricular approach. The teaching of thinking processes especially appropriate for gifted learners is open for serious criticism unless the strategies are combined with meaningful content.

In the regular classroom, the role of the teacher seeking to meet the needs of gifted learners should be similar to that of matchmaker. The teacher seeks to find ways to develop appropriate processes and use the content prescribed in tangential curriculum. The provision of enrichment activities that expand on regular curricular content for the gifted student in the regular classroom could thwart one of the frequent criticisms of the pull-out program model: Seldom does a close relationship exist between what is taught and experienced in the program for gifted students and the remainder of the students' academic program (Cox, Daniel, & Boston, 1985).

Although the ideal and most appropriate learning environment for gifted students should include daily contact with peers of similar ability levels (at least for a portion of the day), the facts cannot be ignored. Most gifted students still spend a portion of each day in the regular classroom. This situation is even more prevalent in school locales where the issue of ability grouping has threatened the use of homogeneous grouping of students, except for the occasional special class or advanced placement class. Likewise, recent concerns over the identification and placement of underrepresented students in programs for the gifted due to impartial assessment measures, an oversight of qualified dually exceptional students, and limited conceptions of giftedness have fueled the need for all teachers to take responsibility for challenging bright learners within the regular classroom. In the remainder of this chapter I offer the reader practical suggestions for the application of process differentiation within the regular classroom by defining 10 specific process modifications and, in many cases, sharing an example appropriate to the regular classroom.

HIGHER LEVEL THINKING SKILLS

One of the most frequently discussed elements of process differentiation for gifted learners is the use of questions and activities designed to develop higher level thinking skills. Our knowledge of the learning characteristics of gifted learners includes the fact that many of these students demonstrate advanced reasoning abilities, ask intelligent questions, and have a desire for knowledge (Terman, 1925; Witty, 1958). Newland (1976) found recurring behaviors that included early discovery of cause-and-effect relationships, a keen sense of observation, and high levels of concentration. When designing lessons that define various levels of thinking, the use of taxonomies can help ensure that students are given the chance to answer questions that require advanced reasoning skills and divergent responses.

Most teachers are familiar with the cognitive domain of Bloom's (1956) Taxonomy of Educational Objectives, which provides a hierarchical order that can be used to evaluate educational objectives and learning activities. When this taxonomy is used for lesson planning in a heterogeneous grouping, a stronger emphasis on questions and activities based on analysis, synthesis, and evaluation needs to be made for gifted learners. Many textbook materials now include labels for questions and exercises according to this popular taxonomy. Use of Bloom's Taxonomy can help the teacher in the regular classroom select activities or questions that are varied in both complexity and use of thinking skills.

The following example is taken from a fourth-grade lesson in which the focus is the role of inventions in today's society. The variety of questions produced using Bloom's Taxonomy illustrates the extensions that can be made with a single topic:

1. What are some inventions that are an accepted part of today's society? (Knowledge)
2. How would you know something is an invention? (Comprehension)
3. Give an example of one invention that led to another invention. (Application)
4. What stages does an invention go through before becoming a part of our daily lives? (Analysis)
5. Develop a sketch or a plan for an invention you believe would be important in your life. (Synthesis)
6. What inventions would you select to put in an Inventor's Hall of Fame? (Evaluation)

When teachers ask a variety of questions, they may save time by offering students a choice by presenting all the questions on an overhead transparency, providing a few moments of thought and reflection, and then giving students an opportunity to respond to those questions that are of most interest to them. The same is true when offering classroom activities based on various levels of this taxonomy or other similar models. In fact, teachers should take serious note of the activities suggested by individual students, as these suggestions often could be added as possible activity choices available to all students and particularly suitable for gifted students. Teachers interested in ensuring similar variety in the area of affective skills are encouraged to use Krathwohl's Affective Taxonomy (Krathwohl, Bloom, & Masia, 1964) or Kohlberg's (1966) Levels of Moral Reasoning.

Research by Guilford (1956) provided the impetus for the development of the Structure of Intellect (SOI), which described a multidimensional model of intelligence that included 120 separate thinking processes. Meeker (1969) later developed tests, workbooks, and activities that a teacher can use to profile a student's strengths and weaknesses and then select appropriate learning materials that correspond to the student's needs. Within the regular classroom, these curriculum materials can serve as valuable skill builders for all students and still provide some of the challenge needed by gifted students to practice higher, more sophisticated levels of thinking. Research conducted by Meeker (1985b) indicated that students can increase their academic achievements as measured by standardized achievement tests, whereas studies by Torrance (1977) indicated that remediation areas also can be strengthened by working through areas of strength.

The philosophy behind the SOI test and materials is important to consider in classrooms with heterogeneous groups of students. The notion that intelligence does not consist of a single dimension has received renewed support from educators who discuss "multiple intelligences" (Gardner, 1983). Regardless of the identification policies existing in a given school district, the use of classroom activities and questions designed to stimulate different intelligences or skills can provide both gifted students and regular students with a greater chance for success.

For example, based on the operational levels of Guilford's (1956) model, the following questions could be asked after presenting a grid showing the impact of various forms of transportation on different aspects of our lives, such as family life and natural resources:

Transportation Mode	Natural Resources	Family Life	Work Life	Communities
Ships				
Planes				
Cars				
Trains				

1. Which form of transportation caused the greatest change in our natural resources? (Cognitive/memory)
2. Using the results of this grid, what questions should scientists ask before fully developing interplanetary travel? (Convergent)
3. In what ways could the negative impacts of transportation modes be diminished in the future? (Divergent)
4. What are the most serious problems that face us as technology continues to result in new ways to live our lives? (Evaluation)

Large cards posted on the back of the classroom wall on which each level of a taxonomy, Guilford's or Bloom's, is listed provides support for spontaneous questions and activities that are varied, and encourages higher levels of thinking. An important point to remember when using any type of taxonomy is that, although the higher levels are considered more appropriate for use with gifted learners, these students need to practice all levels of thinking. Understanding the cyclical nature of the taxonomy, as discussed by Clark (1985), can help students begin to see connections and relationships in the world around them. For instance, in the previous example, the discussion might end in some observations about psychological variables (e.g., autonomy or habit-bound behaviors) that could be entered into the grid; thus, the analysis of the impact of transportation may be revisited. Another cycle can be seen when students learn new facts to add to existing knowledge. Visual charts that show the properties of a certain chemical can be revisited every time new information is added to the student's knowledge base. In social studies, a main idea may be introduced, such as the following: The interaction between the people and their environment influences the way in which they meet their needs. During the course of several years, that main idea may be revisited as students study American Indians, the Middle East, the local community, and particular regions of the United States.

EVIDENCE OF REASONING

The need for learning about evidence of reasoning and training in thinking processes can be met in the regular classroom by asking questions that require students to explain how they arrived at a solution. Math and science teachers have been doing this for years when they give students extra credit for showing their work. Credit and reinforcements are deserved for the logical and creative approach that the student takes to arrive at the answer, not only for the correct answer. The more opportunities all students are given to observe how others have arrived at solutions, the more comfortable the students can become with analyzing their own thinking patterns. Students who tend to be intuitive in their responses differ from those who are driven by logic. Fact gatherers are different from consensus seekers. Both students and teachers can share on the bulletin board examples of different ways of reaching conclusions, using excerpts from biographies and news items.

Maker (1981), however, cautioned that teachers should avoid the constant use of "why" when asking about thinking process. The tone of voice and the manner of the questions are important, as are the words in the question. Many teachers and parents ask "why" when they want to point out faulty reasoning or when they disagree with the students' responses.

OPEN-ENDED QUESTIONS

The strategies developed by Taba, Durkin, Fraenkel, and McNaughton (1971) provide specific processes teachers can employ. Through the use of structured, open-ended, but focused questions, students are led through a series of sequential intellectual tasks. The philosophy underlying Taba's work—that all students can develop abstract reasoning skills—provides support for use of process strategies in the regular classroom. Students who have leadership abilities may be interested in serving as facilitators in discussions after they become familiar with the four strategies: concept development, interpretation of data, application of generalizations, and resolution of conflict.

The use of open-ended questions and activities is another example of how process differentiation for gifted learners could take place in the regular classroom. Taba and colleagues (1971) give excellent guidelines in this area. Their discussion includes examples of questions that are too open, such as, ''What will we talk about today, students?'' as well as closed questions that do not allow many students to enter a discussion, such as, ''What was the carpenter using to pound the nail into the boards?'' A happy medium can be struck with open-ended questions, such as, ''What did you notice about the new home we saw being built yesterday?'' Open-ended questions are not only less threatening to students because of multiple possible answers, but they also invite students to enter a discussion with pieces of information that are associated with the discussion topic. The teacher may not even know what student experiences or previous knowledge can be brought to the discussion, but questions can serve as invitational vehicles.

Kerry (1980) offered a hierarchy of question types for use in the regular classroom. I have illustrated the use of this hierarchy in Figure 11.1, using a class discussion on George Washington Carver. One more type of question could be added to this list. When students are asked to generate additional questions, they enter a state of perplexity that creates a phenomenon of imbalance in students rather than a false sense of closure on the topic. Therefore, the teacher might appropriately close the discussion with, ''If George Washington Carver was able to visit our class, what questions would you ask him?''

What keeps teachers from using open-ended questions in their classes? One factor is limited time constraints. If teachers have not planned for a lengthy discussion, they often fear that something else will be slighted that day. However, strict adherence to a lesson plan results in ignoring many ''teachable moments'' and diminishes the importance of student-initiated learning and motivation. A compromise might include building discussion time into the schedule to be used as needed during the week. In addition, when students are really motivated about a topic, required material can be covered in a shorter amount of time or as a way to provide more time for discussions.

Another negative response to the use of open-ended questions is the fear of moving into an area of discussion in which the teacher does not have a strong information base. When a teacher is willing to admit that learning is a lifetime process that can be enjoyed cooperatively, a positive role model has been presented. Modeling an open attitude can eliminate embarrassing moments when a gifted learner knows more than the teacher does about a particular subject. In conclusion, the teacher's attitude plays a strong role in the appropriate use of questions.

PACING

Ward (1961) and Keating (1976) reminded us that gifted students learn at a rate different from that of other groups of students. Studies on the effects of acceleration have shown that many gifted learners have lasting positive gains from being allowed to learn at a quicker pace than average learners (Kulick & Kulick, 1984). How many

Question Analysis Chart

Question Type	Explanation
1. Data-recall questions	Requires remembering
What was the name given to George Washington Carver's laboratory?	
2. Naming questions	Lacks insight
Name 10 peanut products developed by George Washington Carver.	
3. Observation questions	Requires minimal understanding
What obstacles did George Washington Carver overcome as a black scientist?	
4. Control questions	Modifies behavior
How will you remember George Washington Carver's scientific contribution to the farming community?	
5. Psuedo-questions	Conveys expected answer
Were George Washington Carver's accomplishments inspirational to black people?	
6. Hypothesis-generating questions	Involves speculation
Would George Washington Carver have been famous if he was white?	
7. Reasoning questions	Requires rationale
Why did George Washington Carver want to preserve the small family farm?	
8. Personal response questions	Invites personal opinions
What, in your opinion, was George Washington Carver's greatest accomplishment?	
9. Discriminatory questions	Requires weighing of pros and cons
Which of George Washington Carver's discoveries was the most significant, those evolving from the sweet potato or the peanut?	
10. Problem-solving questions	Demands finding ways to answer questions
If you were to design a memorial for George Washington Carver, what sources would you study for inspiration?	

Figure 11.1 Question Analysis Chart.

adults can remember a childhood experience of holding their fingers at the place in the reader where the rest of the class was still reading? However, when acceleration methods are used as the only solutions for accommodating these differences, important elements of the learning process may be overlooked or slighted. Many gifted children demonstrate a need to slow down the pace in order to spend more time investigating a topic or developing a product. Their use of intense levels of concentration can enrich our world with technological advancements and creative masterpieces. Appropriate pacing is a crucial element in the heterogeneous classroom, which can be used not only for slower learning students but also to develop independent learning habits in all students.

Pacing also involves the use of appropriate "wait time" during class discussions. We do not all have a wonderful idea at the same time. A number of classes for gifted students use a technique called boundary breaking. This technique allows students to respond to a question that does not have a right or wrong answer. Students also are allowed to "pass" if they need more time to respond to the question. Technically, a child who wishes to give an answer later in the week also should be given the chance to share his or her opinions in an environment in which incubation and reflection time are respected.

Some teachers elect to put thought-provoking questions on the chalkboard, such as, "If you could make only one suggestion to our city council, what would it be?" Students are given the remainder of the week to think about the question. If they share the question with others outside the classroom, they may bring additional thoughts and opinions to the discussion when it commences later in the week.

The use of appropriate pacing requires the teacher to demonstrate flexibility when implementing plans and schedules. Letting a gifted learner proceed to the next chapter may be the only way to maintain a student's interest when the rest of the class is moving at a slower pace. The same flexibility is needed to allow a student who expresses real interest in learning more about the topic to make a detour and work independently or with a small group of peers. The student can catch up with the rest of the class later. This policy can, of course, be taken to the extreme. One student recalls taking a whole geometry course independently in the back of the algebra class. Although the student appreciated the challenge of learning new material, she had to rely on self-correcting programmed workbook materials in lieu of teacher–student interaction.

To implement the wide variety of strategies recommended for differentiating process within the regular classroom, the teacher may need to "compact" or "streamline" the curriculum. Not only does compacting provide additional time for the pursuit of topics of interest or detailed investigations, but it also can help teachers to eliminate the type of boredom caused by assignments that are too easy or too routine. Gifted learners seem to have an uncanny ability to discern "busywork" from relevant work and may react to the former by engaging the teacher in power struggles, producing shoddy work, or demonstrating inappropriate classroom behaviors.

Renzulli, Smith, and Reis (1982) recommended that teachers become familiar with the planned content and intended objectives of the instruction and use careful diagnosis to determine which students have mastered successfully the specific competencies necessary to meet the instructional objectives. Curriculum compacting helps teachers examine curriculum areas to be considered for compacting, procedures for compacting basic material, and opportunities for acceleration and/or enrichment activities. Although frequent use of this technique may require additional time on the part of the teacher, the definitive assessment data collected are useful for cluster grouping within the classroom. For example, a teacher planning to instruct the class on the steps involved in the scientific method may develop a sequencing task in which students arrange each step in an order reflective of the scientific method, labeling each step. Those who complete this activity successfully will be allowed to design and implement an experiment to test the properties of talcum powder using the scientific method.

SELF-DIRECTED LEARNING OPPORTUNITIES

When appropriate acceleration and enrichment activities are provided following compacting, students' needs and interests should be taken into consideration.

An assignment that is seen as boring by the students involved also may be perceived as an attempt to isolate them from the rest of the group or as simply more busy-work. Gifted learners can be encouraged to develop their own decision-making skills when choices are offered for acceleration and enrichment activities. The students' suggestions for additional choices can and should be included as alternatives to the teacher's selections.

The use of contracts may be helpful in enhancing communication between the teacher and the students involved when an elaborate project is being planned. Teachers who have become accustomed to control may find that the contract can serve as a transitional stage between teacher direction and freedom of choice for students. A simple example of such a contract is provided in Figure 11.2.

When an opportunity exists for gifted learners to share the results of their projects with the rest of the class, the entire class benefits. However, sharing can be accomplished without always having to designate class time for reports. Students sometimes enjoy investigating a topic of interest without having to develop a complex written product. Sharing can be accomplished through informal question-and-answer sessions, slide presentations, or bulletin board displays. Even a note on the board proclaiming Johnny as the "classroom expert" on the subject of butterflies can initiate desirable interactions between students.

Not only do students practice decision making when they select a topic for independent study, but they also develop working styles during the project's duration. When a student identifies appropriate resource people to assist her in her project, she has practiced networking skills. Likewise, when a student's work is turned down for publication in a professional journal, the experience serves as a valuable lesson on rejection. Therefore, the evaluation process should include working styles in addition to the normal grading criteria. Knowing that these elements are considered dur-

Project Contract

Name _____

Date _____

1. Briefly describe the project you are planning.
2. What do you already know about your project topic?
3. What do you want to learn from this project?
   What questions on the topic do you intend to answer with this project?
4. What materials or resources do you intend to use?
5. In what ways can I provide assistance to you on this project?
6. What are some obstacles that you may encounter with this project?
7. What people or outside resources do you intend to use?
8. How do you plan to share the results of your project with an appropriate audience?
9. List the stages involved in this project along with estimated dates of completion.
10. What questions do you still have regarding the project?

Figure 11.2 Example of Project Contract.

ing the evaluation process reduces the stress that many gifted, perfectionistic students experience, and can help to keep parents from completing projects for their children.

Particularly as the national trend toward accountability increases, educators have a new incentive to explore alternative methods of authentic assessment (Perrone, 1991) that can include a focus on working styles, portfolios, and performances, in addition to more traditional methods of evaluation. Teachers can observe the behaviors of students as they are engaged in tasks and structure portfolios that relate to working styles, creative productivity, and skill development.

INDIVIDUAL SKILLS DEVELOPMENT

Daily opportunities exist during which teachers can develop problem-solving skills and leadership ability. When responsibility for decisions regarding classroom routines and procedures are shared, gifted learners begin to develop self-understanding and interpersonal skills, such as negotiating, resolving conflict, and using nonverbal communication. Many teachers have special responsibilities that they delegate to students on a rotating basis to help highlight their individual skills: organizing materials, planning a fieldtrip, writing thank you letters to guest speakers, monitoring daily events to post on the bulletin board, or gathering resources for learning experiences.

Kaplan (1979) proposed that research skills include activities and abilities needed for acquiring, interpreting, and reporting both old and new information. Maker (1982a) suggested that the types of research practiced by professionals in a field can be modified for use with even very young students. For example, when students in a kindergarten class are asked to decide if ants will go toward a pile of sugar or a pile of salt, they are practicing some of the basic elements of hypothesis formation and testing. The use of a tape recorder can allow second graders to gather and record daily observations of the class pet's behavior and, thus, engage in descriptive research. Correlational research can begin at a level that involves only the number of teeth missing and ages of students. The teaching of research provides an introduction for students, and specifically gifted students, to the ongoing world of questions and the methods we use to seek answers.

Research skills can be used as supplements to the required curriculum or in lieu of required assignments, but such activities need not be extremely time-consuming for the teacher. A number of quality curriculum materials exist that can be used as a guide for students to follow in their research projects. A learning center that is designed to encourage students to probe unanswered questions raised during discussions of the regular curriculum content can provide timely and important research opportunities.

Research reveals that development of personal skills can help individuals become self-actualized and better able to appreciate similarities and differences between people (Sisk & Shallcross, 1985). Use of a journal can help personalize and individualize development of these skills because writing in a journal is a private conversation between the student and the teacher, and it provides a setting in which communication and feedback are nonthreatening. Use of journals can help gifted learners establish personal goals and receive feedback on their progress. For example, topics could include (a) constructing a dialogue with a friend or relative set in the 21st century, (b) writing from the point of view of someone not in the United States, and (c) describing a self-portrait set in the future.

Teachers also can find teachable moments involving personal skills development within the curriculum content. Bibliotherapy, for example, is one technique in which literature is used to help students develop self-understanding, as well as decision-making and problem-solving skills. The use of books to practice problem-solving skills builds on gifted learners' attraction to books and their ability to imagine that they are the characters experiencing the problem. Students can experience vicariously the possible solutions to problems without suffering consequences (Sisk, 1987). The teacher's role is to organize structured time for students to discuss various aspects of the story using questions that promote a variety of thinking skills. In some situations, community volunteers, the school librarian, or older students may wish to facilitate discussion groups involving students who have read the same book.

INQUIRY LEARNING

One characteristic of bibliotherapy lessons is that students are permitted to reach their own conclusions. Students gain unique insights by encountering the character's problem. The insights occur when students view the facts and make their own generalizations that can be tested in other hypothetical or real situations. Use of this approach encourages students to take a more active and autonomous role in the learning process and is a method that can be used in other instructional situations. Inquiry learning, as it is called, builds on several characteristics of gifted students, such as their independence in thought and action, their boredom with routine, their desire for order, and their competitiveness. When the teacher is not the dispenser of all information and the students are allowed to use their skills of observation to discover facts and generalizations, learning becomes similar to a game in which gifted learners can take control of their own destiny. On a simple level, this process can be observed in young children who are attracted to number sequence games and work searches. The answers are already present. One needs only to find a pattern, and discover a generalization that can be tested easily.

The teacher's role changes from data giver to data validator in an inquiry learning situation. For instance, in some cases, the teacher may respond only by answering "yes" or "no" to the students' questions as they work to discover the patterns or generalization (Suchman, 1966). This inquiry method is particularly meaningful in science, an area in which careful observation combined with questioning skills can lead students to make their own discoveries.

Just as an inquiry or discovery may excite some learners, it can be frustrating and unfamiliar to students who are accustomed to being "spoon-fed" facts and data for later "regurgitation." These students will need gradual exposure to "real thinking." They will need multiple examples of problems based on everyday life that will give them the opportunity to practice these skills. Typically, educators have placed this strategy in a category for gifted learners or purchased a packaged curriculum in which inquiry skills are taught in isolated units and workbook pages. Yet, as our society increases in complexity, the need to train students in the logic of questioning becomes more urgent.

FREEDOM OF CHOICE

Another process differentiation recommended for gifted students is freedom of choice. Teachers can provide freedom of choice through independent projects, cooperative learning activities, or learning centers. Many learning center materials can now be purchased that offer a variety of activities based on particular taxonomies and learning models.

Using a model such as Taylor's (1968) Multiple Talent Approach can encourage students to select activities from a variety of skill areas that include communication, decision making, forecasting, planning, implementing, discerning opportunities, academic, human relations, and productive thinking. The nine talents that Taylor described in his model are based on the world of work. One would not assume that a student would excel in all of these areas. However, Taylor believed that a large percentage of students would be considered talented if educators included his talent areas in the curriculum. He also believed that self-concept would highly correlate to the successes that students experienced as they used those talents in which they exhibited natural ability. Combined with freedom of choice for the students, Taylor's model is appropriate for use in meeting the needs of gifted learners in the regular classroom.

Although many gifted learners view freedom of choice as a license for unleashing their own creativity, not all students respond in the same manner. At first, the simplest choices may provoke frustration and discomfort. The teacher can assist by gradually introducing limited choices (e.g., poem or picture, activity 1 or 2, etc.), later opening up more opportunities for students comfortable with their own decision-making skills.

DEVELOPMENT OF CREATIVITY

The types of activities that emerge naturally from the use of a model such as Taylor's are also appropriate vehicles for developing creativity. Both Bloom's (1956) Taxonomy and Guilford's (1956) model also include elements that encourage the use of creativity through synthesis and divergent thinking. Models such as Feldhusen and Kolloff's (1978) Three Stage Model for Enrichment, Renzulli's (1977) Enrichment Triad Model, and Treffinger's (1980) Creative Learning Model all provide useful structure for introducing basic skills and strategies of creative thinking.

Feldhusen and Treffinger (1985) provided educators with a useful guide to both models and resources applicable to teaching creativity and problem solving. They review such models as that developed by Parnes (1967, cited in Feldhusen & Treffinger, 1985), which engages the individual in a six-stage creative problem-solving model. These steps include mess finding, data finding, problem finding, idea finding, solution finding, and acceptance finding.

Many teachers also find Williams's (1970) Teaching Strategies for Thinking and Feeling helpful in designing activities and questions that encourage the following characteristics of creative thinking:

Cognitive	Affective
Fluency of ideas	Curiosity
Flexibility of thinking	Risk taking
Elaboration	Complexity
Originality	Imagination

The following are questions based on this model that might be used in the context of a middle grade–level social studies unit on women leaders:

1. *Fluency*—Make a list of all the female political leaders you can recall.
2. *Flexibility*—What positions are held by the leaders you identified? What positions are not represented on your list? Why might that gap exist?
3. *Elaboration*—Select one female political leader from the past and share one of her accomplishments in detail with the class.
4. *Originality*—Describe what the first female president of the United States will be like.
5. *Curiosity*—Take five major political decisions made by male leaders and decide how you think female leaders would have reacted.
6. *Risk taking*—Develop a slogan for the first female president of the United States and share it with the class.
7. *Complexity*—Study the platform issues for an upcoming election and predict what differences of opinion there would be if one of your female teachers were to run for the office. Argue whether you think these differences are related to gender.
8. *Imagination*—Draw a series of political cartoons capturing the American reaction to a female president.

OPPORTUNITIES FOR GROUP INTERACTION

Many gifted students demonstrate natural leadership skills within the classroom and seek opportunities for interaction with other students during classroom experiences. Others need the structure of activities that will require them to interact within a group. A number of strategies typically suggested for use in programs for gifted students are appropriate for use in the regular classroom. The teacher may find that many average students also will enjoy the opportunity for interaction. The students' work together may exceed their individual performances on solitary activities.

The use of role-playing can be incorporated into discussions very simply by defining roles for students that may represent differing points of view. The role of an observer also is important and can help students analyze human interactions as they occur. A discussion about the various roles that people typically play in group settings may be helpful to older students. A good college textbook on group dynamics can provide the basic content for the discussion.

When role-playing is combined with group tasks that involve decision-making situations based on real-life issues, and that use rules and objectives, the activity is known as a simulation game. The use of simulation games in the regular classroom can offer students with leadership abilities needed opportunities to develop skills such as conflict resolution and consensus forming. Simulated group activities can also develop students' communication skills and provide a change in the learning process.

In designing a simulation game, Reid (1961) suggested that the following be established:

- Name of the game
- Statement of the problem
- Objectives of the game
- Characteristics and their goals
- A point in time
- Resources
- Rules and their administration
- Evaluation and feedback

CONCLUSION

Although the ideas suggested in this chapter represent many techniques and strategies traditionally recommended for use with gifted students, I believe that many other students may benefit from classes that offer the unique approaches and variety often found in programs for gifted students.

When a teacher makes the personal commitment to meet the needs of gifted learners in the regular classroom, some exciting changes can occur. Students previously perceived as average or below-average learners can begin to identify with a different group of role models. Frequently, teachers report being surprised by the talents and skills that begin to emerge in these students when a different approach is tried in the classroom. A process-differentiated approach also helps create a living tapestry of students working productively on different projects and on different levels, which approximates the environment found in the adult world.

Fortunately, more and more educators are becoming less and less concerned with the selection and exclusion of students for various programs or activities and more concerned with meeting students' needs (Treffinger, 1982). The gifted student can and will prosper in the regular classroom when the teacher modifies the instructional strategies to accommodate differences in learning styles, rates, and preferences. Then, within the context of each gifted student's day, the regular classroom becomes an important place where unique talents and contributions are valued and encouraged.

154   CURRICULUM DIFFERENTIATION

REFERENCES

Bloom, B. S. (Ed.). (1956). *Taxonomy of educational objectives. Cognitive domain.* New York: David McKay.

Clark, B. (1985). *Growing up gifted.* Columbus, OH: Merrill.

Cox, J., Daniel, N., & Boston, B. (1985). *Educating able learners: Programs and promising practices.* Austin: University of Texas Press.

Feldhusen, J. F., & Kolloff, M. B. (1978). A three stage model for gifted education. *G/C/T, 1,* 3–5, 53–58.

Feldhusen, J. F., & Treffinger, D. J. (1985). *Creative thinking and problem solving in gifted education.* Dubuque, IA: Kendall/Hunt.

Gardner, H. (1983). *Frames of mind.* New York: Basic Books.

Guilford, J. P. (1956). The structure of the intellect. *Psychological Bulletin, 53,* 267–293.

Kaplan, S. N. (1979). *Inservice training manual: Activities for developing curriculum for the gifted and talented.* Ventura, CA: Office of Ventura County Superintendent of Schools.

Keating, D. (1976). *Intellectual talent: Research and development.* Baltimore: Johns Hopkins University Press.

Kerry, T. (1980). Teaching strategies for bright pupils. In D. Jackson (Ed.), *Curriculum development for the gifted* (pp. 160–169). Guilford, CT: Special Learning Corporation.

Kohlberg, L. (1966). Moral education in the schools: A developmental view. *The School Review, 74,* 1–29.

Krathwohl, D. R., Bloom, B. S., & Masia, B. B. (1964). *Taxonomy of educational objectives: Affective domain.* New York: David McKay.

Kulick, J. A., & Kulick, C. C. (1984). Effects of accelerated instruction of students. *Review of Educational Research, 54,* 409–425.

Maker, C. J. (1981). Curriculum development for the gifted: Basic principles. *New Horizons in Education, 64,* 18–24.

Maker, C. J. (1982a). *Curriculum development for the gifted.* Austin, TX: PRO-ED.

Maker, C. J. (1982b). *Teaching models in education of the gifted.* Austin, TX: PRO-ED.

Meeker, M. N. (1985a). *Brain research: The necessity for separating sites, actions and functions.* Excerpts from presentation to Neurobiology Conference of Extraordinary Giftedness, New York.

Meeker, M. N. (1985b). SOI. In A. Costa (Ed.), *Developing minds: A resource book for teaching thinking* (pp. 187–193). Alexandria, VA: Association for Supervision and Curriculum Development.

Newland, T. E. (1976). *The gifted in socio-educational perspective.* Englewood Cliffs, NJ: Prentice-Hall.

Perrone, V. (1991). Moving toward more powerful assessment. In V. Perrone (Ed.), *Expanding student assessment.* Association for Supervision and Curriculum Development. Alexandria, VA.

Reid, A. (1961). *Turn to page 84.* Unpublished paper, Glencoe, MN.

Renzulli, J. S. (1977). *The enrichment triad model: A guide for developing defensible programs for the gifted and talented.* Wethersford, CT: Creative Learning Press.

Renzulli, J. S., & Reis, S. M. (1985). Scope and sequence approach to process development. *G/C/T, 37,* 2–6.

Renzulli, J. S., Smith, L. H., & Reis, S. M. (1982). Curriculum compacting: An essential strategy for working with gifted students. *The Elementary School Journal, 82,* 185–194.

Sisk, D. A. (1987). *Creative teaching of the gifted.* New York: McGraw-Hill.

Sisk, D. A., & Shallcross, D. J. (1985). *The growing person* (2nd ed.). Englewood Cliffs, NJ: Prentice-Hall.

Suchman, J. R. (1966). *Developing inquiry.* Chicago: Inquiry Development Program, Science Research Associates.

Taba, H., Durkin, M. C., Fraenkel, J. R., & McNaughton, A. H. (1971). *A teacher's handbook to elementary social studies: An inductive approach.* Reading, MA: Addison-Wesley.

Taylor, C. W. (1968). The multiple talent approach. *The Instructor, 77,* 142–146.

Terman, L. M. (1925). *Genetic studies of genius (Vol. 1): Mental and physical traits of a thousand gifted children.* Palo Alto, CA: Stanford University Press.

Torrance, E. P. (1977). *Discovery and nurturance of giftedness in the culturally different.* Reston, VA: Council for Exceptional Children.

Treffinger, D. J. (1980). *Encouraging creative learning for the gifted and talented.* Ventura, CA: Ventura County Superintendent of Schools, LTI Publications.

Treffinger, D. J. (1982). Gifted students, regular classrooms: Sixty ingredients for a better blend. *The Elementary School Journal, 82,* 267–272.

VanTassel-Baska, J. (1985). Appropriate curriculum for the gifted. In J. Feldhusen (Ed.), *Toward excellence in gifted education* (pp. 45–67). Denver: Love.

Ward, V. (1961). *Educating the gifted: An axiomatic approach.* Columbus, OH: Merrill.

Williams, F. (1970). *Classroom ideas for encouraging thinking and feeling.* Buffalo, NY: D.O.K.

Witty, P. (1958). Who are the gifted? In N. B. Henry (Ed.), *Education of the gifted: The fifty-seventh yearbook of the National Society for the Study of Education* (Part II, pp. 41–63). Chicago: University of Chicago Press.

12

A Critique of Rosselli's "Process Differentiation": Beyond Models

Diane Orzechowski-Harland

"Teaching to everyone's needs" as expressed by Rosselli in the previous chapter certainly is a lofty goal, which may seem overwhelming in the context of the regular classroom teacher's role and responsibilities. Hanging on the wall of the front office in a school I visited recently was a poster presenting the following goal statement: "Our greatest contribution is to be sure there is a teacher in every classroom who cares that every student every day learns and grows and feels like a real human being" (Clifton, 1976). One must wonder how a kindergarten teacher with 60 to 70 students, or a junior or senior high school teacher with 100 to 200 students could embrace these goals with serious intent.

Fear of failure, confusion, and anger are responses of teachers and administrators that create emotional barriers to achieving these goals. Nevertheless, "meeting the needs of students" currently seems to be the philosophical foundation from which public school policy and programs emerge. The purpose of the remaining content of this paper is to diffuse negative responses on the part of the reader by presenting a rationale for the emergence of this philosophical foundation and ideas to make the task manageable.

WHAT IS BEING DONE HERE?

College students enter teacher-training programs expecting to learn how to teach and to become credentialed teachers. Once in the working world, they quickly learn that teachers are expected to teach, learn, counsel (students and parents), apply first aid, organize carnivals, scavenge materials, act as student advocates in cases of abuse and neglect, chaperone dances, and perform a host of other responsibilities, including meeting a wide variety of academic needs thought to have been the responsibility of specialists over the past three decades. For years, regular classroom teachers have been told to leave remediation, modification, and acceleration to the specialists.

Now, they are being told something quite different: to modify curriculum and instruction to meet students' individual cognitive needs.

The curricular needs of students at differing cognitive levels have been addressed in a variety of ways, including establishment of grade levels associated with curriculum that increases in complexity and variety, academic programs for exceptional students, and the use of specialists in the areas of basic skills (e.g., reading and math). A thrust toward differentiating basic curriculum to meet the cognitive needs of students initially came over 15 years ago with the passage of PL 94–142. One of the provisions mandated to assure that curriculum is differentiated for students with handicapping conditions, from what is experienced by the mainstream of students, is an Individualized Education Program (IEP). This provision is evidence of a belief that certain biological and/or emotional conditions (e.g., learning disabilities, mental retardation, behavior disorders) negatively affect students so that they have difficulty learning from what has been traditional instruction in regular classroom settings.

Expanding knowledge about metacognition and learning style preferences has raised the awareness of educators that no single profile exists of a learner to which all instruction should be shaped. In any given classroom, students representing a variety of learning styles and preferences are enrolled, and students perform at differing cognitive levels and demonstrate a variety of cognitive abilities. In any given classroom (regular or specialized), a variety of cognitive needs must be addressed by the teacher.

In the previous chapter, Rosselli has presented an abundance of worthwhile information about, suggestions for, and examples of ways to use and/or modify traditional curriculum to meet instructional and other academic needs of both gifted students and regular students. Knowledge of this type, indeed, is crucial in developing and implementing curriculum to meet the variety of instructional and academic needs of today's students. My experience in working with over 70 teachers in their classrooms over a 3-year period and in teaching undergraduates and graduate students enrolled in college-level education courses leads me to support her opinion that ''many regular classroom teachers already may use successfully'' these strategies and principles.

This same experience, however, also leads me to believe that three critical issues need to be addressed when teachers are faced with the challenge of differentiating curriculum to meet the cognitive needs of gifted students, in any classroom. These three issues are (a) the importance of understanding one's own thinking style processes and preferences and their impact on curriculum development, (b) the challenge of selecting the most appropriate strategies to introduce and implement in a systematic way, and (c) becoming skilled in using strategies that are unfamiliar.

UNDERSTANDING YOUR OWN THINKING

Logically, we can assume that teachers teach best the skills they perform best, understand well, and enjoy. Having personal knowledge of and experience in using targeted skills adds to a teacher's ability to develop these skills in students. Lacking personal knowledge of and experience in using targeted skills handicaps the teacher and the students. Think about it! Are you right-brain or left-brain dominant (Wonder & Donovan, 1984), analytical or intuitive? Do you prefer convergent or divergent thinking tasks? Is your thinking style abstract/random or concrete/sequential (Gregoric, 1985)? Do you *see* words when you think? Perhaps you *hear* words or sounds instead, or *sense* images. Understanding yourself in this manner is a primary step toward being able to understand your students' cognitive abilities and styles in preparation for meeting their cognitive needs.

Most of my college-level students (experienced teachers and preservice teachers) had not thought about their own thinking processes, styles, or preferences prior to taking my classes. Interestingly, a common response on evaluations from these students is, "This was the first time I've ever had to really think in a course." Whether the intent of my instruction is to teach my college-level or primary grade–level students a specific thinking strategy or some other content, I always describe the model I propose to use, and identify for them the kind of thinking required for its implementation. For students unfamiliar with the subject of thinking, this practice introduces them to vocabulary necessary for discussing thinking. For students familiar with the subject of thinking, this practice establishes my expectations for their performance during the instruction.

Assessing your own thinking style, preference, strengths, and weaknesses can help you understand why some students have difficulty in comprehending instruction and performing tasks during any given lesson or unit. Knowing these personal characteristics is helpful in the development and implementation of a comprehensive curriculum.

EENIE, MEENIE, MYNIE, MOE

Emphasis on developing thinking skills in students is evident in the number of instructional and administrative models available to educators for creating and implementing curriculum specific to this subject. Most of the models found in the literature about modifying curriculum for gifted students (Maker, 1982) are highlighted in Rosselli's article. Two other models promoted for use by all teachers in the school district where I work include Barry Beyer's (1987) model, Direct Teaching of Thinking, and Marzano and Arredondo's (1986) Tactics for Thinking. Teachers are exposed to these strategies through workshops or demonstration lessons.

After taking advantage during a single school year of inservice training in more than seven instructional models—including Hilda Taba questioning strategies (Schiever, 1991), Creative Problem Solving techniques (Noller, Parnes, & Biondi, 1976), Tactics for Thinking (Marzano & Arredondo, 1986), Odyssey of the Mind (Micklus, 1984), Direct Teaching of Thinking (Beyer, 1977), Mathematics Their Way (Baratta-Lorton, 1976), and Whole Language Approach to Reading (Newman, 1985)—teachers in this district formally complained of frustration and burnout from trying to internalize and implement all of them. While serving on a districtwide task force, I witnessed the confusion and anger brought about by the lack of a systematic plan to incorporate higher level thinking into a curriculum and the attempt to do too much too fast.

The recommendation from the teachers' representatives was that the district administrators choose one or two models they consider most important to incorporate into the curriculum first, and focus on them for the entire year. Part of this focus should be an evaluation of the model's acceptance and effectiveness districtwide, or in one or two pilot study schools, before attempting to experiment with other models.

Beyond specific leadership of this type, look at your districtwide curriculum goals. Assess the degree to which they include the development of the skills identified in Rosselli's chapter. Think about how you attempt to meet these goals, and ask other teachers how they accomplish them. Idea sharing and material sharing are commonplace among the teachers with whom I work. Teachers who are proficient in assessing and developing specific types of thinking skills demonstrate their talent by teaching a lesson in a colleague's class upon request.

Additionally, examine your unit and lesson-plan goals. Identify the type of thinking you are requiring of your students, and assess the comprehensiveness of your curriculum. What is the ratio of closed to open-ended oral and written questions to which your students are expected to respond daily? How many of your curricular activities provide opportunities for all students to perform at their varying cognitive developmental levels?

Most teachers are familiar with Jean Piaget's theory of cognitive development, and curriculum development often is based on it. This paradigm can be useful as a guide in developing activities at age-related cognitive levels, but caution should be taken not to overlook students who demonstrate cognitive leaps to levels beyond what might be expected. Simply asking a question to elicit a response beyond the level at which most of your students think can provide students who are cognitively advanced with the opportunity to perform at their level without intimidating the other students.

Occasionally at the beginning of a unit, teachers will discover that one or two of their students know more about a subject than the teacher expects the others to learn. Also, one can be certain that the cognitively advanced students in the class will be able to learn the required information at a faster pace than the other students. In addition to using contracts when planning an elaborate project as described in Rosselli's chapter, these are examples of when contracts can be used to benefit gifted students in regular classrooms.

The more familiar a teacher is with different instructional and administrative models, the easier the task becomes of choosing which model to use at any point in curriculum development or implementation. Inservice training programs, peer tutoring/coaching, and team teaching are ways to help teachers choose and learn teaching models, and already have been mentioned in this chapter.

MONEY, MONEY, MONEY

Part of district administrators' focus needs to be on providing continuous support for teachers who attempt to learn about and use unfamiliar models. How many paid conference days are provided for teachers in your district? How frequently are experts in thinking skills contracted for inservice training? How are teachers in your district encouraged to develop innovative skills? Are they rewarded commensurate to their development in this area? How is their desire and willingness to help each other develop these skills supported?

Bruce Joyce (in an interview by Brandt, 1987) concluded from his research that a teacher needs to practice a new strategy 30 times, while receiving feedback on effectiveness, before internalizing the strategy. Skill development requires effort, energy, and time on the part of those desiring it; however, time, energy, and effort are valuable commodities. Districts with philosophy statements implying that teachers are expected to be omnipotent, also must be willing to pay for the development of expertise expected.

Administrators must examine to what degree they encourage or discourage risk taking on the part of their faculty through evaluation measures. For example, they can examine to what degree teachers' salaries are dependent upon achievement test scores, and determine how this measure of accountability relates to the district's thinking skills goals and objectives.

Rosselli states that "process differentiation is not dependent on . . . school board decisions" (p. 139). Perhaps it is not in the sense that the provider of this type of direct service is the teacher, and in that the teacher ultimately facilitates what happens in the classroom. However, much of what a teacher does in the classroom is dictated by external forces (e.g., state school boards, local school boards, curriculum development committees). These same forces are expecting teachers to perform a variety of roles in meeting the needs of students, including academic or intellectual development and more. I would argue that, unless the forces establishing these expectations are willing to meet the needs of teachers in support of their continuous development in a fluctuating field, the cognitive development needs of the gifted will go unmet.

REFERENCES

Baratta-Lorton, M. (1976). *Mathematics their way.* Menlo Park, CA: Addison-Wesley.
Beyer, B. K. (1987). *Practical strategies for the teaching of thinking.* Boston: Allyn & Bacon.
Brandt, R. S. (1987). On teachers coaching teachers: A conversation with Bruce Joyce. *Educational Leadership, 44*(5), 4-11.
Clifton, D. O. (1976). [Poster]. Lincoln, NE: Selection Research.
Gregoric, A. F. (1985). *Gregoric style delineator: A self-assessment instrument for adults.* Maynard, MA: Gabriel Systems.
Maker, C. J. (1982). *Teaching models in education of the gifted.* Austin, TX: PRO-ED.
Marzano, R. J., & Arredondo, D. E. (1986). *Tactics for thinking.* Aurora, CO: Association for Supervision and Curriculum Development.
Micklus, C. S. (1984). *Odyssey of the mind: problems to develop creativity.* Glassboro, NJ: Creative Competitions.
Newman, J. M. (Ed.). (1985). *Whole language: Theory in use.* New York: Praeger.
Noller, R. B., Parnes, S. J., & Biondi, A. M. (1976). *Creative action book.* New York: Scribner.
Schiever, S. W. (1991). *A comprehensive approach to teaching thinking.* Boston: Allyn & Bacon.
Wonder, J., & Donovan, P. (1984). *Whole-brain thinking.* New York: Morrow.

13

Differentiating Products for the Gifted and Talented: The Encouragement of Independent Learning

Sally M. Reis
Gina D. Schack

One of the most unfortunate by-products of the ease with which most bright students master the regular curriculum in our schools is that they learn to expend minimum effort to earn the highest possible grades. This accomplishment results in many bright students learning to go through school without working very hard. Many of these students can master the regular curriculum in their classrooms in a fraction of the time this mastery takes for other students, which can provide both frustrations and opportunities for classroom and subject area teachers. Students who are capable of mastering the regular curriculum at a faster pace have the *time* to engage in alternate activities and tasks. One of the most rewarding uses of this time is for students to become involved in independent study, which encourages self-directed learning, as well as a love for delving into a self-selected topic.

Too few students in our country, however, learn the process of independent study or have the opportunity to become involved in producing differentiated products. At the secondary level, the only exposure that many students have to independent study is the assignment of a term paper on a predetermined topic. At the elementary level, some students who are involved in programs for the gifted and talented are encouraged to pursue independent study. Unfortunately, these students usually are not taught *how* to develop differentiated products through independent study and complete their study by merely writing reports.

How, then, can the process of independent study be taught by classroom, subject area, or resource teachers of the gifted? What steps can students undertake to complete independent study successfully? We provide in this chapter strategies for teachers to use in encouraging and instructing students in the art of independent investigations and the creation of differentiated products. These strategies have been field-tested and revised, and have been proven to be effective in helping teachers facilitate independent or small group projects.

The benefits of independent study (Reis, 1981; Renzulli, 1977a; Renzulli, Reis, & Smith, 1981; Torrance, 1962; Treffinger, 1980) have long been recognized by educators of the gifted. Preferences of gifted students for becoming involved in independent study also have been demonstrated through research (Burns, 1987; Stewart, 1981). Unfortunately, most gifted students have virtually no experience with independent research; instead, they usually follow traditional student study habits. The following examples provide a contrast between two approaches to students' independent work: Susan reads books and pamphlets about drug abuse among teenagers and writes a report. Elizabeth locates members of her school's drug subculture and interviews them about their lives, values, attitudes, and behaviors, then organizes interested others into developing a substance abuse program based on her findings. What is the difference between these two independent study products?

One obvious—and important—difference is the creative productive dimension of Elizabeth's project, which is missing in Susan's report. Elizabeth's effort creates new knowledge rather than reinterpreting old, and uses this new information to make a positive contribution to society. A second difference, which may influence the first one, is the use of advanced-level methodology in the gathering and analyzing of raw data. Elizabeth acted like a practicing professional, using anthropologists' techniques of ethnographic interviewing and qualitative analysis. Although both students have "done research," the quality of Elizabeth's process and product is clearly superior. Her project displays both creative productivity and evidence of advanced mastery of content in the social sciences. The teaching of the methodologies of practicing professionals can escalate both the ambitions and the abilities of our students in their pursuits.

Much of an educator's time currently is spent teaching students "knowledge of"—*that* a particular topic or discipline exists—and "knowledge about"—*what* has been learned in the discipline or area. Very little time is spent on "knowledge how"—*how* professionals learn to work in their particular disciplines (Renzulli, 1988). This "knowledge how" not only will enable students to better understand the content of the discipline, but also will teach them the process of becoming independent investigators in their own right. For this reason, teaching students the methodologies and processes of a discipline can result in greater challenge and a truly differentiated education appropriate for gifted students.

We believe that a goal of independent study should be to expose students to the joys of creative productivity. Society celebrates the inventors, writers, scientists, composers, artists, leaders, and others who have made valuable contributions. On a "junior level," educators do this as well, with science and social studies fairs, invention conventions, problem-solving competitions, writing contests and magazines for student work, and local and national recognition of students' accomplishments in the arts. Clearly, our society values those who, in fulfilling themselves, make creative contributions. Indeed, Renzulli (1978) proposed creative productivity as a definition of giftedness. Therefore, a sensible question to ask is, How can educators in general and teachers of gifted students in particular help more students become creative producers?

Twelve steps can be undertaken to teach students how to produce qualitatively different products. These steps have emerged throughout 15 years of working with above-average students in classrooms and a resource room setting in a program based on focusing student interests into manageable study products. The steps are not necessarily sequential, and some steps may be eliminated if students have previous mastery of ways to accomplish the objective of the task.

Teachers should first instruct students in these steps for independent research and learning. The steps can be modified for use with primary students or introduced as written for upper elementary or secondary students. In a heterogeneous classroom, the methodology of independent research can be taught to identified gifted students, introduced to the top reading group (usually above-average students), or even brought into the entire classroom. When the latter approach is used, a positive response and the desire to follow through usually is an excellent way to *identify* students capable of developing behaviors associated with giftedness (Renzulli & Reis, 1985). Various degrees of response may be found from students of various ability levels. Our experience has shown us that students in the upper ability range have the greatest potential for developing high-quality differentiated products as a result of independent learning (Reis, 1981), but that fact should not deter us from teaching the process to all students in a regular classroom setting.

Primary students can be encouraged to develop a differentiated product by following the same process in a slightly modified manner. They can concentrate on an interest area, find a question or a problem to investigate, develop a simple plan with a series of steps, use multiple resources and differentiated methodology, and evaluate their own work. Gifted first graders with whom we have worked have learned to analyze raw data by writing a survey, gathering and tabulating results, and presenting their findings in a table or chart. This methodology must be taught to them, and qualitatively different products must be expected and encouraged from them. To do this, time must be set aside in a regular classroom or a resource room for this type of student work to be accomplished. Quite often, the need for extra time is another reason why differentiated products can be accomplished more easily by bright students than others, as they master the basic curriculum and complete assignments more quickly.

If teachers cannot spend the time needed to teach the independent learning process discussed in this chapter, they may adapt some of the steps to attempt to differentiate products they assign gifted students in their classroom. Encouraging students to find a question to research and a problem on which to focus (Step 3) *instead* of completing a predetermined report or assignment will help in this process. Of crucial importance in the differentiation of products is the introduction of methodology (Step 6). When a teacher, for example, who knows that a student is interested in nature study, helps the student to acquire *The Amateur Naturalist's Handbook* (see Brown, 1980, in Appendix 13.A), the student will learn the methods used by a naturalist to study and collect live specimens and the various range of products to be developed based on this process. In our experiences with students, the introduction of a book like this often has resulted in the creation of a differential product, escalated well beyond what the student would have produced by using encyclopedic references.

In other words, the process of teaching methodology in a different manner than is generally used in most classrooms often is responsible for the development of differentiated products. The process described in this chapter has proven to be an effective way to achieve this goal.

TWELVE STEPS TO PRODUCING QUALITATIVELY DIFFERENTIATED PRODUCTS

Step 1: Assess, Find, or Create Student Interests

Students should be encouraged *and* allowed to select a topic in which they have an intense interest. Too often, independent study is mistakenly confused with doing a research or term paper based on the subject area class in which the paper is assigned. If this occurs, we cannot expect a student to become involved actively in a topic in which he or she displays little or no interest. For example, a student who has a passionate interest in artificial intelligence and spends all of his or her free time devouring books on this topic probably will not expend high energy or commitment on a report on Shakespeare for an honors English class. Even when the class assignment affords students a choice of topics to investigate, few demonstrate genuine interest in the one they ultimately choose. This may be an unfortunate side effect of the limited curriculum taught in schools. Students seldom are exposed to many of the disciplines within the larger field, and these are often areas of great interest to gifted students. When taught the methodologies of sociologists, botanists, statisticians, or poll-takers, for example, students also gain an introduction to new fields of inquiry, new questions, and new ways to approach problems, which will lead to differentiated products.

Students' interests may need to be sparked by exposure to new topics or disciplines of study or by extensions of the regular curriculum. An interesting observation about student interests is that they decline as students age. Primary-aged students have many interests that they would like to pursue; junior and senior high school students indicate less interest in topics. In some cases, interests can be created by the administration of an open-ended instrument, such as *The Interest-A-Lyzer* (Renzulli, 1977b), the scheduling of high-interest speakers, or the introduction of high-interest topics into the regular curriculum.

Casual interests may or may not be appropriate for independent study. If a student's interests and questions about a topic can be addressed in a brief review of available references, this topic probably is not an area that will result in an extensive research project. Whether a topic is a casual or long-term interest often can be ascertained by an interview with the student.

Step 2: Conduct an Interview to Determine the Strength of the Interest

Several important topics should be dealt with at the time of the student interview. The teacher should try to assess how much interest is really present for further pursuit of the topics. Several questions may be asked that will lead the teacher to determine whether a true interest is being pursued. If the investigation or interest involves journalism, for example, and the student wants to produce a monthly elementary school newspaper, the following questions might be asked at an initial student interview:

1. How long have you been interested in journalism?
2. What sources have you contacted to learn more about this subject?
3. Have you ever tried to publish a class or neighborhood newspaper? If not, why?
4. Have you ever tried to visit our local newspaper?
5. Do you know any other students or adults who are interested in this topic?
6. Have you looked at any books or talked with anyone who might help you get started on a monthly newspaper? If I can help you find a couple of books or someone to talk to about this project, do you think this might give you some ideas?
7. How did you become interested in this topic?

Questions such as these will help to assess interest and commitment to the topic in mind. The last question is especially important, because we want to be certain that the interest is in fact the student's! If, for example, the student responded that he or she had not contacted any sources, or read any books, or made any attempt in any way to learn more about journalism, one might question whether it would be an appropriate topic to pursue at this time. Every attempt should be made to encourage the interest and assist the student in finding information about the interest. If, however, these attempts do not generate the type of follow-up that should be required to produce a differentiated product, one would be unreasonable to expect that a student should or would want to continue in this endeavor.

To analyze further the student's desire to begin work, questions about procedures also may be asked. If the idea for the monthly newspaper is being discussed, the teacher should, at this point, ask questions that will reveal whether the student has thought about the task commitment that will be required to complete the product:

1. How do you think you should get started?
2. How many hours do you think you will need to organize completely a monthly school newspaper?
3. How many other students do you think you will need to involve?
4. How will you recruit reporters?
5. How can you reproduce your newspaper?
6. What ideas do you have that might help you to develop a newspaper that is somewhat different from others you have seen?

Questions such as these will help the teacher determine if the student has really considered the amount of work involved in the actual completion of the independent study. If the student indicates that he or she has only an hour a month outside of school to spend on this product, efforts should be undertaken to provide suggestions for how more time might be spent pursuing this idea both at home and in school. A procedure such as curriculum compacting (Renzulli & Reis, 1985) often frees up several hours a week for gifted students in the regular classroom to spend time producing a differentiated product. A student often will not know how to develop a newspaper that is different from other student efforts. Knowing *how* is the crucial step in producing a differentiated product; at this time, the methodology of how to produce something of higher quality can be introduced.

Many students also have only a vague idea about what kind of interest they have when they begin an independent project. Very few students actually have an idea for a final product in an initial interview. Indeed, many students think only of writing a report because that is traditionally what has been expected of them in school. If an interest is strong, students can be taught to focus their ideas to develop a particular question to research. The product can be determined at a later time.

Step 3: Help Students Find a Question or Questions to Research

This step in teaching the process of differentiating products also is referred to as problem finding and focusing. Most teachers have little difficulty recognizing general families of interest—scientific, historical, literary, mathematical, musical, athletic. However, problems arise when they attempt to capitalize on these general interests and use them as the starting point for (a) focusing on a specific manifestation of general interests, and (b) structuring specific interests into researchable problems. How teachers deal with interests, both general and specific, is crucial and, if handled improperly, will undoubtedly get students off on the wrong track.

We know of one youngster, for example, who expressed an unusual interest in sharks. The teacher appreciated the child's enthusiasm and reacted in what he thought was an appropriate fashion: "I'm glad that you have such a great interest in sharks. Why don't you do a report about sharks?" Those awful words, "do a report" led to an inevitable end result—another summary of facts and drawings based entirely on information copied from encyclopedias and "all-about" books. Although the student prepared a very neat, accurate report, her major investigative activity was looking up and summarizing already existing information. Although previous (background) information is always an important starting point for any investigative endeavor, one of our goals in independent study is to help youngsters extend their work beyond the usual kinds of reporting that often result when teachers and students view this process as merely looking up information. Some training in reporting is a necessary part of good education for all students. Indeed, the pursuit of new knowledge always should begin with a review of what already is known about a given topic. The end result of independent study for gifted students, however, should be a creative contribution that is beyond the already existing information typically found in encyclopedias and all-about books.

How can teachers help students learn to focus problems and become involved in more advanced types of creative and productive projects? The first step is to help students ask the kinds of questions routinely raised by persons who do investigative research *within* particular fields of knowledge. At this point, however, we are faced with a practical problem. Because most teachers are not themselves well versed in asking the right questions about specific fields of study, they cannot be expected to generate appropriate questions in *all* fields of study that their students might want to investigate. Teachers, therefore, must assist students in obtaining the methodological books (or resource persons, if available) that provide these important questions. In other words, if students want to ask the right questions about problem focusing in anthropology, then they must begin by looking at techniques used by anthropologists. Every field of organized knowledge can be defined, in part, by its methodology. In every case, this methodology can be found in certain kinds of guidebooks or manuals. These ''how-to'' books are the keys to escalating studies beyond the traditional report writing approach; therefore, we devote a later section of this chapter to procedures for identifying and making the best use of how-to books. Unfortunately, many of these books are not included ordinarily in elementary or high school libraries because of their advanced nature, but the fact that they are not easily available does not mean that able students cannot make appropriate use of at least selected parts of advanced materials.

Teachers can avoid the error of confusing traditional reporting with investigations by keeping the concept of raw data in mind. Raw data can be thought of as relatively unorganized bits and pieces of information that can be gathered and analyzed to reach a conclusion, discover a principle, support an argument, or create a unique product or presentation. (In a certain sense, even a poet uses new combinations of words, ideas, and feelings as ''raw data'' to create an original poem.) The ways in which researchers use data and the purposes toward which the collection of data is directed are important considerations in defining a differentiated product for gifted students. In the following examples, we try to highlight important steps and key concepts in problem focusing by noting these concerns in brackets.

Example 1

Jason's teacher was aware of his special interest in anything and everything having to do with science. [Keep in mind that science is an area rather than a problem.] She provided him with several copies of *Popular Science* and asked him to review and select the articles he liked best. [This is a good example of Type I exploratory activity because these magazines include many topics not ordinarily covered in the regular science curriculum.]

When the teacher asked Jason if he would like to follow up any article by doing some research of his own, he selected the area of hydroponic gardening. [The general area of science has now been narrowed somewhat, but hydroponic gardening is a topic rather than a problem.] The teacher obtained *Hydroponic Gardening* by

R. Birdwell (1974, Santa Barbara, CA: Woodbridge Press) from the county library, and Jason practically "devoured" it in one night.

Through discussion with his teacher, Jason developed the idea of growing corn under varying conditions. His research question became, Will corn grow at different rates when macronutrients are varied while other conditions stay constant? He constructed several growing trays using paper milk cartons and obtained the necessary nutrients from his chemistry set, a high school chemistry teacher, and a university extension agent with whom he made contact through assistance from his teacher. By varying the amounts of certain macronutrients (nitrogen, phosphorus, potassium) and keeping other conditions constant [good research procedures], he was able to observe different rates of growth. He kept meticulous records and recorded weekly measurements [data] of growth rates and plant "health" [more data]. He also photographed plants grown under varying conditions by placing a standard growth-grid chart behind each plant [visual data]. Graphics and statistical summaries were prepared [data summary and analysis] and a written report was developed [communication of results]. Jason also organized an audiovisual presentation of his work [another mode of communication].

Example 2

Jennie, a student who had become interested in a possible historical study involving a local, state, or regional area, had only a vague idea of what she wanted to research. Her teacher found that she needed to help Jennie focus her interest into what became a manageable investigation. Her teacher found certain questions to be very helpful in focusing Jennie's historical investigation. Although the following questions generally involve local history, they also may be applied in the study of county, regional, or state history. They may be expanded or modified to motivate students at all grade levels.

1. What was here before the city?
2. Who was the first settler of our town? Where could you find a written biography of him or her?
3. In what ways have natural disasters changed our town?
4. Which was the first church in our city? Who built it and when?
5. What folklore is associated with our city, our region, or our county?
6. How did certain historical events affect the people of our area? (For example, the Civil War, World Wars I and II.)
7. What famous person has come from our area? Where could you find a written biography of that person? How has that person's contribution had an impact on our city?
8. Who was the town's first elected official?
9. What was life like for employees of our town's early factories?
10. How did the clothing styles change over the years?
11. What is the oldest building in this area?
12. What is the history of that building?

13. What historically significant sites are in this city?
14. What would life have been like to be (student's age) in our town in the 16th, 17th, 18th, or 19th century?
15. When were written documents or records of our town first kept?
16. Where could you find a written history of our city, region, county, or state?

Jennie eventually focused on developing a written history of her county, which had not previously existed, thus creating a product that was very different from her original rather simple idea of doing a report on the first settlers in her city.

Step 4: Develop a Written Plan

Once students have chosen a question or a series of questions, they should be encouraged to develop a written plan. Some teachers who have been successful in facilitating independent projects use a contract with students; others prefer the use of a student journal or log. The Management Plan (Figure 13.1) (Renzulli, 1977a) also has been an effective way to help organize ideas and develop a time line.

The Management Plan is an educational "device" with a format not very different from the procedures or "ways of thinking" followed by the first-hand inquirer. The adult inquirer intuitively engages in certain activities described on the Management Plan. For example, a sociologist working on an attitude survey may not actually list his or her intended audiences; however, the writer usually has a fairly good idea of the journals to which his or her results may be submitted and of the professional societies or organizations to whom such a research paper might be presented.

After the student has identified a general area in which he or she would like to do advanced-level work and has used appropriate problem-focusing techniques, the student can begin to fill in the material requested in the box entitled "Specific Area of Study." A great deal of careful thought should be given to completing this box because all subsequent activities will reflect the degree of clarity with which the problem is focused and stated. The teacher and student(s) should attempt to answer the three questions listed in the box by using a frame of reference that characterizes the actual thinking of a real investigator who is pursuing a particular problem in his or her field. If such a frame of reference is not apparent to teacher or student, a community resource person who knows that field and/or a methodology book will help to start them on the right track.

The two boxes labeled "Intended Audiences" and "Intended Product(s) and Outlets" are designed to help "steer" the student toward thinking about the final form that his or her investigation will take and about the audiences potentially concerned with the results. The answers to the questions in these boxes are derived from the role and purpose of the first-hand inquirer discussed above.

The two larger boxes on the Management Plan (i.e., "Getting Started" and "Methodological Resources and Activities") are intended to provide a "running account" of the procedures and resources that will be used throughout the investigative activity. Both boxes should be completed cooperatively by the teacher and

MANAGEMENT PLAN FOR INDIVIDUAL AND SMALL GROUP INVESTIGATIONS
(Actual Size: 11" × 17")

Prepared by: Joseph S. Renzulli
Linda H. Smith

NAME _____ GRADE _____

TEACHER _____ SCHOOL _____

Beginning Date _____

Estimated
Ending Date _____

Progress Reports
Due On Following Dates _____

GENERAL AREA(S) OF STUDY (Check all that apply)

___ Language Arts/Humanities	___ Science	Personal and
___ Social Studies	___ Music	___ Social Development
___ Mathematics	___ Art	___ Other (Specify) _____
		___ Other (Specify) _____

SPECIFIC AREA OF STUDY Write a brief description of the problem that you plan to investigate. What are the objectives of your investigation? What do you hope to find out?

METHODOLOGICAL RESOURCES AND ACTIVITIES List the names and addresses of persons who might provide assistance in attacking this problem. List the how-to-do-it books that are available in this area of study. List other resources (films, collections, exhibits, etc.) and special equipment (e.g., camera, transit, tape recorder, questionnaire, etc.). Keep a continuous record of all activities that are a part of this investigation.

INTENDED AUDIENCES Which individuals or groups would be most interested in the findings? List the organized groups (clubs, societies, teams) at the local, regional, state, and national levels. What are the names and addresses of contact persons in these groups? When and where do they meet?

1. _____
2. _____
3. _____
4. _____
5. _____

INTENDED PRODUCT(S) AND OUTLETS What form(s) will the final product take? How, when, and where will you communicate the results of your investigation to an appropriate audience(s)? What outlet vehicles (journals, conferences, art shows, etc.) are typically used by professionals in this field?

GETTING STARTED What are the first steps you should take to begin this investigation? What types of information or data will be needed to solve the problem? If "raw data," how can it be gathered, classified, and presented? If you plan to use already categorized information or data, where is it located and how can you obtain what you need?

Figure 13.1 Management Plan.

student, and modifications should be made as new activities are followed through and as a greater variety of resources are brought to the student's attention. A "mushrooming effect" often takes place as the student becomes more familiar with the resources in a given area of study, and the greater variety of resources, in turn, enables the student to advance the level of sophistication that is brought to bear upon a particular problem.

The completion of the "Getting Started" and "Methodological Resources" boxes often will depend on the teacher's familiarity with appropriate resource guides in given areas of study. For example, if a youngster is studying the attitudes of other students about an issue such as dress code regulations, an interviewer's manual and/or guidebook for constructing attitude questionnaires will be a key resource. In many cases, these types of references provide the step-by-step procedures that will assist students in completing the "Getting Started" box and the activities section of the "Methodological Resources" box.

In certain respects, the two larger boxes on the Management Plan should parallel one another. In the "Getting Started" box, the student should list the early steps necessary for beginning an investigation and the types of information that will be needed to pursue the study, at least in the initial stages. Because early success is an important factor for students' continued motivation to complete their studies, teachers must work very closely with youngsters in helping them to complete this box. The information in the box can serve as a checklist for determining whether a student is heading in the right direction. This information also can assist in setting target dates for progress reports. In certain instances, a student may want to lay out the entire plan in the "Getting Started" box; in other cases, the plan may begin in this box and be continued in the "Methodological Resources" box. In view of the wide variety of topics that students may choose to pursue and the many variations in methodology that characterize various areas of study, a rigid prescription for completing these two boxes of the Management Plan is difficult to outline. In certain instances, students may wish to design their studies through the use of a flowchart and record their activities in a log or notebook. Whenever space does not permit the recording of necessary information, the reverse side of the Management Plan can be used and/or additional pages can be appended.

Step 5: Help Students Locate Multiple Resources and Continue Working on the Topic

In addition to exposing students to problem focusing through the methods described earlier, how-to books should be located to help provide advanced content and methodological assistance. Students should be directed also to the numerous resources at their disposal *beyond* encyclopedic references. These resources include, but are not limited to, textbooks, biographies and autobiographies, how-to books, periodicals, films, letters, surveys, telephone calls and personal interviews, almanacs, atlases, and many others. Teachers should encourage students to use many different types of resources in researching their topic.

Step 6: Provide Methodological Assistance

Mindful of the ever-increasing amount of information in the world and the rate at which information is changing and growing, Toffler (1974), Naisbitt (1982), and others have suggested that appropriate preparation for the world of the future would be to teach students how to access and evaluate existing knowledge and create new knowledge. Writers in the field of futuristics seem to agree that people will face an information explosion of major proportions, technological changes that are difficult to anticipate, and the prospect of preparing for several different jobs in their lifetimes. Faced with the impossibility of keeping track of all that is known, people will instead need the ability to locate information, evaluate its worth, and apply it to current problems. Those who are able to use and create knowledge, rather than those able to recall possibly outdated information, will best be prepared for the future. While specific "knowledge about" changes quickly, especially in the sciences, "knowledge how" represents a way for people to evaluate, use, and create new information.

Methodological assistance means helping students to acquire and make appropriate use of the specific data-gathering tools and investigative techniques that are the standard and necessary methods for authentic research in particular fields of study. If a problem is well defined and focused, the correct guidance by teachers during this phase of a study can almost guarantee that students will be first-hand investigators rather than reporters. This step of the process involves shifting our emphasis from learning *about* topics to learning *how* one gathers, categorizes, analyzes, and evaluates information in particular fields. During this crucial time of independent research, teachers can almost guarantee that student products will be differentiated by the methodological assistance and instruction they receive.

Every field of knowledge is characterized, in part, by certain kinds of raw data. New contributions are made in a field when investigators apply well-defined methods to the process of "making sense" out of previously random bits and pieces of information. Although some investigations require levels of sophistication and equipment far beyond the reach of younger students, almost every field of knowledge has entry- and junior-level data-gathering opportunities. At this stage, teachers need to provide some examples of the independent study process; the teacher's role is to help students identify, locate, and obtain resource materials and/or persons that can provide assistance in the appropriate use of investigative techniques. In some cases, teachers may have to consult with librarians or professionals within a field for advice about where and how to find resource materials. Professional assistance also may be needed to translate complex concepts into ideas students can understand. Although methodological assistance is a major part of the teacher's responsibility, to expect teachers to have mastered a large number of investigative techniques is neither necessary nor realistic. A good general background and orientation toward the overall nature of research is necessary, but the most important skill is the ability to know where and how to help a student obtain the right kind of material and the willingness to locate the necessary resources for students.

For elementary classroom and secondary subject area teachers, the first step in learning about methodologies involves identifying the disciplines within the subject being taught—the "-ologies" and "-ographies" of the field. Some examples are the following:

Social sciences—history, geography, economics, sociology, political science, anthropology, psychology, theology, philosophy

Sciences—biology, microbiology, botany, zoology, ornithology, herpetology, entomology, oceanography, ecology, biochemistry, chemistry, physics, astronomy, geology, meteorology

Language arts (modes of communication)—fiction writing, journalism, playwriting, literary criticism, poetry, cartooning, drawing, graphics, photography, cinematography, drama, oratory, debate, storytelling, mime, dance, songwriting, music

Mathematics—number theory, statistics, probability, geometry, topology, logic, calculus, mathematical modeling

Once the disciplines have been identified, teachers can focus on areas of interest to many students (based on information from an interest inventory) or areas with wider applicability. One example of a process skill that would prove useful in almost any independent project is research methodology, including such tasks as problem finding and focusing, research question and hypothesis generation, research design, data gathering and analysis, and dissemination of results.

Once interest areas have been chosen, teachers should help the student to identify methodologies used within the particular discipline. How can teachers learn about methodologies with which they are not already familiar? One possibility is to become experts themselves, taking courses or working with experts for periods of time. Another would be to take the time to interview or shadow experts as they work. However, both of these options seem unlikely for most teachers. One idea, which seems both practical and effective, is the use of how-to books that explain the methodologies of practicing professionals in terms that students and/or teachers can understand. A few are texts, but most are published as trade books, intended for a general audience. Good how-to books should include the following:

1. Information about the structure of the field
2. Procedures for problem finding and focusing
3. Specific methodological skills of the discipline
4. Suggestions for investigations students could pursue
5. Suggestions for format/communication of findings

Using a how-to book as a source of professional expertise for students who already have identified an area of potential investigation is an excellent way of upgrading the quality of independent study products. Depending on the student's ability and the book's readability, teachers may choose to have the student work with the book independently, to teach the techniques, or to work with the student while using the book as a resource. The book might provide suggestions for research or real-world problems to be solved. The book should provide guidance and instruction in professional-level methodologies that the student can use to carry out the project after a problem has been brought into focus. Finally, the book might have information about appropriate audiences and formats for communicating findings.

If students have not yet identified areas for further exploration, how-to books could suggest methodological lessons or mini-courses that would introduce students to new topics and processes to generate interest. For example, Fink and Kosecoff's (1985) how-to book could provide the basis for a series of lessons about public opinion polling, including sample selection, poll construction, interviewing techniques, and data analysis, sparking students' interest in a variety of areas. Potential projects might include polling peers or the general population about a topic of interest, investigating the effect of polls on local elections, doing market research for a business venture, conducting in-depth interviews, or working for a candidate or interest group.

If the goal is this kind of project, however, teachers need to conduct "debriefing discussions" with students to help them see the relationship between the methodologies they are learning and personal interests, real-world problems (Renzulli, 1977a), and areas of potential investigation. Teachers can ask the following questions to stimulate interest in further exploration:

1. How does this field relate to something in which you are already interested? (Use forced connections to see the relationship of the methodology to students' personal interests, no matter how remote they may seem at first.)
2. What are some unsolved problems in this area? What are some issues currently being considered by professionals in this field?
3. If you were interested in solving a problem in this area, what kinds of things could you do?
4. What problems in our school or community are related to this field?
5. How would you use these methodologies to solve a problem of interest to you?

Examples of how-to books that have been used extensively may provide insight into how independent study may be aided by the acquisition of these books. Appendix 13.A includes brief descriptions of eight exemplary how-to books in five areas: science, social science, research methodology, modes of communication, and inventing, designing, and other interests. As of this writing, all still are being published. Having a small library of how-to books within a classroom or school library will enable teachers to encourage students to pursue the process of developing differentiated final products.

Step 7: Help Students Decide Which Question(s) to Answer

Once students have learned about the disciplines, become more aware of their interests, and identified the methodology, they often are able to make a decision about which question or area they want to research. In addition, students often begin investigations when they see how particular methodologies make possible the pursuit of a previous area of interest. A teacher introduced a lesson about controlled experiments as a way to test hypotheses to a sixth-grade class composed of identified above-average students. Following this lesson, one student excitedly told her classroom that she now saw how she could win the argument with her mother about listening to music while doing homework. She wanted to design an experiment in which the class did academic work under conditions of both music and silence. As a result of the methodological lesson, Sasha knew that all conditions except music had to be held constant—the students, length of study time, difficulty of task, setting, and other variables. If, after this experiment, no significant differences were found in the quality of student work, Sasha would have found support for her hypothesis.

Sasha did indeed pursue her investigations. After deciding on an appropriate academic task and choosing the music, she enlisted her classmates in the experiment. To her disappointment, the results were not what she had hoped they would be. The positive outcome, however, was that Sasha acted like a "junior practicing professional" in an area of interest as a result of instruction in research methodology.

Step 8: Provide Managerial Assistance

Managerial assistance involves helping students to "make arrangements" for obtaining the types of data and resources necessary for independent investigations. Setting up an interview with a public official, arranging for the distribution of a questionnaire to students or parents, and providing transportation to a place where data will be gathered are all examples of managerial functions fulfilled by teachers. Additional activities might include gaining access to laboratories or computer centers, arranging for the use of a college library, helping students to gain access to a telephone or photocopying machine, and driving downtown to pick up some photographic materials or electronic parts. The teacher's responsibilities in this regard are similar to the combined roles of research assistant, advocate, ombudsman, campaign strategist, and enthusiastic friend. At this stage of product development, the student should be the leader and emerging expert, while the teacher assumes a supportive rather than authoritative posture. The teacher's typical comments should be, "What can I do to help you? Are you having any problems? Do you need to get a book from the university library? Would you like to bounce a few ideas off me? In what ways might we explore raising the money you need for solar cells?"

The major purpose of the managerial role is to help the student stay on track and keep moving toward each intermediate goal and its accomplishment. A planned strategy for bringing the teacher up to date on progress between meetings will create a vehicle for fulfilling the managerial role. A log, notebook, or annotated time line are good examples of such vehicles. Also, this procedure should involve a review and analysis of the Management Plan or any other written plan being kept by the student.

Step 9: Identify Final Products and Audiences

Finding an audience is regarded by some theorists (Renzulli, 1977a) as the key to improving the quality of products and developing effective ways of communicating their results with interested others. We also believe that a sense of audience is a primary contributor to the creation of task commitment and the concern for excellence and quality that we have witnessed in many high-quality products resulting from independent study projects.

Attention must be given to helping students find appropriate outlets and audiences for their most creative efforts. This concern is modeled once again after the *modus operandi* of creative and productive individuals. If we could sum up in as few words as possible the *raison d'être* of highly creative artists and scholars, it would certainly be *impact upon audience.* Creativity is a source of personal satisfaction and self-expression, but a great many of the rewards come from bringing about desired changes in the human condition. The writer hopes to influence thoughts and emotions, the scientist carries out research to find better ways to contribute to the knowledge of his or her field, and artists create products to enrich the lives of those who view their works. Teachers can help young people to acquire this orientation by encouraging them to develop a sense of audience from the earliest stages of an independent investigation.

The teacher's role regarding outlets and audiences is to help students take a small but often neglected step in the overall process of product development, which is to consider how people typically communicate results or products within given fields of the arts and sciences. In Table 13.1 is a listing of possible products by discipline. Final products also should be determined by student self-selection and interest. Students interested in media or film should not be forced to write an article. Once a product has been identified, audiences should be explored. For teachers to have the names of all possible audiences and outlets at their fingertips is neither necessary nor practical; however, persons programming for advanced-ability youngsters need to find out about audiences and outlets in the community. What historical societies or conversation groups are in the community? Do they publish newsletters or have regularly scheduled meetings? Would they be receptive to including a student's article in their newsletter or perhaps having a student present the results of his or her research at one of their meetings? How-to books also may be used to provide guidance in identifying products and audiences.

Although school and local audiences are obvious starting points in the search for outlet vehicles, teachers should help students gain a perspective for other outlet vehicles and audiences. Many organizations, for example, prepare newsletters and journals at the state and national levels. These organizations usually are receptive to high-quality contributions by young people. Similarly, state and national magazines often carry outstanding work by young people. Whenever student products show unusually high levels of excellence, students should be encouraged to contact one of the publishing companies and magazines that specialize in or are receptive to the contributions of young writers, artists, and researchers. Just as gifted athletes extend their involvement into larger and larger fields of competition, so also should our most able young scholars and artists be encouraged to reach beyond the local levels of success they have achieved. This process involves an element of risk taking and the chance that one's work will not be accepted in the wider arenas of publication and dissemination. If, for example, a student completes a detailed and well-

Table 13.1 Outlet Vehicles for Differentiated Student Products

Literary
  Literary magazine (prose or poetry)
  Newspaper for school or class
  Class reporter for school newspaper
  Collections of local folklore (*Foxfire*)
  Book reviews of childrens' books for children, by children
  Storytelling
  Puppeteers
  Student editorials on a series of topics
  Kids' page in a city newspaper
  Series of books or stories
  Classbook or yearbook
  Calendar book
  Greeting cards (including original poetry)
  Original play and production
  Poetry readings
  Study of foreign languages
  Organizer of story hour in local or school library
  Comic book or comic book series
  Organization of debate society
  Monologue, sound track, or script

Mathematical
  Contributor of math puzzles, quizzes, games for children's sections in newspapers, magazines
  Editor/founder of computer magazine or newsletter
  Math consultant for school
  Editor of math magazine, newsletter
  Organizer of metrics conversion movement
  Original computer programming
  Programming book
  Graphics (original use of) films

Media
  Children's television show
  Children's radio show
  Children's reviews (books, movie) on local news shows
  Photo exhibit (talking)
  Pictorial tour
  Photo essay
  Designing advertisement (literary magazine)
  Slide/tape show on self-selected topic

Artistic
  Displays, exhibits
  Greeting cards
  Sculpture
  Illustrated books
  Animation
  Cartooning

(Continued)

Table 13.1 *(Continued)*

Musical, dance
  Books on life of famous composer
  Original music, lyrics
  Electronic music (original)
  Musical instrument construction
  Historical investigation of folk songs
  Movement—history of dance, costumes

Historical and social sciences
  Roving historian series in newspaper
  ''Remember when'' column in newspaper
  Establishment of historical society
  Establishment of an oral history tape library
  Published collection of local folklore and historical highlight stories
  Published history (written, taped, pictorial)
  Historical walking tour of a city
  Film on historical topic
  Historical monologue
  Historical play based on theme
  Historical board game
  Presentation of historical research topic (World War II, etc.)
  Slide/tape presentation of historical research
  Starting your own business
  Investigation of local elections
  Electronic light board explaining historical battle, etc.
  Talking time line of a decade (specific time period)
  Tour of local historical homes
  Investigate a vacant lot
  Create a ''hall'' of local historical figures
  Archaeological dig
  Anthropological study (comparison of/within groups)

Scientific
  Science journal
  Daily meteorologist posting weather conditions
  Science column in newspaper
  Science 'slot' in kids television show
  Organizer at a natural museum
  Science consultant for school
  ''Science Wizard'' (experimenters)
  Science fair
  Establishment of a nature walk
  Animal behavior study
  Any prolonged experimentation involving manipulation of variables
  Microscopic study involving slides
  Classification guide to natural habitats
  Acid rain study
  Future study of natural conditions
  Book on pond life

(Continued)

Table 13.1 *(Continued)*

Aquarium study/study of different ecosystems
Science article submitted to national magazines
Plan a trip to national parks (travelogue)
Working model of a heart
Working model of a solar home
Working model of a windmill

documented historical biography about a famous local suffragette, an element of success has been built in by beginning the process at the local or school level. At the same time, the opportunity for a real-world experience has been built in by helping young people to learn about the rigors and challenges of the creative producer as he or she attempts to reach out to wider audiences in the country, state, or nation.

Step 10: Offer Encouragement, Praise, and Critical Assistance

Even the most experienced researchers, writers, and creative producers need feedback from persons who can reflect objectively upon a given piece of work. For young scholars who are having initial experiences in the often frustrating task of first-hand inquiry, this feedback must be given in a firm but sensitive manner. The major theme or idea underlying the feedback process is that almost everything can be improved in varying degrees through revisions, rewriting, and attention to details, both large and small. This message must be conveyed to students without harsh criticism or discouraging comments. Each student must be made to feel that the teacher's most important concern is to help the aspiring artist or scholar reach the highest possible level of excellence. Just as a champion athlete or dancer knows that a rigorous coach has the performer's best interests at heart, so also must students learn that critical feedback is a major service that good teachers must offer.

Bright students often are unaccustomed to any criticism being offered about their work. Therefore, encouragement must be given throughout the process, and students must understand that all professionals regard feedback as a necessary, although sometimes unpleasant, way to improve their work.

Step 11: Escalate the Process

The teacher should view his or her role in the feedback process as that of a "resident escalator." Sensitive and specific recommendations about how particular aspects of the work can be improved will help the aspiring scholar to move slowly but surely toward higher and higher levels of product excellence. Every effort should be made to pinpoint specific areas for suggested changes. This approach will help students avoid discouragement and reconfirm a belief in the overall value of their endeavors.

How many of us have encouraged students to do research, only to have them return with a synthesis of magazine articles (at best) or encyclopedia references? Even when we encouraged students to go one step farther and do surveys, how often have we found that each polled the same 10 friends or classmates? Bright students should not be blamed for using simple or unimaginative methods when they are not taught more advanced or appropriate ones.

If teachers want students to act like first-hand researchers, they must teach students how these people operate. Students need to understand how to identify and phrase research questions and hypotheses, design research that will answer their research questions appropriately, gather and analyze data in an unbiased manner, draw conclusions, and communicate their results effectively. Although the specifics change from discipline to discipline, all professionals use the research process in their work. Authors may state their premises less formally than scientists, and may gather data through observations and introspection rather than experimentation, but the underlying processes are similar.

Step 12: Evaluate

An almost universal characteristic of students of all ages is a desire to know how they will be evaluated or "graded." We would like to begin by saying that we strongly discourage the formal grading of products resulting from independent study[1]. No letter grade, number, or percentage can reflect accurately the comprehensive types of knowledge, creativity, and task commitment developed within the context of the independent study. At the same time, however, evaluation and feedback are important parts of the overall process of promoting growth through this type of enrichment experience, and therefore students should understand thoroughly the procedures that will be used to evaluate their work.

We believe students and teachers should both be involved in the evaluation process. Additionally, if an outside resource person or mentor has been involved in the development of the product, he or she should be asked to provide evaluation input.

The Student Product Assessment Form (SPAF) (Figure 13.2) (Renzulli & Reis, 1985) was the result of a comprehensive instrument development research project (Reis, 1981) that was directed toward establishing the reliability and validity of this instrument and documenting the quality of products that were produced by various groups of students participating in programs for advanced-ability students. The validity and reliability of the SPAF were established through a year-long series of studies, using a technique developed by Ebel (1951). Levels of agreement among raters on individual items of the scale ranged from 86.4% to 100%. By having a group of raters assess the same set of products on two occasions, with a period of time between ratings, we established a reliability coefficient of .96 for the instrument. Information about the reliability of this instrument should be brought to the attention of decision makers to establish the credibility of this approach to the evaluation of student products. In other words, when questions about ''hard data'' and objectivity are raised, the fact that a research-based instrument of proven value is being used will help overcome many of the concerns that traditionally are raised about the merits of various approaches to evaluation.

The instrument is composed of 15 items designed to address both individual aspects and overall excellence of products. Each item contains a single characteristic on which raters should focus their attention. Items 1 through 8 are divided into three related parts:

1. *The key concept*—This concept is always presented first and is printed in large type. It should serve to focus the rater's attention on the main idea or characteristic being evaluated.
2. *The item description*—Following the key concept are one or more descriptive statements about how the characteristic might be reflected in the student's product.
3. *Examples*—To help clarify the meaning of the items, an actual example of the student's work is provided. These examples are intended to elaborate upon the meaning of both the key concept and the item description. The examples are presented after each item description.

Item 9 contains seven different components, providing an overall assessment of the product. When completing the ratings for this assessment of a student's product, raters attempt to evaluate the product in terms of their own values and certain characteristics that indicate the quality, aesthetics, utility, and function of the overall contribution. In other words, raters are encouraged to consider the product as a whole (globally) in Item 9, and to use their own judgment and rely upon their own guided subjective opinions when completing this component of the assessment.

The best way to help students gain an appreciation for the ways in which their work will be evaluated is to conduct a series of orientation sessions organized around SPAF. Two or three examples of completed student products that highlight varying levels of quality on the respective scales from the SPAF instrument will help students to gain an appreciation for the factors involved in the assessment and examples of the manifestation of each factor. In many ways, these sessions represent an excellent way to teach students about the nature of an advanced product expected from gifted students and the difference between a traditional report on the one hand and a product resulting from a first-hand investigative activity on the other.

Numerous forms have been developed to help students in evaluating their own work. An effective and simple questionnaire (Renzulli & Reis, 1985) has been used successfully for 10 years in a program for gifted students based on *The Enrichment Triad Model* and includes these questions:

1. What were your feelings about working on your project?
2. What were some of the things you learned while working on your project?
3. Were you satisfied with final product? In what ways?
4. What were some of the ways you were helped on your project?

Student Product Assessment Form
Summary Sheet

Name(s) _____ Date _____

District _____ School _____

Teacher _____ Grade _____ Sex _____

Product (Title and/or Brief Description) _____

_____

Number of Weeks Student(s) worked on Product _____

FACTORS	RATING*	NOT APPLICABLE
1. Early Statement of Purpose	_____	_____
2. Problems Focusing	_____	_____
3. Level of Resources	_____	_____
4. Diversity of Resources	_____	_____
5. Appropriateness of Resources	_____	_____
6. Logic, Sequence, and Transition	_____	_____
7. Action Orientation	_____	_____
8. Audience	_____	_____
9. Overall Assessment	_____	_____
A. Originality of the Idea	_____	_____
B. Achieved Objectives Stated in Plan	_____	
C. Advanced Familiarity with Subject	_____	
D. Quality Beyond Age/Grade Level	_____	
E. Care, Attention to Detail, etc.	_____	
F. Time, Effort, Energy	_____	
G. Original Contribution	_____	

Comments:

Person Completing This Form _____

*Rating Scales: Factors 1-8

   5 - To a great extent
   3 - Somewhat
   1 - To a limited extent

Factor 9A-9G

   5 = Outstanding
   4 = Above Average
   3 = Average
   2 = Below Average
   1 = Poor

Figure 13.2 Student Product Assessment Form.

5. Do you think you might like to work on another product in the future? What ideas do you have for this product?

CONCLUSION

One of the most difficult challenges faced by educators in developing programs and activities for gifted students is helping students to get started on developing appropriate differentiated products. This type of work represents qualitatively different learning experiences. Therefore, teachers need to realize that they themselves must engage in some activities that are different from the activities that define the traditional teacher's role. This point cannot be overemphasized. Fostering *differential* types of learning experiences through the use of ordinary teaching methods is impossible. If we want young people "to think, feel, and do" like practicing professionals (or first-hand inquirers), then we as teachers also must learn how to raise a few of the questions that professionals ask about the nature and function of their own work. In other words, we must go one step beyond the typical questions that teachers ordinarily raise in problem-focusing situations and move on to *product* focusing.

Raising these questions serves two major purposes. The first obviously is to focus upon differentiated products and target audiences. The second purpose is somewhat less direct, but equally crucial: Teachers must begin to help youngsters think, feel, and believe that they *can* be creative producers. Almost everything children do in school casts them in the role of lesson learners. Even when working on so-called research reports, the student nearly always perceives his or her purpose as that of "finding out about . . ." One need only ask youngsters *why* they are working on a particular report. Invariably, they reply, "To find out *about* the eating habits of the gray squirrel (or *about* the exports of Brazil, or *about* the Battle of Gettysburg)." Finding out about things is part of the process of investigation—all student and adult inquirers do it—but the big difference is that practicing professionals do it for a purpose *beyond* merely finding out something for its own sake.

Encouraging the development of self-selected products through self-directed independent study is not an easy process. Many bright students are content to produce merely another report about a topic. Taking the steps in this chapter will encourage students to go beyond reporting in developing differentiated products. Our goal in doing this is

> larger than the products students prepare or the methods they learn in pursuing their self-selected problems. The largest goal is that students begin to think, feel and do like creative producers. Our most potentially able young artists and scholars must develop the attitude that has reinforced the essence of creative people since the beginning of time: I can do . . . I can be . . . I can create. (Renzulli & Reis, 1985)

Appendix 13.A

Resource Section of "How-To" Books

SCIENCE

Brown, V. (1980). *The amateur naturalist's handbook.* Englewood Cliffs, NJ: Prentice-Hall. (Grades 6–12)

This book has three sections dedicated to beginners, students, and advanced learners. Beginning naturalists will benefit from information about animals, plants, rocks, and minerals, and ways to collect each, as well as an introduction to climate and ecology. Student naturalists will find more detailed information for collecting and studying live plant and animal specimens, as well as the advanced study of rocks and minerals, climate, and ecology.

Wentworth, D. F., Couchman, J. K., MacBean, J. C., & Stecker, A. (1975). *Ecology in your community.* Toronto: Holt, Rinehart & Winston. (Grades 3–7)

This book is an introduction to the study of ecology through hands-on investigations and data collection. Many suggestions and examples of observation and record keeping are given, with questions to help students analyze what they find. Topics include habitats, communities, interdependence, and adaptation.

SOCIAL SCIENCE

The American Genealogical Research Institute Staff. (1975). *How to trace your family tree.* New York: Doubleday. (Grades 7–12)

Written by those in the know, this book provides for the novice all that is needed to begin a family history project. Included are guides to all kinds of records: library; local, state, and federal government sources; churches; newspapers; and organizations. Additional chapters about using your family as a source and various ways to organize findings make things simple for the first-time genealogist.

RESEARCH METHODOLOGY

Bunker, B., Pearlson, H., & Schulz, J. (1975). *The student's guide to conducting social science research.* New York: Human Sciences Press. (Grades 5–10)

In the introduction, research is related to real-life experience; then a nine-step approach to research is provided. Later chapters include explanations of research design, hypothesis testing, surveys, observation, and experiments. Hands-on experience with data-gathering methods is provided through ready-to-use activities.

Kramer, S. (1987). *How to think like a scientist.* New York: Crowell. (Grades 2–5)

In this delightful book, the scientific method is explained in terms young children can understand. Examples are given of each of the five steps in the scientific method: asking a question, gathering information, forming a hypothesis, testing the hypothesis, and telling others what you found. In addition to providing a great example illustrating the use of treatment and control groups, the book includes a chapter helpful to students in finding questions they might want to answer.

Carey, H., & Greenberg, J. (1983). *How to use primary sources.* New York: Franklin Watts. (Grades 5–10)

Students are helped to go beyond the usual library sources through explanations of how to gather information from interviews, paintings, and museums.

MODES OF COMMUNICATION

Henderson, K. (1986). *Market guide for young writers.* Sandusky, MI: Savage. (Grades 5–12)

Many books have been written to teach children how to write; this one is designed to help them get published. Included are sections about preparing the manuscript and entering contests, short essays by children who have published, annotated lists of publications and contests open to young writers, and additional references. In a final chapter, answers are given to the questions asked most frequently by young writers.

INVENTING, DESIGNING, AND OTHER INTERESTS

Caney, S. (1985). *Steven Caney's invention book.* New York: Workman. (Grades 4–12)

In this book, Caney shares everything prospective young inventors need to know, from inspiration to marketing. Steps include getting started, the inventor's workshop, keeping a notebook, planning, prototypes, names, patents, and marketing.

REFERENCES

Burns, D. E. (1987). *The effects of group training activities on students' creative productivity.* Unpublished doctoral dissertation, The University of Connecticut, Storrs.

Ebel, R. L. (1951). Estimation of the reliability of ratings. *Psychometrika, 16,* 407–424.

Fink, A., & Kosecoff, J. (1985). *How to conduct surveys: A step-by-step guide.* Newbury Park, CA: Sage.

Naisbitt, J. (1982). *Megatrends.* New York: Warner Bros.

Reis, S. M. (1981). *An analysis of the productivity of gifted students participating in programs using the revolving door identification model.* Unpublished doctoral dissertation, The University of Connecticut, Storrs.

Renzulli, J. S. (1977a). *The enrichment triad model: A guide for defensible programs for the gifted.* Mansfield Center, CT: Creative Learning Press.

Renzulli, J. S. (1977b). *The interest-a-lyzer.* Mansfield Center, CT: Creative Learning Press.

Renzulli, J. S. (1978). What makes giftedness? Reexamining a definition. *Phi Delta Kappan, 60,* 180–184, 261.

Renzulli, J. S. (1988). The multiple menu model for developing differentiated curriculum for the gifted and talented. *Gifted Child Quarterly, 32*(3), 298–309.

Renzulli, J. S., & Reis, S. M. (1985). *The schoolwide enrichment model: A comprehensive plan for educational excellence.* Mansfield Center, CT: Creative Learning Press.

Renzulli, J. S., Reis, S. M., & Smith, L. H. (1981). *The revolving door identification model.* Mansfield Center, CT: Creative Learning Press.

Renzulli, J. S., & Smith, L. H. (1977). *The management plan for individual and small group investigations of real problems.* Mansfield Center, CT: Creative Learning Press.

Stewart, E. D. (1981). Learning styles among gifted students: Instructional technique preferences. *Exceptional Children, 48,* 134–139.

Toffler, A. (1974). *Learning for tomorrow.* New York: Random House.

Torrance, E. P. (1962). *Guiding creative talent.* Englewood Cliffs, NJ: Prentice-Hall.

Treffinger, D. J. (1980). *Encouraging creative learning for the gifted and talented.* Ventura, CA: Ventura County Superintendent of Schools, LTI Publication.

14

Critique of Reis
and Schack's
"Differentiating Products
for the Gifted
and Talented"

Sandy Lethem

Independent study is one of the most promising areas for developing differentiated curriculum for gifted students because it builds upon the students' desires and needs for self-initiated learning. For many years, researchers have shown that students will learn better and be more motivated if involved in their own learning (Treffinger, 1975). Through independent study, gifted students can acquire motivations and skills that they will use to continue learning throughout life.

In the previous chapter, Reis and Schack provide strategies for teachers to use in encouraging and instructing students to develop independent investigations and to create differentiated products. They give sound suggestions for encouraging students to go beyond reporting in developing these products.

Truly, students usually are not taught how to pursue an independent project and merely end up writing a knowledge-level report as a final product. However, before introducing elementary gifted students to an independent study program, the teacher must give the students practice in making informed, logical, and appropriate uses of information, rather than simply acquiring it. Practice in making valid generalizations, grasping underlying principles, evaluating ideas, transforming existing information, deciding about relevant and irrelevant facts all will help the gifted student be capable of meaningful independent study (Lethem, Osborn, & Zmuda, 1981).

The 12 steps devised by Reis and Schack to teach students how to produce qualitatively different products have great merit. Several of the steps need expanding, particularly when used by the elementary teacher of the gifted. In the following section, I take a closer look at the 12 steps.

REIS AND SCHACK'S 12 STEPS

Step 1: Assess, Find, or Create Student Interests

The term *independent study* indicates to me that the topic to be selected is not a blanket assignment to all students. Therefore, the topic would not be selected from subject areas within the general curriculum. Such overall assignments may have value, but not within the realm of true independent study. The elementary gifted student often is interested in a wide range of topics. Reis and Schack have suggested that these interests narrow or lessen as the student grows older. Perhaps this is the result of inappropriate education practices!

Certainly, open-ended surveys and instruments such as *The Interest-A-Lyzer* (Renzulli, 1977) should be a starting place. Such instruments should be used as a planned strategy for helping the student focus upon those subjects of interest or potential interest. Exposure to general discussions and guest speakers concerned with high-interest topics also is valid. For the elementary student, however, more exploration often is needed. Brainstorming potential interest areas can help the elementary student explore his or her own ideas and feelings about areas of potential interest. Simply seeing the list of brainstormed topics increase will stimulate new ideas. Also, the development of a file or collection of research topics is important. The elementary student needs to be aware of what has interested other students in past years. By looking through the collection of topics and research proposals, students may discover unexplored ideas and areas of potential interest. Helping the student focus on areas of intense interest is a vital first step in developing the independent learner.

Step 2: Conduct an Interview to Determine the Strength of the Interest

Teachers must ascertain whether a student's interest in a specific topic is strong enough to result in an extensive research project. This task, however, is time-consuming. For the resource room teacher with few students or the regular classroom teacher with one or two students who are just beginning their independent study, such interviews are manageable. For the teacher of a self-contained classroom of highly gifted students to set aside the time for 16 or more in-depth interviews about potential topics of interest is difficult. Within my elementary classroom, designed for identified gifted students with high academic ability and IQs of 145 or above, conducting 16 such interviews often is impossible.

One alternative to the individual interview is to group the students with related areas of interest for a discussion of the interview questions. For example, the teacher can meet with the 2 or 3 students interested in various aspects of historical topics, or scientific topics, to discuss the hows and whys of their interests. Questions about research procedures and the ways and means of the research may be similar, and often one student's ideas will stimulate the other students' thinking. Ideas about the end product and the means of presentation often are best explored within the small group. With careful questioning, a teacher can help several students concurrently to analyze their interests and their desire to research a topic area.

Sometimes, in an effort to save time, a teacher will have students write answers to the interview. Directing students to write the answers to the interview questions is not as effective as having them respond verbally. Writing responses to the questions may inhibit the student's thinking, and for the very young student it is too time-consuming. Also, the beginning researcher may not know how and why the interest is important to him or her without having the advantage of questions being restated and the ideas discussed within the small group. If the written interview method is used, the student needs to have ample time to think about the questions before writing his or her thoughts and feelings. The use of such a method would, perhaps, save a little teacher time during the school day; however, responding to the students' ideas in writing would necessitate much additional time on the part of the teacher, and responsing to the students' ideas is essential. The acknowledgment of students' thoughts and feelings gives validation to their ideas, and will help establish valuable personal trust in decision making. The most efficient way for a teacher to accomplish this is the personal interview. Writing a response to each child's written interview is very time-consuming, but it does have the advantage of establishing a written record of the interaction. As a teacher of a self-contained class, I seldom have the time to respond in writing, and the personal interview seems most appropriate. The important point is for the student to feel secure about the choice of topic for his or her research. Feeling secure about the topic choice will enable the student to move easily into the next step of the independent study process.

Step 3: Help Students Find a Question or Questions to Research

Once an independent study topic has been selected, helping the student to focus on the problem for study and to determine the questions to be researched is essential. Although determining the questions to be researched is necessary for all students, it is particularly important for the elementary student who is just beginning to learn about research. Developing research questions enables the student to identify the limits of the investigation and to know when enough information, or data, has been gathered.

Each student should develop a proposal for a research project, stating the topic and the specific questions for investigation. A resource box of the topic ideas and research questions might be established. In addition to being useful to students who are having difficulty finding a specific topic of interest, the topic box enables the student to keep track of the direction of the investigation, and to know the limits of the study. A 5 × 8 inch card box works fine and provides a way to save the research questions and proposals from one year to the next.

A beginning researcher, in second grade, designed the following card for his first independent study. It is typical of elementary school–level independent study research proposals.

Topic: Air Pollution
Research Questions:

1. What is air pollution?
2. What causes air pollution?
3. What problems are caused by polluted air?
4. What is being done about air pollution?
5. How is Albuquerque affected by air pollution?

Having the research proposal card helped this student to focus on specific areas of the broad topic, air pollution, and to limit his investigation to specific questions. Because he was a beginning student in independent study, knowing he had gathered enough information and raw data when each of the five questions was answered was important.

An upper elementary student conducting an independent study for the first time developed the following proposal for her study of wolves:

Topic: The Mexican Wolf
Research Questions:

1. What is the lifestyle of the wolf in its natural environment?
2. How does the behavior of the male differ from that of the female?
3. What is the current status of the Mexican Wolf?
4. What is the plan to reintroduce the Mexican Wolf into a natural environment?
5. What are the pros and cons of this plan?
6. How will the reintroduction of the wolf impact the environment?

This research proposal goes beyond gathering background information about the wolf, although that is a necessary part of the initial research. The student has extended her questioning to reflect a current social issue facing environmentalists and endangered species advocates in her state. With such questions, even the elementary researcher can deal with an issue of importance to society.

Reis and Schack repeatedly stress the importance of using how-to books to escalate studies beyond the traditional knowledge-level report. I, too, feel these books have merit. Although they seldom are included in a school library, they can be obtained. A small collection of such resources, along with many books on various topics, would be a well-used addition to any class with gifted students. Meeting with experts in the chosen field of interest is perhaps the best way to acquire the methodology needed for student research. Being able to talk with people who are working in the specific area of the student's research is extremely important. However, at this early stage of question development, students seldom have enough background information on their chosen topic to discuss fluently the area of research.

Discussing with an environmentalist the ways to discover the impact of a wolf reintroduction plan cannot take place unless the student has accurate general information about wolves. Too often teachers direct students to experts before the students have enough background information to be able to question, probe, and process the valuable information available to them. For this reason, I suggest that students keep their research questions in the rewriting stage while they gather needed background information. Then, after initial research, they can talk with the experts, study the how-to books, and develop the methodology necessary to complete the research.

Step 4: Develop a Written Plan

The development of a written plan is essential to keep the student focused on the direction of his or her independent study. Reis and Schack suggest the use of Renzulli and Smith's Management Plan. This is a complex management plan, giving valuable information and direction to the student when it is complete. For very young students, and even older beginning researchers, use of a simplified management contract would be wise (see Figure 14.1). Much of the same information is acquired, but the format is very simple and not at all confusing to the young elementary student. As with the more complex plan suggested by Reis and Schack, this contract should be completed cooperatively by the teacher and the student, and should be modified as new resources are brought to the student's attention.

Step 5: Help Students Locate Multiple Resources and Continue Working on the Topic

After the topic and research questions have been selected, the student should begin to gather information, data, and reference materials. Obtaining essential information for any independent study necessitates having access to material beyond encyclopedic references. A search of the classroom library and magazine files is an important first step in gathering data. Using the school library, public libraries, and the university library should follow. Finding experts on the topic from the general community also is necessary. Developing the means to collect raw data, and beginning the raw data collection, should be accomplished early in the independent study.

Reis and Schack neglect to make suggestions concerning the recording of the collected information; however, this step is important in the development of basic research skills. "Keeping track" of information in a usable manner is necessary as the student gathers, categorizes, analyzes, and evaluates information in a specific field. Too often the beginning researcher is not taught this skill.

As information is gathered, surveys are developed, and raw data are collected, notes must be taken. Some teachers feel it is important, even at the beginning levels of independent study, to develop the skill of taking notes on file cards. Others feel taking notes in a spiral notebook is sufficient. However, the advantage of having note cards that provide one major fact per card, properly categorized and labeled, seems worthwhile when developing the topical outline for use in the student presentation or final product. These cards can be manipulated, organized, and reorganized into the various areas of the outline.

As information is recorded, whatever the method, the teacher must stress that note taking is not copying directly from the source of information. Each student

Independent Study Management Contract

Student Name _____

General Topic of Study _____

Specific Research Questions _____

_____

_____

_____

_____

Brief Description of the Problem to Be Investigated:
(What do I hope to find out?)

Intended Audiences:
(Who would be most interested in my findings? List the group(s) and names/addresses of contact person(s).)

Intended Products and Presentation:
(How will I share the results of my investigation?)

Resource Persons:
(Who are experts that might help my study? List names/addresses.)

Data Collection:
(What type of data will be needed? How will I collect it?)

Presentation:
(When will I present my results? How much time will I need?)

Evaluation:
(What means of evaluation will I use?)

_____   _____

Student Signature   Date

_____

Figure 14.1 Independent Study Management Contract.

should put the ideas into his or her own words. When using note cards, every card should include the following items:

1. A short label to categorize the information it contains
2. The information, in note form, not using complete sentences, except for a necessary direct quotation
3. The source of the information, including the author's last name and page number

For the student to keep track of the references used, he or she should maintain throughout the independent study a bibliography card of each source, or a list of references, personal communications, and the location of needed charts and graphs. Even though the final product will not be a written one, good organization of the gathered information is essential and some of the same skills used in writing a good paper apply.

Students of today have access to more information than any previous generation. To establish valid generalizations, use underlying principles, and transform existing information, the student must have experiences with evaluating ideas, and deciding about relevant and irrelevant facts. Such practice must precede the initial independent study, and might be considered the very beginning of providing methodological assistance to the student.

Step 6: Provide Methodological Assistance

Providing good methodological assistance is probably the weakest link in programs of independent study. Many teachers of the gifted have not acquired the skills themselves, and consequently cannot assist their students. To help students develop life-long independent learning skills and be prepared for our ever-complex future, the "knowledge how" to acquire and make appropriate use of the specific data-gathering tools and investigative techniques is essential. Reis and Schack have covered this topic thoroughly.

Step 7: Help Students Decide Which Question(s) to Answer

After students have focused their interests and become involved with the methodology of their chosen topic area, they should reexamine the questions developed earlier. Often the questions thought to be of importance no longer apply, and additional questions need to be asked. Returning to the original research proposal, evaluating the proposed questions, and restating the questions to be researched are often necessary.

Step 8: Provide Managerial Assistance

I concur with Reis and Schack's tenent that the major purpose of the managerial role is to help the student stay on track and move toward the accomplishment of each intermediate goal. However, Reis and Schack seem to have the teacher carrying the burden of the workload. Although the teacher must be supportive throughout the entire process and facilitate some of the activities, the student must be prepared to assume maximum responsibility for obtaining the needed information.

For example, Reis and Schack suggest that the teacher might set up an interview with a public official. How much more valuable it would be to the student to obtain the necessary skills to arrange the interview. Using role-playing with an old telephone is an easy way to teach students how to make arrangements to meet with public officials, university professors, or other experts in various fields. Once the student is competent on the telephone and has planned the request carefully, even the youngest researcher can request politely to have a meeting with an expert. I have taught second-grade students the appropriate skills to request and obtain appointments with environmental experts and political officials.

An older elementary student, researching urban landscaping problems, arranged a meeting with the mayor during school time. He was able to leave school, use public transportation to arrive at the mayor's office on time, and return after his appointment, well pleased with his success. Assuming the responsibility for making such arrangements is important to students; however, the teacher needs to teach students "how" to accomplish the task.

Students must be well versed in proper interview techniques to meet successfully with an expert in their field of interest. The following suggestions need to be included in the instruction:

1. Have ample background information to discuss your topic.
2. Make appointments well ahead of time.
3. Be prompt and polite.
4. If arrangements for the interview have been made by telephone, correspond about the purpose of your visit and any specific information you might need. This will enable the person who will be interviewed to prepare needed statistics.
5. Prepare three or more open-ended questions to be answered by the expert.
6. Bring a pad and pencil to record responses. Use a tape recorder, if you wish, but request permission of the person being interviewed.
7. Thank the interviewee and leave promptly.

Learning correct methodology also extends to learning to use the copy machine correctly, and having the freedom to use it when needed; being able to obtain materials from libraries; distributing surveys; and the like. If the learning environment for gifted students has been modified to facilitate independence, the student will be able to assume more and more of the responsibility for the research investigations. With proper instruction, even the youngest students can achieve most aspects of information gathering (except those requiring driving). Of course, the teacher continues to play a vital role as supportive advocate, available for idea discussion and planning.

Step 9: Identify Final Products and Audiences

Finding a real and meaningful audience for the final product is necessary to every independent study. This is not always an easy task, but it is one that needs careful consideration by teacher and student. Although beginning research presentations may use the class as an audience, the student and the teacher need to realize that a real problem, when investigated thoroughly, deserves a real audience. Teacher–

student discussions can analyze the area of study and determine potential audiences during the preparation of the management plan or contract. The suggestions can be finalized into firm plans as the final product emerges. The meaningful audience may be a special population of the school, clubs within the school, or special groups within the local community, the state, or the nation. Reis and Schack provide a list of outlet vehicles for student products. Student–teacher discussions may generate additional ideas.

Students who research a real problem can make a significant contribution to society. For example, one sixth-grade student in my class was researching water problems in New Mexico. Refining her interests and research questions narrowed her research to the Jemez Water Project in northern New Mexico. The background information and raw data collected by this young student were excellent. She had researched a societal problem, and then presented her findings to the community most concerned with the problem by means of a town meeting. Her research contributed significantly to the decisions reached by the community. Although a sixth grader, she had made a real contribution to society.

Often the final product takes the form of a presentation to a specific audience. Preparation for a research presentation takes time and skill. Effective visual material (graphs, charts, maps, mounted pictures, time lines, displays, etc.) should be prepared explaining the major points of the research. Development of high-quality visual materials does not come easily to most elementary and middle school students. Teacher-directed lessons concerning layout, design, lettering, and mounting are very important. High-quality visual aids enhance any research presentation, giving clarity to important points. Low-quality, messy, carelessly created visual aids detract from the presentation and cause the audience to question the quality or the depth of the research.

In addition to creating original materials for the visual aids, each student needs to organize the verbal portion of the presentation. The three sections of the presentation (introduction, body, conclusion) must flow smoothly from one to another. The introduction literally introduces the topic to the audience. It should attract the attention of the audience and set the scene for the entire presentation. The research problem should be stated clearly, and in a manner that will hold the attention of the audience. The body is the main section of the research presentation. If the research was conducted thoroughly, and the student is familiar with the information, the body of the presentation is not difficult to organize. The student probably will know more about the topic than will be reported. Telling everything one knows is not necessary. However, selecting those items that seem most interesting and most important for presentation is necessary. In the conclusion of the presentation, one should summarize the important evidence presented in the body, review the major ideas of the research, and answer the specific questions of the research proposal. A good conclusion helps the audience remember the main points of the research. It also helps the student to combine the ideas into one concluding idea or answer to the basic research question. Such synthesis is important.

The following suggestions should be used as the student prepares for the presentation before an audience.

1. Know your material. If you have to read from notes or memorize material, your knowledge of the topic is slight. You need to know your subject so well that you feel as much at home with it as riding your bike.

2. Use an outline to organize your presentation. You might want to jot down key words to keep you on track during the presentation. Using an outline card in this way is not the same as reading from note cards or memorizing a prepared speech.

3. In giving your presentation, you will be either sitting or standing, facing your audience. Undoubtedly, you will be nervous. Do not allow this nervousness to upset you. Nervousness is normal. It means you are "keyed up." Take a deep breath and begin!

4. Look at your audience as you give your presentation. Talk directly to them. Do not look at the floor, ceiling, or tabletop, and do not try to hide behind your notes or display materials!

5. Speak clearly. When giving your presentation, speak in a clear, strong voice, so all can hear you. Speak slowly enough so all can understand you. Pause from time to time to allow an important idea to reach the audience.

6. Organize your presentation so that you tell certain important and interesting things about your research study. Don't try to tell everything you know about the topic. During the questioning period at the end of the conclusion, you will have an opportunity to show how well informed you are on your subject!

7. Practice. After your presentation is organized and ready to go, practice the entire presentation. Give your presentation before an audience at home, several times; work in front of a mirror; share it with your pet turtle; find some way to practice the presentation. Practice enough that you will be relaxed, knowledgeable, and professional before your real audience.

8. Save your notes. They may be valuable to you in later years, as a basis for an essay, a science fair project, or further research!

Independent study communication skills, particularly when dealing with a real audience, require specific instruction and practice. Such instruction often is lacking in the classroom. Teachers would be wise to give students practice in expressing a particular idea in the various forms of media—demonstrative, representational, and symbolic (Atwood, 1974)—to experience the differences and the uses for each. All three media types are important in communicating the results of an independent study to an audience.

Step 10: Offer Encouragement, Praise, and Critical Assistance

Feedback is vital to all creators, from the most novice researcher to the most seasoned professional. Reis and Schack stress the idea underlying the feedback process that almost everything can be improved in varying degrees through revisions, rewriting, and attention to details. This message must be conveyed to students without harsh criticism or discouraging comments. Students need to feel that the teacher is making a genuine attempt to understand and is attending to the student's ideas. Having displayed acceptance and encouragement, the teacher can ask the student to explain, elaborate, and clarify ideas. Through this process of critical thinking about the product, the idea of revisions and improvements can be discussed together. The student should feel the satisfaction of having produced his or her best effort. Helping the student to achieve that best effort is an important role of the teacher.

Step 11: Escalate the Process

To achieve at the highest possible level, with the highest quality of work, each student must be encouraged to reach upward and onward. One should not allow the student researcher to be satisfied with mediocre work. To do so is a disservice to the gifted student. If the student has the necessary tools, if the methodology and the how-to's have been part of the independent study process, the final product should be of the highest quality. If good rapport, including a sense of respect on the part of both teacher and student, has been established, the idea of product escalation will be easier to achieve.

Step 12: Evaluate

Although Reis and Schack discourage the formal grading of products resulting from independent study, public school policies often deem otherwise. Truly, no letter grade, number, or percentage can accurately reflect the comprehensive knowledge, creativity, and task commitment that has been gained through independent study. Nevertheless, grades seem to be part of the requirements of public education as it stands today.

The Student Product Assessment Form (SPAF) shared by Reis and Schack seems to be very appropriate for product evaluation. The research behind the development of the SPAF gives it validity and reliability. The instrument helps evaluate the quality of final products, and gives value to the process of independent research. The process is important; the value of independent study is not limited to the merits of the final product.

Criteria for evaluating the final product and its presentation should be developed by the student and the teacher as part of the preliminary work. Each student should be aware of that criteria during the independent study, and during the preparation for the research presentation. Working jointly with the SPAF, or a teacher–student devised comment sheet, is necessary. Reis and Schack use orientation sessions organized around the SPAF to help students gain an appreciation for the ways in which their work will be evaluated. More information concerning the SPAF and the orientation sessions is needed, but the ideas seem very sound.

All students should use self-evaluative techniques to evaluate their own products and presentations. Students should use the same forms, or the same criteria, as the other evaluators. Students should attempt to match the assessments of others, rather than compare the two perceptions. Differences can be resolved through discussion. Differences in perception might be very apparent when a student presenter feels the main ideas of the research were stressed, whereas the peer evaluator, or the teacher, feels the opposite to be true. A short meeting to discuss the main ideas and their inclusion in the presentation could help the presenter to improve his or her ability to bring the main points of the research into focus. Such a learning situation has a benefit to both the student, who may need to be more specific, and the evaluator, who may have inappropriate expectations.

Peer evaluation is an aspect of independent study evaluation that deserves specific consideration. The student audience can evaluate those presentations and products shared with the class. A simple 5-point rating scale with room for peer comments can be devised easily, based on the previously established evaluation criteria. The peer evaluation form should be developed with the students to include the desirable characteristics of public speaking and the appropriate use of audiovisual materials. Figure 14.2 was developed with upper elementary students as a generic form, for use with all oral presentations. When using this form for independent study peer evaluation, the class discusses, early in the research process, the points to be evaluated, and each student is well aware of the requirements as he or she plans the oral presentation.

Elementary students, especially, benefit from peer evaluations. Receiving input from each member of the audience can be very rewarding. Students should save these peer evaluation forms, using them to improve the quality of future oral presentations. If several peers give a low rating on the labeling of visual aids, for example, the teacher and the student can work together to strengthen the skills of appropriate labeling, lettering, and layout of future visual aids. In addition, the task of completing an evaluation form at the end of each presentation helps keep the student audience "in tune" with the presentation. Appropriate audience behavior and respectful listening skills also need to be discussed and developed within each student.

Students making presentations to an outside audience should develop specific means of evaluating their presentations. Different audiences may tend to evaluate the product or presentation in different ways, depending upon their point of view. However, all audiences will judge the product or the research results by the clarity and efficiency of the presentation. A simulated role-playing situation can be arranged within the class if students are not able to make their research presentations before a real audience, or as a practice session before the real audience presentation. Students should be encouraged to look at the product or the results of the independent study from several viewpoints and to think carefully about the criteria that different audiences may apply in judging it. These criteria might then be used as a guide for the teacher, the student, and other classmates to evaluate the presentation.

The evaluation of each independent study product is extremely important. Feedback gained from the evaluation process will enable the student to think creatively and critically about the independent study product, and to apply the knowledge gained to future work.

CONCLUSION

The strategies developed by Reis and Schack seem very useful to the educator facilitating independent studies. These strategies will result in differentiated products, if used within a learning environment modified especially for the gifted student.

Oral Presentation Peer Evaluation

Student _____

Date _____   Peer Evaluator _____

Topic of Presentation _____

NUMERICAL RATING = 1 (lowest) – 5 (highest)
Please circle one rating for each statement.

MECHANICS

1. Student was well acquainted with topic.   1   2   3   4   5

2. Presentation was well organized.   1   2   3   4   5

3. Main ideas of the research were stressed.   1   2   3   4   5

4. Presentation was directed to the audience.   1   2   3   4   5

5. Notes or topical outline were used appropriately. 1   2   3   4   5

6. Student spoke in a clear, easy to hear, voice.   1   2   3   4   5

7. Presentation included a specific introduction.   1   2   3   4   5

8. Presentation included a defined conclusion.   1   2   3   4   5

9. Conclusion summarized main points of the research. 1   2   3   4   5

10. Student answered questions asked by audience.   1   2   3   4   5

11. Presentation held the interest of the audience. 1   2   3   4   5

12. Audience learned from the presentation.   1   2   3   4   5

AUDIOVISUAL MATERIAL

13. Audio materials were used to enhance main ideas.   N/A   1   2   3   4   5

14. Audio materials clarified important points.   N/A   1   2   3   4   5

15. Audio materials were well planned and well made.   N/A   1   2   3   4   5

16. Visual materials illustrated main ideas.   N/A   1   2   3   4   5

17. Visual materials were used to clarify ideas.   N/A   1   2   3   4   5

18. Visual materials were used throughout
    presentation.   N/A   1   2   3   4   5

19. Visual materials were well labeled.   N/A   1   2   3   4   5

20. Visual materials were readable and clear.   N/A   1   2   3   4   5

Total Points_____

Comments:

Figure 14.2 Sample Peer Evaluation Form.

Several components of Reis and Schack's strategies needed to be expanded, especially for the teacher of beginning researchers, or elementary gifted students. I discussed these areas, based on my experiences working directly with gifted students since 1961. In addition, I shared some practical guidelines for independent study presentations. Pre-independent studies instruction is needed to prepare the student for using the vast quantity of available information, as well as to learn how to collect and make use of raw data.

Reis and Schack seem to be directing educators to provide the instruction and the support needed to develop creative, meaningful contributors to our society. This goal surely emphasizes the importance of providing a means of developing one's full potential as a gifted student.

REFERENCES

Atwood, B. S. (1974). *Building independent learning skills.* Palo Alto, CA: Education Today.

Lethem, S., Osborn, M. & Zmuda, R. (1981). *The four component curriculum — the resource seminar class.* Unpublished paper.

Renzulli, J. S. (1977). *The interest-a-lyzer.* Mansfield Center, CT: Creative Learning Press.

Treffinger, D. J. (1975). Teaching for self-directed learning: A priority for the gifted and talented. *The Gifted Child Quarterly, 19,* 46–59.

Differentiating the Learning Environment for Gifted Students

Shirley W. Schiever

The premise that certain elements are critical to the learning environment is basic to all education. These elements are necessary for students to learn, whether the learning is basic factual information to be memorized or advanced abstract concepts to be formed. The characteristics and needs of gifted students, however, require that modifications be made in their learning environment. In this chapter, I discuss first the critical elements of the general learning environment and then those necessary for the gifted learner. Each element is examined, and examples or explanations are given. The reader will notice an overlapping of ideas at times; because elements of the classroom environment are complex and interrelated, they defy treatment as discrete entities.

CLASSROOM CLIMATE – ALL CLASSROOMS

The tapestry of classroom learning is woven on the frame of classroom climate. The teacher who establishes a structure with known, consistent boundaries allows this tapestry to develop and become rich, varied, and exciting. Such a structure of clearly defined rules and procedures is critical and underlies positive classroom experiences. When discipline is either inconsistent or harsh, when rules are unreasonable or when they vary, when students have freedom without responsibility or no freedom, then intellectual, social, and emotional development are not nurtured. Such a classroom is a sterile place, despised and dreaded by student and teacher alike.

I believe that elements critical to all effective learning environments include the following: (a) psychological, emotional, and physical safety; (b) the valuing of and excitement about ideas and learning; and (c) stimulating and challenging educational experiences. I discuss each of these elements in an attempt to demonstrate the appropriate modifications for classroom environments.

Safety

Safety in the classroom involves the following: (a) respect of the teacher for the students, the students for the teacher, and the students for each other; (b) appreciation of personal, ethnic, and social differences; and (c) fair, consistent, and firm discipline that establishes boundaries allowing freedom within prescribed limits.

Safety is a basic need; students cannot learn effectively when they are worried about being humiliated or physically harmed by the teacher or other students. Students who feel valued as individuals and as part of the class can take intellectual risks; those who know they may be the target of put-downs by either the other students or the teacher are not likely to take the risk of offering a new idea or adding to an existing one. Teachers can build a supportive environment by modeling acceptance of individual differences and contributions, even unusual ones; and by making clear that students are expected to be accepting of each other's thoughts, feelings, and opinions. Acceptable classroom behavior cannot include hurting other people, either their feelings or their bodies. The ''put-down'' is the basic fare of the television sitcom; students benefit by an awareness of how pervasive the practice is and how destructive of good thinking and positive feelings.

Another element of the safe environment is the acceptance and valuing of ethnic and cultural differences. As members of an increasingly multiethnic and multicultural society, students must learn that such differences are neither right nor wrong, but merely differences. Furthermore, they must come to understand the strengths of various cultures, and what each of us can learn from other cultures. From such understanding, appreciation will develop.

Assisting students in learning how to handle conflicts also will contribute to their psychological safety. Teachers should hold guided discussions of conflict situations similar to those experienced by students (e.g., bullying, name calling, exclusion by a clique, or destruction of personal property). Allowing students to explore the varied feelings of those involved in such conflicts and possible alternative actions and resulting consequences will help students to develop processes to deal with such situations when they arise. These coping skills may be especially valuable in light of the fact that conflicts on television and in many homes are responded to with physical force. Students must understand that they are surrounded by choices and that just as *no action* is a choice, so is the *type* of action taken.

Most people who become teachers like children. They believe they know how to relate to young people, and to convey their care and concern to students. However, my observation is that at times teachers unknowingly behave in ways that humiliate children and devalue their feelings. Remarks such as, ''Do you mean to tell me that a big boy (or a smart girl) like *you* doesn't know . . . ?'' humiliate the student. The teacher may forget the remark immediately, or consider it as teasing; the student may feel like a hopeless person and an outcast for the rest of the day . . . or longer.

Discipline is the invisible glue that bonds a group and allows it to develop a group personality. Discipline also contributes to an environment that nurtures unique personalities within the group. Teachers who establish a structure that allows discipline to remain invisible are able to channel their own energy and that of the students for productive thinking and learning. When students discover that rules and boundaries change without apparent reason or in response to whining or other inappropriate behavior, the classroom unit will disintegrate. Students will expend their energies on testing the limits, and teachers will spend their energy on attempting to gain control. Rules can be flexible, but an underlying consistency and logic must accompany the flexibility. For example, a classroom rule that students may move about the room in appropriate ways and at appropriate times is a flexible rule. Consistent enforcement of the rule prohibits running at any time, requires limited movement during seatwork time, and allows freedom of movement when students are using learning centers or engaged in other activities requiring free movement. Through consistent enforcement, students will learn to recognize and accept the inevitable consequences of inappropriate behavior.

Valuing of and Excitement with Learning

Students spend a significant portion of their time in a classroom. If this time is well spent, they see value in what they are doing and its relevance to real life. The curriculum must include the required content and processes, and teachers must establish the value of what is taught and its link or relationship to students' lives. Equally important, however, is the value teachers place on what is to be taught and the excitement they feel about learning and the learning process.

Teachers who are excited about learning—both their own and that of the students—convey this excitement in many ways, some rather subtle. Open interest in student progress and joy when a skill is mastered or a concept formed are obvious markers of a teacher's level of intellectual excitement. A less obvious but no less accurate indication of the value placed on learning is how efficiently classroom time is managed. Teachers who truly believe that an incredible number of exciting and worthwhile learning experiences should be provided for students reflect this belief by using classroom management techniques that allow the nitty-gritty, housekeeping tasks to be accomplished quickly and with as little disruption of the instructional routine as possible. I am not saying that such a person is inflexible, merely that he or she considers contact time with students as extremely valuable, a time when skills are learned and concepts are formed and, therefore, a time that is to be guarded jealously. Students always know when their teacher really believes that learning is exciting. Teachers' overt behaviors, such as eye contact, facial expression, and active listening, in addition to their body language, informal remarks, and structure of each class period and each day, communicate to students whether learning is seen as an exciting endeavor. The teacher's attitude can communicate that class time is too valuable to be wasted—by anyone.

Stimulating and Challenging Educational Experiences

Libraries contain an abundance of books, journal articles, and magazines focusing on curriculum. Many teachers attempt to make school learning experiences appropriate and interesting, as well as relevant to the student and to district requirements. Administrators, school boards, and parents express concern about students not only learning the basics, but becoming life-long learners. Nevertheless, the majority of students express varying degrees of disdain, boredom, and/or bare tolerance of the time they must spend in school (Goodlad, 1984; National Commission on Excellence in Education, 1983). Some observations and possible remedies follow.

Generally speaking, textbooks are deadly dull. They can be read and understood by the ''average'' student at a given grade level, and many are beautiful, with colorful and eye-catching illustrations and attractive displays and format. However, in most cases, the content is shallow and uninteresting, and the suggested activities and teacher questions are at the rote memory level. Not only is no real thinking required, but these texts contain very little to think about!

Textbooks are state- and district-adopted, and the teacher is accountable for teaching the concepts presented and skills identified therein, so the dilemma is difficult and complex. Teachers *can* teach the required skills and content in a stimulating and challenging way. The following are suggestions of ways to do this:

1. Most content-area textbooks contain lists of the important concepts covered. Concentrate on these concepts, and find ways to teach the concepts through (a) providing hands-on experiences and activities, (b) relating everyday experiences from the students' lives to the concept, or (c) using audiovisual materials and/or resource people from the community. For example, to develop the concept of social structure, elementary curriculum can include setting up and observing an ant farm; films on bees, fish, birds, and mammals that live in groups; shared experiences of differing family structures; and speakers on varied aspects of the local community structure. Middle school and high school students might investigate and/or visit and observe social agencies in action, follow a local trial from beginning to end, listen to guest speakers on related topics, and eventually consider differing state and national social systems and structures. The thread of concrete experiences and relevancy can run throughout curriculum, from kindergarten through high school.

2. Capitalize on every experience. For example, when planning a field trip, be sure that students understand what the purpose of the outing is and *what they are responsible for learning* from the trip. At certain ages, students might be required to take notes on specified aspects of the trip, to record observations, and/or to make evaluations of the experience or what was observed. For example, students making a trip to a regional science fair should be required to (a) observe landmarks, terrain, or notable architectural features en route to the fair; (b) describe and/or draw or diagram and evaluate three to five of the exhibits; and (c) make a written overall evaluation of the field trip as an educational experience. Small booklets with lined and unlined paper within can be assembled easily as a travelogue. Language arts skill development the following week could center on the field trip, and spelling words might be related to the concept and experience. Using the above example,

words such as *observation, hypothesis, photosynthesis,* or *campus* (if the fair had been held on a high school or university campus) might be included. If a field trip, a speaker, and a film all focus on a particular concept, through a discussion, a teacher can pull together the information and examine similarities and differences or conflicting data. For example, a study of local environmental problems might include a variety of audiovisual aids and written material, as well as speakers who hold different views of solutions or key issues. The class might refer to textbooks to see how information presented there compares with other sources. As a consummating activity, the teacher could lead the students in an interpretation of data discussion (Schiever, 1991), wherein causes and/or effects of (differing) data are inferred, conclusions drawn, and generalizations made.

3. Encourage every student in the classroom to stretch his or her cognitive abilities every day. One way to do this is to incorporate questioning techniques that encourage thinking at the higher cognitive levels. Ten generic principles of questioning can be applied to every content area, classroom and playground social problem or situation, and informal interaction between teachers and students. Students soon begin to use the modeled questions, and the effect is exponential. The 10 principles follow:

Written or Oral Questions

1. Questions are focused to give direction to the responses and to the discussion as a whole. The focus should lead to the predetermined purpose of the discussion or written exercise. For example, ''What happened on our field trip yesterday?'' is not sufficiently focused. A more focused question is, ''What examples of positive or potentially harmful uses of the environment did you observe on our field trip yesterday?''

2. Questions are open ended. Open questions have no predetermined ''right'' answer and they cannot be answered by ''yes'' or ''no.'' Whereas closed questions may be useful in establishing the existence of a factual knowledge base, they do not require higher level thinking. Open-ended question stems include the following: ''In what ways . . . ?'' ''How are these similar/ different . . . ?'' ''What if . . . ?'' ''What pattern do you see . . . ?'' and ''What are the causes/effects of . . . ?''

3. Responses require the *use,* or processing, of information. Focused, open-ended questions (e.g.,''Based on our discussion or unit of study, what do you believe is the most important effect of slavery?'') require students to process information.

4. Proof or reasoning questions (''Why do you say . . . ?'' or ''What evidence do you have . . . ?'') are asked when students make inferences, conclusions, or generalizations, or when they give opinions. When asked orally, such questions must be asked in a nonthreatening manner.

Discussion—Oral Questions

5. Wait time is allowed before the focus question is repeated. If students are to process information, time must be allowed for this processing. Waiting even 3 to 5 seconds for a response or between responses increases the

number and level of responses and decreases discipline problems (Rowe, 1974). Students who are thinking about the discussion topic are not distracting other students or acting out.

6. Discussion is paced appropriately. Pacing includes wait time, but an additional factor is "lifting" the discussion to a higher level when a given level has been explored sufficiently. A discussion that is paced too rapidly is as lethal to student attention and participation as one that is paced too slowly. Teachers must be sensitive to student responses and behavior to pace discussions effectively.

7. Individual student responses are accepted *without comment by the teacher.* If the response is incorrect or irrelevant, the other students are likely to catch the error and comment; both the original contributor and the student who sees a flaw should be asked for proof or reasoning when this happens. Accepting good ideas without comment is difficult for teachers, who many times have been trained to give lavish positive reinforcement. Pronouncing an idea as "good" or "fantastic" reinforces the concept that the teacher has the official and last word on what is good (right) and what is not. This practice also may act as a constricting force on responses. After hearing someone else's idea praised, students may feel that their own idea would not be so highly valued (Carin & Sund, 1978) or that the answer being sought has been given. Rewarding the entire group for collective effort, ideas, and thinking fosters camaraderie and produces no negative side effects. Individuals receive reinforcement by having their ideas listened to by the teacher and responded to and expanded on by the other students.

8. Student responses should not be repeated by the teacher. At least two things may happen when the teacher consistently repeats everything the students say: The students can become lazy listeners, and the teacher may, without meaning to, rephrase and/or edit student responses. In the latter case, ideas are then filtered through the teacher's frame of reference and perceptions rather than the students'. For example, if a student were to respond, "people who don't work," and the teacher were to say, "people who are lazy," the teacher's interpretation of the phrase "don't work" has been interjected. In such an instance, the student may have been thinking of persons who are unemployed, or unemployable due to lack of skills or a handicapping condition. Most students will not correct a teacher who has misinterpreted their meaning, but they are less likely to offer ideas when they know everything will be reframed by the teacher.

9. The teacher should seek a variety of ideas and encourage students to interact with and build on each other's ideas. Seeking a variety of ideas requires eliciting negative and positive aspects of situations and differing viewpoints or types of data. Students learn from each other, and encouraging student interaction allows them the opportunity to learn content from each other, as well as to discover each other's thinking processes. For example, in a discussion focusing on the effects of the use of disposable products (e.g., disposable soft drink containers), the teacher should seek both positive and

negative effects and encourage student comments such as "Susie said they're more sanitary, but they also can cause more disease, because when a plastic soda bottle is thrown out, some soda might stay in there and germs can grow and if people pick it up, they might get sick."

10. The teacher, as facilitator of a discussion designed to develop higher levels of thinking, should seek clarification or extension of student responses as needed. When students use a term that may be open to differing interpretations or is not generally known, they should be asked to explain what the term means or to give an example of the phenomenon indicated by the term. For example, if a student were to use a term such as *high technology,* the teacher should ask what is meant by the term or request an example (e.g., of how high technology causes pollution). When the level of a student response offers the possibility of lifting the discussion or expanding its scope, the teacher should be aware of and act on the opportunity.

Creating stimulating and challenging educational experiences requires that the teacher spend extra time and effort and exercise some creativity. Many ways to stimulate and challenge are possible; three have been suggested. Teachers may focus on concepts, capitalize on experiences, and use specified questioning techniques; or they may devise other techniques, congruent with their teaching style and the learning styles of their students.

The elements discussed above—psychological, emotional, and physical safety; the valuing of, and excitement about, ideas and learning; and stimulating and challenging educational experiences—should be part of every student's school experience. The characteristics of the gifted student, by definition, dictate learning needs that differ significantly from those of most students. Therefore, the learning environment requires modifications to allow these needs to be met.

LEARNING ENVIRONMENT MODIFICATIONS
FOR THE GIFTED LEARNER

All human characteristics, from intellectual abilities to personality traits, can be seen as occurring in individuals somewhere on a continuum that ranges from little potential or capacity to highly developed ability in the given characteristic. For example, the ability and desire for self-direction, while very strong in many gifted students, is not necessarily a characteristic of *all* students, which poses a problem for the classroom teacher. The gifted students need to be encouraged to be self-directed and taught the requisite skills, whereas other students may feel far more comfortable and learn more efficiently in a teacher-directed atmosphere. Managing these discrepancies poses a significant challenge to the teacher.

Providing an appropriate learning environment for the gifted student within the regular classroom requires the equivalent of a juggling act—maintaining and managing the curriculum and environment for a wide variety of needs and abilities. Based on the characteristics of gifted students, Maker (1982a) listed six modifications of the learning environment necessary for the gifted learner: (a) student centered, (b) encouraging of independence, (c) open, (d) accepting, (e) complex, and (f) offering high mobility. Each of these is discussed in light of its implementation in the regular classroom.

The Student-Centered Classroom

The student-centered classroom is the opposite of the teacher-centered class. In student-centered classrooms, students' ideas are valued and initiative is encouraged; teachers view themselves as "guides on the side," rather than dispensers of knowledge. Students are in the process of learning to manage their own learning, handle classroom conflicts, make and enforce necessary rules, and create bulletin boards and other displays that reflect their interests and skills.

To develop a student-centered classroom, the teacher needs to convey, in a variety of ways, the importance of the students' ideas and interests. Whole class or small group discussions incorporating the principles given above communicate the value placed on these ideas and interests and encourage student-to-student interactions. Students can be asked for input on ways to extend or implement the required curriculum, the organization of class activities such as field trips or parties, designing and putting up bulletin board displays, and the formation of a fair set of rules governing certain student activities (e.g., the use of athletic equipment). In essence, the classroom needs to become a reflection of the personalities, interests, and abilities of the students rather than the teacher. Because all students benefit from some degree of student centeredness, this dimension is not difficult to implement in the regular classroom. The challenge lies in providing the appropriate degree of student centeredness for a wide variety of needs.

The Classroom that Encourages Independence

All students should develop independence; gifted students have a need, felt or unfelt, to become independent life-long learners and producers of knowledge. Additionally, the gifted have the capacity to become self-directed in many aspects of their lives; the school experience should make possible and develop this capacity.

In the classroom, the teacher can develop independence by giving the students options or choices and providing the structure necessary to support these options or choices. For example, the teacher might give to the whole class a brief overview of the requirements for a unit of study in a given content area. He or she could outline the necessary knowledge base and skills, the material to be covered in class, the way it will be covered, and some possible extensions or expansions that individuals or small groups of students might undertake. The class should be asked for more ideas for extensions, and a time set when the teacher "would like to meet" with the gifted students *and anyone else who is interested in an extended study of this topic.* When the small group meets, the discussion should center on helping students choose topics for further investigation that will be interesting and/or useful to them. Further time should be spent discussing how individuals or small groups might evaluate their work, and what and how information will be shared with the entire class. The teacher then needs to schedule student conferences to draw up contracts that specify the student(s) involved, learning objectives, a time line, and an evaluation procedure and criteria for evaluation, as well as how the information will be shared and with whom. Less teacher time is required for student conferences when pairs or groups of students make contracts together. Requiring a parent's or guardian's signature on the contract as well as the student's may open up resources, as well as communicate to the parent part of what is happening at school.

The advantages of taking (or making) precious classroom time to initiate and follow up on this procedure accrue to both the gifted and the nongifted learners. All students are being offered an extension of the basic curriculum, either through direct participation or through the sharing process. Furthermore, a student who has a consuming interest in a particular topic but who otherwise is an average or below-average student, may have the opportunity of working with one or more gifted students and not only learning from them, but *teaching* them as well. Sharing this information with others may be the first experience for such a student in ''shining'' for others.

Possible problems of such a plan include how to handle gifted but unmotivated students who prefer to do very well on what is required but not to stretch their abilities. Perhaps in such a case the teacher could require that students undertake a minimal number of extra projects, in their strongest areas, encouraging (or requiring, if necessary) a gradual increase in the number and the scope of the projects, so the student is not only developing independence but experiencing intellectual challenges.

Encouraging independence seems deceptively easy, because all students should be growing more independent daily. The difficulty for the classroom teacher lies in the heterogeneity of the group. Levels of, and the capacity for, independence vary significantly within specific groups. The teacher must be aware not only of the present level of self-sufficiency skills, but also of the need for systematic opportunities for growth. Two models that help teachers to assess and develop independence in students are Treffinger's Self-Directed Learning Model (Maker, 1982b) and Betts's Autonomous Learner Model (Betts, 1985).

The Open Classroom

The learning needs and characteristics of most gifted students require an open classroom, one that is psychologically and physically open to a variety of ideas, materials, problems, people, viewpoints, and resources. The difference between an open and a closed classroom is the extent to which restrictions affect the environment (Maker, 1982a); that is, an open classroom will have the fewest possible restrictions on ideas, materials, problems, and topics allowed in the classroom.

Creating a classroom that is open enough to allow for maximum development of the gifted yet structured enough to provide direction and a level of comfort for the other students is indeed a challenge. The classroom structure must be firm but flexible, with ingress and egress of varied resources and materials, without disrupting the basic curriculum. Encouraging all students to develop an appropriate level of independence and individualizing learning experiences help to make such a structure workable. However, classroom time restrictions may seem insurmountable. How can time be allotted for enriching activities, when some students need every moment of the school day to work on basic skills? The teacher has to make a difficult professional decision and weigh each experience in terms of its value to the class as a whole and the amount of time required.

The other aspect of openness, allowing students to go outside the classroom for learning, also presents a dilemma. Some students may be motivated to complete regular classroom work if sorties into the outside world for research and varied experience are held as rewards for completing assignments. However, the gifted underachiever or procrastinator may miss many relevant, interesting, and motivating experiences, and the slower students may begin to resent the gifted students and the whole system. Again, teachers must make a professional appraisal of a complex situation and act accordingly.

One step the teacher can take that presents few foreseeable complications is to incorporate open-ended questions into every aspect of the students' experience, and to include a number of open-ended learning experiences for all students. For example, the question, "Why do we have to have laws?" could lead to an (open-ended) investigation of school, organization, and community rules and laws. Students might interview school personnel, other students, leaders of youth groups, and community leaders to gather data on the reasons for and evolution of rules and laws. The activity is open ended because, although the teacher knows the purpose of the investigations and discussions that will ensue, the end result, or group conclusions and/or generalizations, is not known. The students who are not gifted may not be as comfortable as the gifted with open-endedness, and may not develop the concepts to as great a depth, but the experience will be beneficial for them without leaving a residue of resentment or negative feelings.

The teacher's attitude is the overriding factor in the openness of the classroom. If teachers are open to new experiences for themselves as well as for the students, are flexible and accepting of student differences in abilities and learning styles, and are determined that the classroom shall be as open as appropriate for students, the classroom will be supportive of the gifted students'—and all students'—needs. Teachers who are open to new experiences will allow both sides of controversial issues to be aired in their classrooms, and may invite speakers to address the pros and cons of such issues as organ transplants or extraordinary life-saving measures. For younger students, local issues, such as the environmental impact of a proposed industry, can be explored in breadth and depth. Teachers who invite open discussion of varying views of such issues provide a model of personal and professional openness for their students, as well as the opportunity for provocative and possibly contradictory information to be processed.

The Accepting Classroom

Maker (1982a) defined acceptance as the absence of judgment and listed three elements as important in the accepting dimension of classroom climate: attempting to understand, timing, and evaluation rather than judgment. These three elements are related, but each reflects a somewhat different emphasis. Each is considered in the context of the regular classroom.

Attempting to understand requires a genuine attempt to understand the students' attitudes, values, feelings, and beliefs. Teachers must shed stereotypical views and accept differences in ability, culture, and ethnicity. The regular classroom frequently encompasses an extremely wide range of ability levels, as well as representatives from a variety of cultural and ethnic groups. What teachers may need to work on more intensely than their own acceptance of differences is the *students'* acceptance and respect for these differences. For example, I remember a sixth-grade class that consisted of a variety of ethnic and cultural groups, but only one Asian student. The other boys liked Hop Sing (not his real name) and included him in their activities, but called him "Chink." When I spoke to the leader of the dominant group of boys, he protested Hop Sing "didn't mind" the name and knew they were only kidding. Nevertheless, I outlawed the use of the term and began a series of stories, filmstrips, films, and ensuing discussions on individual, ethnic, and cultural differences. One purpose of the activities was to explore affective issues, such as how it feels to be different, to be called a name, to be part of a group, to call someone a name, and so on. Gradually, the class members began to show more respect for each other, and name calling, ridicule, and put-downs decreased dramatically. Modeling acceptance is important, and class discussions of issues, feelings, and attitudes related to differences will help students to focus more on commonalities than on differences.

The second element of the accepting classroom, timing, refers to *when* evaluations are made. Adults have their agendas and schedules to meet, and therefore frequently evaluate a student before the student feels ready. This premature evaluation may occur when a single idea is pronounced as impractical, or when a report must be evaluated before semester grades can be determined. Students need to understand that times exist when judgment will and should be deferred and other instances when evaluation must occur in conjunction with an external time limit. The evaluation of reports or other grade-related projects usually is controlled by quarterly or semester schedules. Students might agree to complete a specified number of steps before the end of the grading period and help develop criteria by which the unfinished project can be evaluated fairly, so the teacher can meet the necessary deadlines, without alienating students or discouraging them so the project is never finished.

Evaluation, the third element of the accepting classroom, is a constructive exercise, an assessment of strengths and weaknesses and suggestions for improvement. Koberg and Bagnall (1976) offered these steps for constructive criticism (evaluation): (a) Begin with two positive reinforcements: "Your choice of topic is unique—I learned from your project!" "This report is well organized." (b) Insert your criticism: "You didn't use as many resources as we had agreed on—the depth is disappointing.'' (c) Add one more positive reinforcement: ''You always have so many good ideas.'' (d) Finish with a ray of hope: ''When you plan your next project, I would be happy to help you develop a daily time line so you will have time to fulfill your agreement.''

Using these steps in the regular classroom is beneficial for all students; the teacher need only remember to approach evaluation in this way. Instead of the paper's ''bleeding'' with red marks and the resulting discouragement, students will feel that improvement is possible and the teacher is on their side. Evaluation should make students feel that they are part of a team that is concerned with planning their education and that skills and content can be mastered.

Complexity of the Classroom Environment

Complexity includes the physical environment and the tasks students perform, and is a difficult modification to make in the regular classroom. Adding a variety of stimuli is beneficial for the gifted students, but may prohibit many other students from concentrating on the task at hand. A simple classroom environment, however, may be detrimental to the gifted. The teacher is faced with difficult choices.

One way to provide for differing student needs is to have a corner or nook of the classroom that is somewhat separate from the rest of the room where stimulating, complex materials and objects are kept. Clear and consistent rules about when the nook may be used or inhabited by students must be established, and all the teacher's creativity will be called into play in defining or leading the students to define these rules.

In some schools, the library may be a resource room with a skillful librarian available, as well as a variety of materials and challenges. In such a case, teachers can make arrangements for gifted students to spend time in this complex environment. The disadvantages inherent in this arrangement are that some students who are not identified as gifted might profit from exposure to the complexity, and the gifted students will see the complex materials and experiences as something separate from their classroom experiences. Neither of these suggestions (a nook or a provision for library time) allows for the degree of complexity gifted students need, but they both offer ways of providing greater complexity than exists in most classrooms.

Classroom Mobility

Classroom mobility is the amount of movement allowed and encouraged by the teacher. This movement is physiological, with consideration of large and small muscle use; physical, with elements of movement in and out of the classroom; and psychological, with students being grouped in different ways for various reasons and purposes.

The gifted student from the regular classroom may go to a different class for math, reading, or other content area classes. This movement allows for the development of skills at a higher level than the age-grade, as well as interaction with other students with advanced knowledge and skills and, sometimes, a teacher with a greater depth of knowledge in a particular content area. The disadvantages are the scheduling required, the flexibility that is inevitably lost, and the possible loss of involvement by the classroom teacher with the student's progress in the particular content area.

When teachers group students for activities, the groups should be flexible. Group membership should be sometimes on the basis of ability, sometimes interest, and sometimes purposely to include a variety of strengths and weaknesses. From such flexible grouping, the gifted may have opportunities to interact with other bright students, with others of varying abilities but similar interests, and with those who will allow the gifted student to develop and exercise organizational and leadership skills. All students will benefit from being in a variety of groups, and from discovering that everyone has strengths and weaknesses and can contribute to group effectiveness.

Ideally, the gifted student should be able to move from the classroom to the community as needed for investigations and other experiences. The regular classroom lends itself to allowing the gifted students to conduct research within the school, but not the entire community. Students may make surveys in other classes or in the school at large, or they may use staff and student body as resources for other investigations. Mobility outside the school is usually restricted to those activities that may be appropriate for an entire group or to experiences provided by parents.

Some types of mobility are far easier to accomplish in the regular classroom than others. Flexible grouping and activities providing movement within the classroom are simple to implement; community investigation might be impossible. The teacher should be aware of the need, however, and use existing situations and opportunities that develop to provide mobility for the gifted student.

CONCLUSION

Earlier in this chapter, a comparison was drawn between a juggler and the regular classroom teacher. Even the brief consideration herein of the daily concerns and challenges teachers face in trying to meet the needs of their students confirms the aptness of the juggler analogy. Gallagher (1975) stated that teaching gifted students must become less of an art and more of a science, and I agree. However, I am struck by the art required to balance and deliver what science, or research, prescribes. Educational research has resulted in an increased body of knowledge, the identification of more subcategories of students, and recommended teaching strategies. Furthermore, mainstreaming students with mental handicaps to provide the least restrictive learning environment increases the range of abilities and needs, and therefore the teaching demands, in the regular classroom. Each forward movement seems to add another element to an already prodigious list of elements with which the teacher is dealing, and each addition is exponential in its effects on and implications for classroom planning. In view of this complexity, I suggest that the effective classroom teacher is a person who has mastered the art *and* the science of teaching. The science of teaching is choosing what is to be taught and deciding how it will be taught; the art is being able to juggle all the elements.

REFERENCES

Betts, G. T. (1985). *Autonomous learner model.* Greeley, CO: Autonomous Learning Publications and Specialists.

Carin, A., & Sund, R. B. (1978). *Creative questioning and sensitive listening techniques.* Columbus, OH: Merrill.

Gallagher, J. J. (1975). *Teaching the gifted child* (2nd ed.). Boston: Allyn & Bacon.

Goodlad, J. I. (1984). *A place called school.* New York: McGraw-Hill.

Koberg, D., & Bagnall, J. (1976). *The universal traveler.* Los Altos, CA: William Kaufmann.

Maker, C. J. (1982a). *Curriculum development for the gifted.* Austin, TX: PRO-ED.

Maker, C. J. (1982b). *Teaching models in education of the gifted.* Austin, TX: PRO-ED.

National Commission on Excellence in Education. (1983). *A nation at risk: The imperative for educational reform.* Washington, DC: U.S. Government Printing Office.

Rowe, M. B. (1974). Relation of wait-time and rewards to the development of language, logic, and fact control: Part I. Wait time. *Journal of Research and Science Teaching, 11,* 81–94.

Schiever, S. W. (1991). *A comprehensive guide to teaching thinking.* Boston: Allyn and Bacon.

16

Creating and Maintaining a Responsive Environment for Gifted Students

Dorothy A. Sisk

During the past few years, educators have gained new insights into the nature of giftedness, and teachers have been encouraged to supplement their knowledge by learning the underlying reasons why differentiated learning is required for gifted students. However, societal expectations have not always been conducive to program planning and development for gifted students. A number of false assumptions about gifted students have been exposed only recently. These assumptions include many myths: Gifted students will somehow experience success on their own; they are not exceptional students and do not require special educational programs and services; they already receive sufficient extra attention to their needs; and if education does address their needs, gifted students will form an elitist group. The current notion that the development of the unique qualities in all learners should be encouraged, concentrating on their subsequent responsibility to all of society, is reflected in the previous chapter in Schiever's approach to differentiating the learning environment for gifted students by first identifying what is necessary for all classrooms to become more effective.

The common elements that Schiever identifies as critical to psychological, emotional, and physical safety are addressed by Abraham H. Maslow (1954) in *Motivation and Personality* (see Figure 16.1). He listed five categories of basic needs that should be considered when planning and implementing programs for all students. Maslow identified physiological needs or drives and stated that these needs are to be met before the learner is capable of meeting or motivated to meet other needs. As the general profile of today's student continues to change, with greater numbers of our youngsters growing up in single-family homes, living below the poverty level of economic standards, and coming from different cultures, this basic need becomes crucial to good education.

Maslow listed safety needs as the need for security, stability, dependency, protection; and freedom from fear, anxiety, and chaos as his second level of basic needs.

Self-Actualization of Higher Abilities

↑

Self-Esteem and Competence

|

Belonging

|

Security

|

Physical

Figure 16.1 Maslow's Hierarchy of Needs.

Advanced cognitive ability notwithstanding, gifted students also have a preference for a safe, orderly, predictable, and organized environment, as noted by Schiever. The next level that Maslow identified is belongingness and love needs. He stated that all learners possess a basic hunger for positive affective relationships with others. Again, this need is crucial to gifted students who may feel alienated from others because of their unique differences. Gifted students also have a strong desire to rise above their feelings of aloneness, strangeness, and loneliness. One way in which their learning environment can be modified is to provide supportive peers with whom they can experience healthy social and emotional growth.

Maslow listed esteem needs next and stated that all students have a desire to experience a firmly based and stable evaluation of themselves, for self-respect and self-esteem. This basic need for esteem includes a desire for achievement, for feeling adequate, and for mastery of and competence in educational experiences. Included in Maslow's esteem needs for gifted students would be the need for independence and the need to experience freedom of growth in learning experiences. Maslow reminded us that satisfaction of the esteem needs produces feelings of self-confidence, self-worth, a sense of one's personal strength, and capability and adequacy to become useful and necessary in today's society.

Self-actualization is the last level of Maslow's hierarchy, and the need for self-actualization is manifested in students' desires to find peace with themselves. This last stage is essential for gifted students in that they need to experience the fulfillment of their potential and to feel that they have attained their aspirations.

Schiever lists the valuing of and excitement about ideas and learning as a need for all students. This need was discussed by Cox, Daniel, and Boston (1985) in the final report of the national study on giftedness conducted by the Richardson Foundation in Fort Worth, Texas, and was reflected in their recommendation that excellence be rewarded in the schools. With so many youngsters coming from homes and environments that do not reward excellence or reflect excitement about ideas and learning, the role of the teacher as a model becomes significant. Intellectual excitement can be brought about for all youngsters by being given encouragement and opportunities to question, to experience freedom to experiment and freedom to reflect, and to develop complex and intense thinking. This intellectual excitement can be intensified further through providing supportive experts, peers, and professionals. I agree with this need and add the need for a supportive environment. This type of environment includes opportunities to identify real problems and to find solutions, as well as to experience complex levels of feelings.

The last characteristic common to all students' learning needs for classroom climate identified by Schiever is providing stimulating and challenging educational experiences. Again, I would like to see all students receive more opportunities to become independent learners and thinkers, and one way to accomplish this is for teachers to be provided more freedom. Teachers need freedom to develop personalized strategies for learning in their students. Coupled with this need is the need for teachers to be encouraged to provide students with the freedom to pursue areas of personal interest. Teacher freedom requires administrators who will encourage teachers to go beyond the standardized curriculum.

For years, as a classroom teacher and teacher trainer, I have advocated for many of the basic notions and strategies that have been identified as appropriate for gifted students to be applicable and effective for *all* students. Schiever makes this point quite well.

The questioning techniques that Schiever identifies certainly would encourage thinking at the higher cognitive levels. However, teachers of gifted students need to go beyond the basic thinking skills, such as observation, correspondence, classification, and seriation, to what can be called integrated thinking skills (Popp, Robinson, & Robinson, 1974), which include (a) logical multiplication, (b) compensatory thinking, (c) proportional thinking, (d) correlational thinking, and (e) probabilistic thinking. Thinking skills for gifted students are differentiated in that they call for more complexity of thinking. Gifted students need to be encouraged to learn more sophisticated organizers and to apply these to specialized models of thinking, such as inquiry models, problem-solving models, and decision-making models.

Basic thinking skills include *observation* as the ability to use all of the senses to identify the characteristics of objects or events; *correspondence* as the skill of matching objects or events or groups of objects or events (at this level, students determine whether two sets are equivalent by one-to-one matching and perhaps constructing proportional sets through one-to-many correspondence); *classification* as the placing of objects or events into groups on the basis of similarities; and *seriation* as the ordering of objects and events on the basis of differences in some characteristic (this procedure occurs when students are given a group of objects and are to seriate them along one dimension, then reseriate them along other dimensions). Gifted students, however, are capable of operating at higher levels of thinking, such as the integrated thinking skills listed above.

Logical multiplication involves treating objects or events in terms of two dimensions at the same time, such as cross-classification and *compensatory thinking,* which includes dealing with the notion of equilibrium and changes in equilibrium. When gifted students are given an operation that upsets equilibrium in a system, they can restore equilibrium by reversing the process or performing the same operation to another part of the system or by performing a different operation having an effect opposite and equal to the initial operation.

Proportional thinking is thinking that involves determining the magnitudes of groups in relation to each other. Proportional thinking also encourages gifted students to deal with such complex notions as velocity, percentage, interest, discount, and commission.

Another type of thinking that gifted students need to master is *correlational thinking,* which helps them to make allowances for cases that deviate from what is expected to be regular or normal. In using correlational thinking, changes in one variable are related to changes in another variable. Correlational thinking involves identifying a relationship when it exists, indicating the direction of the relationship (whether it is positive or negative), and indicating the strength of the relationship.

Finally, gifted students can profit from *probabilistic thinking,* in which they determine the likelihood of a given event's occurring again. Probability involves determining the proportion of successful events and nonsuccessful events. This type of thinking can become an introductory device to more traditional treatment of probability in the study of statistics.

THINKING MODELS

Basic Inquiry Model

Use of three generic models that interact with the questioning skills proposed would help provide the challenging learning environment required by gifted students. These models are the basic inquiry model, the basic decision-making model, and the basic problem-solving model (see Figure 16.2).

In the basic inquiry model, the gifted student is provided a wide array of exploratory activities, encouraged to pose a suitable question that can be studied and researched, directed to generate a range of alternatives that might answer the question, and instructed to collect information on each alternative. At this point, the gifted student can pose a conclusion based on the accumulated information about which alternative provides the best solution. The student decides if the conclusion adequately answers the leading questions, and then organizes a clear expression and presentation of the conclusion. Finally, the student assesses the appropriateness of the conclusion.

Basic Problem-Solving Model

In the basic problem-solving model, the gifted student identifies a problem or deficiency in a situation. Then the student formulates a question that can help clarify the issue. The student generates a range of reasonable alternatives to solve the problem, collects information on each alternative, and arrives at a conclusion based

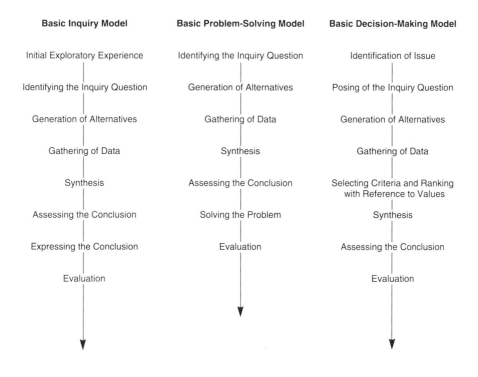

Figure 16.2 Three Models of Thinking.

on the information that represents the best answer. Then the student decides whether the conclusion adequately answers the original question and solves the problem. The final step is the actual solving of the problem and deciding if the solution is appropriate.

Basic Decision-Making Model

In the basic decision-making model, the gifted student identifies an issue; formulates a question to clarify the difficulty or issue; and then applies common sense, beliefs, interests, and/or policy to generate reasonable answers to the question. Next, the student uses this information to select the criteria or standards for evaluating the alternatives and ranks the criteria. When the student arrives at the best decision for the present, he or she judges whether the decision or conclusion will be suitable for the future. Finally, the student takes action to implement the decision, and evaluates the suitability of the conclusion and the success of the action.

MODIFICATIONS OF THE LEARNING ENVIRONMENT

Schiever, in identifying modifications of the learning environment, lists the six modifications of the learning environment that Maker (1982) reported, that is, that the learning environment (a) be student centered, (b) encourage independence, (c) be open, (d) be accepting, (e) be complex, and (f) offer high mobility. I agree with the importance of all of these modifications and add two more: interdependence and encouraging creativity.

Interdependence

In encouraging interdependence, teachers of the gifted would be concentrating on offering a learning environment that supports learning behavior that can be called consultative learning. Consultative learning is characterized by an interactive teaching–learning process. The breadth of learning experienced in special programs for gifted students generally requires that these students interact with other children, experts, and professionals. Consequently, the skills of interdependence, including interaction, need to be developed and nurtured. The following descriptors characterize the interdependent student: interactive, responsible, cooperative, tolerant, respectful, personable, communicative, and trusting.

Teachers who are keen on developing interdependence in their gifted students will concentrate on developing a sense of community in the learners and will offer many educational opportunities for gifted students to learn cooperatively. Having gifted students learn together can be accomplished by encouraging them to identify topics that relate to the regular classroom work that will provide opportunities for the content and product to be differentiated, with an emphasis on depth. The coplanning also can involve topics of interest that are unrelated to the regular curriculum and that will differentiate content and product. When gifted students work together with other students to explore and learn cooperatively, they learn some very basic skills. They learn to accept responsibility for their own learning, to assume ownership of that learning, and to gain power over their learning. Consultative education is cooperative education and also can include working with community members who have specialized knowledge and skills that may not be available in the school setting. When students colearn with others, they are involved in selecting, planning, investigating, monitoring, reporting, and evaluating.

Encouraging Creativity

To create an environment for encouraging and developing creativity, teachers need to be engaged in providing learning opportunities for creative exploration of real problems, exploration of complex levels of feeling in a stimulating and supportive environment and emphasizing creative production. The creative student would be anticipatory, curious, imaginative, visionary, risk taking, adventurous, inventive, and idealistic.

Although gifted students have the potential to become creative and productive people, creativity and the independence that accompanies it must be nurtured through learning experiences. What education of gifted students demands is a process by which teachers can observe the students' behaviors, recognize their unique characteristics, and identify their concomitant needs. All of this information about the gifted students' needs, abilities, interests, and aspirations then can be used to plan effective learning for gifted students.

In a presentation on gifted learners, Cawelti (1988) reported on research-based characteristics of effective schools and teachers. Teachers who are endeavoring to create an appropriate learning environment for gifted students will find his major points noteworthy. He reported that effective teachers demonstrate the following behaviors:

1. Hold high expectations for students.
2. Provide frequent monitoring of student progress.
3. Create a classroom climate for learning that can be characterized as businesslike with an achievement orientation.
4. Provide materials at the appropriate level of difficulty, neither too hard nor too easy.
5. Routinize classroom management skills that will help ensure adequate time on task.
6. Provide opportunity to learn criterion materials.

In essence, Cawelti suggested that a classroom atmosphere that is individualized, uses mastery of subject matter as a criterion, and wastes neither teacher nor student time could be provided by teachers who demonstrate the characteristics listed above. However, I would add two more characteristics to the above list:

1. Provide opportunities for students to develop resourcefulness, adaptability, and creativity in learning and living.
2. Provide opportunities for students to experience satisfaction from consultative learning and from cosharing and in the participation with others in learning.

An appropriate learning environment for gifted students will encourage creative production through a physical setting that exudes creativity, and will include a teacher who has a desire to foster and develop specific characteristics in gifted students (see Figure 16.3). Gifted students represent a unique minority in all races, all nationalities, all cultures, both sexes, and all levels of society. When society nurtures and develops the potential of gifted students, society also gains individuals who are capable of enriching life through sharing their knowledge and skills. The inquiring and creative minds of gifted students are our hope for the future. They will contribute to the development and maintenance of a productive society. We need their information, their intelligence, and their imagination. Through establishing appropriate learning environments for gifted students, teachers can help ensure that gifted students experience education that is relevant, innovative, and cohesive.

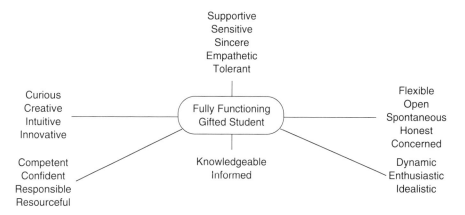

Figure 16.3 Characteristics of Fully Functioning Gifted Students.

REFERENCES

Cawelti, G. (1988, January). *Effective teacher behaviors.* Paper presented at the National Leadership Training Institute, Austin, TX.

Cox, J., Daniel, N., & Boston, B. (1985). *Educating able learners.* Austin, TX: University of Texas Press.

Maker, J. (1982). *Curriculum development for the gifted.* Austin TX: PRO-ED.

Maslow, A. H. (1954). *Motivation and personality.* New York: Harper.

Popp, L. A., Robinson, J. P., & Robinson, F. G. (1974). *Basic thinking skills.* St. Catharines: The Ontario Institute for Studies in Education, Niagara Centre.

PART IV

CLASSROOM MANAGEMENT SYSTEMS AND TECHNIQUES

The key question addressed in Part IV is "How can regular classroom teachers manage their classrooms to enable them to meet the needs of 25 to 30 children with a variety of talents and abilities?" With this question in mind, reading the chapters in this part, I had the recurring image of the seven blind men examining the elephant. As the story goes, each described the elephant differently, depending on what part he touched. The one standing at the tail thought an elephant must look like a rope, whereas the one at the elephant's side thought it must look like a wall.

Like the blind men, the authors in Part IV have offered a variety of answers to the question, and their answers seem to result from very different perspectives of the "elephant" called "management." Like the blind men's descriptions, none is wrong, but each considered alone is incomplete. Unlike the blind men, fortunately, the authors recognize their different perspectives and understand that other, equally valid, perspectives exist.

In her critique of Hazel Feldhusen's lead article on individualization, Margie Kitano calls attention to the differences in their perspectives, noting that Feldhusen's approach is consistent with a process definition of individualization (i.e., individualization involves the process of one-to-one instruction). Kitano then presents an alternative definition of individualization, in which the focus is on the result rather than the means of achieving the result: Children receive instruction consistent with their individual needs. This definition is called a "curriculum-based" approach by Kitano, and she demonstrates how this perspective results in somewhat different techniques from Feldhusen's, which could be called a "task-based" approach.

223

The two views of individualization can be seen as resulting from two perspectives of management, and examined in the writings of other authors in the section. A process- or task-based definition of management would include descriptions of the tasks or processes involved in management of instruction, whereas a curriculum- or results-based definition would consist of descriptions of the kinds of differentiation needed to meet the needs of all the learners in a classroom.

Chapter 17, the first in this section, includes suggestions from both perspectives. Janet Conroy recommends that teachers employ such techniques as cluster grouping of gifted students, acceleration/flexible pacing, dual enrollment, independent study, employment of a counselor–advocate, individually prescribed instruction (IPI), and mentorships. These methods, when supplemented by general processes, such as teaching and practicing routines, extensive prior planning, consistency, and positive attitudes, can result in a classroom in which a variety of needs are met. The "ends" or results recommended by Conroy are schools similar to corporations, classrooms with a pleasant visual climate, and an accepting, positive psychological atmosphere. Different learning styles are accommodated, and gifted students are provided with challenges and interactions with peers at similar levels of ability.

Mary Vuke, in her critique of Conroy's chapter, seems to have more of a curriculum-based focus, recommending the use of Taylor's and Williams's models to guide in the recognition and development of a wide variety of talents and abilities in the classroom. She reminds educators to examine the assumptions they make about gifted students, and cautions against assuming that they all possess most of the traits attributed to the gifted, or that they will be gifted in all subject areas. Vuke does not ignore processes needed to achieve the recommended ends, however, and suggests that principals establish a climate of cooperation among teachers, and assist them in developing needed skills. Some skills or processes considered important are defining expectations clearly, developing different expectations for different types of tasks, assessing a variety of student attributes, and teaching time management methods to students.

Feldhusen recommends the use of cluster seating, learning centers and resource materials, student planning of daily and weekly learning experiences, room meetings, freedom of movement, extensive use of volunteers, close monitoring of students' learning, and effective record keeping. Curriculum-based recommendations are individualized learning of basic skills, fostering thinking skills (creative writing, problem solving, and higher levels of Bloom's Taxonomy) within the context of the subject areas taught. She also recommends balanced treatment of basic disciplines and the arts.

A slightly different emphasis is provided by Kitano, although she does not disagree with the recommendations made by Feldhusen. In the curriculum-based plan for individualization she describes, Kitano identifies two approaches. First, a comprehensive curriculum plan based on a well-defined philosophy is developed spanning several years. Within this plan, individualization for gifted students can be accomplished by including content areas or concepts different from those required in the regular curriculum, and by allowing and encouraging gifted students to pursue these different concepts after mastering the regular curriculum. A second approach is to use the regular curriculum and concepts as the framework, and to provide for differentiation through different activities and different student responses to the same activities. Kitano ends her chapter with a list of questions teachers can ask themselves about all learning activities they design. She provides suggestions and examples of methods to achieve curriculum-based individualization throughout the chapter.

In their lead chapter on learning centers, Roseanne Lopez and Joy MacKenzie have a dual focus on means and ends, by describing what kinds of learning centers teachers should develop to accommodate the diverse needs of a variety of learners. Teachers are encouraged to involve students in all phases of the process of developing and using learning centers, including keeping records of their own progress, designing and evaluating learning centers, and reflecting upon and evaluating their own learning. To achieve the goal of differentiating for gifted students by modifying the depth, scope, pace, and self-directedness of expectations using learning centers, the authors recommend that teachers (a) become facilitators; (b) understand the type of thinking required for center activities, and help students to understand also; (c) provide multimedia materials needed for research and production; (d) start slowly; (e) develop "proactive" management strategies; (f) establish clear classroom rules; (g) hold individual conferences; (h) observe and keep anecdotal records of student behavior; and (i) engage the help of volunteers.

Two of the questions Helen Follis answers in her critique show her dual focus on means and ends. She first presents and answers a question related to outcomes: "How can gifted students benefit from learning centers in the regular classroom?" She then focuses on the process: "How does a teacher develop and manage a learning center for gifted students in a heterogeneous classroom?" She recommends 10 clear, specific steps and provides examples of how these steps can be implemented. Follis recommends a management scheme, examines topics appropriate for development in a learning center, and suggests ways for gifted students to manage their time effectively in a learning center.

Through the varied perspectives presented in this section, educators can develop a clear, complete understanding of classroom management techniques to meet the needs of gifted students. Like the perceptions of the blind men, the perspectives of these authors are different and offer us different views. However, unlike the blind men, these authors can see beyond the limited perspectives of their viewpoints, and have identified for us some elements common to the management of instruction for bright students in a regular classroom setting:

1. Extensive preplanning and continuous "practice" of strategies are required to prevent problems.
2. Clear expectations with clearly delineated consequences are needed for those who do and do not meet these expectations.
3. Cooperative effort and responsibility assumed by teachers, students, administrators, volunteers, and parents are necessary elements of a classroom management system.
4. Flexibility in teacher roles and responsibilities facilitates success.

5. Differentiation in what is taught, methods used to teach, and products expected can be used to meet the variety of student needs and interests.
6. No one technique or system can be used to meet the needs of all gifted students.
7. Students must be involved in establishing their own goals, creating and selecting learning experiences, and evaluating and recording their progress.

Webster's (1984) dictionary defines *management* as "the act, manner, or practice of managing, supervising, or controlling" (p. 722). Rodale's (1978) *The Synonym Finder* provides an interesting list of synonyms for management: regulation, administration, superintendence, supervision, direction, control, government, command, leadership, oversight, care, charge, conduct, guidance, treatment (p. 702). The chapters in this section, although varied, still do not provide a complete description of effective classroom management; the reader is encouraged to read other sections of the book, noticing additional perspectives and suggestions. Of particular relevance to teachers are Parts III, Curriculum Differentiation, and V, Programs and Models for Extending Learning Beyond the Classroom. Administrators will find additional recommendations for schoolwide management in Part II.

Finally, I believe all authors will agree, and I concur, that the classroom teacher has a complex and varied role in the management process. I shall make no attempt to describe or summarize that role. I simply offer a list of synonyms for *manager* from my favorite writing tool, Rodale's (1978) *The Synonym Finder:* helmsman, pilot, fugelman, gerent, leader, organizer, master, governor, mayor, adviser, mastermind, Rasputin, power behind the throne, guide, cicerone, dragoman, proctor, administrator, executive, superintendent, supervisor, boss, chief, overseer, foreman, director, straw boss, skipper, kingpin, controller, comptroller, treasurer, husband, steward, major-domo, seneschal, housekeeper, factor, agent (p. 702). I invite you to add your own synonyms to this list!

REFERENCES

Rodale, J. I. (Ed.). (1978). *The synonym finder.* Emmaus, PA: Rodale Press.
Webster's II New Riverside University Dictionary, (1984). Boston, MA: Houghton Mifflin.

17

Classroom Management: An Expanded View

Janet Conroy

MANAGERS IN SCHOOLS

In schools, a number of employees are perceived as "bosses," authority figures, and disciplinarians. These persons range from the school secretary to the librarian to the school nurse. The classroom teacher is perceived to have the bulk of the responsibility for management; he or she is with the students most of the time and is responsible for student learning outcomes. Without common "goals" or a "philosophy of management" directed by the principal and shared by others, however, one teacher's effort to discipline or manage instruction will be isolated and less effective if the entire school is not geared toward shared policies for student objectives and outcomes.

Schoolwide management issues need far more attention in teacher and administrator preparation. One must not assume that teachers enter their jobs with all skills necessary to manage a classroom effectively. Supervisors should diagnose teachers' strengths and weaknesses, and offer training in developing needed skills. With the help of a supportive principal, teachers can take pride in continued improvement of management skills. The best assistance can be found in other classrooms and from other experienced teachers. A principal can offer to take a beginning teacher's class for a 30-minute segment, to allow him or her to see how a colleague handles management problems.

Administrators also may not enter their jobs with the skills necessary for effective management or supervision. For example, prospective administrators seldom receive special training in what to look for in a program for the gifted. At many universities, evaluation is taught as if the same standards should be used to evaluate all teachers, including those teaching in special programs. Because special skills and endorsements are needed, and are defined clearly for such positions as librarian, school psychologist, teacher of special education, and teacher of the gifted, administrators need to know the standards that should be used to assess the effectiveness of these specialists. Principals need basic knowledge of how each special program functions, and what curricula and methods of instruction are appropriate.

As instructional leader, the principal is responsible for hiring, training, monitoring, and evaluating the staff. Teachers are responsible for training, monitoring, and evaluating students. Both principals and teachers manage 30 or more individuals. Peters and Waterman (1982) found that in top-performing companies, such as Hewlett Packard and IBM, informal and casual communication from managers was demonstrated to be more effective than management by rules and deadlines. The authors called it "management by walking around." School principals-in-training at Northern Arizona University learn the concept of management by walking around. They learn that effective principals visit classrooms, talk to students and teachers, and demonstrate active monitoring of the school (Lemley, 1990). Principals who walk around see what is going on in classrooms and are able to provide informal support and assistance to students and staff. A recent study by Goertz, Lemley, and Dereshiwsky (1991) indicates that effective principals are creative leaders who demonstrate passion, originality, goal setting, flexibility in problem solving, a wide range of interests, intelligence, independence, and the talent for motivating others. Effective leadership consists of more than being a manager.

Teachers watch their instructional leader closely. If the principal supports differentiated instruction for gifted students, teachers know it. Teachers observe the principal talking with students, parents, teachers, and other administrators about the program. If the principal takes no stand on an issue, or avoids it because he or she is not informed, the teachers are left without important leadership.

Gifted students constitute a special interest group. Parents of gifted students sometimes are quite vocal. In many states, laws protect the right of gifted students to an appropriate education. Administrators, parents, and teachers on district planning committees should become informed of the laws and rules governing the education of gifted students in their state. District administrators need to take a stand and be clear in their beliefs about education of the gifted to respond to parent and community concerns. If district and local school administrators do *not* have a strong commitment to ability-appropriate curriculum for gifted students, the needs of gifted children are likely to be addressed only minimally.

A principal takes direction on many issues from the superintendent, who in turn responds to the school board. The way gifted students are to be served often becomes a political issue because of active involvement of parents and board members. If the board and superintendent support programming for gifted students, principals and teachers will follow their lead. Quality programs for the gifted are found in districts and schools with a strong commitment to serving the academic and social–emotional needs of gifted students.

The principal sets the pace and the tone for the school. If he or she takes an active management role and communicates positive attitudes and high expectations for staff and students, staff members will rise to the challenge. If the principal and other key administrators support differentiated education for gifted students, the program will be free to sprout wings. If the principal is uninformed or noncommittal about appropriate education for gifted students, the program may have limited success.

Teachers in situations without needed program support from their principal need to take the initiative to build support for themselves. Some teachers get support by "dropping in" to visit the principal or another teacher. They talk about what is going on in their program and share ideas. All teachers need to interact with other staff members and their principal—about management concerns, about individual students, and about curriculum. Support and sharing make a stronger school. According to Maslow (1970), individuals are more free to develop creative potential when other human needs, such as the need to belong, are met. A sense of belonging is important in schools.

Schools today are undergoing various types of restructuring. In some schools, the result is shared decision making by teachers and administrators. Teacher representatives in such schools will have increasing input in decisions that affect the management of the school, including budget items, course offerings, and schedules. Teacher communication about schoolwide management issues results in common policies for student management. A common "mission" or philosophy can help define a consistent position on certain issues.

Teachers, staff, and administrators all share responsibility for establishing a positive learning environment for students. In a school designed for successful learning, classroom management strategies will be an extension of schoolwide management beliefs. A strong instructional leader will provide guidance and support for all special programs, including those serving gifted students.

SCHOOLS AS CORPORATIONS

Both schools and businesses are improved by well-educated and experienced employees. In business, efficiency is rewarded through raises; ineffective employees are dismissed or counseled into other jobs. In contrast, teacher salaries are based on years in the system plus credit for additional coursework or hours of inservice education. Both effective and ineffective teachers move up on the salary scale according to longevity. Although career ladder and other teacher incentive programs are being piloted in many areas, no agreed-upon system has yet emerged for rewarding outstanding teachers.

In businesses, employees with outstanding skills are recognized, are called upon to educate colleagues, and are rewarded with benefits not afforded other workers. Every employee reports to a manager, who evaluates the employee's skills. At quarterly evaluation conferences, the employee is asked about personal goals. A career development plan is written. If the employee wants to develop skills in a new area, such as marketing or research, the employee (with backing from the manager) attends workshops on the topic of interest for an extended period of time before moving to the new job. Potential managers are "groomed" and offered additional training at company expense. If the employee is viewed by his or her manager as prospective manager material, he or she is sent to workshops and classes to learn new management skills. The company may invest thousands of dollars in training an employee believed to have management potential. When training is completed, the employee may be asked to move to one of several locations. If such a move occurs, the company helps with moving expenses. IBM receives maximum productivity from its employees through the use of this career development plan, along with training and flexibility (Pam Osterhout, IBM, Tucson, AZ, personal interview, 1987).

Managers in schools also encourage productivity from their employees through training, usually in the form of coursework or inservice education. However, training in the form of academic coursework is generally taken at the teacher's expense and is accomplished outside of school (evening or summer classes). When teachers wish to attend workshops or conferences, their employers may not provide released time or substitutes, resulting in teachers taking personal leave to attend such events. On the other hand, some employees are paid for training when the district needs something such as additional teachers with an endorsement to teach English as a Second Language (ESL). Great differences exist within and among districts in the degree of support offered for teacher education.

Teacher salaries suffer compared with salaries of professionals in business with comparable university educations (e.g., master of business administration holders or certified public accountants). Not only do wide variations exist in teacher base-level salaries among districts and across states, but variances in salary credits are common when experienced teachers relocate. When a teacher moves to another city or state, he or she is most likely not credited for years of experience, but hired at a salary equal to that of teachers with much less experience. In Arizona, for instance, the policy of the majority of school districts is to credit a newly hired, but experienced teacher who has 10, 15, or 20 years experience with only 5 years on the salary scale. This practice results in a critical loss of income for teachers who wish to move to a new setting, or who are forced to move due to personal circumstances. It probably causes many excellent teachers to leave the profession for jobs in business or industry. This phenomenon does little to encourage teachers to seek new growth experiences in other jobs in other school districts. For job security, teachers must stay where they are, something that often does not fit with family or personal growth goals or the need for a change. Health profession workers, attorneys, engineers, and other highly trained professionals can move to other parts of the country and expect to earn salaries commensurate with their experience.

Although teachers and administrators have management responsibilities of similar difficulty (they merely supervise different age groups), school administrator salaries often are more than double teacher salaries. With the trend toward shared decision making in schools, teachers will be more involved in decisions formerly left to the principal. As teachers assume more responsibility for management of schools, and as the diversity of their skill is recognized, they may receive pay more in line with their responsibilities.

Another interesting comparison between business and industry can be made in numbers of employees supervised. The average IBM manager has 10 employees to supervise and monitor (Pam Osterhout, IBM, personal interview, 1987), whereas managers in education supervise people that number from 30 (an elementary teacher with 30 students) to 80 (a principal with 80 faculty members) to more than 100 (a middle school or high school teacher with five classes of 20 to 35 students per day). Educators in public and private schools have difficult and complex management jobs, regardless of the level or type of management.

Both education and business must be accountable. Workers in business are responsible for production, sales, and customer satisfaction; educators are accountable for students' mastery of the curriculum, and for producing responsible citizens and employees for the workforce of the future. Both schools and businesses work toward the goals of excellence and efficiency. Both are mindful of equity issues and may not discriminate against groups or individuals. Managers in both business and education have similar jobs: They must monitor, supervise, train, and "coach" their students or employees toward certain goals, objectives, and time lines to satisfy clients, stockholders, and consumers of their products, which, in the case of education, includes higher education, employers, and the community at large. In addition, managers in both business and education want quality work from those they teach and supervise.

The similarities between business and education seem greater than the differences. Perhaps when communities and legislators recognize the diverse and difficult tasks and complex skills needed for producing effective schools, effective teachers, and effective learners, educators will be rewarded with status (both in pay and in respect) equal to that of other professions requiring extensive management skills. The products of education—skilled citizens and workers of the future—are certainly as important to society as the computers produced by IBM.

MANAGEMENT IN THE HETEROGENEOUS CLASSROOM

Elementary teachers not only must teach and monitor behavior and routines such as lining up for lunch and recess, but also must plan and evaluate different levels of instruction to meet the needs of all the varied abilities of students. Secondary teachers must plan for five different groups of students coming in and out daily, each with mixed abilities unless they have a special advanced class. Both groups of teachers have difficulty simultaneously (a) covering mandated curriculum with the average students, (b) differentiating instruction to challenge gifted students, and (c) remediating instruction for students who are achieving below grade level. Teachers will need special skills and materials to plan appropriate differentiated curriculum for advanced students, as well as for students below grade level.

In the regular classroom, some children with special needs will leave the room periodically to attend resource programs. Students in ESL, learning disabilities (LD), and Chapter 1 reading programs may leave the room from 45 minutes to 2 hours or more. When these students return, the teacher is expected to fill in the gaps, and otherwise meet their special needs. Clearly, the regular classroom teacher has a difficult job planning and managing instruction for all the special needs students and the spread of learning abilities in the classroom. A teacher faced with many levels of instruction to manage may be tempted to use gifted students to help teach other students. This practice, if used regularly, exploits the abilities of gifted students rather than meeting their learning needs, and should be avoided.

Can the needs of gifted students be met in a heterogeneous classroom? The issue is widely debated, and concerns parents and teachers alike. McDaniel and Gallagher debate this issue in Chapters 1 and 2 of this volume. A plausible response is that the general *enrichment* needs of gifted students probably can be met in the regular classroom with additional materials and a commitment from the teacher (Gallagher, 1985), but a truly differentiated or accelerated curriculum provided on a full-time basis will be difficult if not impossible to implement in the regular classroom. Gallagher wrote

> The problems that seem to weigh most heavily . . . are the lack of depth in content train-
> ing of the teacher; the impressive range of intellectual ability in the heterogenous elemen-
> tary class, with the consequent heavy demands for multiple planning by the teacher; and
> the teacher's limited amount of time to work at the high conceptual level for the bright-
> est children in the group. (p. 350)

If gifted students are to be taught in the regular classroom, teachers must be committed to providing an appropriate and stimulating curriculum, and administrators must be committed to providing training and assistance for teachers. One way to provide training and assistance is to hire a specialist or consultant whose primary responsibility is to assist teachers with curriculum and materials for gifted students.

That the needs of *highly gifted* students will be met in the regular classroom is unlikely. Gallagher, Greenman, Karnes, and King (1960) looked at highly gifted students in an elementary school setting in which assistance was provided to regular classroom teachers working with gifted children. Recommendations in this study were that additional diagnostic help from a psychologist, additional curriculum help from a specialist, and a program of grouping all were needed.

One might ask why educators are choosing to meet the needs of gifted students in the regular classroom rather than through a weekly pull-out program or a daily special class in reading or math. The major concern seems to be money. One teacher salary is needed to hire each specialist to work with gifted students in a pull-out resource model, or to work with teachers in a districtwide or school consultative model. The program for the gifted is one area in which cutbacks can be made by serving the students in the regular classroom. Educators seem to believe that gifted students can make it on their own, that they do not need a special class. The danger of this line of thinking, however, is that teachers might revert to some of the previously unsuccessful ways of serving gifted students, and have them do "more" or work "faster," neither of which addresses adequately the need for gifted students to have a differentiated and more complex curriculum.

Another factor behind the move to serve gifted students in the regular class-room may be the general ambivalence our society seems to have toward high-ability students (Gallagher, 1985). In other words, if we provide separate special classes for gifted students, we will be going against our country's democratic and egalitarian ideals. Yet when a student is highly talented in athletics or music, the student is offered special training. Unless educational and community leaders take a strong stand in support of programs for gifted students, ambivalence and confusion will continue as to how these students are to be taught.

The use of certain classroom management strategies enables teachers to provide part-time acceleration and part-time ability grouping for gifted students in the regular classroom. According to J. Feldhusen's (1989) synthesis of research, support exists for both *acceleration* (defined as providing instruction comparable to achievement and readiness levels) and *ability grouping* (defined as grouping with other gifted peers at least part of the time). Research on acceleration shows that gifted students reach higher levels of achievement with acceleration and suffer no detrimental effects (Brody & Benbow, 1987; J. Feldhusen, 1989). Evidence indicates that acceleration and ability grouping are both positive and productive for gifted students.

To manage adequately the needs of gifted students in a classroom of widely varying abilities, the teacher needs to plan varied and challenging activities. For every curriculum unit, the teacher needs to develop extension and enrichment activities appropriate to ability levels of the students, including the gifted students. He or she can manage instruction by dividing blocks of time and by grouping the students. While some students have small group instruction with the teacher, others work in learning centers, and others do self-directed activities. The teacher can vary the groups, sometimes providing direct instruction to the whole class, and sometimes working with smaller groups within the class. For the gifted students, the teacher can "compact" the curriculum, allowing them to master it in a shorter time, and then "enrich" or "extend" the curriculum with in-depth assignments that encourage synthesis of concepts or development of thinking skills or creativity related to the content.

Few regular classroom teachers receive special training in strategies to manage the intellectual needs of gifted students. A special endorsement or certificate in education of the gifted in most states requires 15 to 36 hours of combined coursework and inservice, to include such content as educational foundations, creativity, curriculum models, methods, and evaluation. To "manage" curriculum needs of the gifted, teachers need some training. Because many teachers lack coursework in classroom management, and specifically how to manage the needs of the gifted in the regular classroom, an introduction to the general components of classroom management is presented, followed by strategies and adaptations for managing the instruction of gifted students in the regular classroom.

Components of Classroom Management

Classroom management is, most simply, *time management,* the teacher's organization and use of classroom time, for both instruction and routine tasks, such as sharpening pencils or passing out papers. Time management means careful planning for what the teacher wants to have happen, both in the curriculum and in student behaviors. It means approaching the day as if it were a workshop in which each 15-minute segment, including occasional breaks, needs to be planned.

Classroom management also is *behavior management*. The teacher sets guidelines and standards for student behavior and for interactions in the classroom. He or she outlines standards for desirable behavior, describes behavior that is not acceptable, and defines consequences for the misbehavior.

Classroom management in a broader sense is the *planning and management of instruction* by designing an appropriate educational program with a basic curriculum while also planning for the interests, abilities, and needs of individual students. Instructional management is a means for the teacher to assist students to learn and work together productively in the classroom.

Another element of classroom management is *classroom climate*. Climate is the atmosphere set by the teachers, staff, administrators, and students toward learning and toward others. Classroom climate is an attitude of caring about students. It is friendliness. Climate affects students and classrooms, and is a *joint responsibility* of all school personnel. An effective school with a positive climate for learning depends in part on administrative and staff "togetherness," sometimes called *school spirit* or *morale*.

The integration of the management components mentioned above reflect the individual teacher's "teaching style" and result in the teacher's "reputation." The components are found in all classrooms, whether the classroom demonstrates effective management or something less. In a well-managed classroom, the components seem to work without teacher effort. When one observes several classrooms, and notices slight differences in management techniques, however, the existence of the separate components and the effort needed to structure them become more apparent.

The Well-Managed Classroom

A well-managed classroom has a sense of order and purpose. Students are "engaged" in their learning, whether writing at desks, reading in small groups, listening to audiotapes with headphones, or working in a cooperative group. The teacher has organized the work so students know what to do, and little time is wasted. Respect among students for their teacher and fellow students is obvious. Instructional time is used well. The teacher is in charge, although quietly. Rules are understood and are followed, and the teacher has no need to "bark" orders or reprimands. The teacher reinforces desirable behaviors by saying, "I like the way John is working" or "Thank you, Susan, for helping Mary Jo." Management in such a classroom looks easy, but time and effort are required for these behaviors to become automatic for the students.

In a poorly managed classroom, one might see children playing catch with their pencils in the back of the room when the teacher is not looking. One child pokes another, causing a stir, which the teacher has to stop. When recess time comes, children push and shove to be first in line, and one child cries because another hit him. The difference between the two classrooms is that in the first the teacher has taken time to structure and implement components of classroom management. She has talked about each of the routines, "taught" the routines by having the children practice doing them until they are mastered to her satisfaction, and reinforced the routines by complimenting the children for behaving in the way she had planned. In the second classroom, the teacher has been concerned only about the content that needs to be taught and has not thought of needed procedures or rules for behavior. Students in this class do what they feel like doing, because no consistent instruction is provided by the teacher to remind them of appropriate behavior.

In a well-managed kindergarten class I observed, students arrived in the morning, took a reading book from the library corner, sat in a circle on the rug, and started reading or looking at books quietly. They were not talking to each other. Obviously, they knew what their teacher expected. This teacher had taught her students this routine so she could have a few minutes to take attendance and talk with any parents who might want to talk with her when they left their child at school. When she was ready, the children were in their circle waiting to begin the day. This management strategy was developed because the teacher thought of what she needed—some flexible time to talk with parents—and what the children needed to get ready to start the day. She planned a strategy that would meet both needs. She probably spent several weeks teaching the strategy, through reminders, until it became automatic for the students. This example of classroom management shows how to make time for the teacher and for the students, and teaches students to be responsible members of a group.

Planning for Effective Management

Classroom management begins in teachers' minds long before the first day of school. The teacher pictures mentally what he or she wants in the "ideal classroom," then designs procedures to support the plan (Evertson, Emmer, Clements, Sanford, & Worsham, 1984a, 1984b). During the planning process, the teacher first imagines the instructional patterns (e.g., lecture, discussion, group work, learning centers) he or she will use. The teacher answers several questions: Will different groups be doing different types of activities? Will desks be in rows or in groups? Will the room be visually stimulating? What student behaviors will be needed to implement instructional methods? (Battista, 1984).

Planning Routines

Standard procedures and routines for taking attendance, reporting to reading groups, turning in papers, collecting lunch money, and lining up for recess will help students know what is expected. Teaching the routines and having students practice them will enable students to do them automatically. A mistake teachers often make is to talk about the rules once, but fail to have students practice in the same way they would a content lesson. For example, a teacher might say, "Today we are going to practice coming to reading groups quietly. When I ring the bell, I want the red group to come up quietly.'' After several practices, students will know what is expected. Most teachers who establish these routines ultimately save time, although extra time is needed to establish and teach routines initially.

Planning and Organizing for Responsibilities

In addition to providing important content instruction, teachers should expose students to important societal concepts, such as rules, responsibilities, time lines and due dates, and evaluation of work. Teachers help students develop good work habits to prepare for further study and the world of work; they teach behaviors and skills such as listening, following directions, cooperation, teamwork, and leadership. They model these behaviors and attitudes themselves, and set standards in these areas for how they want students to behave. For example, students are not allowed to call fellow students derogatory names. A teacher, on hearing one student call another a derogatory name, responds, ''In this class, we do not talk that way about others.'' The teacher repeatedly models respect toward all students by his or her own behavior and reinforces through both words and actions how he or she expects students to behave toward one another. The teacher also teaches students to handle work responsibilities. Students take turns with jobs such as cleaning the pet hamster cage, watering plants, wiping off counters, and taking attendance sheets to the office. All students are responsible for finishing their work and for cleaning up after an activity. A rule of thumb for the teacher might be, ''Don't do anything for a child that he can do for himself'' (Dinkmeyer, McKay & Dinkmeyer, 1980). A student who has not finished a task for which he or she is responsible may need to miss a few minutes of recess. Logical and natural consequences are used rather than a system of rewards and punishments, thus allowing the student to take responsibility for his or her behavior (Dreikurs & Soltz, 1964).

Planning for Management Skills

Many books and articles have been written about management, and classes are taught at teacher training institutions. One of the best ways for teachers to learn and improve management skills is to observe master teachers at work. Administrators can help by taking a teacher's class for 15 or 20 minutes to allow a teacher to observe another classroom. Some schools have coaching teams in which a group of teachers agrees to work together to help one another by observing, making suggestions, and offering assistance. These teams also may serve as teacher evaluation teams, or can tailor assistance to specific weak areas. When a spirit of teamwork exists, this kind of shared teacher coaching is not seen as threatening. In some school systems with career ladder evaluation, teacher coaching is used with great success.

Planning for Attitude and Style

Teachers develop a personal teaching and management style based on their educational philosophy and experience, as well as personal attitudes and beliefs (Battista, 1984). Think back to an influential teacher or one who seemed effective, and recall things about that teacher that stay in memory. Are they the routines used for attendance or discipline, or the general attitude toward teaching students and learning? What would be four words to describe this teacher? Do the words address subject area content? Personal style? Classroom management?

I recall a sixth-grade teacher years ago who literally threw a book at a boy in the back of the room who was disturbing the class. I do not remember what he did. I do know he was a slow learner and looked for attention in ways other than through his academic work. I remember how shocked we were when this teacher yelled, turned red, and threw the book. The boy ducked, the book crashed through the window, and landed on the grass below. The room was silent. Geography ended for the day as this student was dragged away to the principal's office. What is interesting is that I remember this teacher's frustrations with discipline more than I remember any geography she taught. Words I would use to describe her would be *strict, unpredictable, temperamental,* and *emotional.* These words describe her style and reputation, not her subject area. Another teacher I recall, my eighth-grade math teacher, is memorable because she made that subject enjoyable for me for the first time. She made it a game. I could succeed by trying. I didn't get bored with the drill. This teacher had one row competing against the other using timed tests and math drills. She taught us to subtract long columns of money in these row teams using rapid subtraction methods she said we would later use to balance checkbooks. Class moved at a fast pace. Words that come to mind for her are *organized, effective, enthusiastic,* and *demanding.* These words reflect her management style and reputation, but also her content area.

Planning a Positive Work Atmosphere

Students work best when they feel safe and the atmosphere is friendly and positive. The visual classroom is an important and sometimes overlooked aspect of classroom management. Students need a pleasant and orderly setting with a variety of things for visual interest. The room may have bulletin boards, posters, plants, mobiles, small animals to study, learning centers, bookcases, an art corner, and/or a reading corner. Desks may be arranged in a circle, in study groups, or in two sets of rows facing each other. Desk arrangement should facilitate the type of student interaction being encouraged. For example, a circle, semicircle, or U-shaped arrangement facilitates group discussions; small groupings of desks facilitate cooperative learning groups; and rows facing the teacher facilitate teacher lecture or large group instruction. H. Feldhusen (1990) suggested that moving away from continuous straight row seating encourages students to work independently in small groups on problem solving or on projects, and deemphasizes the teacher as the sole source of information. It teaches students to be in charge of their own learning. A study by Rosenfield, Lambert, and Black (1985) found that semicircle or cluster seating results in more on-task behavior than does traditional straight row seating. Both the room arrangement and bulletin boards should be changed periodically for variety, and to reflect new subject area content being studied.

Planning for Student Interaction

For learning to take place, students need to feel free to take risks and ask questions. Teachers should build an atmosphere in which students know they will be free from ridicule or harsh criticism. Three words for the teacher that help build this kind of atmosphere are *firm, fair,* and *friendly* (Harriet Sheridan, Carleton College lecture, 1963). The teacher should establish firm guidelines for student behavior in the classroom, model fairness with all students, and insist that students treat one another with respect and friendship (teachers also must model these behaviors). Many teachers post important rules for the classroom, such as "listen when others speak" and "respect other people and property." Teachers often ask students to help develop the rules as the need arises. For example, if a student takes something from another student, the teacher asks the class if a rule is needed, and, if so, what it should be. Regardless of how rules are determined, students need to understand both the rules and the rationale behind them. The teacher might lead a discussion by asking, "What would happen if no one listened when others were speaking?" or "What would school be like if everyone called everyone else names?" Teachers should be prepared to enforce rules and to be sure students understand consequences if rules are broken. The student who misbehaves seriously might be asked to stay in a few minutes at recess. Serious misbehavior could result in a visit to the principal's office, where perhaps a special behavioral contract would be written to be signed by the student, the teacher, and the principal. Students also can be asked to assist in developing consequences for misbehavior.

Planning for Instruction

Effective instruction includes individualization (see Chapters 19 and 20) or modification of the curriculum for students with special needs, such as handicaps, learning disabilities, and attention deficits, and for students who are gifted. Equal opportunity means that instruction must be appropriate for varying abilities. Instructional management strategies ensure that time on task for learning is maximized for all students.

If lessons are appropriate to students' abilities and learning styles, students will be able to learn better, and will be eager to move on to the next task. Sometimes teachers need to provide nontraditional strategies to accommodate learning style differences. A student with a learning disability in writing might be allowed to complete assignments or take tests by tape-recording the answers to questions. A gifted student can do an extension or adaptation of an assignment that requires higher level thinking processes (see Chapters 11 and 12) and thus challenges his or her abilities.

The National State Leadership Training Institute for Gifted and Talented recommends consideration of the following elements when planning instruction for gifted students (Kaplan, 1979): (a) *pacing*—allowing students to progress according to their abilities; (b) *scheduling*—allowing students to schedule their own time; (c) *environment*—selecting or creating environments that enhance or match interests and abilities of the students; (d) *instructional strategies*—selecting strategies that match the student's needs, interests, and abilities; (e) *learning styles*—allowing students to choose learning experiences that match preferred learning styles and interests; and (f) *use of material*—selecting material at an appropriate level of complexity and stimulating the use of new and different input sources. Kaplan (1979) further suggested that to provide the needed flexibility in scheduling instruction for gifted students, a teacher may *borrow* or *rearrange* time from other subject areas, or may *extend* the time a student is allowed to work on a project.

Planning for Positive Attitudes

Purkey (1971) isolated four factors of student self-concepts as important classroom features: relating, asserting, investing, and coping. He designed a checklist in which school personnel reflect upon how well people talk and listen to one another in the school: Do students talk to students, students to teachers, and teachers to teachers? (relating). Do people feel free to share their feelings? (asserting). Do people feel safe trying or suggesting new things? (investing). Do people care and offer to help when others need it? (coping).

All students learn best in an environment they perceive as supportive. Gifted students, with their intensity and idealism, are particularly sensitive to teacher attitude and style. They prefer teachers who are encouraging and may be inhibited by those who are rigid and authoritarian (Clark, 1988).

Students are sensitive to what they perceive as negative attitudes of teachers. They often say, "He doesn't like me," or "She's not fair." The teacher who builds a positive classroom atmosphere for students is comfortable with himself or herself, confident, and self-assured; genuinely likes students; and can look at himself or herself and situations with a sense of humor. Students respond well to teachers who are firm, fair, and friendly. Teachers who demonstrate anger, sarcasm, and put-downs are perceived by students as negative. For example, a high school advanced placement science teacher may take pride in making tests extremely difficult and rigorous. He or she puts nothing on the test that has been in the chapter just studied, but makes the problems complex applications of chapter material. As students arrive on the day of the test, the teacher says with enjoyment, "You are all going to flunk this. I'll bet you don't get a single one right." Some students are able to ignore these comments and proceed to work on the test. Others experience a "block." Optimum learning does not occur in an atmosphere of tension, with students on edge wondering when the teacher may make a new sarcastic comment. Students in classrooms of such teachers may be afraid to risk, afraid to give an answer that might be wrong, or afraid they will fail. The teacher could design the same test, but present it as a challenge to the students, telling them he or she has confidence they will meet the challenge. Students' attitudes toward both the teacher and the test will be completely different. An in-depth discussion of classroom environments for gifted students is beyond the scope of this chapter, but can be found in Chapters 15 and 16.

Planning for Equity

Students have a right to be taught by teachers who relate and respond equally to all students—male, female, and those from different ethnic backgrounds. Educators have been remiss, sometimes unknowingly, in this area for some time. Discrimination and unfair treatment can be very subtle. The male science teacher who uses sarcasm in class also may make it harder for females than males to achieve in his classroom. I have seen classes in which girls ask a question of a male teacher, and the teacher ignores the question. Later in the class, a boy asks a similar question, which the teacher answers. This teacher does not know he is treating students of the opposite sex differently, but the girls sense that to succeed in his class they have to be twice as persistent and twice as competent as the boys. Gifted girls may not always be assertive or strong enough to operate in this way.

Planning for Differentiation of the Curriculum

Teachers planning for multilevel instruction in their classrooms should first plan the regular curriculum, and then modify the *content, process, product, environment,* and *affect* to make instruction more appropriate for gifted students (Kaplan, 1986). Many suggestions for differentiation of the curriculum are found in Part III (Chapters 9 to 16). Gifted students learn faster and are good thinkers. Classroom teachers always have tried to accommodate students who finish early by giving them "more" or "extra" work, or by "using" the students to run errands or help other students. Such responsibilities are likely to foster resentment in gifted students. Many gifted students in public schools would rather hide their abilities than stand out as the one who finishes early or is perceived as the "teacher's pet."

Gifted students have the following curricular needs: (a) *acceleration*—for work that matches their achievement level and for continuous progress; (b) *adaptation*—for more abstract, broad-based, interdisciplinary connections, or creative approaches to regular curriculum; (c) *enrichment*—for exposure to new topic areas and ideas; (d) *independent study*—for learning more about topics of interest to them; and (e) *affective topics*—for social and emotional growth and increased awareness of self and others. Whether gifted students are served in a daily or weekly resource room or pull-out program, or in a special class, they have needs pertaining to their giftedness all day every day (Cox, Daniel, & Boston, 1985). Even when gifted students go to a special class, experiencing appropriate curriculum in the regular classroom is essential.

Cluster Grouping

Grouping five to eight gifted students in a "cluster group" in the same classroom allows the teacher to address some of the above curricular needs by working directly with the gifted group. It also allows the gifted students to interact with one another. In cluster grouping, the teacher is the coach, sometimes working with small groups and sometimes with the whole class. The teacher will sometimes work with gifted students, instructing their small group while others work independently. Sometimes he or she will work with another group while gifted students work independently. The teacher will do whole class instruction primarily when introducing a unit. He or she will need to determine what all students should know, compact that into a smaller time frame for the gifted cluster, and use the time gained to offer enrichment, independent study, or other differentiated curriculum. When cluster grouping and cooperative learning strategies are combined in classes, gifted students can work some of the time in their own cooperative group with a more complex problem, and some of the time with heterogeneous groups. Gifted students need to work with students of mixed abilities to learn cooperative and leadership skills. However, if gifted students are placed in cooperative learning groups such that they are *always* the intellectual leaders, their own needs for intellectual challenge will not be met. Most adults work with various groups, some of which are made up of those with similar needs, skills, and abilities, and some of which are made up of those with widely different skills, needs, and abilities. Students need to develop cooperative and leadership skills in a variety of situations similar to what they will encounter as adults.

Cluster grouping allows gifted and talented students to interact with students who are their intellectual as well as chronological peers. Furthermore, projects completed by the cluster group of gifted students may result in spin-offs for the regular students. For example, suppose the class is studying dinosaurs. The teacher introduces the unit with a National Geographic videotape and whole class instruction. Students are then grouped cooperatively to study the various types of dinosaurs and make dioramas for display in the library. Gifted students are included in heterogeneous groups for this activity. Then, as groups finish their dioramas and written reports, the teacher works with the cluster of gifted students explaining a historical time line. The gifted students then work on making a historical time line for the room to show when dinosaurs lived in relation to other life, such as mammals, birds, and fish. This activity represents appropriate differentiation. It includes greater breadth, depth, and interdisciplinary connections (history, math, geology). Gifted students could be asked to share their time line and findings with the class, resulting in benefits to the class. Advantages of cluster grouping for primary gifted children are that children do not leave the room, and they frequently may do activities with heterogeneous groups within the class. Cluster grouping essentially is part-time ability grouping within the classroom. With a trained teacher skilled in managing groups, it can be very effective.

Planning for the Cluster Group

In most regular sixth-grade math classes, the teacher will cover several units, from review of computation to fractions and percentages. Average students will need the full number of teaching cycles to master the concepts before the test. Gifted students may be able to take the test after the first teaching cycle. Once gifted students have demonstrated mastery, they should move on to more difficult or complex applications of the principles just learned, or to a related enrichment project. Within the cluster group format, a teacher may provide *acceleration, enrichment,* or other options. The teacher needs to evaluate gifted students on criteria that match the subtasks of their cluster work, as well as mastery of the common curriculum. Gifted students may not have all the same tasks as the regular students (as the curriculum has been compacted for them), and will have additional, different tasks.

A good deal of advance thinking, planning, and creativity is necessary to implement successfully the cluster grouping approach for gifted students. The following is an example of 1 week's schedule for math activities in a sixth-grade class using cluster grouping:

Monday: Regular students—introduce two-digit multiplication. Gifted students— Same. Teacher gives all members of class an outline of the entire week of math seatwork and homework assignments ending with a test on Friday.

Tuesday: Regular students—Review concepts presented Monday, guided practice. Gifted students—Teacher introduces some enrichment material, including math logic problems. Gifted students work on these as soon as they have mastered the concepts of the other problems. Teacher assigns their group to come up with some story problems and logic problems related to the week's concepts. Teacher then assists regular students in doing seatwork. Although gifted students are responsible for the test Friday and for specific portions of the homework throughout the week, such as every third problem, they choose to use class time working on the enrichment or a group project.

Wednesday: Regular students—Introduce three-digit multiplication. Gifted students—Listen to explanation of concepts, demonstrate that they can do three problems correctly, and continue with enrichment project. Teacher moves between both groups.

Thursday: Regular students—Review and guided practice in seatwork, with introduction of story problems. Gifted students—Do three of six story problems and continue enrichment activities.

Friday: Regular and gifted students—Take unit test on two- and three-digit multiplication. Test has application story problems. One challange problem is more difficult. It is designed for the gifted students, but others may try it.

Planning for Acceleration and Flexible Pacing

If acceleration is appropriate for a gifted student or a group of students, the teacher must plan the amount of acceleration and communicate with teachers at the next higher level regarding this decision and its implications for the teachers who will have the student(s) next year. For example, if one or more students in the sixth grade complete all sixth-grade math work and get partly through the seventh-grade math curriculum, will next year's seventh-grade teacher agree to continue the acceleration process? Will this be possible? If the sixth graders *finish* the seventh-grade math curriculum, will they be allowed to take eighth-grade math in seventh grade? Teachers and school administrators need to discuss and agree on the answers to these questions before a program of acceleration is begun. Cooperation and commitment to this sort of pacing is beneficial to gifted students and will help future gifted students. Dialogue among different levels of math teachers will be beneficial in the articulation of math concepts. The district-level coordinator of the program for the gifted may work with elementary teachers, or with math, science, and language departments districtwide, to develop precedent and policies related to acceleration. Sometimes pressure from parents of individual gifted students has been a factor in persuading administrators to support acceleration. When students are accelerated, their grades are based on individual criteria. A separate section is set up in the grade book for students who are doing accelerated work.

At the secondary level, a sample policy for acceleration might read like this: "Students who complete high school algebra in the eighth grade will be asked to take the high school year-end algebra exam at the end of eighth grade. If students demonstrate mastery, by passing the exam with a grade of 85% or better, credit and a grade for the algebra class will appear on their high school transcripts at the end of the freshman year." This policy would need to be discussed and agreed upon by the high school math department.

Some gifted students may wish to finish high school in 3 years by taking a heavier than usual class load, attending summer school, or taking college or correspondence classes. Social and emotional issues should be discussed with the student and parents before electing such an accelerated plan. Another option for talented high school students is to take a college or correspondence class concurrently with high school classes, "banking" college credits for future use, or, if high school credit is needed, such college credit could be given on a petition basis as a "dual credit" on the high school transcript. Courses that might substitute in this way would be courses already listed in the high school curriculum, such as economics, American or world history, or a foreign language. This sort of flexibility is appreciated by gifted high school students.

Flexible pacing as a variation of acceleration works very well with gifted elementary students and is similar to concurrent enrollment for high school students. In this service delivery model, the gifted elementary student spends some time with his or her own grade level, and part of the time with a higher grade level. For example, a third-grade student gifted in the area of math might go to a fourth- or fifth-grade teacher willing to include the student for math lessons in place of third-grade math, which the student already has mastered and finds too easy. Flexible pacing works well for highly gifted students; it enables them to stay with age peers for social–emotional development at recess and in certain core subjects, and to be with intellectual peers for certain subjects. I know of a student who has been allowed to follow this pattern for 6 consecutive years. In first grade, he took part of his work with second graders. In sixth grade, he was spending half his day at the junior high. Flexible pacing has worked very well for this student. His parents and teachers felt he needed the intellectual stimulation of more challenging work, but believed strongly that he also needed social and emotional development with his own age group. The result of flexible pacing was that he was accepted by other students in both grades. His cognitive and affective needs were met. This student was fortunate that his parents were able to work with the school to plan such a program to meet his needs (Barbara Kraver, personal interview, 1988).

Planning for Enrichment

The teacher may choose to do enrichment or "extension of the curriculum." An example of enrichment in math is to introduce more difficult story problems or have the gifted students write their own story problems relating to everyday applications of math concepts. The teacher also might introduce logic problems, commercial math enrichment materials, or math-related computer software. Another option for the teacher would be to adapt the curriculum to include higher level thinking skills—analysis, synthesis, and evaluation. For example, students are assigned math applications, such as making a chart illustrating multiplication patterns, or estimating and figuring square footage of items in the room. A separate section of the grade book is used to indicate assignments and criteria for evaluation. For 1 week's math activities, gifted students would receive a grade on the regular classwork, as well as separate grades for the enrichment work. The teacher develops forms similar to those in Godfrey's (1986) Appendix B to assist in evaluation.

The previous example in sixth-grade math illustrates curriculum compacting, that is, shortening time for the gifted students to cover the content. The time saved is used for other activities. The ease of compacting depends on whether the teacher has lessons planned in advance, and can determine which work will be compacted for the gifted students. Teachers who are new to the process of differentiating instruction for gifted students should start in one subject area, and add others as they are able. Many teachers report that once they use dual classroom management, they find the process effective and students accept more responsibility for their own learning. Other options for gifted students in cluster program models are learning centers, enrichment folders, contracts, commercial learning packets designed for gifted students, independent study, and career exploration. A number of these options are discussed elsewhere in this volume.

Individually Paced Instruction

In individually paced instruction (IPI), students work at their own pace. Students set their own time lines and achieve mastery before advancing. The teacher acts as guide or coach, and students choose the order and method of learning (Pirozzo, 1987). The work is laid out sequentially in charts, folders, notebooks, computer software, or sequential lab experiments. Lessons may be designed with "challenge questions" for gifted students. IPI can be used within the framework of clusters or with an entire class in certain subjects, such as math or computers. Independent study projects can be partially managed with a cluster of gifted students using this system. In this system, the teacher monitors and gives frequent feedback to the student.

IPI has many advantages. Students who work at their own pace work independently. The element of competition for grades is removed as students compete against themselves. Students take the time they need to master the material; slower students may review or relearn, or get needed help from the teacher, while gifted students are spared needless repetition and move quickly through the material. Students have responsibility and control over their own learning. Work to be done is prescribed clearly, as are the criteria needed to achieve certain grades. Student motivation is improved; students who perceive they have control of their learning and grades are motivated to ask questions for understanding and mastery. The problem of makeup work following absences is eliminated. The teacher, freed from lecturing, is available to move around the room to answer questions, evaluate completed work, record grades as students finish, and provide assistance as needed. The teacher needs only minimal planning time to organize materials for the next week's or next day's lessons, although he or she may need to set out equipment and materials needed for each day's labs.

One disadvantage of IPI is that the teacher must have lessons, materials, tests, and labs sequentially planned for the entire year. Materials are coded by color or number so students can move on without having to ask the teacher what to do each time a unit is completed. Grades are entered each time a lesson or test is completed. Lab work, computer software, books, and supplemental materials must be readily available. Lab procedures must be stated clearly. The teacher writes the lessons and labs clearly and developmentally in the notebooks so that new concepts build on previous concepts and understandings. Lessons have built-in self-checks so students may check understandings before completing the unit test.

Another disadvantage of IPI is that the students will be scattered throughout the curriculum; different students will be doing a number of different tasks at any given time. One might think that students might be tempted to "goof off" when given this much freedom, but teachers report that peer pressure is strong enough to keep students on track (Bretini Cooper, personal interview, 1988, Tucson, Arizona, Flowing Wells School District). Students see that their choices affect their progress. Because students may be tempted to depend on other students, or copy from a friend, guidelines and policies need to be developed concerning when students will work together (e.g., for class assignments, but not on tests).

Subjects that lend themselves well to IPI are those with structure or a natural sequence of learning, such as spelling, vocabulary, math computation, or word processing. Grammar, science facts and problems, geography, history, computer work, foreign language, and nearly all vocational subjects (e.g., sewing, cooking, typing, auto shop, photography, and welding) adapt well to IPI. These subjects can be organized so that students are asked to complete tasks, assignments, labs, or projects with a certain percentage of mastery before advancing to the next task or assignment. History and geography can be individually paced for facts, dates, and time lines, but will need to incorporate class discussion to develop other understandings. If gifted students are to practice higher levels of thinking, they must have some structured learning experiences in which concepts are expressed through teacher-led group discussion.

Cooperative Learning: A Team Approach

In traditional classrooms, students sit in rows facing the teacher. They listen and depend on the teacher to teach. They compete with other students for grades, and have little or no incentive to work together. In *Control Theory in the Classroom,* William Glasser (1986) argued for changing this system to one of learning teams in which the team itself builds student motivation. Glasser suggested that all individuals act and behave based on four psychological needs: belonging, power, freedom, and fun. A good school, he says, is one in which students believe that if they work, some of these needs will be met. Glasser noted that these four needs are met in sports, drama, or debate far better than in the typical classroom, particularly in middle and high school. He commented that students want and need more power and control over their learning, and that cooperative learning allows students to take control of their learning while developing a sense of pride and interdependence similar to that found on an athletic team. He argued that when schools use cooperative teams to teach, the slow students will become involved, and the faster students will develop important leadership skills.

In *Control Theory*, Glasser outlined a theoretical base for this approach. He said students misbehave in the classroom because one or more of their psychological needs is not being met. We cannot make students learn through punishment; students must have choices. Everyone tries to control life experiences. When we blame others for our own anxiety or anger, we are wrong. If we admit we are actively choosing to be anxious or angry, that it was our choice, then we have power to change. One reason cooperative learning teams are effective is that students can no longer put the responsibility for their learning on the teacher. Students work with peers who need their input; they are responsible to themselves and to the team.

In cooperative learning teams, the teacher assigns small groups of students to do an assignment together. According to Johnson and Johnson (1984), the teacher using this strategy must structure into the assignments elements of *positive inter-dependence* (we sink or swim together) and *individual accountability* (I am responsible to myself). To achieve both elements, teachers award grades based on both individual and group effort. Many ways are devised to structure both long-term and short-term assignments, using cooperative learning. For example, a language arts prewriting assignment is based on discussion of students' own thoughts prior to reading a story, followed with reading, discussion, and writing. The teacher first divides students into groups of four. Each group contains a mix of slow, average, and bright students. The topic is life in the future. The students individually imagine themselves about to take a time-travel trip to the future and prepare a list of items they will take, with justification and costs listed. Next, each student writes a letter or proposal requesting the items needed (individual accountability). After completing the proposal, each student checks the written work of two others in the group for content and grammatical errors (collaboration). The story about time travel is read. Each student then writes a composition, stating his or her opinion about whether the main character made the right decisions in what to take on the trip (individual accountability). A group grade (positive interdependence) is figured. Each group starts with a possible 100 points. Five points are subtracted for each grammatical error on any paper in the group; 20 bonus points are given if each member of the group gives a clear interpretation of the story in his or her individual essay (individual accountability). Motivation to work collectively as a group is built in because all grades are higher if the group grade is higher. The teacher changes the groups often enough to ensure that students have an equal chance to get higher grades. Student grades are determined by averaging group and individual grades (Glasser, 1986, p. 99).

Benefits of cooperative learning as an instructional management system include the development of cooperative skills, social skills, and leadership skills. No discipline problems are evident, because no power struggle is needed with the teacher; students are working for and with their peers, not for the teacher. Students practice interdependence. For the teacher, seven groups are easier to monitor than 28 individuals. Lessons carry over from one day to the next. In whole class instruction, lessons often are short and finished in one period or less, with papers turned in for grades. In cooperative learning, assignments are longer term; students explore concepts in depth and have more opportunities to use higher level thinking skills. As the teacher monitors groups, he or she needs to encourage students to solve problems within the group rather than to solve their problems for them. Some teachers find changing from "director" of learning to "coach" a difficult task. Teachers also may find the greater amounts of noise and movement in the classroom that go along with cooperative group work to be difficult to accept at first. With time, however, teachers usually see that the benefits outweigh this perceived disadvantage.

One disadvantage of the cooperative learning approach for gifted students is that if teachers group gifted students with academically average or slow students, the gifted students never get a chance to see how far they can go with an assignment. Gifted students need to be with other gifted students some of the time to spark and challenge one another. If groupings are always heterogeneous, gifted students may come to resent having to work with slower students on every assignment. Gifted students should be allowed to work in cooperative groups with one another some of the time if their own academic needs are to be considered.

In cooperative learning situations, grades are minimized and learning outcomes stressed. Grades reflect both individual and group achievement. Student self-evaluation, in which students tell what they learned, also is beneficial.

CREATIVE AND ACADEMIC COMPETITIONS

Creative and academic competitions, such as Odyssey of the Mind, Future Problem Solving, Knowledgemasters, Wordmasters, Math Olympiad, and Academic Decathlon, provide a framework for students to work together cooperatively to solve problems and come up with products, results, skits, or written solutions. These products are judged by standard criteria against those of other student teams or groups. In the case of Odyssey of the Mind, student teams take their skit or product to a regional competition in which teams from other schools compete in an all-day event with several divisions. In Future Problem Solving, students learn a problem-solving process through a series of practice problems. The final team solution is submitted in written form for evaluation, feedback, and assignment of points. In Academic Decathlon, teams of students are judged in speech, essay, and eight other academic content areas against other teams. Winning teams from many of these programs compete at state and national levels. (For addresses of these competitions, see Appendix 17.A.)

These programs may be used with heterogeneous groups, as well as with high-ability groups, but were designed primarily to meet the needs of gifted students. Average students may become frustrated with the difficulty of the problems and the competition. Creative competitions are excellent illustrations of the concept of differentiation for gifted students because they involve abstract content and real audiences. Creative competitions offer opportunities for gifted students to interact with other gifted students, to learn problem-solving and communication skills, and to develop leadership and group skills. A concern with these programs is that they may become the only program for gifted students in the school. An effective program for gifted students operates with many components and options in the curriculum, never as one isolated activity.

Record Keeping and Contracts

A good system of records helps teachers track student progress, report to parents, and plan for instruction. Involving students in record keeping helps them take responsibility for their work (Godfrey, 1976). A simple yet effective method of helping young children keep track of their work is to make a sheet with 10 outlined stars, numbered to correspond to various tasks. As students complete each task, they are given a star sticker to paste over the corresponding space on the record sheet (H. Feldhusen, 1990). Another way for the teacher to record students' progress is to keep a notebook with a separate page for each child, and maintain written notes on the student's work in each subject. A method that allows for individualizing competencies for each child is to keep a separate sheet for each student listing competencies and objectives that are tailored to that child's unique strengths and needs. As the student works on each objective, the teacher marks beside the objective to signify (a) *introduction* of the competency, (b) *beginning competency,* and (c) *mastery.* Students keep a duplicate progress sheet and mark their own mastery level by each objective. Students bring their sheets to a weekly conference with the teacher.

A popular way to track the progress of an entire class is to list student names on the left side of a grid, list competencies along the top, and check or date the appropriate box when a student completes the competency or the assignment. This method allows the teacher to see quickly which student is missing assignments or needs extra help. When students are working on independent studies, special record-keeping devices are needed to encourage student responsibility while keeping the teacher apprised of what the student has been doing (Kaplan, Kaplan, Madsen, & Taylor, 1980). The teacher might construct a bulletin board of a giant thermometer and use the degrees of the thermometer to represent student progress through the steps of the independent study (Kaplan et al., 1980). Each student might have an individual thermometer on which to list the steps of his or her study; additionally, a giant thermometer might represent the entire class, with student names at different points on the thermometer. Another method to help both student and teacher is the daily log. Students record progress in the log, and the teacher collects and reads the logs periodically. Additional ideas for record keeping are found in Appendix 17.B. Teachers are encouraged to use a variety of record-keeping devices for different purposes.

Contracts are another useful tool for helping children to manage their own learning. Contracts represent a commitment from the student to follow a course of action or complete certain tasks (Kaplan et al., 1980). A reading contract might include spaces for pages read, questions to be answered, summary cards to be completed, or cassettes for a listening station. A contract for a science experiment might have spaces for a hypothesis; equipment or tests used; observations and discoveries made; data collected or things measured, weighed, counted, or drawn; and student evaluation or comments following the experiment. Sometimes teachers find a contract useful in helping a student to manage nonproductive or problematic behavior, such as an attendance or homework problem. Teachers should adapt contracts to fit both the student and the content area addressed. Two sample contracts are shown in Appendix 17.B. Commercial materials with contracts also are available for teachers to use or adapt to fit specific needs.

GRADES AND ACCOUNTABILITY FOR GIFTED STUDENTS

Keys to successful curriculum planning and classroom management for gifted students are *flexibility, advocacy,* with *accountability.* An imaginative teacher who understands and is an advocate for gifted students will try to find challenging activities for students. A word of caution is needed, however. Some gifted students are manipulators. These students would like to do as they please, study a topic until they are tired, switch topics or subjects repeatedly, and go to the next counselor or teacher if the first will not change the schedule or listen to the students. Students need to negotiate within school policies for what is reasonable and possible. We must not allow gifted students to manipulate the environment unproductively. Independent study, mentorships, and other flexible program options are important learning experiences for gifted students, but should not provide an excuse for students to operate entirely without direction. To monitor independent study, teachers can require periodic progress reports, daily logs, and teacher conferences. Students working in a community internship must go to work according to a schedule, just as if this were a real job. Gifted students often are charmers, capable of overloading their schedules, then pleading to get out of commitments. We are not doing gifted students a favor if we let them get away with lame excuses. Rules and expectations need to be explained at the beginning of the semester, and applied consistently and fairly throughout. A contract may be signed by all parties involved in the internship or independent study. The supervising teacher will monitor internships and independent study by talking with the community sponsors and the student regularly. Problems need to be addressed before they become serious. Additional suggestions for managing independent study, mentorships, and internships are contained in Section V (Chapters 23 through 28).

Gifted students deserve challenging learning opportunities. These students often go through the elementary and middle school years without challenge and without ever taking home a book. Gifted students may complete high school without learning to study or doing any difficult thinking or writing. Some gifted students first experience a need to study and do homework in college. College may be frustrating for the gifted student whose elementary and secondary school experience is too easy. For this reason, appropriate activities—challenging work, including study skills, time management, and accountability—must be structured for gifted students during their early school years.

MANAGEMENT STRATEGIES FOR GIFTED STUDENTS IN SECONDARY SCHOOLS

A parent once called me to complain that her gifted son, who had completed the entire BASIC computer course in the first 5 weeks of class, had been told by the principal that he would simply have to sit in class for the remainder of the semester to receive credit for the class. The principal cited state law about Average Daily Membership (ADM) to justify his position. In Arizona, the ADM student count is taken on the 100th day of school and is the number on which state aid to schools is based. Surely this student would be counted, whether he was in this class or another. If we are in the business of educating bright students, we must be flexible. This student could have been given additional computer software to learn (Advanced BASIC or PASCAL), could audit another class already in session, or could do independent study. Registration and transcript problems could be handled as a "special situation." If a student is ready to move on, he or she should be permitted to register for a second class and get credit for both classes in the same semester if he or she does the work for both. By requiring a student to sit through the rest of a semester in a class that has been completed, the student is penalized for being industrious. The issue is not one of attendance; the important issue is the learning accomplished and the appropriate educational experience for each child.

MORE IDEAS FOR SERVING
SECONDARY GIFTED STUDENTS

The format of most high school class periods—a 55-minute class period and a 9-week grading period—is restrictive. Many high school subjects could be taught in varying time frames. Some subjects, such as typing, lend themselves to shorter time blocks. Others, such as college writing or advanced placement history, would benefit from an occasional 90-minute period. An economics class might meet 3 days a week rather than 5. Given that most schools are restricted to the present format, why not allow gifted students to double register for or attend more classes? For example, allow the student who finishes BASIC in the first few weeks to continue studies with PASCAL, either through teacher direction or independently. Allow another student gifted in foreign language acquisition to attend French class on Monday, Wednesday, and Friday, and to work on independent study or a community internship on Tuesday and Thursday. Allow students interested in electronics to attend classes at the local community college, and return to campus for other classes. For concurrent enrollment, give dual credit if the student needs the credit to graduate; otherwise, let the student accumulate college credits early.

A SECONDARY COUNSELOR/ADVOCATE FOR GIFTED STUDENTS

I was fortunate to work for a time in a school district as a part-time secondary counselor–advocate for gifted high school students. My job consisted of academic and career guidance with gifted students using a 4-year plan as a tool. My duties included setting up and monitoring internships and job shadowing experiences for career exploration, planning special seminars and field trips, facilitating concurrent enrollment at the local community college or the university, coordinating the advanced placement testing program, monitoring independent study programs in cooperation with a content area teacher, and facilitating all enrichment or acceleration opportunities for gifted students. Students were not expected to know of these opportunities on their own; the counselor–advocate role in part was to match student needs and interests with available opportunities. Sometimes an opportunity needed to be created. The counselor–advocate was housed in the counseling department, in which the position fell under the larger ''umbrella'' of services offered there, such as counseling and college planning. As a management strategy for gifted students, it worked beautifully, and could be copied successfully by other school districts willing to create such a position.

CONCLUSION

The strategies discussed in this chapter are all options for managing the needs of gifted students in the regular classroom. Teachers should experiment with them, and use them interchangeably to discover which system works best within a given curricular structure and format, and with their own personal teaching style. Teachers who have a briefcase full of management strategies will be able to meet the needs of these students better than those who have only one. If one strategy does not work, another can be tried. Teachers who understand the characteristics and needs of gifted students, who are flexible and creative in their approaches, who differentiate their curriculum to make it appropriate, and who allow gifted students to make decisions about their own learning, will be meeting the needs of these students.

Appendix 17.A

Academic Competitions

Future Problem Solving
202 E. Washington, Suite 10
Ann Arbor, MI 48104-2017
(313) 998-7876

Knowledgemasters
Academic Hall
P.O. Box 998
Durango, CO 81302
(800) 321-9218

Math Olympiad
125 Merle Ave.
Oceanside, NJ 11572-2211

Odyssey of the Mind
P.O. Box 27
Glassboro, NJ 08028

United States Academic Decathlon
11145 183rd St.
Cerritos, CA 90701
(213) 809-4995

Wordmasters
2213 E. Allendale Ave.
Allendale, NJ 07401
(201) 327-4201

Appendix 17.B

Sample Record-Keeping Tool and Contracts

SAMPLE RECORD-KEEPING TOOL

Name: _____

Reading Skills	Below Average	Average	Above Average
Recognizes word meanings			
Notes details			
Identifies main idea			
Notes logical sequence			
Distinguishes cause–effect			
Reads critically			
Recognizes literary devices			
Skims for varied purposes			
Classifies information			
Identifies part of a book			
Uses an index			
Uses card catalog			
Uses dictionary properly			
Reads maps/globes			
Reads charts, graphs			
Uses other data sources			

Appendix 17.B (Continued)

SAMPLE MATH CONTRACT

Name: _____ on dates _____
agrees to do the following math activities:

1. In my math book I will work on pages _____.
2. In the learning station I will do three math tasks.
3. Choose two of the following for checking my math skills:
    Worksheets
    Math lab materials (cuisinaire rods, attribute blocks, tangrams)
    Computer program
Completed on: _____

                    Student signature _____

                    Teacher signature _____

Appendix 17.B (Continued)

SAMPLE READING CONTRACT

Contract Agreement

Name: _____ Class: _____

1. I agree to read the book I have chosen. I will read the entire book.
2. I will show consideration for others by reading the book quietly.
3. As I find new words, I will write them on my bookmark. At the end of each reading period, I will transfer my new words from the bookmark to my vocabulary list.
4. I agree to have at least one conference each week with my teacher in order to
   a. review contract work
   b. summarize what I have read
   c. talk about my book (story, characters, settings, meanings, etc.)
5. I agree to do the entire contract: vocabulary list, frames to draw characters of the book, and drawing and description of the book's setting.

Name of book: _____
Date due: _____
Signed: _____
on the _____ day of _____, 19_____
Date completed: _____
Teacher comments: _____
_____
_____

Note. From *Contracts for Individualized Instruction* by L. Godfrey (1976), Menlo Park, CA: Individualized Books. Copyright 1976 by Individualized Books Publishing Co. Reprinted by permission.

REFERENCES

Battista, N. (1984). *Effective management for positive achievement in the classroom.* Phoenix, AZ: Universal Dimensions.

Brody, L., & Benbow, C. (1987). Accelerative strategies: How effective are they for the gifted? *Gifted Child Quarterly, 31,* 105–109.

Clark, B. (1988). *Growing up gifted* (3rd ed.). New York: Macmillan.

Cox, J., Daniel, N., & Boston, B. (1985). *Educating able learners: Programs and promising practices.* Austin: University of Texas Press.

Dinkmeyer, D., McKay, G., & Dinkmeyer, D., Jr. (1980). *Systematic training for effective teaching: Teachers' handbook.* Circle Pines, MN: American Guidance Service.

Dreikurs, R., & Soltz, R. (1964). *Children: The challenge.* New York: Penguin.

Evertson, C., Emmer, E., Clements, B., Sanford, J., & Worsham, M. (1984a). *Classroom management for elementary teachers.* Englewood Cliffs, NJ: Prentice-Hall.

Evertson, C., Emmer, E. T., Clements, B., Sanford, J., & Worsham, M. (1984b). *Classroom management for secondary teachers.* Englewood Cliffs, NJ: Prentice-Hall.

Feldhusen, H. (1990). *Individualized teaching of gifted children in regular classrooms.* Buffalo, NY: D.O.K. Publishers.

Feldhusen, J. (1989). Synthesis of research on gifted youth. *Education Leadership, 46,* 6–11.

Gallagher, J., Greenman, M., Karnes, M., & King, A. (1960). Individual classroom adjustments for gifted children in elementary schools. *Exceptional Children, 26,* 409–422.

Gallagher, J. (1985). *Teaching the talented child* (3rd ed.). Boston: Allyn & Bacon.

Glasser, W. (1986). *Control theory in the classroom.* New York: Harper and Row.

Godfrey, L. (1976). *Contracts for individualized instruction.* Menlo Park, CA: Individualized Books.

Goertz, M., Lemley, R., & Dereshiwsky, M. (1991, October). *The relationship of leader effectiveness and selected traits of creativity.* Unpublished paper presented at Arizona Educational Research Organization Conference. Flagstaff, AZ.

Johnson, D. W., & Johnson, R. T. (1984). *Cooperation in the classroom.* Minneapolis: University of Minnesota Press.

Kaplan, S. (1979). *Inservice training manual: Activities for developing curriculum for the gifted/talented.* Ventura, CA: Office of the Ventura County Superintendent of Schools.

Kaplan, S. (1986, March). *Classroom management for gifted in the regular classroom.* Workshop in Lincoln, NE. National State Leadership Training Institute for Gifted and Talented. Ventura, CA: Office of the Ventura County Superintendent of Schools.

Kaplan, S., Kaplan, J., Madsen, S., & Taylor, B. (1980). *Change for children: Ideas and activities for individualizing learning.* Pacific Palisades, CA: Goodyear.

Lemley, R. (1990). *Leadership.* Unpublished lecture, Northern Arizona University, Flagstaff.

Maslow, A. (1970). *Motivation and personality* (2nd ed.). New York: Harper and Row.

Peters, T., & Waterman, R. (1982). *In search of excellence: Lesson from America's best run companies.* New York: Warner Books.

Pirozzo, R. (1987). Breaking away: A self directed independent approach to learning science. *Gifted Child Today, 10,* 22–24.

Purkey, W. W. (1971). *Self concept and school achievement.* Englewood Cliffs, NJ: Prentice-Hall.

Rosenfield, P., Lambert, N., & Black, A. (1985). Desk arrangement effects on pupil classroom behavior. *Journal of Educational Psychology, 77*(1), 101–108.

Sheridan, H. (1963). *Classroom management.* Unpublished lecture, Carleton College, Northfield, Minnesota.

18

Critique of Conroy's "Classroom Management: An Expanded View"

Mary Vuke

How can regular classroom teachers meet the diversified needs of students in their classrooms? In the previous chapter, Conroy proposes several suggestions for managing schools and classrooms to meet the needs of students with a variety of talents and abilities. In this chapter, I comment on some of Conroy's suggestions.

MANAGEMENT OF SCHOOLS

Conroy writes that schools should be run as a business whose product is learning. This excellent idea would impact positively on education in terms of efficiency, accountability, and quality. Running a business efficiently requires accountability on the part of all employees. Under this premise, all school personnel, as well as students, would be expected to carry out their responsibilities efficiently and to the best of their ability. Teachers should be accountable for teaching the required curriculum objectives appropriate for their classrooms. Administrators and teachers must be jointly responsible for providing an atmosphere to enable students to learn.

Administrators should be chosen for their ability to manage other people, not merely finances, transportation, and physical plants. As each principal accepts responsiblity for teachers' performances, education becomes more efficient. Teachers need to feel the support of their supervisors, as well as of their fellow teachers. A principal must set the school climate to be one of cooperation and mutual support for the purpose of providing quality education for all students. If the school climate is one of efficiency and seriousness toward excellence in teaching and learning, the job of learning can be efficient.

Students also should be held accountable for their own learning and behavior. In the business world, workers are expected to do their jobs efficiently, cooperate and get along with other employees, and take direction from managers. Because a student's job is to learn, all students should be expected to learn to the best of their ability and to cooperate with other students and their teachers. Students also should be accountable for demonstrating what they have learned, just as employees must demonstrate their ability to complete a task satisfactorily.

If educators have set the goal of preparing students for adult life, running schools as a business would give students a realistic view of the world of work. Job-related skills, such as accountability, time management, and cooperation, would be a part of the school curriculum. This realistic approach would receive support from parents, as well as students, because it would prepare youth for the real world of work.

CLASSROOM MANAGEMENT

Conroy lists four areas of classroom management: behavior management, time management, instructional management, and classroom climate. Expecting regular classroom teachers to demonstrate various management techniques requires the acceptance of certain assumptions.

Assumptions About Teachers

Many teachers do not have the skills to manage an efficient classroom. Teacher training programs have been sorely lacking in the teaching of behavior management, and time management is almost unheard of as a skill teachers should master. Teacher training programs need to emphasize diagnosing students' individual needs so teachers can manage instruction appropriately to meet each student's needs. In teacher training programs, instruction in creating positive classroom climates that encourage students to learn and think is neglected. Assuming that teachers naturally have the skills to manage behavior, time, instruction, and classroom climate is unrealistic. Teachers need to develop these skills, and an appropriate evaluation of these abilities should be devised.

Behavior management is extremely important, but difficult. Many teachers would not consider teaching students to do such simple things as sharpening their pencils appropriately. However, when teachers take the time to define clearly their expectations about all these daily chores that need to be carried out in a classroom, more time is available for the students' all-important task of learning the core curriculum.

Different kinds of behavior are required for different classroom activities. Four types of activities usually are conducted in classrooms: individual work, whole group discussion, small group work, and whole group instruction. Discussing behaviors and posting lists of behaviors expected for each type of activity would define clearly what is expected of each student during each activity. Classrooms will run efficiently when the teacher points out the type of activity and, therefore, what behavior is expected before each lesson.

Time management must be flexible. As a teacher, I have observed that 15-minute time segments are optimal for large group lessons. However, the teacher must be prepared to be flexible in executing each lesson. Flexibility may be required by the instructional material or by the students' reactions to the material.

Elementary school students commonly complain that their teachers talk too much, especially during science and social studies lessons. Students assume a passive role in classrooms in which the teacher talks more than 40% of the time (Maker, 1982a). Teachers who talk less than 40% of the time encourage students to become more involved in and excited about the curriculum. Student participation gives the teacher the opportunity to assess students' abilities and knowledge informally. By scheduling activities for 15-minute periods, teachers can monitor their talking time and strive to increase students' participation time.

Teachers are taught to translate assessments into instructional management; however, many teacher-training programs neglect instruction in the needs of gifted students, as well as of other students with special needs. As the diversified needs of the students in a classroom become apparent, teachers must plan to use instruction and teaching methods that will meet those needs. In classrooms of 25 to 30 students, planning for all students' needs is a monumental task, especially for a teacher untrained in recognizing special needs. School administrators must provide support to classroom teachers in the form of inservice training and assistance from master teachers. Characteristics and needs of gifted learners and other learners with special needs should be the topic of inservice training and discussion among the school staff. Administrators also must provide time for classroom teachers to do the detailed planning required to meet the needs of all students.

The classroom climate is important, but not isolated from the climate of the school. If the school's major goal is learning, the climate of each classroom will improve. The entire staff must support a commitment to quality education. Parental support also is essential to creating a climate for quality education.

Assumptions About Gifted Students

Even though lists of characteristics of gifted students have been generated, assuming that all gifted students possess all of those characteristics would be a disservice to them and other students. Conroy suggests several strategies to use with gifted students in the regular classroom, but classroom teachers must not assume that all gifted students will be ready for those strategies in all subjects.

Gifted children usually can generalize and transfer ideas from one context to another, work comfortably with abstract ideas, and synthesize diverse information to a greater degree than can other children (Clark, 1983). However, high achievers and creatively gifted students may have different characteristics or a combination of these and other characteristics. Teachers must be aware of all their students' learning characteristics to adjust the content and activities in the classroom to meet the needs of the students and anticipate possible problems in the learning environment. This is an extremely tall order for a teacher in a classroom of 25 to 30 students.

Teachers should assess the skills of each student very carefully (Clark, 1983). Some students may have high ability in an area without having the necessary skills to perform specific tasks the teacher expects of the gifted students in his or her classroom. Other students may have high ability in one area and not in another.

Teachers need to assess the independent study skills of each student and provide instruction for each student as necessary. Students need to master research skills to investigate a topic independently. Each research skill needs to be taught ad practiced. Teachers must provide opportunities for students to practice these skills and give support to all students as they are mastering the skill. A detailed explanation of ways to assess and develop independent study skills is presented in Chapters 27 and 28.

Students also must learn time management. Teachers should give specific instruction in a variety of study skills so students can choose the ones that make their learning more efficient. Another way students can develop time management skills is by working on individual contracts. Contracts should be designed to give students many choices in activities, sequences of activities, and deadlines. Conferences between teacher and individual students will help the students recognize their own ability and/or need to manage their time. As students become more proficient at managing their time, they can be given more choices about deadlines. Students can also improve the way they use their time by keeping track of what they do with their time. Writing about what they accomplished in a journal every day and keeping track of the amount of time they are on task or not on task also are ways to improve students' time management skills.

Underachieving gifted students present a difficult problem for teachers. Such children may be aggressive because of their frustrations in dealing with other people and their own special needs (Clark, 1983). Many underachievers withdraw in classroom situations or choose goals that are not in line with their interests and abilities. These students require an extra amount of patience and support. Regular classroom teachers should seek support for these children from counselors, parents, and teachers experienced and educated in techniques for dealing with underachievers.

Cluster grouping within the regular classroom must be very flexible. Students should be moved in and out of cluster groups based on their abilities in *each* subject area. Cluster grouping and cooperative learning require interactions among students. For student interaction to be successful, supervised practice is required. For projects to be completed successfully, students must respect others' opinions and be willing to participate in the group. Completing a group project requires skills such as the ability to follow a leader, task commitment, and time management (Clark, 1986; Maker, 1982a).

MORE SUGGESTIONS FOR INSTRUCTION

Calvin Taylor (1968, cited in Maker, 1982b) suggested that all kids are potentially gifted. Taylor proposed reforming school systems to enhance the development of talents, such as creativity, communication, planning, forecasting, and decision making. Taylor's Multiple Talent Approach defines these talents, and demonstrates methods for developing and implementing these talents within the regular curriculum. This approach provides a positive way of looking at all children and a useful framework for planning to meet the diversified needs of students.

To implement Taylor's Multiple Talent Approach, the teacher must plan learning experiences in each area of talent Taylor proposes. By getting all students involved in these experiences, the teacher is able to assess individuals' strengths and weaknesses. Students can be encouraged to develop strengths and minimize weaknesses as the teacher plans for new learning experiences. This model can be used effectively in a regular classroom setting.

Frank E. Williams (1970, cited in Maker, 1982b) suggests Teaching Strategies for Thinking and Feeling. His model combines three basic elements: student behaviors, curriculum, and teacher behaviors. The purpose of Williams's model is to encourage and recognize creativity in all children by individualizing the basic elements according to each child's talents and skills.

The first step to implementing Williams's model is to determine thinking and feeling characteristics of each child. This assessment is used to develop a profile of creative behaviors in each student. These profiles are interpreted by the teacher to develop a generalized approach for each student. Then the teacher must select teaching strategies to use with the whole group, as well as with the individual child. This approach is time-consuming, especially during the assessment and while developing the profiles; however, it provides teachers with an instructional model for meeting all students' needs.

CONCLUSION

To meet the diversified needs of all students in a classroom, a teacher must recognize and assess the needs of each student. A teacher must manage behavior, time, and instruction, while creating a positive classroom climate. Each teacher needs training and support to complete this task. Schools need to be restructured to run more efficiently. Educators must call for and work toward reduced class sizes, improved administration support, increased flexibility in scheduling, and emotional support for themselves and their students. Only with a firm commitment to excellence in education from administrators, teachers, parents, and students can this model learning environment become a reality.

REFERENCES

Clark, B. (1983). *Growing up gifted* (2nd ed.). Columbus, OH: Merrill.
Clark, B. (1986). *Optimizing learning: The intergrative education model in the classroom.* New York: Merrill.
Maker, C. J. (1982a). *Curriculum development for the gifted.* Austin, TX: PRO-ED.
Maker, C. J. (1982b). *Teaching models in education of the gifted.* Austin, TX: PRO-ED.

19

Individualized Teaching
of the Gifted
in Regular Classrooms

Hazel J. Feldhusen

The major needs of gifted and talented students include challenging instruction at a level and pace that fit their abilities and interests, and creative, dynamic teachers who can provide generative learning experiences for them. Generative learning means that students are themselves actively involved in the learning process, dealing with skills and concepts simultaneously. Learning how to learn means that they are learning the skills of thinking and developing motivational patterns and learning styles appropriate to their talents and abilities. This learning can best be accomplished in the context of the traditional disciplines of science, mathematics, language arts, literature, and social studies, with a high degree of individualization to fit the precocity of each child or cluster of children. Individualization for the gifted student is needed whether he or she is enrolled in a special full-time class for the gifted, is part of a cluster of gifted students in a regular heterogeneous classroom, or is the single gifted child in a regular classroom setting.

Giftedness is potential, and the process of identifying such potential must be oriented to looking for signs of future growth, not merely current accomplishments. Potential for future growth is best shown by students who exhibit a high degree of independence and self-direction in learning, who reason well, who have intense interests that lead to in-depth reading and investigations, who exhibit curiosity and questioning behavior, and who show advanced levels of conceptual ability. Achievement and intelligence tests alone are not adequate measures of giftedness. The identification process must include substantial input from teachers and parents, who have the best opportunities to observe the child in a variety of intellectually demanding situations. Appropriate rating scales, combined with test scores, can provide the evaluation information for a selection committee to make a professional judgment concerning a child's potential giftedness. Sheer addition of numbers is never adequate. A committee of knowledgeable professionals should decide.

My own delivery system is a regular heterogeneous classroom of 20 second-grade children in which 2 to 5 very bright or gifted youngsters are enrolled each year. My major goals for these gifted youngsters follow: (H. J. Feldhusen, 1986):

1. Master basic skills and concepts at levels commensurate with their abilities
2. Develop enthusiasm for reading in a variety of literary forms
3. Develop independence and self-direction in learning
4. Learn to work in small groups
5. Develop positive self-concepts

SYSTEM COMPONENTS

The major components of my system are the following (H. J. Feldhusen, 1986):

1. A cluster seating arrangement
2. Extensive use of learning centers and resource materials
3. Student involvement in planning their own daily learning activities
4. Highly individualized arrangement for learning of basic skills
5. Room meetings to involve students in problem identification and solving
6. Fostering thinking skills
7. Much freedom of movement
8. Balanced treatment of the basic disciplines and the arts
9. Extensive use of volunteers
10. Close monitoring of student learning and effective record keeping

Cluster Seating

I learned about the great potential of cluster seating very early in my teaching career. The several advantages over row seating are that it fosters cooperative learning, enhances social development, heightens children's morale, encourages assistance to one another in learning, and motivates children through their observation of one another's progress. What a joy to read confirming evidence in the study by Rosenfield, Lambert, and Black (1985), who found that cluster seating produced more productive behavior than did row seating in the elementary classroom.

I group children into clusters of three or four, as shown in Figure 19.1. Their rectangular desktops make a tablelike configuration. From the beginning of the school year, I discuss in weekly room meetings with the students a variety of topics having to do with self-direction, cooperative learning, social interaction, and dealing with problem behaviors. Time and patience are needed to help children learn how to function well in the cluster seating arrangement with the related freedom of movement in the classroom. However, gifted youngsters seem to master this arrangement quickly and to thrive on the freedom of movement.

Cluster seating is particularly effective in accommodating individual learning styles. Some children learn best working with one or two other children. Some need

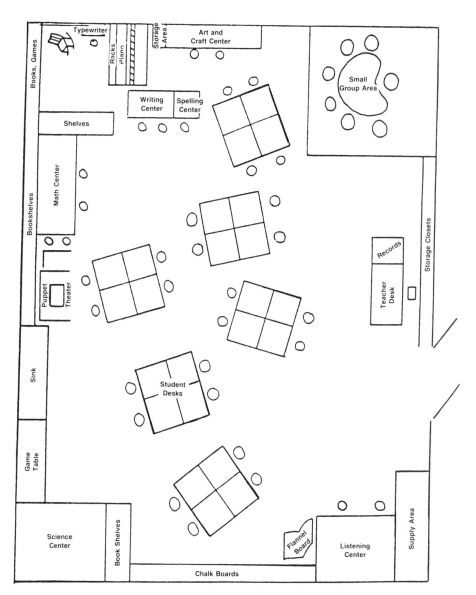

Figure 19.1 Diagram of Classroom.

movement now and then. Some need to be able to vocalize their learning activities. Row seating blocks communication, is antisocial, and tends to inhibit movement. My successes with cluster seating can be duplicated with a table arrangement, but I prefer desks that hold books and materials. Use of desks saves time because students are not running back and forth to storage units.

Cluster seating enhances learning by fostering student interaction during instructional activities, and it makes for a happier classroom. Occasionally, scrapes occur when I create clusters of incompatible children. Then I have to regroup. Some children also object at first because they are accustomed to row seating. After a while, however, they all learn to function well in cluster seating and they love it.

Learning Centers and Resource Materials

To teach well, I need a large variety of instructional materials and good learning centers. Because children learn in varied ways, different materials are needed to accommodate their differences. For instance, Sara learns about the structure of teeth from an audio self-instructional program in my science center, whereas Mark prefers to read a book about the structure of teeth. Each learning center houses a variety of materials. Centers for reading, creative writing, science, mathematics, and short-term special topics are found in my classroom. Many resources are needed in the centers. A good guide to instructional materials is the book *Creative Thinking and Problem Solving in Gifted Education* by J. F. Feldhusen and Treffinger (1985). In their Chapter 6, they listed and described 76 books and materials that are all useful in individualized teaching of the gifted. My book (H. J. Feldhusen, 1986) also lists many good resources.

The children learn to access materials in the centers and from files in the room so that they do not have to depend on me for every step as they go about learning. The centers are aesthetically appealing and motivating places to lure or draw children into the learning process. In each center, all children can work as fast as they are able, and at a level appropriate to their achievements. The centers also afford many opportunities for extended or enrichment learning, such as in-depth projects, problem solving, or small group activities. The centers offer excellent opportunities for individualized and small group learning, development of self-direction skills, and experiencing joy and a sense of accomplishment in learning.

Students Plan Their Own Daily Learning Activities

To achieve the goal of independence and self-direction in learning, the children begin each day by planning their own learning activities. However, the plan often includes the morning only because we frequently do whole class activities in the afternoon. This is our ''learning agreement system.'' A list of centers and activities available or operating each day is posted on a large chart. The children examine the chart, think over their own needs, plan the order, schedule time, and record on a form their activities for the morning. One child's schedule might be similar to the following list:

1. Work on subtraction in math center
2. Go to reading center
3. Work on spelling
4. Work on science project in center
5. Creative writing
6. Reading group
7. Art project
8. Main library

A social studies center is available for morning projects, but the entire class works in science, social studies, and writing during the afternoon.

When the children plan their own morning activities, I try to get around to check their plans to assure that they allot ample time to work in all the basic areas of the curriculum and in areas where they may have special needs. For the gifted students, this means helping them select and pursue extended or enriched learning activities. In math and science, the students develop special problem-solving projects. In reading, the children are helped to find suitable high-level books appropriate to their special interests.

The children grow throughout the year in their ability to plan well. By spring, the gifted children are able to transcend daily planning and plan a week at a time. This individual planning gives the students a sense of internal control that shows clearly in their pride as they go about learning in the classroom.

Individualized Learning of Basic Skills

Gifted children and slow learners must be able to pursue the learning of basic skills at a level and pace that fits their current achievement levels. To help them accomplish this goal, I need many instructional resources that can be accessed easily to fit each child. The Apple II computer can be of service in math, language skills, and writing. Special kits and activities for math, spelling, reading, punctuation, and handwriting are located in learning centers.

To monitor their progress as closely as possible, I check worksheets the children do each day. For Tommy, who is gifted, I try to make sure that he is working on activities in each skill area at an appropriate level; however, if he rushes his work and grows careless, I can determine whether he needs special assistance by monitoring his worksheets.

A wealth of material is available to accommodate individualized learning and children's learning styles. A specialized library at Purdue University contains instructional materials to use with gifted children. The librarian, with the aid of her computerized retrieval system, provides excellent assistance in finding good materials for gifted students. J. F. Feldhusen and Treffinger's (1985) book has been a valuable guide in selecting good materials to individualize instruction in my class, and my book (H. J. Feldhusen, 1986) provides a list and description of all the materials and resources used in my classroom.

Room Meetings

From Glasser (1969), I learned the concept of room meetings. The purposes of the room meetings are to identify and solve social and learning problems children are experiencing in the classroom, and to develop in the children a sense of autonomy or self-control. Meetings are held about once a week, and we begin by brainstorming difficulties, troubles, or problems: someone keeps spelling lesson cards in his desk, Mary talks mean to some of the boys in the classroom, Shawn takes too long on the computer, and the librarian has not been able to help the gifted cluster with its special project on Indian arts and crafts. When all problems are articulated, we brainstorm and discuss possible solutions. The meeting always concludes with a definite plan of action.

Much of the time, room meetings focus on social aspects of living, working, and "funning" together in the classroom. I want the room to be a pleasant and intellectually stimulating place for all children, but especially to be intellectually challenging for the gifted. An excellent climate for learning is developed through our room meetings.

Fostering Thinking Skills

A major goal of my system for teaching gifted children in a regular classroom is to help them develop higher level thinking skills. The principal areas of thinking developed through the system are creative writing, problem solving, and the higher levels of Bloom's (1956) Taxonomy. All of the work in developing thinking skills is done in the context of teaching language arts, science, social studies, and mathematics. For example, I see creative writing as developing creativity in language arts.

We deal with creativity often in the form of brainstorming ideas: "What are all the things you would have wanted to bring with you if you were a pilgrim on the Mayflower?" "Rewrite these numbers in as many combinations as possible." "What are all the soil and climate factors that might influence the growth of our beans?" The gifted children or the cluster of gifted students is expected to develop longer and more elaborate lists than the other students.

Elaboration is encouraged through creative writing and in group story writing activities. Originality is solicited in the writing of newspaper article titles. Risk taking is encouraged through trying different approaches to solving math problems. The whole range of creative thinking skills is addressed, and gifted children specifically are stimulated to undertake higher level activities in this area.

Creative writing requires creative thinking, logical sequencing, imaging, and elaboration of characters. All of the students' writing projects grow out of knowledge-input experiences, such as classroom speakers, library research, or field trips. I feel strongly that children should develop their writing out of knowledge-generating experiences. Gifted children start with larger knowledge bases and acquire much more from classroom activities than do children who are not gifted. For example, when she learned that an expert on robotics from Purdue University was going to be a guest speaker, Sandy immediately told us about all the things she already had read on robotics. She attended carefully to the speaker, and then wrote a lengthy story about Robby the Robot.

Problem-solving activities can be infused in all areas of the curriculum. Because they need far less time on basic skills, gifted children are able to do much more work on problem solving than do average students. My cluster of gifted students is working on a problem concerning the dimensions of the Mayflower, Sean is working on a science problem in astronomy, and Nelly is working on some math problem-solving activities in *Problem Solving: A Basic Mathematical Goal* (Meiring, 1982). The gifted students elect on their learning plans each day to spend more time in problem solving, or I guide them to it.

The top three levels of Bloom's (1956) Taxonomy—analysis, synthesis, and evaluation—can be used to develop curriculum and as a guide for project activities. Although gifted students need to develop a knowledge base, comprehension, and application skills, these levels are embedded in teaching basic subject matter. The three higher levels build on those bases. At the analysis level, three gifted children are comparing the background problems of the pilgrims and the Vietnamese as immigrants. Sean and Nelly are designing a science project on the growth of bean plants (synthesis). Mary is evaluating a story she wrote with criteria I supplied. In the course of a year, substantial growth can be observed in the thinking of the gifted students, and reasonable growth can be observed in all the students in my classroom.

Freedom of Movement

A good skill for children in general to learn is to control their own movement and to move about the classroom freely in pursuit of learning. Gifted children are precocious; that is, they are far advanced in basic skills compared with children of average ability, and they are loaded with ideas and interests. Thus, they need freedom to explore, examine, go, and read, and generally to indulge their curiosity. They should be free to go to the school library whenever they have a need to get information or explore ideas. All such movement should be done in a quiet and orderly manner in respect of the learning activities of the other students. Children can learn to control their own behavior to that end. Gifted children thrive in the open classroom and profit tremendously through being able to guide and facilitate their own learning.

In my model, the children plan for themselves the order in which they will participate in learning activities and the amount of time they will spend in each activity. Those activities include time in learning centers, time at their own seats, time working in small groups, or trips to the library. They learn to go about these activities quietly and in an orderly manner because we have rules, discussed in room meetings, which state and reinforce these ideas. The freedom of movement is especially helpful to some children whose learning styles are more action oriented, but the general affective tone of the classroom experience is enhanced when children do not feel bound to their seats. Childhood is a time of action, movement, and exploration, and the classroom should be a place where those inclinations can be expressed productively in pursuit of learning.

Balanced Treatment of the Basic Disciplines and the Arts

Basic knowledge needs to be learned in science, language arts, social studies, and mathematics, as well as in art and music. All of these areas are a part of the curriculum in my individualized classroom. I expect gifted children to go far beyond basic skills levels for their grade level, so many supplementary learning materials can be used to help them extend their knowledge and comprehension. Materials from higher grade levels (acceleration), as well as creativity, problem-solving, and project enrichment activities, are used to meet the needs of the gifted, just as below–grade-level materials and activities are used for children who are functioning below grade level. An essential ingredient in sustaining motivation and positive attitudes about schoolwork is to let the gifted operate at a more challenging level. Holding bright children in the lockstep or giving them only on-grade enrichment activities fosters boredom and destroys their motivation to learn. The bottom line is that children need to be challenged in school and helped to meet the challenges. Then they feel good about learning and develop positive self-concepts as learners.

As an example, Brad is a bright second grader. He started cursive writing early because he showed an interest, and he did very well on the first writing activities I gave him. Brad also is precocious in math. He completed all of the second-grade math curriculum after 2 months of school. Thus, I started him in division, advanced multiplication, and fractions, and again found that he could learn the new material with no difficulty. I also have introduced some enrichment problem-solving activities and some extra creative writing into his daily plans, and he seems to love and thrive on both of them.

Gifted children must get balanced exposure to all areas of the curriculum. Some, like Tina, would like to spend all their time on reading and writing and avoid science and math. Tina is allowed to devote a lot of her time to reading and creative writing, but I also check her learning agreement to ensure that she does not omit math and science, and I make special efforts to build her interest in the latter by selecting special materials.

Extensive Use of Volunteers

Some teachers are quick to tell me that my system is not feasible because they would not have time to do it properly. Admittedly, somewhat more time is required than with group instruction, but one can become more efficient in use or management of time, and one can obtain auxiliary help. Time management books are readily available, as are workshops or inservice on the topic. These management workshops and materials are very helpful in learning ways to operate more efficiently, but extra help still is needed, so I use volunteers. In my school district, volunteers are used widely.

Parent volunteers are sought at the parent room meeting shortly after school opens. I tell them that I can use help (a) with the Junior Great Books Program; (b) with clerical activities (e.g., typing, cutting, pasting, copying); (c) in working with individuals and small groups; (d) in assisting children in the learning center (a place for extended and remedial learning) with cassette tapes and computers; and (e) in helping with field trips. Parent volunteers are augmented by some college and university students who come to my class for special kinds of practicum experiences connected with courses they are taking.

As an illustration, while we were studying endangered species, one parent worked with a small group of gifted children in writing a play. She also led them through rehearsals of the play, helped them create costumes and a setting, and directed production of the play. Another parent arranged all the details of a trip to a historical museum. Still another worked with several gifted children on planning a hypothetical trip to Japan as a part of a unit on Japan that is taught each year.

Volunteers make possible the extension of my contacts with gifted children, and their presence as nonprofessional partners in teaching is welcome. A bit of time is needed to get ready for the volunteers and to guide their work, but the payoffs for the children, and especially for the gifted, are abundant. The children also appreciate the diversity of human contacts.

Close Monitoring of Students' Learning and Effective Record Keeping

In an individualized learning situation, close monitoring of student progress is needed. The situation is complex, however, because children are working at a wider range of levels and on a wider variety of activities than what is generally found in the regular classroom. The mastery learning techniques suggest that different types of material should be used when children fail to master an idea or skill the first time. Switching from print to audio media or to a game or to a hands-on activity might be just what is needed for a gifted child who does not thrive on workbook exercises. However, the variety of levels and materials being used complicates efforts to keep track of each child's progress. Thus, much time is spent checking papers, watching children at work, checking quizzes and short tests, and talking with children about their work. Their learning agreements are examined daily to make sure that the students are selecting appropriate activities.

I need to monitor the work of students in the gifted cluster in my room on advanced skill learning activities, on problem solving and projects, and in their reading. I do not want them to languish or to scatter their efforts, so I must monitor closely and offer guidance.

One example is Michelle, who was inclined to take on more activities than she could handle. At one time, she was reading four books, writing two stories, designing a science experiment, and doing several math problem-solving activities. She needed help to focus on a smaller set of activities so that she could be successful.

My record-keeping systems consist of card records for each child in each subject. The children help in checking their own work (I spot-check their efforts), and in the upper grades they can assist in recording grades or performance levels. I have also experimented with a card-sort record-keeping system that made it possible to pull up all the cards of the gifted children who had already mastered a skill or concept before introducing them to a higher level project activity. However, I found the system too cumbersome and abandoned it.

A special record-keeping system also is used, which consists of one 5 × 8 inch card for each child. Personal things related to the child's needs or problems that should be addressed are recorded on the cards. For example, on the card for Sean, I noted at the beginning of the third month that I should introduce him to multiplication of three-digit by two-digit numbers, long division, and complex story problems. Sean was extremely precocious in math, and my special record reminded me that I must attend to his readiness for higher level work.

Sally was precocious verbally. I noted on her special card during the fifth month that I should introduce her to some books by Beverly Cleary. Some of Cleary's books are appropriate for the fourth- to seventh-grade level. I also noted that Sally might profit from a longer writing project.

Teachers need to monitor children's work closely so that they can guide students to appropriate learning experiences that fit achievement levels, interests, and needs. Good records are needed to help the teacher select appropriate higher level materials and activities for gifted students so that they will be challenged properly and will achieve at the highest levels of which they are capable.

CONCLUSION

My system for individualized teaching of the gifted in a regular classroom is complex but manageable. My book (H. J. Feldhusen, 1986) spells out the details of daily operations, and provides references for the teaching materials I use. The achievement levels attained by children in my classes are very high. Several of my gifted children achieved at 7.2 grade level. All of the children develop a true love of reading because of the emphasis I place on techniques to develop positive attitudes toward reading. Above all, students learn to operate independently and to guide their own learning activities. I work closely with the gifted students, helping them to achieve at the highest possible levels, and yet to have time for enriching experiences in problem solving, projects, games, and writing. The system works well for me and has been adopted by other teachers. It is one good way to meet the needs of the gifted in the regular classroom.

REFERENCES

Bloom, B. S. (1956). *Taxonomy of educational objectives. Cognitive domain, Handbook I.* New York: David McKay.

Feldhusen, H. J. (1986). *Individualized teaching of gifted children in regular classrooms.* Buffalo, NY: DOK Publishers.

Feldhusen, J. F., & Treffinger, D. J. (1985). *Creative thinking and problem solving in gifted education* (3rd ed.). Dubuque, IA: Kendall-Hunt.

Glasser, W. (1969). *Schools without failure.* New York: Harper & Row.

Meiring, S. (1982). *Problem solving: A basic mathematical goal* (Books 1 and 2). Palo Alto, CA: Dale Seymour Press.

Rosenfield, P., Lambert, N. M., & Black, A. (1985). Desk arrangement effects on pupil classroom behavior. *Journal of Educational Psychology, 77*(1), 101–108.

20

Critique of Feldhusen's "Individualized Teaching of the Gifted in Regular Classrooms"

Margie K. Kitano

Feldhusen's approach to individualized teaching of gifted children in the regular elementary classroom has many advantages for both gifted and average children. The unique components of cluster seating, self-planning of learning activities, and freedom of movement logically support children's development of independence, self-directed learning, and sense of personal control over their learning. Availability of the same opportunities to all children in the classroom enhances all children's educational experience and limits perceptions that the gifted children receive special treatment. Although Feldhusen presents no specific evaluation data, the record-keeping system appears to promote close monitoring of children's progress. In short, Feldhusen presents a viable model for meeting gifted children's individual needs in the regular classroom.

My affinity for Feldhusen's model makes difficult a "critique" in the sense of presenting a radically divergent viewpoint. Instead, in this critique, I present (a) an analysis of implicit assumptions, (b) a discussion of potential problems and limitations in the implementation of Feldhusen's model, and (c) an alternative strategy for individualizing instruction in the regular classroom.

ASSUMPTIONS REGARDING INDIVIDUALIZATION

Feldhusen's discussion of her approach to individualizing instruction for the gifted assumes a common definition of individualization and that individualization enhances gifted children's learning. Specifically, she implies that individualization involves the process of one-to-one instruction. An alternative definition focuses on the ends rather than the means: Children receive instruction consistent with their individual needs—their different learning styles, receptive and expressive modalities, and academic objectives. Defined in this way, the goals of individualization can be achieved through small group or even whole group activities.

Feldhusen's approach to individualization, in which children establish individual daily plans and work independently, is consistent with a process definition. The model relies on "extensive use of learning centers and resource materials," including computers and special kits for math, spelling, reading, punctuation, and handwriting. Logically, such individualized instruction would appear more effective for any group of learners than would nonindividualized instruction. Yet little empirical data are available to support or refute this assumption for gifted or average children. In fact, Brophy (1986) concluded from his review of research that reliance on individualized learning modules and other materials-based approaches is less effective in producing achievement than the teacher's active instruction. Where individualization means that students work on their own for extended time periods, "even bright and well-motivated students develop incomplete or erroneous concepts" (Brophy, 1986, p. 1071). Implicit assumptions that individualization requires one-to-one instruction and is effective for gifted children, although logical, require critical examination.

POTENTIAL PROBLEMS AND LIMITATIONS

As Feldhusen cautions, her model for individualizing instruction in the regular classroom requires excellent time management, use of volunteers, and careful record keeping. Possible problems in implementing the model include (a) conflicts with teacher style and (b) gaps in skill and knowledge acquisition.

Conflict with Teaching Style

Just as children's individual differences demand a variety of instructional techniques, teachers' individual differences require a range of pedagogical models. Whereas some teachers will enjoy the challenges of Feldhusen's model, others may be more comfortable with traditional seating arrangements, limited movement, and greater teacher control over learning activities, particularly as class size and student variability increase. Teachers who implement Feldhusen's model may need to prepare children for the transition to traditional classrooms, where even the "action-oriented" child will be required to remain seated for long periods. Although childhood is indeed a time of action, movement, and exploration, some educators and parents suggest that the discipline and delay of gratification required by traditional classrooms reflect real-world demands. As Feldhusen notes, Rosenfield, Lambert, and Black's (1985) study on desk arrangement indicated that fifth- and sixth-grade students seated in clusters engaged in significantly more on-task behavior than did those seated in rows. However, in this study, a circle arrangement produced more on-task behavior than either clusters or rows; on-task behavior was defined as participation in brainstorming discussions (listening, commenting). The conclusions of the study cannot be generalized to include nondiscussion behavior.

In addition, appropriate use of parent volunteers often involves preparation of specific instructions for parents, training in questioning and response strategies, and delicate interpersonal communications. For example, volunteers who are untrained with regard to specific objectives and techniques may use convergent rather than divergent questioning during a creativity lesson. In some cases, children behave negatively when their parents are in the classroom, and the parents' presence may interfere with their children's learning. Clearly, parent volunteers can significantly enhance educational programs. Effective use of parent volunteers requires teacher preparation and parent training.

Gaps in Skill and Knowledge Acquisition

As Feldhusen emphasizes, programs in which children are encouraged to acquire basic skills and concepts through independent learning must include effective record keeping to monitor each child's progress. Other elements critical to children's skill and knowledge acquisition missing from Feldhusen's discussion are a guiding districtwide philosophy concerning gifted children's education, comprehensive curriculum planning, well-articulated scope and sequence, and periodic criterion-referenced assessment to determine progress and detect gaps in learning. How Feldhusen's model fits within the context of a district's total educational plan for gifted children is unclear; especially unclear are procedures necessary for articulation. For example, what are the guiding parameters within which children can plan their activities? If a child chooses accelerated learning in mathematics, what accommodations are available after the child leaves Feldhusen's classroom? If children demonstrate mastery of basic mathematics and language arts skills commensurate with their chronological age, can they select any project of their interest? Or does a flexible core curriculum exist that guides the teacher in providing and limiting options?

In short, Feldhusen's model provides a physical and temporal structure for encouraging individualized activities. The major limitations to the model stem from presentation of the structure without an overall philosophical and curricular context.

ALTERNATIVE STRATEGIES FOR INDIVIDUALIZATION

An alternative approach to individualizing instruction for gifted children in a regular classroom emphasizes curricular, rather than structural, accommodations within the context of a comprehensive curriculum plan. Comprehensive, long-term planning of educational experiences for the gifted is an imperative; a curriculum for gifted students should designate the main content or subject matter for those students over a number of years (Kitano & Kirby, 1986). A preliminary working draft of standards for programs for gifted students (Parke, 1987) includes the following statement: "An ideal program for gifted and talented students is articulated and comprehensive from preschool to post-secondary'' (p. 19). Another standard is that the curriculum should be based upon a flexible core with the goal of having students become content experts. Maker's (1986) criteria for appropriate scope and sequence include flexibility for gifted students to pursue their interests, integration of higher level thinking processes and sophisticated product development, and building upon and extending the regular curriculum. For the regular classroom, an additional consideration should be to extend opportunities for advanced/enriched learning to all children.

Curriculum-based approaches begin with a comprehensive curriculum plan in which subject matter concepts are identified and articulated over several years. The curriculum plan is based on a well-defined philosophy and provides parameters within which specific objectives and activities can be developed. One curriculum-based option stems from development of a special curriculum for gifted children. The special curriculum might include content areas or concepts different from those required in the regular curriculum. Gifted students in the regular classroom would pursue these topics after or while acquiring regular curriculum knowledge and skills. For example, a district might develop specialized curricula for elementary-aged gifted children in the areas of leadership, the arts, politics, or anthropology. This approach provides differentiated services to gifted children through presentation of content selected to match the characteristics and needs of gifted learners.

In a second curriculum-based approach, the regular curriculum and concepts are used as a framework. Differentiation is provided through activities presented and children's responses. The teacher offers a variety of activities to convey the targeted concept; these activities encourage increasingly more abstract concept acquisition and/or increasingly sophisticated products. The teacher can offer the activities as simultaneous alternatives or may ask all children to engage in all the activities in a sequential manner. Children of all ability levels will be able to participate in the most challenging activities; only the quality of their responses and products will vary.

For example, suppose District X's comprehensive curriculum plan identifies the art concept of color–feeling association and the science concept of energy conservation as important for fourth-grade students. The fourth-grade teacher can individualize instruction by presenting activities that permit children to interact with the concepts in ways commensurate with their differing ability levels. For the concept ''color can be used to communicate feelings,'' the teacher can present activities with increasingly more abstract thinking process demands: categorization, analysis, synthesis/creativity, and evaluation (see Figure 20.1). Children of all ability levels will be able to participate; differentiation will occur in the children's level of response.

The teacher might present the concept ''people can help conserve energy'' through activities that result in different products (see Figure 20.2). Depending on time constraints, all children can be invited to pursue all activities or to select among alternatives. Having three groups of children working on different projects simultaneously may require use of volunteers to supervise the groups. Presenting all activities to the whole group means that gifted children will participate in lower as well

Topic _____ Art Techniques _____

Concept	Processes			
	Level 1 Categorization	Level 2 Analysis	Level 3 Creativity/Synthesis	Level 4 Evaluation
Color can be used to communicate feelings.	Which colors make you feel happy? sad?	Describe how this painting makes you feel. What techniques did the painter use to evoke those feelings?	Paint a picture that conveys the feeling of . . .	How effectively did the artist use color in these paintings? What changes would you suggest to the artist?

Figure 20.1 Individualizing Through Process Differentiation.

Topic _____ Energy

	Products		
Concept	Level 1 List for Home	Level 2 Position Paper for School	Level 3 Model for Community
People can help conserve energy.	Develop a list of ways to conserve energy at home.	Identify sources of energy loss in the school; suggest modifications for conservation; calculate savings.	Plan and construct a model of an energy-efficient community.

Figure 20.2 Individualizing Through Product Differentiation.

as higher level activities. However, research findings suggest that higher level questions are not necessarily better than lower level questions and that the latter may facilitate acquisition of higher level objectives (Brophy, 1986).

Curriculum-based approaches permit teachers to meet individual children's needs through whole group or small group activities directly related to the established scope and sequence. In developing activities, guiding questions include the following:

1. Do the activities include provisions for several ability levels?
2. Do the activities include ways to accommodate a variety of interest areas?
3. Does the design of activities encourage development of sophisticated products?
4. Do the activities provide for the integration of thinking processes with concept development?
5. Are the concepts consistent with the comprehensive curriculum plan?

CONCLUSION

Whether teachers select curricular or structural approaches, serving gifted students in the regular classroom requires specific attention to their preference for complex tasks, facility with abstractions, and greater ability to generalize and to learn from their errors. Recent research on grouping practices (Rogers, 1991) suggests that within-class grouping options produce substantial academic gains when instruction is differentiated.

Feldhusen's model for individualizing instruction of gifted children in the regular classroom focuses on structural accommodations: cluster seating, self-planning, freedom of movement, volunteers, and extensive use of centers and resource materials. These accommodations support gifted children's needs for independence and self-directed learning while providing the same opportunities to children of lesser ability. However, individualization need not occur through individual activities. Defined as meeting individual learner needs, individualization can occur through group activities. An alternative model that emphasizes curricular rather than structural accommodations enables teachers to extend the regular curriculum by providing a variety of activities to convey major concepts. The activities permit process, product, and response differentiation through whole and small group activities. Alternative approaches to individualizing instruction in the regular classroom are needed to accommodate individual teaching styles, philosophies, and preferences.

REFERENCES

Brophy, J. (1986). Teacher influences on student achievement. *American Psychologist, 41,* 1069–1077.

Kitano, M. K., & Kirby, D. F. (1986). *Gifted education: A comprehensive view.* Boston: Little, Brown.

Maker, C. J. (1986). Developing scope and sequence in curriculum. *Gifted Child Quarterly,* *30*(4), 151–158.

Parke, B. N. (1987). *First steps toward program standards in educating the gifted and talented.* Manuscript in preparation. Reston, VA: The Association for Gifted (a division of the Council for Exceptional Children).

Rogers, K. B. (1991, November). The relationship of grouping practices to the education of the gifted and talented learner: Research-based decision making [Abstract]. *National Research Center on the Gifted and Talented Newsletter,* p. 8.

Rosenfield, P., Lambert, N. M., & Black, A. (1985). Desk arrangement effects on pupil classroom behavior. *Journal of Educational Psychology, 77*(1), 101–108.

21

A Learning Center Approach to Individualized Instruction for Gifted Students

Roseanne Lopez
Joy MacKenzie

The learning center approach to individualizing instruction is no panacea of promise by which the problems unique to all types of learners and learning styles can be accommodated. Learning centers may not even be the optimum choice for instruction for all gifted and talented learners. However, a major assertion of our chapter is that instruction through learning centers is one of the most versatile methods for enhancing student thinking, goal setting, and self-direction. This method allows the teacher to integrate the curriculum with a single learning environment to accommodate all types of learners, and is especially appropriate for the education of the gifted student.

CURRICULUM, METHODOLOGY, AND PHILOSOPHY

Educators often conceive of curricula for the gifted too narrowly. Many curriculum adaptations can be defined as "adding on"—longer, harder, more—and they may not achieve the desired outcomes. Curriculum for the gifted, when compared with curriculum for any learner, should not be *more* or *less,* but *different,* because the gifted learner's needs are in many cases *different* from those of other learners. The best education of the gifted consists of curriculum differentiation—a differentiation based on the needs of the individual. Differentiation can be accomplished efficiently and effectively using the learning center approach. The teacher's role in education through centers becomes one of a facilitator. The methods that the teacher selects should allow the learner to accomplish learning goals while being given the opportunity to make choices, explore, and go into depth on a topic or issue.

Designing and implementing curriculum strategies for gifted students who are mainstreamed into the regular education program require a flexible educator who

282

is willing to look beyond the "regular" program into the possibilities that the topics provide for exploration and research. Ideally, every classroom would provide such opportunities for all learners; however, such provisions for gifted students are imperative. When designing a learning center, the teacher first must define what results the students are to achieve, and then decide how those outcomes can be assessed. Although this approach is sound and consistent in its philosophy, it must be well thought out. The outcomes, assessments, and management procedures must be planned in advance to ensure success. Careful planning is necessary for curriculum goals to be met deliberately and developmentally.

ADMINISTRATIVE AND ECONOMIC ADVANTAGES

The learning center approach offers school administrators the opportunity to provide gifted students with appropriate curriculum within the regular classroom setting. Some aspects of the social and emotional development of the gifted learner along with intellectual peer stimulation may need to be dealt with in the overall program and instructional planning. The cost of providing separate programming for gifted students is prohibitive to some schools because appropriate staff must be hired and a classroom must be equipped. For other schools, ability grouping in any form is philosophically inappropriate. Some fear administrators may be accused of "elitism," whereas others believe that research conducted to prove the benefits of dissolving grouping of low-ability students is relevant to the gifted as well. The use of learning centers in the regular classroom should not be seen as a comprehensive approach to meeting the needs of gifted students. All gifted students need to be grouped some of the time with intellectual peers to be challenged fully. Researchers in the area of ability grouping have admitted to their lack of attention to the effects of such grouping on gifted students and, in some cases, have stated that excluding grouping for gifted students may be harmful (Allan, 1991). One advantage of using learning centers is that they allow educators to address part of the needs of gifted students without allocating additional funding for staff, buying additional classroom equipment, or grouping gifted students in self-contained settings.

Educating regular classroom teachers to meet the affective and academic needs of gifted students is an area to which attention must be paid. Staff development must be conducted to facilitate maximum learning. As this approach is implemented in the regular classroom, *all* students will have access to accelerated and enriched curriculum, which ultimately will aid all students in advancing to their highest level of ability.

LEADERSHIP AND STUDENT INVOLVEMENT

Effectively implementing a learning center approach for gifted learners in any school requires a joint effort of the regular classroom teaching staff, a specialist in the area of education of the gifted, and a supportive administrator. All parties must design the program with the needs of the gifted learner in mind. The teacher must be well acquainted with the various characteristics and types of giftedness, and the variety of learning styles that may be encountered. The teacher also should create curriculum plans and choose resources that serve the needs of an integrated, multilevel group of students. The gifted student needs opportunities to experiment and explore abstract ideas and pave new frontiers in thought. Opportunities also should be provided for students to assist in the planning, implementation, and evaluation of progress within the learning center approach. The students can assist in making decisions about topics they would like to investigate, and can assist in gathering resource materials. Real-life research skills are developed that can be generalized into other areas. In implementation, the student is the busy one! However, knowing when to come for teacher assistance is important.

In our experience, many gifted students wait an extraordinarily long time before they ask for assistance, even when presented with a task in which they have little or no expertise. This reluctance may be due in part to their fear of "not knowing." *Knowing* things has been a built-in part of their persona for so long that they are fearful someone will ridicule them for admitting they need assistance. The teacher's establishment of trust and modeling of making mistakes, looking up answers to questions they themselves do not know, and communicating the expectation that assistance will be needed in accomplishing the more difficult tasks, will open up the door for the reluctant student. Making students comfortable in this type of environment, and knowing when they need help, will assist the teacher further in implementing the learning center approach.

Students can help to establish criteria for evaluation of tasks. The teacher should always provide additional criteria so that the students understand the expectations of a variety of audiences. In all cases, students should be made accountable for the record keeping of their progress, with teacher approval. Records can be kept privately in student work folders. Private folders are preferable to more public recording or check-off systems when students will be working on a variety of levels within the same classroom. Teachers must examine the students in their classes and their own philosophy when setting up the management of the records and assessment process. In designing the learning center approach, the leadership team must give each participating staff member the freedom to implement a system that is manageable for him or her, while guiding the process toward success for all students and advancing the opportunities for gifted learners.

THE TEACHER'S ROLE

The teacher's role when using the learning center approach shifts dramatically from that needed in a teacher-directed classroom. The teacher using learning centers becomes a facilitator of learning. Once clear educational outcomes and specific criteria are established, the teacher is free to provide specific assistance throughout the classroom. The teacher's role becomes creative, with multiple opportunities to provide meaningful instruction to individuals, small groups, and the entire class. By becoming a facilitator, the teacher has more time to assess by observation the need to teach specific skills. Sometimes teachers assume that the gifted child has all of the skills necessary to accomplish a certain task; in actuality, however, he or she may not have developed particular skills because they seemed irrelevant previously.

The teacher also must assist the students in understanding the type of thinking required for particular tasks. Making students aware of their thinking and the processes they might use to accomplish a task assists them in becoming self-directed learners. Once students are aware of the uses for particular thinking strategies, they can begin to identify where those strategies can be used outside the classroom and in other educational settings. Such connections make the learning life-long.

When selecting activities for the learning center approach, choosing a wide variety of tasks that require various types and levels of thinking and that appeal to the various types of learners is necessary. Knowledge of the work of many researchers in these areas will assist the teacher in activity design. In *Frames of Mind* (1983), Howard Gardner outlined seven intelligences: linguistic, musical, logical–mathematical, spatial, bodily–kinesthetic, intrapersonal, and interpersonal. The seven intelligences give the teacher a framework for selecting appropriate activities to address the various types of learners. The work of Barbara Clark (1988) in the area of characteristics of various types of giftedness is complementary to Gardner's theory of multiple intelligences. Examining both the intelligences and the possible characteristics that may be encountered in gifted children makes connections for the teacher to those areas that need to be addressed in the learning center classroom through corresponding activities.

Bloom (1956) and Krathwohl, Bloom, and Masia (1964) provided cognitive and affective taxonomies of educational objectives. The taxonomies are easy to understand and provide a useful framework for teachers to use in curriculum writing and examining activities to make certain all levels of thinking are included. Each of the levels of the taxonomies can be addressed in the learning centers through one of the seven intelligences and demonstrated by the appropriately selected activities.

Once the activities are selected based on the criteria set by the teacher (e.g., addresses a particular intelligence, focuses on needs of the gifted), he or she must then decide on the most effective manner in which to communicate the directions to the students. The clearer the directions are in the planning stages of the centers, the more time the teacher will have to spend on actual instruction and one-to-one interaction when the centers are in place. The teacher needs to consider the level being taught and the reading levels of the students. The teacher should not assume that all gifted students are excellent readers. Communication of directions to students needs to occur in a variety of modalities, just as when the teacher operates in a whole group instruction mode. The directions should be written, oral, and, in some cases, diagrammed in pictures so the task is understood by the students. Providing specific criteria for completion of the activity, along with the standard expected, focuses the learner on the desired outcome, thereby encouraging success.

Shifting the role of the teacher, and the planning necessary to select and organize student tasks is time-consuming. Before making final decisions regarding use of learning centers, careful examination of teacher style, desired results, and time allocation should be made. The use of volunteers in classrooms has shown some promise (M. Franklin, personal correspondence, Tucson, AZ, 1991). Often, local retirement communities are cooperative in advertising volunteer opportunities in the schools. Such volunteers can be used in the planning process for development of materials and in the implementation phase for communicating directions. Volunteers can serve as a sounding board for student ideas. Aides (if available) can serve in the same capacity, and students from upper levels can assist as well. Assistance from other students should be designed in consideration of learning outcomes for *all* students involved, not only for those being helped.

RESOURCES

In addition to the human resources already mentioned, the learning center approach requires the compilation of multiple resources for students to be most successful. Research materials, such as magazines, documents, books on the theme being studied, computer searches, various encyclopedias, newspapers, and pictures, must be gathered. The selection of such material is dependent upon the topic or issue being studied.

The teacher also must gather tools for the production of work. Word processors and graphics can be used by the students to produce products that display their learning. Multimedia resources are motivational for the students and encourage creativity. Kits are available from various suppliers that have materials for students to make slides, filmstrips, and more. The video camera is another tool for the students to use in designing their products. Various art materials also are potential sources for product development. Often teachers expect that the students will be able to select a medium and produce the work without instruction; however, this usually is not the case. Specific lessons on layout, use of electronic equipment, examples of uses of various media, and techniques in marketing ideas are essential.

Funding comes into play when deciding what resources to purchase. After the teacher selects a theme, he or she should review catalogs and determine the materials that would be essential for the students to achieve the targeted outcome. Each year, additional purchases can be made that enhance the collection. Many materials are available free of charge from education departments of large corporations and non-profit interest groups, although they usually are accompanied by a sales pitch. Even the sales pitch can serve as a teaching tool in the learning center. Information demonstrating a variety of viewpoints can serve as excellent starters for discussion and writing. Teachers should make and distribute a list of needs. Students have a wealth of connections in the community, and many people have access to material and information at little or no cost. For teachers who decide to purchase materials, however, buyer beware! Many publishers have hit the market of educators of the gifted by producing attractive packages *labeled with the right words,* but without the appropriate substance. To avoid purchasing inappropriate materials, teachers should take advantage of those companies that allow teachers to preview materials before paying for them.

LEARNING CENTER DEFINED

A learning center is a physical space, not necessarily stationary, that accommodates the body of ''academic'' components needed to teach a given skill, idea, or group of skills related to a particular content area or blend of content areas. The character and design of learning centers may vary greatly to provide the kinds of space, materials, and methods of presentation needed to accommodate the experiences or tasks particular to the content of each center. The following checklist includes basic characteristics of successful learning centers and ''rules of thumb'' to consider. This list is not specific to gifted students, but is meant for every type of learner. The use of the list enables teachers to assess many facets of the learning center approach, and may serve as an important tool for the planning team as it sets the stage for student learning.

Focus

- Students know what they will learn.
- Students know what they will be able to do or demonstrate.

Assessments

- Criteria are established and student input is solicited.
- Evaluation is congruent with stated focus or outcome.
- Assessment provides useful information for the student and the teacher.
- Assessment includes student self-reflection.

Activity Selection

- Needs of the various levels of learners are met.
- A balance is achieved among activity types (i.e., hands-on, reading, writing, group work, listening).
- Activity types address various intelligences and learning styles or allow for varied product development.
- All thinking levels are addressed.
- Activities are sequenced when appropriate.

Communication

- Center introduction is planned to enhance student interest and understanding.
- Clear written and oral directions are prepared.

Motivation

- The center catches the eye as the students walk in the room.
- The center may have an intriguing quality or sense of mystery.

- Learners are invited to sit and ponder the possibilities in a comfortable setting.
- The center is nonthreatening.
- Activities change or are added periodically.
- Student choice is provided within the parameters of the center.
- The center capitalizes on student interests.
- Thought-provoking questions are asked.

Learner Involvement

- Activities are relevant to the learner (A MUST!).
- Pairings and/or small group work are allowed.

Time

- Limits are established, yet flexibility is in place.
- Expanded opportunity for student work time is given.
- Transitions are short when work time is over.

Management

- Clear behavioral expectations are communicated.
- Alternative work areas are provided and allowed.
- Traffic flow is arranged.
- Record keeping is clear to the students.

DIFFERENTIATION FOR GIFTED STUDENTS

Once the stage is set for a learning center–oriented classroom, differentiation for the gifted within the regular classroom setting is relatively minor. The activities for gifted students need to be as carefully designed and as clearly explained as any others. The differences lie in the *depth, scope, pace,* and *self-directedness* of the expectations. The process and product may be differentiated at the same time. The gifted student will be able to complete activities at the higher levels of cognitive and affective skill at an earlier point in instruction than some of their nongifted peers. A regular classroom teacher must be aware of the myth that gifted children can "make it on their own" within a learning center classroom. An effective facilitator prepares carefully for the gifted students and seeks out additional resources, checks for accuracy, and develops student strengths while the students move at a faster pace. Students should be encouraged to seek out their own resources and to continue their learning by finding connections in other content areas or real-life experiences to enhance further the value of the learning in the center. Such behavior encourages transfer and fosters life-long learning (Perkins & Salomon, 1988).

IMPLEMENTATION

A teacher is given a class of 25 to 30 heterogeneous students, several of whom have been identified as gifted. How does the teacher implement a full-scale, whole class learning center approach to individualized learning? The task may appear formidable!

Beginning this approach on day one with the entire class, *all* day, in *every* subject, although not impossible, would be a major undertaking, even for the most masterful of teachers. This is especially true at the elementary classroom level. For most teachers, and especially for those unaccustomed to working with learning centers, participation in this program, for both student and staff, needs to be introduced and practiced in small pieces. Teachers should begin with one or two content areas, one thematic unit of study, a particular time period, or one learning level. Then, the program can be expanded until all the pieces are operative and working smoothly as an integrated whole. The process is similar to learning to spin plates on poles—becoming acquainted with the feel of the plates, learning to spin, then learning to anticipate how long each plate can endure without additional reinforcement. Should a plate fall, the teacher should pick up the pieces by sharing the problem with the students and brainstorm possible solutions. A shared decision will be owned by the learners and therefore be long lasting.

Preparing the students for this new format and establishing the technical details require proactive classroom management (Gettinger, 1988). Teachers should review the checklist of characteristics of effective learning centers. If motivating activities are included for all types of learners, and students dart into the room asking when they can start, behavior problems (for most students) will be minimal. Behavioral expectations should be clearly established. Teachers should review their own expectations about what a classroom should look like. A learning center classroom will not always be quiet. The noise should be that of students talking to one another about what they are doing and asking one another for assistance. Freedom of movement will be important for students to exhibit self-directed behavior. They will need to get up and get resources, ask an opinion of a friend, use equipment and supplies, and use all the classroom space for the projects that come as a result of their learning. This all sounds fine, but some students, for a variety of reasons, are unable to cope with a less structured environment. For those children, a slow progression from working in one area to free access to all the space may be helpful. Some students may require much stricter parameters, such as a behavioral contract, to be successful. We use a set of rules called Classroom Rights (unknown author). A simple gesture toward the poster in the room helps some students remember their responsibility as a member of the classroom community. The original "rights" have been expanded by the students:

> I have a right to learn about myself in this room; this means that I will be free to express my feelings without being interrupted or punished.
> I have a right to hear and be heard in this room; this means that no one will yell, scream, shout, or make loud noises.

I have a right to get help when I need it. The assistance may come from books or other resources, from another student, or from an adult.

I have a right to be myself in this room; this means that no one will treat me unfairly because I am black or white, fat or thin, tall or short, boy or girl.

I have a right to be safe in this room; this means that no one will hit me, kick me, punch me, or hurt me. Also, I can express my feelings in this room without fear that those ideas, opinions, and feelings will be repeated outside this room.

I have a right to be happy and to be treated with compassion in this room; this means that no one will laugh at me or hurt my feelings.

Learning center classrooms look like workshops or even an artist's studio at times. The appearance of the room can be troublesome to teachers who are comfortable with desks in rows and materials in neat stacks. Finding a balance between a "mess" and a functional work environment takes cooperation between the teacher and the students, all of whom must take responsibility for maintenance of the centers so that all the students have the necessary supplies and materials. The students should be introduced to the centers by having them see where all the essential resources and materials are to be stored. Once everyone understands that it is important for everything to be put back in place so that tasks can be accomplished, few problems will be encountered. The teacher must check at the end of each center time to be sure that the necessary supplies are available. In addition, supplies that would allow students to develop creative products should be on hand. Most of these things are affectionately referred to as "junk": egg cartons, yarn, spools, scrap matting, paints, buttons, and other items found in an attic or storage shed! With the teacher as the facilitator and the student as worker, the shared responsibility instills a valuable work ethic in the student, and saves the teacher precious time that will be needed for planning.

GETTING STUDENTS STARTED AND ASSESSING PROGRESS

Once the stage has been set, the centers are in order, and behavioral expectations are in place, the fun begins! Each student should set clear goals related to his or her particular needs. The teacher serves as a guide in this process. For example, each student in the classroom may be given a record sheet on which to record progress. The teacher sits with each student during an exploratory session and helps the student to choose what activities to do and the sequence in which they should be accomplished. As the teacher talks to each student, learning is customized. These brief talks can be accomplished successfully if the teacher has preassessed each student based on the outcomes that will be desired, knows the student learning style, and knows the strengths and weaknesses of each learner.

To illustrate a goal-setting conference with a gifted student within a learning center classroom, a brief case study and dialogue are included here. Carlos is a fifth-grade Hispanic male. He was identified as gifted on both verbal and quantitative measures. His strong intelligences seem to be in the logical–mathematical, linguistic, and interpersonal areas. The centers and subsequent activities for the unit being taught in his classroom involve the theme "perspectives." Three main centers have been established for all the students. In the writing center, students can select an activity that has them writing a story or poem from another person's or animal's point of view. A number of skills activities are designed to assist the students in their writing. Another center in the classroom has a social studies–humanities focus in which students have the chance to explore various historical events in America. Activities range from answering comprehension questions to writing critiques of the decisions made by our nation's leaders. A third center focuses on mathematical concepts. Activities range from manipulating geometric shapes and angles on a computer to conducting neighborhood surveys about what grocery store actually offers the best prices.

The teacher in this case sits down with Carlos and his center outline for the unit in which each center activity is described carefully and what he should be able to do upon completion of the learning experiences is outlined clearly. The teacher then begins to help Carlos set goals that are appropriate to his needs:

Teacher: Carlos, your goals for this unit are due soon. Let's talk about them for a while. Have you had a chance to explore each of the centers?

Carlos: Yes. I like the one where we can find out about history.

Teacher: Great! I bet you will find other things you like, too. Let's talk about the history one for a moment. What interests you most about that center?

Carlos: I am interested in the Vietnam War. I would like to find out more about it. Maybe the Persian Gulf Crisis, too.

Teacher: Your interests will fit nicely with our theme "perspectives." When you think of the word "perspective" and the interests you mentioned, what does it make you think of?

Carlos: Well, everyone has a perspective on wars. I like them . . . well you know what I mean . . . they are not good all of the time but . . .

Teacher: Who might not like them?

Carlos: My mom. The people that have to fight. The people who have family that dies in them.

Teacher: What could you do to find out more about people's perspectives on these wars?

Carlos: Well, I could ask them. Maybe me and my friends can make a movie about what people think about war.

Teacher: Let's write down a couple of goals for you. Your movie idea sounds great! What do you need to know before you can make a movie about people's perspectives on war?

Carlos: I can already use the camera!

Teacher: Yes, you mastered that on one other project. What else do you need to know?

Carlos: Well, I don't know enough about Vietnam. I watched everything on television about the Persian Gulf . . .

Teacher: What can you do to show what you will learn about Vietnam and what you already know about the Persian Gulf?

  Carlos: Maybe I could do a speech for the class.

Teacher: That sounds like it could go along with your movie. What are some ways we could evaluate your movie and your speech?

  Carlos: Well, I guess we could ask the students who hear the speech and the ones who watch the movie to tell what they think of it.

Teacher: Yes, that would be helpful. What else could we do?

  Carlos: I don't know . . . Maybe you could look at the movie and listen to the speech, and tell me what you think.

Teacher: I certainly will. Now, Carlos, what would be some things all of us, including you, could look for that would help us determine the quality of these products, and help you do them better the next time?

The resulting goals, and the criteria/methods for evaluation, which were expansions of center topics for Carlos, may have looked something like this:

  Goal: Carlos will compare the Vietnam War to the Persian Gulf War. He will give a speech to the class in which he explains the comparisons.

Evaluation: Students, teacher, and Carlos will evaluate the speech based on accuracy of information, clarity of and support for comparisons made, organization of ideas, effectiveness of presentation, and other criteria Carlos may add later.

  Goal: With a small group of students, Carlos will interview community members about their perspectives on one of the wars. The interviews will be taped and developed into a short movie.

Evaluation: Everyone who watches the movie will be asked to tell how effective it is in showing various perspectives of war, and how it could be improved if done again.

Carlos now is free to use the information in the centers to accomplish his goals. He knows how his products will be evaluated. The teacher in this case may need to offer assistance in locating other resources as needed.

Once the students' goals have been set with the teacher's approval, ongoing assessment of progress is needed. Teacher observation and subsequent anecdotal records can help to document students' progress toward their goals. Such records help the teacher identify patterns and assist in planning for alternative approaches to having the student accomplish the center tasks. Observations should center around the evaluation criteria and the specific goals set. Similar observations or evaluations of complex final projects can be made by community experts in the field of study addressed by the unit. Such community contacts can result in mentoring relationships for the gifted students in the classroom.

Student self-reflection and evaluation can serve as useful assessment tools to increase student metacognition and improve student performance. If self-reflection is to be used, the students must understand the purpose of the activity and see the relevance before it will be successful. Self-reflection must be ongoing and not seen as a culminating activity. It needs to have a clear tie to the expected learning outcomes and the goals that were set by the learner. Students can answer questions in a log or journal, or separate worksheets can be developed for this purpose. Some questions that may assist the students in self-reflection might be the following:

- What do you like best about this piece of work? What are the strengths?
- What thinking or other skills you have acquired are illustrated in this work?
- If you could go on with this work, what would you do next?
- What do you know now that you didn't know before?
- How does the learning that has taken place here fit into other situations outside this classroom?
- What will you do next?

As students engage in reflective activities, they reveal perceptions and purposes behind their work that may not be evident in the product or through observation (Howard, 1990):

- What students believe they have done well in a piece of work
- What the students value in the learning or work
- The students' own goals and interests as learners
- The students' strategies for completion of a task and their awareness of strategies
- What the students understand about the concepts taught

Student perceptions are vital to the teacher using learning centers. The role of the facilitator requires that the teacher have a clear notion of each student's needs to best guide progress.

Student self-evaluation is imperative if students are to feel that learning is truly "theirs." Self-evaluations typically occur at points of culmination, such as the completion of a project or as the student masters particular concepts. If grading is to be used, self-evaluation should play a part in the final grade. The evaluation is based upon the established criteria set out and posted prior to the student's beginning the task. Self-evaluation can be in chart form, with a Likert scale for each of several criteria, or it may be based on a more holistic approach by using a rubric with student explanation of their judgment. Using the goals established for Carlos in the example above, the self-evaluation formats shown in Figures 21.1 and 21.2 may help to clarify this concept. Assessment is an inherent part of a successful learning center classroom. The key to the success lies in having clear goals set by the student and the teacher, clear criteria and standards preset, and ongoing student reflection on their progress.

Name: Carlos C.

Activity: Speech comparing two wars

Criteria	Scale
1. Demonstrates flexibility	1 2 3 4
2. Compares two elements of the concept	1 2 3 4
3. Shows evidence of synthesis	1 2 3 4
4. Relates to outside of classroom	1 2 3 4
5. Information presented is accurate	1 2 3 4

Comments:

Descriptors for ranges:
1—Limited evidence of this criterion
2—Evidence of this criterion is satisfactory
3—Evidence of this criterion is clear
4—Exemplary/model demonstration of this criterion

Figure 21.1 Chart Form for Self-Evaluation with Likert Scale.

CONCLUSION

Initiating and implementing learning centers in the classroom requires careful planning based on current student learning research. Facilitating a classroom with this design allows the teacher to become a guide in the child's educational process, thereby giving the students the opportunities to become more self-directed learners. Assessment procedures should be for the purposes of planning and goal setting for the student and the teacher. The learning center approach should not be seen as the only solution for serving gifted students. All aspects of every child's giftedness must be considered when developing suitable programs, including their need to be grouped with other gifted students part of the time to facilitate interaction and stimulate their thinking and reasoning abilities. In addition, the social and emotional needs of gifted learners is of particular importance. Although learning centers can address these areas, they may not be the best method in which to ensure progress.

Review the work you have just completed. Select the rubric level that *generally* best describes your results.

Level 4—The work has evidence of higher levels of thinking either affectively or cognitively. Examples of how this learning was used or will be used outside the classroom is evident. Self-direction was demonstrated throughout the work on this piece. The information is accurate and informative. Evidence of synthesis is present.

Level 3—The work has evidence of application-level thinking and shows that you can demonstrate your learning by providing examples of uses of the learned concepts. Teacher direction was necessary for the tasks to be completed. The information presented is accurate and informative, indicating full understanding of the material.

Level 2—The work presented indicates that you fully understand the material presented and can present the facts in an organized fashion. Lack of application or other higher thinking levels is evident. Teacher direction was necessary throughout the process.

Level 1—The work shows a presentation of basic knowledge-level information. You did not apply the concepts and your knowledge base may be weak or inaccurate.

Rubric level for this work: ____

Explanation for selection of level: (Be sure to cite examples from your work or the process you went through to complete the task that support your decision.)

Figure 21.2 Self-Evaluation Using Rubric Scoring and Assessment.

Learning centers carefully planned to address all thinking levels and styles can offer every student the opportunity for high-level achievement. Differentiation for the gifted student is accomplished by differentiation of criteria and goals.

REFERENCES

Allan, S. (1991). Ability grouping research reviews: What do they say about grouping and the gifted? *Educational Leadership, 48,* 60–65.

Bloom, B. (1956). *Taxonomy of educational objectives: Cognitive domain.* New York: David McKay.

Clark, B. (1988). *Growing up gifted.* Columbus, OH: Merrill.

Gardner, H. (1983). *Frames of mind.* New York: Basic Books.

Gettinger, M. (1988). Methods of proactive classroom management. *School Psychology Review, 17,* 227–242.

Howard, K. (1990, Spring). Making the writing portfolio real. *The Quarterly,* pp. 4–8.

Krathwohl, D., Bloom, B., & Masia, B. (1964). *Taxonomy of educational objectives. Handbook II: Affective domain.* New York: David McKay.

Perkins, D., & Salomon, G. (1988, September). Teaching for transfer. *Educational Leadership,* pp. 22–31.

22

A Step-by-Step Plan for Developing Learning Centers

Helen D. Follis

The focus of this chapter is on examining critically Lopez and MacKenzie's assertions about the use of learning centers to meet the educational needs of gifted students enrolled in a heterogeneous classroom. The purpose of this critique is to examine the ideas presented by Lopez and MacKenzie in light of their practicality and feasibility for implementation by the classroom teacher.

Lopez and MacKenzie offer a good general background on the development of learning centers for the classroom. Their remarks on the use of learning centers to benefit gifted students in a heterogeneous classroom are insightful and appropriate, especially as they pertain to providing gifted students with a program that is integrated into the total classroom environment and directly related to curriculum goals.

Lopez and MacKenzie's definition of a learning center, as well as their criteria for a successful center, should be helpful to teachers and administrators. Their outline for developing a center gives teachers a blueprint to follow. When developing and implementing my own learning centers, however, I felt the need for more structured guidance in the form of examples and detailed management techniques. I wanted to know *how* students would engage in goal-setting activities, and *what* the teacher must do to manage a learning center with 30 students.

I do not believe that a learning center approach in a heterogeneous classroom is sufficient to meet the programming needs of the majority of gifted children. Individualized instruction via learning centers throughout the curriculum (which implies learning centers established and functioning in all curricular areas—a massive undertaking for a classroom teacher) requires the engineering of a teacher who is trained and skilled in meeting the needs of gifted students. If the teacher lacks the skills necessary for implementing the methods under consideration, the program will not be effective (Maker, 1982).

In each of the classroom's centers/content areas, teachers must highlight for the gifted the concepts at the level of their abilities, as well as the skills and strategies necessary for them to become independent learners (Gallagher, 1985). Goals and objectives must be charted for the gifted, which reflect their intellectual characteristics, as well as the content, process, and product of the area(s) of study (Sisk, 1987).

Although learning centers may be an effective approach for gifted students in a heterogeneous classroom, these able students need to spend time with each other to exchange ideas, to be challenged by, and to interact with their intellectual peers (Kolloff & Feldhusen, 1981).

Teachers must be trained and skilled not only in identifying gifted students, but also in balancing these students' educational needs and unique characteristics to make the most of their experience in a heterogeneous classroom.

The following section is a reaction to Lopez and MacKenzie's ideas on the development and implementation of classroom learning centers for gifted students. Additional detail is provided to facilitate the use of learning centers by classroom teachers to help meet the programming needs of gifted students in a heterogeneous classroom. The critique will follow the pattern established by a line of questions raised in reaction to Lopez and MacKenzie's text.

DEVELOPING THE LEARNING CENTERS

How can gifted students benefit from a learning center format in the regular classroom? The use of learning centers can benefit all students, as well as help teachers meet the unique needs of gifted students in the regular classroom. Learning centers provide a vehicle for individualizing instruction in the regular classroom. Specific assignments within the center can be adapted to meet the needs of students at different ability levels. This flexibility allows all students to be exposed to required content with assignments adapted to meet their own unique educational needs. Gifted students in general require less time to master the regular classroom curriculum. They benefit from assignments that allow them to apply higher level thinking skills to concepts contained in or related to the curriculum; they can develop and apply creative and/or critical thinking skills to areas of emphasis within the curriculum. Gifted students with a skill/conceptual deficiency benefit from participation in appropriate learning centers. Through prescriptive assignments, they can strengthen deficient areas.

Learning centers can be designed to involve gifted students in a range of activities requiring different outcomes. Teachers can vary the processes and products of classroom learning centers to allow students to experience activities requiring different modes of participation in any of the content areas. For example, in a third-grade science center on fish students might be required to observe fish in a tank and compare and contrast the behavior and appearance of different fish, look at fish scales under the microscope and write a description of what is seen, create a story or poem about fish, diagram the parts of a fish, use references to describe how fish reproduce, and create a three-dimensional life-sized model of a particular fish. These activities involve students not only in reading, but also in drawing, diagraming, researching, building, observing, and writing. Teachers can work with their students to develop an understanding of learning styles, helping children to identify and practice appropriate learning behavior.

Learning centers can help gifted students acquire life skills for thinking, solving problems, and locating information. Centers can be designed to incorporate a variety of useful "instructional materials" from telephone books to maps to the newspaper. These sources of information can help students find information about a specific content area. An extension of the fish center might be to use the phone book to locate a fish expert to interview, or study ocean maps to determine the location of the best environment for different kinds of fish, or use the newspaper to find information about environmental hazards to ocean life.

Learning centers allow gifted students to be proactive learners. As they work in a learning center format, students make choices, proceed through a variety of activities, keep track of their progress, and evaluate their results. Students gain experience in planning, decision making, and evaluating the results of those decisions. Also, they learn how to make better decisions in the future.

How does a teacher develop and manage a learning center for gifted students in a heterogeneous classroom? Lopez and MacKenzie offer a fine blueprint for learning center development. To make the most of this blueprint, teachers need to structure a format for the learning center within the context of the heterogeneous classroom.

Students, both gifted and nongifted, enjoy and benefit from a variety of classroom experiences. In addition to the classroom learning centers, time should be scheduled for both large and small group instruction, discussion, individual student conferences, quiet reading, independent study, and problem solving. A learning center can be implemented for gifted and nongifted students to meet a perceived need and/or to develop a skill, concept, or area of study within the curriculum.

Assume that a classroom contains all the components listed above except learning centers. The following guidelines are designed to help teachers begin to implement a learning center approach to meet the needs of gifted students in a heterogeneous classroom. This does not mean that all instruction will be handled through the learning center, or that learning centers constitute an ideal vehicle for instruction of gifted students in the regular classroom. Rather, these guidelines are intended to supplement Lopez and MacKenzie's theoretical base and facilitate classroom teachers in developing learning centers that will be effective in helping to meet the needs of bright students assigned primarily to a heterogeneous classroom.

1. Begin by isolating a content area or unit of study for the focus of the first learning center. Choose an area that will allow for a variety of related activities to be included in the center. Select an area with which students have a degree of familiarity—the first center is easier to manage if it is not designed to introduce an area of study to the students. This does not mean that classroom learning centers will be used only for review. Centers can be excellent vehicles for providing exploratory activities designed to introduce or familiarize students with content. For the first center, choose a topic with which students are acquainted. For example,

second graders traditionally study school and community helpers. This concept might be introduced better through discussion and observation activities than in a center. After students have participated in discussion and exploratory activities, center activities focusing around the community and various roles played by key helping individuals would be both appropriate and exciting to students. At this point, differentiation for the gifted could occur easily and naturally, with gifted students channeled toward activities requiring a higher level of convergent as well as divergent production. For example, nongifted students might list school helpers and identify the names and faces of those helpers in their school. Gifted students could develop a list of questions to use in an interview with school helpers to determine what they do in their jobs. They could schedule and conduct the interviews and share the results with their class.

2. Outline goals and objectives for the learning center. If the center reflects curricular goals and objectives, students will be mastering the required curriculum as they engage in learning experiences designed to meet their educational needs. Curriculum developed for gifted students should reveal an awareness of the characteristics and learning needs of this population. Part III of this volume contains many suggestions for differentiating the curriculum for the gifted.

3. Select activities that will enable students to achieve the identified goals and objectives. Consult the goals and objectives for gifted students as you design activities for them to complete. Implement and evaluate these initial activities before designing additional activities for this center. Students' success or failure to achieve the objectives will provide valuable clues as to the appropriateness of the activities in this learning center. Additional activities can be modified to reflect the results of this evaluation.

4. Collect resources and/or materials necessary for students to complete the activities of the learning center. Assemble materials in containers that are easily organized and straightened. Allow for sufficient space at the center for display of materials and resources and student work space. If possible, locate the center near a bulletin board or display area. Visual aids and/or directions are most helpful if posted in a prominent place. Provide a table (or study carrel) and chairs if students are to work at the center.

5. Write clear directions for students at the center and post in a prominent place. Refer to these directions during the initial introduction to the center and subsequently as needed.

6. Arrange the center as attractively as possible, including relevant eye-catching artwork, posters, illustrations, and clear, succinct directions. Unveil the center only when it is ready to be implemented.

7. Develop all management tools and techniques before the center is unveiled. Decide how students will record their work in the center and how the results of their work will be evaluated and recorded. Following are some questions to consider:

- How will you know when students have achieved the objectives of the center?

- How will you know if some students have not finished their work at the center? How will you deal with these students?

- How will you communicate different assignments within the center to students of different ability levels?
- Will you assign grades to student work?
- Will you record the grades in your grade book?
- Will these grades be part of the grades students receive on their report cards?
- Will students be allowed to work at their own speed throughout the center?
- Will students be allowed to work in pairs or groups?

8. When all process questions have been dealt with, introduce students to the learning center. Make sure they have a clear understanding of expectations for their performance at the center. Discuss the manner in which they should work, the requirements for written work and/or record keeping, and any other concerns that will affect their performance in the center.

9. Develop a learning center time line. Decide how long each center will be in use in the classroom. Set a time limit for student participation at each center. Be realistic, and understand that this work style may be new to some students. Set reasonable goals and be consistent in expectations. If goals or expectations change, all persons involved must be informed of the change and how they will be affected by this change. Involve gifted students in determining their own goals, objectives, and time lines for each center. Allow them to make suggestions and design learning centers of their own.

10. Enjoy sharing this opportunity for learning with the students. Be patient as they learn to be self-directed. Teach students the skills they need to know. Students who have survived up to this point in a totally teacher-directed environment will need coaching on how to operate in a learning center. They will need to know how to keep records, how to document their participation, and how to set their own goals and make plans for completing their work.

A SUGGESTED MANAGEMENT SCHEME

Experimentation will indicate the management strategies that work best with specific gifted students. To begin, teachers should determine how to communicate differentiated assignments to students of different ability levels. One possibility is to color code assignments, activity cards, and/or directions so that students know which assignments within the center are designed for them. The color coding should be explained at the introduction of the learning center.

Another possibility is to provide individual prescriptions for students in a folder or activity booklet to be used in the center. This would allow for teacher analysis of individual needs in making assignments at the center. This would also be more time-consuming for the teacher. Student conferences scheduled on a regular basis would facilitate record keeping of this nature. Assignments could be adjusted and monitored as needed during brief, regularly scheduled meetings with students to document progress and pinpoint areas of strength and/or need.

Still another possibility is to develop different centers for students according to their ability level in the subject under consideration. This provision would require the teacher to develop a greater number of specialized centers to meet the variety of needs within the class. This approach may be on target when working with a specific skill or concept or with students who are clustered in their achievement of a given objective.

Designing and managing learning centers is a challenging, but rewarding, task for both teachers and students. The task requires a commitment to provide additional time, resources, flexibility, and record keeping to allow the learning centers to function smoothly. Teachers should conceptualize, organize, implement, and evaluate one learning center before attempting to juggle consecutive and/or simultaneous learning centers. A gradual beginning will give both teachers and students the opportunity to adjust to a different classroom management strategy while maintaining a balance of other instructional activities. Teachers, too, will be able to gauge the appropriateness of the center for their gifted students.

What topics lend themselves to development in a learning center format for gifted students? A learning center can be content specific or interdisciplinary in focus to provide rich curricular experiences for gifted students. Depending on the instructional need, teachers may choose to build a center entirely around a subject area or unit of study, such as electricity. Applications of electricity for gifted intermediate science students could include building a complex electrical circuit, developing an electrical game board, and experimenting with different types of conductors. Interdisciplinary extensions at the same center could involve students in researching the discovery of electricity and early inventions, making an invention using electricity, writing a thank you letter to Thomas Edison, or writing and illustrating a scenario about life in the future without electricity.

A center also could be developed around a central theme, such as conflict. Fifth-grade students involved in a study of colonial America could participate in a variety of activities to illustrate conflict, including the more obvious illustrations found in colonial history. Students could use the newspaper to find illustrations of conflict, observe a classroom or the playground for 20 minutes to document instances of conflict, or conduct a survey to study the frequency and effect of conflict on the playground or in the classroom.

Teachers can develop an interdisciplinary learning center around a central theme, such as change, conflict, or communication. Activities can be developed within each of these themes to involve students in many different content areas. Students can take part in writing, reading, and thinking exercises focusing on a variety of issues or subtopics within each of the above themes.

The learning center can also be structured around curriculum traditionally covered within a given grade level, such as exploration in the fifth grade. This subject matter can be presented appropriately to gifted students by involving them in content and/or process applications through the use of higher order thinking skills. In this manner, learning centers can be developed to accommodate the study of any content area. Activities within these centers could be differentiated to meet the needs of gifted students by involving them in the study of complex real-life issues, the application of higher order thinking skills, problem solving, and independent study. For example, a fifth-grade exploration learning center for gifted students might incorporate the following components: a comparison of ancient and present-day maps, writing about life on a Spanish galleon during the time of Columbus, making a model of a galleon or Viking ship, and developing research questions about an explorer to guide an independent study.

How do gifted students manage their time effectively at a learning center? Both gifted and nongifted students will need a time management scheme to make the most of their learning center experiences in the regular classroom. The teacher can begin by creating a learning center time line, indicating what centers will be implemented during the year and how long each will be in operation.

Hopefully, learning centers will comprise a part of the regular classroom "bill of fare." With this in mind, teachers should determine each student's need to spend time in each center. This decision will be based on the student's ability and needs, as well as the content, process, and product of each learning center under consideration. Gifted students might be allowed to spend more time in a center that offers the opportunity to explore a classroom area of emphasis in greater depth. Perhaps they could substitute time in an appropriate learning center for class instruction on a topic with which they are familiar. However, gifted students should not be scheduled into the learning centers so completely that they are no longer members of the class. They still need to take part in large and small group discussions and group-building activities.

Students will benefit from a time management device, such as a contract. The contract is a signed agreement between teacher and student to complete a given amount of work in a prescribed length of time. Contracts can prescribe instruction effectively for students (Blackburn & Powell, 1976). They can be based on students' needs and/or interests. Student choices may be indicated in the contract, depending on the student's maturity and the material presented in the center.

Contracts should offer students a clear picture of the work that is expected of them. Due dates and other expectations must be outlined clearly. Consequences for failure to keep the contract must be understood before the contract is undertaken.

Each contract must include the following components (Blackburn & Powell, 1976):

1. Objectives to be accomplished, including criteria for mastery of the stated objectives
2. Resources and/or materials to be used in completing the assigned work
3. Alternative assignments or strategies to be completed to achieve the objectives
4. Description of the product or outcome that will indicate that the objective has been achieved

The contract also may include an evaluation component to examine subject matter mastery and time management skills. Student self-evaluation, as well as teacher appraisal of progress, should be incorporated into the evaluation procedures. Students also can be asked to comment on any aspect of the contract and/or learning center. Gifted students could be asked to indicate any changes they would make in negotiating future contracts.

Begin gradually to introduce students to contracts. This approach allows students more independence than they may have had in the past. Initially, students may react to the perceived lack of structure by working furiously or not at all. Given time, most students learn to pace themselves and budget their time.

Allow students the time and independence to learn to make full use of contracts as a management technique. Students need time to work on the assignments indicated in the contract, with regular teacher conferences or checkups to make sure they are performing satisfactorily. If a contract proves to be inappropriate, it can be renegotiated and adapted during the teacher–student conference to fit existing conditions.

Develop a record-keeping system that will accommodate the contracts. File contracts for reference and use them to keep track of students' progress. Plan a regularly scheduled time to evaluate progress and spot-check for problems. This could be part of the teacher–student conference.

The concept and design of learning centers requires students to be able to manage their time efficiently. Even with gifted students, this requirement is not always fulfilled without direct instruction in planning, decision making, and goal setting. With experience, gifted students should be able to help establish their goals for participation in a learning center. They also may draw up their own contracts to submit for teacher approval.

In addition to the above benefits, the contract system can help parents stay current on their child's progress in the classroom. The contracts can be signed by teacher and student, then taken home for a parent signature at the completion of the center. This encourages parent–child interaction on the subject of the contract, and may at last provide a meaningful, accurate answer to the question, "What did you do in school today?" Parents will benefit from a session wherein they are able to examine a contract and discover its function in their child's classroom. This session may be scheduled at a beginning-of-the-year open house or similar activity.

CONCLUSION

Lopez and MacKenzie offer many valuable suggestions for developing learning centers for use with gifted students assigned to a heterogeneous classroom. Their endorsement of the classroom learning center as an effective delivery system for gifted students is supported with good general implementation strategies and a familiarity with the learning center format.

Learning centers will not solve the problems inherent in attempting to meet the needs of gifted students in a heterogeneous classroom. Centers will neither ease the workload of the teacher nor provide the last word in curricular adaptations for gifted students with a wide range of abilities.

To the teacher who is willing to devote time and energy to their preparation, learning centers offer one programming alternative for meeting the needs of gifted students. Gifted students assigned to a heterogeneous classroom can use learning centers to develop independence and time management skills. They can study and learn through activities and strategies that have been prescribed on the basis of their unique needs as gifted individuals.

Gifted students can participate in this program option and still be part of the class, with all the feelings of belonging and possibilities for social and academic interaction that class membership implies. They can go beyond the teacher-developed learning centers by designing and implementing centers of their own—to relate a personal interest to a curricular area or to expose classmates to one of their passions.

Teachers who incorporate a learning center format into their classrooms can plan and implement activities that meet the needs of individual students. They can prescribe curricular adaptations for gifted students based on identified goals and objectives for the academic and personal growth and development of these students. Teachers can broaden the approach to a subject by developing interdisciplinary learning centers to involve gifted students in a wealth of experiences related to a central issue or theme. Teachers can expose gifted students to real-life skills by incorporating skills that are vital to life-long learning into classroom learning centers. Teachers can add a futures perspective to each center, and help students glimpse a better future by learning planning, goal setting, and decision making.

REFERENCES

Blackburn, J. E., & Powell, W. C. (1976). *One at a time all at once: The creative teacher's guide to individualized instruction without anarchy.* Glenview, IL: Scott, Foresman.
Gallagher, J. J. (1985). *Teaching the gifted child.* Newton, MA: Allyn & Bacon.
Kolloff, M. B., & Feldhusen, J. F. (1981, May/June). PACE: An application of the Purdue three stage model. *G/C/T,* pp. 47–50.
Maker, C. J. (1982). *Curriculum development for the gifted.* Austin, TX: PRO-ED.
Sisk, D. (1987). *Creative teaching of the gifted.* New York: McGraw-Hill.

PART V

PROGRAMS AND
MODELS FOR
EXTENDING
LEARNING BEYOND
THE CLASSROOM

Authors of chapters in Part V were asked to describe how certain models (mentorships, internships, and independent study) can be used to extend the learning of gifted students. They were asked to describe the necessary elements of these models, and to provide examples of successful programs in which these models are used. The authors have provided a variety of ideas, recommendations, and examples. Additional resources are suggested for readers who wish to extend their learning beyond this book.

The terms *mentorships, internships,* and *independent study* often are used interchangeably or together to describe programs designed to help teachers provide for the needs of gifted students. Such experiences can augment, supplement, fill gaps, extend learning opportunities beyond the classroom setting and beyond the limitations of a teacher's expertise, and meet students' needs for an individualized program. Although mentorships, internships, and independent study are similar types of programs, they have subtle differences in focus; all three are important components in a comprehensive educational program for gifted students.

Mentorship usually is employed to describe the *relationship* between an adult and a student, whereas *internship* usually is used to denote a particular kind of work experience, often under the supervision of a mentor. *Independent study* is employed to describe a process of student selection of goals, choice of instructional methods, and assessment of progress. Independent study can be done entirely without supervision, with supervision or guidance by a teacher only, with supervision by a teacher and mentor, or with supervision by a mentor alone. Internship experiences can be included or not included in an independent study. One way to examine the differences and similarities among the three types of programs is to use a Venn diagram. As described in this introduction, and in the chapters that follow, the program types could be seen as related in the ways shown in Figure V.1. A mentorship relationship always would be involved in internship experiences, but many other experiences besides internships could (and should) be provided by mentors. Independent study, as a process, could include the other two program types, but could be done in the context of the classroom or with guidance from only the teacher. I have chosen not to show independent study as the all-inclusive program type, even though I recognize that one could view it in this way, because I believe the mentorship relationship is very special, and goes far beyond anything that could be labeled ''study.'' Special mentorship relationships continue long after educational programs end, and expand into areas of life that may seem totally unrelated to school.

In their lead article on mentorships, William Nash, Patricia Haensly, June Scobee Rodgers, and Nilah Wright note that mentoring may be the oldest of instructional models, and that the need for its use is increasing because of the large numbers of students educators now are expected to serve. Gifted students may fail to reach their potential without a mentor, because unusual talent requires intensive personal attention for development. The authors list and discuss four major functions of mentors: (a) enhancing creativity through encouraging, supporting, and protecting the student in academic as well as business settings; (b) shaping careers through exploration, identification, development, and advancement; (c) serving as a role model for a particular talent; and (d) shaping personal growth.

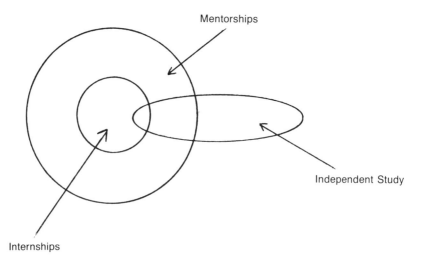

Figure V.1 Illustration of the Relationships Among Program Types.

Jody Batten and Jan Rogers provide support for Nash and colleagues, noting that children have limited opportunities for extended time with individual adults, and when they do have extended time, it usually is social rather than intellectual. Recognition and development of talent is difficult in this climate. These authors agree with the four functions outlined by Nash et al., and provide many examples of ways these functions have been exhibited in the program they describe. Fulfilling the role of enhancing creativity can result in helping students develop products that exceed the expectations of a normal school setting, and when shaping careers, mentors can help students develop a future vision of their "career self." As a role model, the mentor demonstrates both personal and professional qualities; and in the process of shaping personal growth, mentors provide emotional support, enabling students to take on the world on their own terms rather than imitating the mentor.

Batten and Rogers add reciprocity to the four functions described by Nash et al., noting that mentorships contribute to the mutual growth of mentor and protege. The authors provide examples of mentors who have completed their own degrees because they wanted to be good role models for students. Many mentors and students become life-long friends, a relationship that extends far beyond the boundaries of school learning.

In her chapter on internships, Jeannette Bodnar uses the term *mentorship* to describe a program in which students are introduced to a career, but the focus of her chapter is on internships. The focus of an internship, as she describes it, is on identification of strengths and weaknesses within the framework of a career choice. An internship is an intensive work experience, in which students are involved for 20 hours each week for a 17-week period. Their involvement in a concurrent seminar provides exposure to the work experiences of students involved in other settings. Mentors are involved in internships, and may direct the activities of students or supervise those who work with a group of students at a particular agency. The model of internships Bodnar provides has been tested for many years, and is implemented in all high schools in a large southwestern city.

JoAnn Seghini, in her critique of Bodnar's chapter, focuses on ways to enhance the value of the internship experience. She believes that such programs help students to see the value of academic abilities for the world of work, and that they provide a transition from an academic situation to the world of work. Seghini suggests four programs that can augment the internship Bodnar describes, achieving the dual purposes of (a) helping students benefit more from an internship, and (b) involving students who may not have been eligible for internships because of low motivation or excluded due to poor choice of courses in junior high and high school. Seghini recommends a strong counseling component involving students and parents at an early age. She describes how Renzulli's Enrichment Triad Model can be used to provide early exposure to careers, and can involve many members of the community in the education of children at an early age. The Business–Industry–Community Education Partnership she describes is a community-based career exploration program in which seminars, visitations to workplaces and schools, and taped interviews with workers in a variety of career areas are available. The Betts Autonomous Learner Model also is presented; Seghini suggests that it may provide a way to involve special populations of students, helping them to take advantage of programs such as the one described by Bodnar.

Frances Burns, in her lead chapter on independent study, provides readers more information about the Enrichment Triad and Autonomous Learner models. She presents these and two additional models, Self-Directed Learning by Treffinger and a generalized model, as approaches that can guide the development of independent study as a way of meeting the needs of gifted students. Independent study, according to Burns, is a process designed to provide each student an opportunity to select a content or topic to be studied in a "personalized environment." It provides an opportunity for the student to go beyond the classroom while remaining protected and guided by a nurturing adult. Burns provides many suggestions for teachers wishing to implement such models based on her extensive experience as a regular classroom teacher and a teacher of the gifted.

In their critique of Burns's chapter, Reva Friedman and Tom Gallagher remind educators that teaching students to work independently is a goal shared by all phases of education. These authors present a general model of school learning, and discuss what is needed in each of the four components (assessment of entering behavior, goals and objectives, instructional procedures, assessment of outcomes) to make independent learning more effective. Friedman and Gallagher provide more information about the models described in Burns's chapter in the context of this generalized model, and give readers a well-organized analysis of the strengths of these approaches.

At this point, I return to my analysis of the similarities and differences among the three program types or approaches to extending learning presented in this section—mentorships, internships, and independent study—by analyzing them according to the generalized model of school learning provided by Friedman and Gallagher. In this general model, instruction consists of four major components, which are connected and interactive: assessment of entering behavior, goals and objectives, instructional procedures, and assessment of outcomes. Using this general model, the three approaches appear more alike than different. Such an examination, however, can highlight the elements necessary for implementing successful programs. All four components of the general model are necessary, even critical, to the success of mentorships, internships, and independent study. However, subtle differences exist in focus and implementation, and must be considered when designing programs.

I have summarized in Table V.1 the elements considered necessary for successful programs by authors of the lead chapters and the critiques. They are grouped according to the generalized instructional model. Please note that no attempt has been made to be exhaustive in listing elements deemed necessary by all authors. The chart's purpose is comparative.

In all models, selection of students is important, and assessment of particular characteristics (interests, skills, knowledge) related to the program purpose is critical. In the case of independent study, for example, one should not assume that highly motivated, gifted students possess the skills that will enable them to succeed in independent study. They need to be taught skills, such as topic selection, time management, identification of resources, and development of sophisticated products. Students involved in internships must possess certain basic skills and knowledge to be suc-

Table V.1 Necessary Elements of Program Models

Mentorship	*Internship*	*Independent Study*
Assessing Entering Behavior • Selection of students • Assessment of interests and abilities	• Selection of students • Assessment of interests and career-related skills and knowledge	• Assessment of student interests and skills related to independent learning needs
Goals and Objectives • Development of comprehensive plan for programs and individuals • Cooperative decision making	• Development of plan for programs and individuals • Cooperative decision making	• Use of a comprehensive model or plan, with articulation between grade levels, and a specific plan for each learner • Student selection of topics • Focus on identification of independent learning needs as well as content needs/interests
Instructional Procedures • Match of mentor and student • Cooperation from community • Recognition for mentors • Variety of experiences and people • Optional development of a product	• Match of mentor, placement, and student • Cooperation from community members • Recognition for mentors • Variety of placements • Development of a product • High school credit for work • Discussion of work experiences in a group setting • Counseling prior to and during experience • Development of career-related skills prior to experiences at high school level	• Match of procedures, topics, and people • Cooperation among educators involved with student • Variety of materials, resources, and audiences • Development of a sophisticated product • Sequential development of independent study skills
Assessing Outcomes • Evaluation by everyone involved • Evaluation of student progress and the mentorship experience	• Evaluation by everyone involved • Evaluation of student progress and the internship experience	• Emphasis on self-evaluation, but involvement of others • Evaluation of student progress and the independent study experience

cessful in particular placements, because the purpose of the internship is not to substitute for school experiences, but to supplement and extend them. Students involved in the program described by Bodnar must complete extensive applications and career-related interest and skill inventories prior to placement.

Goals and objectives must be developed for the program as a whole, as well as for each student involved on an individual basis. These individual goals are established cooperatively by the mentor, student, teacher, and parents in the case of mentorships and internships, and cooperatively by at least the teacher and student (and sometimes parents and community members) in the case of independent study. Goals and objectives must be based on assessment of student needs and interests, as well as on a realistic view of what can be offered by a mentor or what experiences are available in a work experience setting.

Instructional procedures are wide and varied, depending on the setting and program. Mentors can work with students at school, as in the program described by Batten and Rogers; in the work setting, as described in Bodnar's chapter; or anywhere else, as noted by Nash, Haensly, Scobee-Rodgers, and Wright. Cooperation is needed from the community, and educators must provide recognition for the contributions of mentors and agencies providing experiences for students. Products of students involved in mentorships, internships, and independent study can be shared with other students, teachers, and community agencies. This sharing benefits everyone involved, and provides a real-world audience for students.

In mentorship and internship programs, special emphasis is placed on the "match" between mentor and student, and between work experience setting (in the case of internships) and student. Nash and colleagues discuss the role of the teacher and a committee, and Batten and Rogers elaborate on the use of a committee to make such decisions. All authors also recommend that students and parents participate in committee meetings and take an active role in searching for appropriate mentors. Bodnar describes the responsibilities of a committee in reviewing the student's application materials and recommending an appropriate placement. However, as Nash et al. remind us, a meaningful and productive mentorship occurs only when the match of student and mentor has been appropriate and two people have felt a "spark of intellectual and creative compatibility." Mentors must possess certain characteristics, such as being youth oriented, highly committed, richly qualified (high academic and career expertise), excited about the area of study, and able to relate personally to a gifted student without being threatened. They must believe and be committed to the purpose of education as "transformation," and be willing to "share" themselves.

Assessment of outcomes must be a cooperative effort by all involved, and everyone should be asked to evaluate the experience and the progress of the student involved. In the case of independent study, although emphasis is placed on self-assessment by the student, teachers and others involved need to provide their perspectives on the acquisition of independent learning skills and on the structure or process of independent study.

The teacher's role is critical in the success of mentorships, internships, and independent study. Teachers must be involved in all phases of the learning process, but must be willing to facilitate and guide rather than dictate. This willingness to "step aside" must pervade all phases of the process and must guide communication with all individuals involved. Teachers may find that being guides in the evaluation/assessment of outcomes is more difficult than assuming this role during the instructional phase of the process. However, students must become skilled at self-assessment if they are to become truly independent learners, and they cannot do so if the teacher assumes too much responsibility in the evaluation of learning outcomes.

In performing their crucial roles in the extension of learning of gifted students beyond the classroom and regular curriculum, teachers may find interesting a review of the synonyms of the key descriptors of their duties (Rodale, 1978): to *guide* (p. 390) and to *facilitate* (p. 477).

Guide

lead	orientate	advise
lead the way	put on the right track	counsel
conduct	map out the route	instruct
usher	escort	teach
pilot	convoy	tutor
drive	accompany	tell about
navigate	attend	take under one's wing
hold the reins	chaperon	steer
take the helm	companion	recommend
be at the helm	guard	suggest
direct	watch over	offer an opinion
give directions to	keep an eye on	give a tip
steer toward	look after	hint
head toward	be by one's side	tell what to do
show the way		

Facilitate

ease	lessen	encourage
smooth	abate	further
simplify	reduce	foster
uncomplicate	lighten	open the door for
clear	assist	pave the way for
relieve	aid	make way for
assuage	help	clear the way for
disburden	befriend	support
disencumber	forward	back
alleviate	advance	abet
allay	promote	sustain
mitigate		

The essence of guiding and facilitating is knowing when to do what with which student, and being willing to perform one's role flexibly and caringly.

REFERENCE

Rodale, J. I. (Ed.). (1978). *The synonym finder.* Emmaus, PA: Rodale Press.

23

Mentoring: Extending Learning for Gifted Students

William R. Nash
Patricia A. Haensly
V. June Scobee Rodgers
Nilah L. Wright

In the saga of human experience, events tend to come full circle. This may well be the case with regard to our current educational experimentation to determine successful school programs for gifted children and youth. Although we have developed multiple curriculum models that provide numerous options for educational acceleration and enrichment, attractive and meritorious in and of themselves, we always seem ultimately to realize that the key ingredient for growth and development is a subtle, yet elaborate relationship between the student and teacher. We describe its optimal form as a mentor relationship and quickly realize that we are possibly referring to the oldest of instructional models. In *The Sorcerer's Apprentice,* Boston (1976) explained the ancient Greek origin of the mentor concept:

> In the *Odyssey,* Mentor was the faithful friend of Odysseus, the King of Ithica, entrusted by Odysseus with the care of his household during his absence during the Trojan War. Above and beyond this general responsibility, however, Mentor was the guardian and tutor of Telemachus, Odysseus' son. The goddess Athena assumed Mentor's form and accompanied Telemachus in the search for Odysseus after the war, acting as guide and offering prudent advice. (p. 2)

From Boston's discussion, we readily recognize that Mentor was more than a tutor. He was given the responsibility of "guarding" Telemachus, and his role evolved into that of a "guide" and trusted "adviser" under Athena's influence.

Torrance (1984) noted that "those who have guarded, guided, and taught young persons in such relationships have borne varying labels in other cultures and periods of history with only slightly different meanings" (p. 2). One could argue, in a more

313

general sense, that our historical images, possibly romanticized, of the American pioneer teacher are more akin to the mentor role than today's perception of the teaching profession. The pioneer teacher was often an integral part of small frontier communities, living with different families, trusted as an adviser and source of wisdom, caring for children in times of hardship and even danger, as well as serving as a tutor in the three R's. One could argue further that the current emerging interest in developing mentor programs in school settings is bringing us "full circle" in our continuing efforts to define good teaching.

In this chapter, we provide a philosophical rationale for implementing the mentorship model to extend learning for gifted students. We then focus on functions performed by mentor relationships in a variety of settings, demonstrating how each function, in turn, can be accomplished in an especially relevant manner. A discussion of school-based mentorship programs follows, first a description of the essential elements that must be present in such programs, and then examples of prototype programs.

THE RATIONALE FOR USE OF THE MENTORSHIP MODEL

Today's societal conditions almost "cry out" for opportunities for children to receive individually the sort of consuming instruction and guidance to which the mentor relationship alludes. With our emerging population concentrations, young people find themselves in larger and larger peer group settings with fewer and fewer opportunities for individual contact with teachers (with adults in general, for that matter). Although small schools still can be located, a sizable percentage of junior and senior high schools number students into the thousands. Opportunities to spend extended periods of time in small group and individual instruction occur rarely, except in sports and a few other extracurricular activities. Additionally, many children return each school day to empty homes due to the occupations of commuting parents. These conditions all have led to a society in which children may find their behavior influenced more dramatically by peers than by parents, teachers, and other adults. Teachers and various school personnel sense the alienation from adult life that our young obviously feel in today's world, but they are overcome by the demands of dealing with the sheer numbers and often are frustrated in their attempts to reach the individual student. Thus in the *general sense,* our current interest in the mentoring process may be an attempt to define good teaching in the context of the demands of large group instruction.

In the *specific sense,* educators and researchers who have focused their interests on our gifted and talented student populations are coming to realize that students with unusual abilities not only may develop most favorably under the conditions of a mentor relationship, but also may fail to reach their potential if such an experience is not present. Torrance (1984) observed the following: "For centuries it has been said that almost always, wherever independence and creativity occur and persist and important creative achievements occur, there is some other person who plays the role of mentor, sponsor, patron, or guru" (p. 1). Although any question of "necessary condition" remains open to research, historical documentation does reveal an unusual incidence of mentor relationships in cases of creative genius. As Haensly and Edlind (1986) noted, "Individual success and creative productivity in a wide range of endeavors has frequently been attributed to having a personal mentor" (p. 1). Quick reflection brings to mind such famous relationships as those of Socrates and Plato or Ann Sullivan and Helen Keller.

Why do these relationships appear vital to the protege? We often associate the individual of outstanding creative genius with the time-worn phrase of "marching to his or her own drummer." Could unusual talent, while isolating one from the normal flow in many respects, demand intensive personal attention for development? This paradox suggests two avenues of investigation. First, tremendous talent is by its very nature extremely complex, and thus requires a great deal of disciplined attention to detail and persistent nurturance of learning style to progress to anticipated levels of achievement. At the same time, great emotional stress accompanies complex talent, because it does set one apart from others at tender ages when pressures for conformity and alikeness are strongest. In many ways, being different in exceptional ways exposes one to all sorts of danger. While the mentor guides the development of talent, he or she also guards and protects the protege during difficult and threatening times. In each area, a successful mentor may, as Levinson (1978) concluded, be both a parent and peer, a subtle combination that leads equally to intellectual and emotional support. In fact, Scobee (1986) recommended that parents should consider becoming mentors to their children.

Returning to our general discussion of mentoring as reflecting our concern for effective teaching, we might view our American pioneer teacher as one who intuitively recognized a "parenting" aspect of his or her role and found it to be a source of inspiration. Jesse Stuart (1949) expressed this attitude beautifully in *The Thread that Runs so True,* an autobiographical book about his teaching experiences in a backwoods, one-room schoolhouse. While on a solitary autumn walk in the wilderness, he reflects on teaching:

> I thought if every teacher in every school in America . . . could inspire his pupils with all the power he had, if he could teach them as they had never been taught before to live, to work, to play, and to share, if he could put ambition into their brains and hearts, that would be a great way to make a generation of the greatest citizenry America had ever had. (p. 82)

Stuart's commitment to this concept is revealed dramatically later as he prepares to embark on a trip to his parents' home to obtain more reading materials for his students:

> NOBODY could keep me from starting home. I was determined to go. I needed more novels, books of short stories, books of poems and essays for my pupils to read. . . . It was early in the afternoon, but the dark December skies hung low over the valley, and there were six inches of snow on the ground. I had seventeen miles ahead of me. The only way I could get to my destination was to walk. (p. 83)

He encounters a snowstorm and spends the subzero night in a cornfield inside a makeshift hovel he creates out of fodder shocks, but he survives the trip home for his books. His love and concern for his students are evident. We have little problem expanding his label as ''teacher'' to include ''mentor.''

Whatever our reasons, we currently find ourselves attempting to establish school programs that facilitate the development of mentor relationships, particularly for gifted students. Although the models developed by Boston (1976) and Levinson (1978) have retained the essential psychological quality lifespan characteristics of the original Mentor–Telemachus relationship, numerous logistical variations (i.e., programs for formally arranged mentorships) have arisen. In such programs, the focus is on particular functions of a mentor, often going beyond, or at the very least elaborating on, the roles of teacher, guardian, wise guide, and advocate. The variations reflect an expanding view of the possible functions of sensitive yet powerful mentor–protege relationships, functions that may be inferred from the preceding discussion, and which are elaborated in the following text.

FUNCTIONS PERFORMED THROUGH MENTORSHIPS

Enhancing Creativity

One of the most evident and frequently cited functions that mentors perform is that of *releasing and supporting creativity,* as shown, for example, from the biographical studies of eminent individuals (Goertzel, Goertzel, & Goertzel, 1978). In these biographies, eminence accompanied by outstandingly creative contributions repeatedly was attributed by the individual, or by others, to the influence of a mentor. The specific ways in which a mentor nurtures and maintains the development of creative achievement have been elaborated by Torrance (1984). In his examination of the mentor relationship, he described and supported with 22 years of longitudinal data on the creative achievement of over 200 individuals, the initiation, maturation, and death of mentor relationships, and the particular means that mentors used to enhance creative development. Mentors perform their functions by encouraging and supporting the expression of creative ideas; protecting the protege from the reactions of peers and superiors for enough time to test and modify ideas to acceptable form; keeping situations open enough for originality to occur and persist; and exhorting courage by the protege to pursue valued interests (Torrance, 1984).

Shaughnessy (1983) expanded further on this theme of nurturance of creative ability by mentors with specific admonitions and guidelines for accomplishing the task, directed to parents and teachers who might have the opportunity to serve as mentors or who might be seeking mentors for the youth with whom they work. Some of these guidelines include recognizing the need for mentors for talented youth, and seeking out experts to serve in this role; encouraging the intense pursuit by these youth of a particular interest, rather than wasting energy on becoming well rounded; and encouraging students to free themselves from limitations, well meaning or otherwise, of superiors or peers who suggest inappropriate directions for the use or development of their talents.

Focusing on the corporate world, Zey (1984) described as an imperative function of mentors the promoting of productive innovation, the life blood for successful corporate development. To accomplish that function, Zey continues to work with corporations in establishing formalized provisions for matching incoming personnel with appropriate senior staff members who have had a record of innovative contributions and who have a particular capability for fostering creative invention in others (Zey, 1986). As a business executive stated (quoted in Collins & Scott, 1978), "We don't demand that they do many things in one certain fashion" (p. 101). Flexibility in expectations regarding the nature of task responses thus allows junior personnel to derive creative solutions for problems.

Nurturance of creativity is a particularly important function served by mentors working with school programs. The objectives of most school curricula are so highly oriented toward achievement goals that creativity in thinking and action often is not valued, and may be counterproductive or at cross-purpose with success in the school environment. This dilemma is unfortunate for the individual, because it may diminish potential for unique contributions in adulthood as well as during school years, and unfortunate for a society whose need for innovative problem solving is obvious. Yet, it is a realistic descriptor of much of current thinking about learning and about excellence in the schools. In addition to modeling creative behaviors, mentors in school programs serve as sounding boards for divergent ideas and as reflective listeners, nonjudgmental in their response to the ideas of proteges in contrast to the evaluative nature of most school curricula. Mistakes and trial balloons are viewed by mentors as possible avenues for breakthrough ideas, and are allowed because mentors respect the ideas of their proteges. One protege in a school mentorship program (Edlind & Haensly, 1985) described how "they [mentors] really listen" to my ideas. Another spoke of the probes that her mentor encouraged, "My mentor asks me 'why' all the time—it changes my thinking." Mentors provide a protected relationship within which the protege can take risks without fear of ridicule and rejection. One university professor, describing this function as he saw it with his student protege, stated that he viewed his role (and that of other mentors) as that of "a psychic midwife" responsible for "the bringing forth of a creative being" (Edlind, Haensly, Nash, & Proudfoot, 1983).

Shaping Careers

A second major function, somewhat entwined with the support of creative achievement, involves *career identification, development, and advancement*. The business literature is replete with descriptions of the many facets of this function. Included are the mentor roles of directing goal setting and attainment (Phillips, 1978; Phillips-Jones, 1982) and acquisition of political savvy and corporate culture (Kennedy, 1985); opener of doors and introducer to career networks (Schein, 1978); and sponsorship (Kanter, 1977) and advocacy in career advancement (Collins & Scott,

1978; Roche, 1979). In the helping or service occupations, such as nursing, Hess (1986), Fagan and Fagan (1983), and others (Cameron, 1982; Kelly, 1978; Taylor, 1986) focused on evidence for effective career planning and on attaining career satisfaction through mentorships, as well as on increasing professional productivity. The purpose of the program described by Faddis (1986) is to increase motivation for young minority women to enter emerging professional and nontraditional careers through matching with professionals in those fields. Herrington and Harney (1986) developed a workshop series on mentoring as a tool in career exploration, designed to assist administrators and career counselors from a variety of organizational settings in selecting and implementing mentorship programs.

School mentorship programs, especially designed to attend to the career identification and development function (Borman, Nash, & Colson, 1978), have provided creatively oriented, gifted high school students important insights about and exploration of career possibilities, along with significant early experiences under the guidance of enthusiastic professional representatives (Colson, 1980). In a mentorship program designed especially for the disadvantaged gifted, B. Moore (1978) attempted to identify students from low socioeconomic status families, especially minority students who were from large families or were wards of the court. The goal of this year-long program was to broaden rather than to identify career choices through a guided study of possibilities and exploration with mentors of three professions. Having become aware of the relevance of particular courses and the possible application to their lives, over three-fourths of the students in this program redesigned their high school degree plans. This and other school programs also have demonstrated other career-related effects that mentorships have on such students: (a) affirmation that they do not need to limit their career aspirations and plans too early, (b) knowledge of ways successful professionals interact effectively, (c) development within a protected environment of subsidiary talents to complement a career of interest, and (d) development of a personal ethic and set of standards peculiar to a particular career area (Edlind & Haensly, 1985).

Role Modeling

A third function, related both to creativity nurturance and career development, is that of *role model for a particular talent*. Specific interpersonal and other job-related skills in the field of police work (Fagan, 1985, 1986; Fagan & Ayers, 1985), opportunities for joint projects and for selection of a specialization in the field of home economics (Bolton, 1986), skills for coping with internal politics in student services (Barr & Keating, 1979), and coaching and support of team growth in nursing (Atwood, 1979) all have been shown to be acquired through mentorships. Acquisition of organizational management skills by school principals (Eng, 1986), training learning style and development of communication skills by new teachers (George, 1986), and friendship and enthusiasm for the profession of teaching (Sacks & Wilcox, 1986) have occurred as a function of mentor programs in various educational settings.

A mentor's function as role model has been conceived as particularly important in school-related programs. In an analysis of the role of mentors for the 1964–1968 Presidential Scholars, Kaufmann, Harrel, Milam, Woolverton, & Miller (1986) suggested that the role model function was perceived as important by 61% of the scholars, with (a) enhanced professional and job-related skills resulting from association with a mentor and (b) intellectual stimulation of new ideas and concepts cited by 23% and 7%, respectively, of these scholars. Jackson (1981) described the importance of author mentors to the development of writing skills by her students. As one student in another program (Edlind & Haensly, 1985) commented,

> The knowledge I treasure most is what I gained from watching professionals in my discipline doing their jobs, seeing them respond under pressure, utilizing their skills. . . . This is something I could never have extracted from a textbook or a month of lectures . . . the understanding it takes to be a professional journalist—this alone makes the mentorship program a worthwhile endeavor for me. (p. 56)

Shaping Personal Growth

A fourth function that mentors serve, and the last we mention here, relates to *personal growth and development.* Boston (1976) stated it well by saying that the mentorship should be "a protected relationship in which . . . results can be measured in terms of competencies gained rather than curricular territory covered" (p. 1). Again, the effect on the individual's sense of self-worth and self-directedness is intertwined with creativity nurturance, realization of the potency of particular abilities and skills, and the appropriate placement of those abilities in life plans and careers. Johnson (1980) and K. M. Moore (1982), in the training and professional development literature, stated that strengthening of self-esteem and confidence takes place especially well among those individuals who have had mentors.

The importance of positive self-esteem, and of the awareness by students of how these may be maintained under ordinary and adverse conditions, is addressed *ad infinitum* in the literature on academic achievement. Yet, under the usual conditions of "a place called school" (Goodlad, 1984), enhancement of self-concept does not always seem to have high priority on the agenda. Educators (e.g., Edlind & Haensly, 1985; Gifted Children Task Force, 1985; Schatz, 1986) have found this need met through the mentor in school programs, who serves as an insightful sounding board to help the protege assess objectively his or her strengths and weaknesses. A few comments by students can convey the importance of this function to many gifted students: "I now see myself as more mature, capable, and more able to cope with various problems"; "my mentorship has helped my self-concept for several reasons . . . the perception of myself as someone possessing special gifts"; and "my mentor really cared about *me,* not just the work I might do" (Edlind & Haensly, 1985). Schatz (1986) elaborated on the self-esteem aspect, describing how one child's mentor helped him "to find more to like in himself," and Reddick (1979) described the typical college student's response to having had a mentor as having been helped to understand self, both limitations and unrealized potential.

As suggested by Phillips-Jones (1982), the functions served or the variety and scope of roles that may be played by mentors occur in all manner of helping relationships; thus, these helping relationships should be included under the mentor–protege umbrella. Such a broad view, however, leads to concern that those who plan formal arrangements for mentorships in school programs may fail to understand the rich possibilities of true mentorship and thus be superficial in their planning. Mentorships do not automatically take place when students and adults (potential mentors) are brought together to work; a relationship must have the right circumstances to develop and time to mature to become a fulfilled mentorship. Nevertheless, the view that helping under most auspices is a positive good can underlie our attempts to promote this option for gifted students. The most salient fact, however, is that the functions served by mentorships and described above are as appropriate in extending education for gifted students as they are for the adult professionals in the occupations mentioned.

The critical issues in this discussion become, then, how educators can promote mentorships for gifted students, where and for whom they will best serve, and how mentorships can be introduced, initiated, developed, and maintained within the auspices of programming for gifted students. In the next section, the necessary elements of a school mentorship program are described, followed by a discussion of some of the most frequently used (and some of the more innovative) forms mentorship programs have taken in educating gifted students, with an emphasis on how they have been implemented in classrooms and schools. Brief mention of the need for students to institute searches, and to develop and maintain informal mentorships concludes this section.

SCHOOL-BASED MENTORSHIP PROGRAMS

The Necessary Elements

The success of school-based mentorship programs (no less than those in other settings) is related directly to three components: (a) a special teacher who has the educational qualifications, sensitivity, flexibility, and enthusiasm to facilitate a complex educational arrangement for gifted students; (b) a comprehensive plan for the rationale and logistics of bringing together students (potential proteges) and professionals or experts (potential mentors) under school guidelines for an out-of-school educational experience; and (c) a mentor pool that includes richly qualified, youth-oriented, highly committed individuals with expertise. Adequate time for planning both before and during the program, clear objectives associated with clearly identified needs of students, acknowledged support from the school district (both physical and moral), effective monitoring of student placements, and appropriate recognition of the contribution of mentors are elements that contribute to the differentiation between an outstanding and a mediocre program. At least a year should be allowed for planning a program of this type. Comprehensive planning might well begin with the parallel tasks of assessing the student population and its needs, assessing the community resources for the mentor pool and for assistance with logistics, and locating a teacher for the program. Each of the three basic components and associated guidelines are discussed in the following sections.

A Special Teacher

The teacher–facilitator, a key factor in a school-based program, is the individual who will be responsible for making the match between identified needs of individual students and the way in which extended learning for each gifted student will be implemented. This facilitator also is responsible for seeing that appropriate matches between student–protege and expert–mentor are made, recognizing the effect on protege and mentor of variables such as gender and learning style. To accomplish these tasks, the facilitator must be sensitive to the needs, adolescent mood swings, and temporary periods of indecisiveness of gifted students; knowledgeable about school regulations and times for adherence, as well as the protocol and the niceties of communicating with busy and dedicated professionals; and well informed about the ways in which educational needs of gifted students may be met.

The facilitator should be a master teacher who relates well to students; relates well to other teachers (because many requests for the latter's goodwill and flexibility will be made during mentorships); is not afraid of meeting and communicating with professionals from many fields on their territory; has the vocational background to understand the advantages, limitations, and demands of a variety of professions; and is persistent enough to pursue hazy leads for increasing the mentor pool or acquiring some logistical advantage for the students. The facilitator should be a risk taker, have the time and energy to be in many places much of the time, be enthusiastic enough to energize hesitant students, be able to allay the occasional fears of inadequate mentoring by professionals, and keep the momentum of the program at a high level.

A Comprehensive Plan

A comprehensive program plan must be developed, beginning with determination of the particular educational objectives for the specific group of students. The objectives may range from development of the creative writing skills of an entire class of verbally talented and advanced students, to providing special attention for highly gifted math students, to development of leadership skills among students identified as socially gifted from a specific grade level. The objectives also might include responding to a range of individually identified interests within a designated mentorship course (Silrum & Pullen, 1986) or identified needs for advanced study among gifted students of all ages across many districts (Wenn, 1986). They might address directly Renzulli's Enrichment Triad (Renzulli, 1977), allowing gifted students to carry out Type III projects (individual and small group investigations of real problems) under the guidance of a mentor (Gray & Gray, 1986; Runions, 1980). They also might be structured to bring the disadvantaged gifted into the educational mainstream and decrease school dropouts among at-risk students, by enhancing their self-concept and lifting their educational aspirations through association with college students as mentors (Lanier, 1986; Wiseman, Larke, & Bradley, 1989; Richardson, 1986; Silverstein, 1986).

Visits to other school mentorship programs can supplement reports found in the literature, which should be searched for logistical models that will work well for the specific circumstances that will govern the program being planned. Once these parameters have been defined clearly, and a model for implementation has been decided and adapted, an attitude that success will follow should permeate all remaining planning.

Prior to the program's beginning, everything should be determined, including the way to identify the curriculum base from which the program will stem, transportation details, student and parental liability, and scheduling and its consequences. Public relations must proceed with general school inservice to enlist strong cooperation from other teachers and the administrators, to develop a community support group that can participate in generating ongoing and future mentors, and to construct guidelines—perhaps even a handbook (Fulbright, 1981; Fulbright & McLaughlin, 1985)—for students and for mentors. Effective preplanning with as much ongoing documentation as possible will prepare program advocates to defend effectively the cost and learning effectiveness to school administrators and school boards. This preplanning and documentation is especially necessary in most school districts with this type of off-campus programming.

Mentor Pool

The mentor pool must be a concern prior to all else. If, for example, 30 mentors will be needed for as many students in the area of science, but the school district is in a small community located hundreds of miles from a university or in a rural area with no well-developed industry, expecting to place all these students with appropriate mentors will not be realistic, and the possibility of repeating the program a second year will be unlikely. Flexible scheduling may permit secondary students to be transported to a distant university for a 2-day session once a month, and creative sharing of resources may assemble a small group of students to work with a single mentor, but the mentor pool must complement program objectives.

The Gifted Children's Task Force, in planning an individual-needs–based program for the entire state of Victoria, Australia (Wenn, 1986), launched a mentor search using a media event that attracted 200 people. Within 18 months, 186 students from schools throughout the state had been nominated for the program, 148 mentor volunteers with over 100 specialized interests had been identified, and 105 of the mentors had been matched and were working with 91 of the students.

On a much smaller scale, a visit to the vice president for academic affairs of a university, for example, might precede the posting of a letter to individual departments explaining the program and the manner in which mentors will be sought (Nash & Fulbright, 1984). Personal visits, parent-arranged contacts, and a constant alertness to possible mentors through newspaper and television coverage of professional and community activities can facilitate the mentor search and, again, provide mentor possibilities from a wide variety of disciplines and expertise. If multiple mentors within a discipline are needed, however, one may have to be much more creative in the search and in the match than if only one is needed. For example, each of a group of young budding mathematicians might be placed with an outstanding community college math instructor, an insurance actuary expert, a stockbroker, a computer programmer, a bank president, an older math-talented student, or even an artist who has focused on geometric forms. These placements could be matched to particular side interests of the student and provide experience with a variety of math applications, as well as provide the opportunity to "tune in" to the mathematical thinking of experts with the specialized applications.

As the program continues, the mentor pool must be treated with care, neither overworking individual professionals nor failing to extend recognition to them. Recognition can be both private (e.g., letters copied to superiors who might give added recognition because of this exemplary activity of their employees) and public (e.g., an ad in the local newspaper or a special ceremony).

EXAMPLES OF PROGRAM TYPES

Although learning may be extended for gifted students through a variety of mentorship models and logistical arrangements, we have categorized three particular program types: (a) career exploration, guidance, and development programs; (b) content-based programs, in which the focus is on enrichment in a content area of particular interest to the student; and (c) personal growth programs, in which the focus is on helping a particular group of youths improve self-awareness so that they may aspire to higher educational goals and strive to develop their potential. In the following section, each category is described, with guidelines for implementation, followed by a discussion of specific examples.

Career Exploration Models

One of the most successful models for gifted secondary students is focused on career exploration and is especially oriented to the highly creative student whose giftedness has not necessarily been expressed in high academic achievement (Colson, Borman, & Nash, 1978; Nash, Borman, & Colson, 1980). Although students can be identified for this program using general or specific academic achievement and general intelligence, creative thinking ability and expressed talents are sought. The year-long program is offered in three phases: (a) career guidance laboratory, (b) placement with a university professor in a chosen career area to gain an awareness of the particular parameters of that career, and (c) an internship placement that provides a work-oriented experience. In both the mentorship and internship phases, the student engages in a project under the mentor's guidance, designed to release and nurture creative responses. Evaluation of this program has demonstrated that students and mentors receive many benefits from these formally arranged mentorships (Edlind & Haensly, 1985), not the least of which is recognition and enhancement of creative ability and development of an increasingly positive self-concept for students.

The program that has many modifications for the limitations of particular settings can be offered as a credit-accruing course meeting daily with the mentor and/or at the work site for a 2-hour block of time, with one session per week at the school setting. Self-directedness in the student and sensitive monitoring and resource facilitation by the teacher are critical to the success of this program. Some of the modifications have included 1-day-a-week sessions with the mentor, where the university site is too distant for daily commuting; flexible scheduling of student time with the mentor; provisions of the course during the sophomore or junior year to encourage and permit minority students to construct their high school degree plans more effectively (B. Moore, 1978); and scheduling the course in dual content areas, such as English and history, to satisfy state curricular requirements.

Content-Based Models

A content-based mentorship program is an effective way to provide both acceleration and enrichment in a content area to students with advanced ability or talent at any level of schooling. Used as an option when only a limited number of students will be served, arrangements can be made for the student and mentor to meet at either the school or a designated place for only a portion of the student's class time (1 or 2 days a week, or more for the mature and advanced students). This type of program requires explanations to parents and their permission (as does any valid school program), obtaining necessary transportation assists, and prior planning so that these students will not be penalized for missed work. Any focus on a certain content area for groups of students requires an even more serious search of the community's human resources than the career exploration–based program described previously. After careful matching of student and professional to assure compatibility of style, initial commitments should be formalized by both student and mentor and limited to 5 to 10 sessions. Both should participate in the decision of whether to continue for an extended time period. Initial conferences between teacher and mentor can shape realistic expectations by both students and mentors and facilitate their realization. Periodic contacts by the program facilitator permit prompt recognition of problems and appropriate adjustments. Two examples of content-based mentor arrangements are those described by Jackson (1981) for creative writing and Stanley (1979) for math.

Other content-based mentorships include programs such as *The Mentor Connection* (Silrum & Pullen, 1986), which incorporates a variety of the interests of students and attempts to provide matches with professionals/experts from the appropriate discipline. As stated in the brochure of *The Mentor Connection,* this is an "educational opportunity for high achieving, creative, self-motivated high school students . . . who have 'used up' the resources of a regular high school curriculum." This semester-long program for credit begins with an orientation lab, where the student identifies an interest area, followed by a preparation lab to develop communication skills for interacting with professionals, and is culminated by 8 hours per week in the mentor's workplace for the remainder of the semester. In another interest-based variation, programs have been designed on the Renzulli Enrichment Triad foundation with Type III triad projects carried out under the direction of a mentor (Gray & Gray, 1986). (Independent projects are also carried out in the Nash et al., 1980, career model.) In one of the earlier versions of this type of implementation, advanced students are trained as mentors of other students in a Mentor Academy Program (Runions, 1980), and a community agency supplies additional mentors, all of which is coordinated by a *learning enrichment service* centered in the school (Runions, 1980, 1982).

A variation developed by the Gifted Children's Task Force in Victoria, Australia (Wenn, 1986), to serve students who have been identified as having needs that cannot be met by the regular school curriculum is "a meeting of the minds." Although it appears to be guided by the U.S. definition of the gifted student, the unique aspect of this program has been the intention to avoid identifying *gifted* students (thus circumventing egalitarian educational attitudes in which education for the gifted is viewed in a critical, negative light). The attempt to provide "a special teacher to interact intensively with a special youth" fits well the philosophy described at the outset of this chapter. A second unique aspect of the program is the wide geographic area served by a central organizational unit. The entire state of Victoria provides the identified mentor pool (described earlier) from which mentors are drawn to match with students from any of the public schools in Victoria.

Teachers nominate students with whom they need assistance; for example, a 10-year-old boy who has developed extensive expertise in electrical circuitry and related applications but whose other academic skills are about average for grade level and whose social skills are suffering, or a high school girl who has demonstrated outstanding talent and avid interest in journalism and creative writing. These students might be matched, respectively, with a college graduate student in electrical engineering and with a retired journalist who is a widely published author (actual cases described in the program's promotional material). A committee composed of the youth, teacher, parent, potential mentor, and program representative meets to discuss appropriateness of the match, the program that will be developed between student and mentor, conditions that each will follow, location and schedule for meetings, and the evaluation procedure for the student's progress. The teacher arranges minimal released time from school and excuses from particular assignments so that the student has some time freed for this activity, although the partners are encouraged to meet at other times as well. The authors who document the many successful mentor–protege relationships in this program have indicated that numerous informal meetings occur as well, and that friendships have been established that continue after the school arrangement has terminated.

Personal Growth Models

The personal growth model of mentorship programs indirectly addresses extending learning for gifted students. In this model, the goal is to involve at-risk students with role models who will work to enhance the student's self-concept and raise educational aspirations. One such program in New York (Richardson, 1986) matches college students from the Bronx Community College with high school students who are at risk of dropping out of school. The college student mentors are guided by a coordinator, initially receive college credit, and are assisted by the class as a support group. The high school students are identified as having potential that is not likely to be developed with current levels of academic motivation. A similar type of program has been developed at Texas A&M University (Wiseman et al., 1989) for somewhat younger minority students from economically disadvantaged homes. These students are matched with teacher education majors. Parental involvement and support are sought, and each college student probably continues the relationship over a 3- to 4-year period to provide this role modeling for a particular protege. Students such as these have not necessarily been identified as gifted by their schools, but this is a useful model for gifted students who are underachieving and are potential dropouts.

We would be remiss in omitting mention of one last avenue to mentorships for gifted students: the informally developed arrangement in which the student seeks out an expert for temporary assistance. Often, when a particular mutual attraction is present, a teacher becomes a mentor (Edlind et al., 1983). In many cases, these associations have developed into meaningful relationships that have lasted for years as the youth moves on in his or her educational plan and into a career. We need to make gifted students aware of this rich option and give them guidelines for initiating such potential mentorships. Suggestions may be found in *Mountains to Climb: A Handbook of Resources for the Gifted and Talented* (Haensly & Nash, 1983, pp. 3–4, 55).

CONCLUSION

Extending learning for gifted students through mentorship programs may occur in many forms. Enrichment and acceleration can occur readily when professionals and students are brought together through sensitive and thoughtful matching of interests, learning and teaching styles, communication styles, and other personal characteristics. The logistical modifications for formal mentorship arrangements that can be made to accommodate the specific characteristics of a school district, its clientele, and its population of gifted students are limited only by the creative abilities of planners. The models we have discussed are some of the many theoretical approaches to the task of extending learning through formally arranged mentorships. The examples we have provided demonstrate the variety of ways planners have found to accomplish the task.

The overlying consideration that must surround the models and programs generated is that although we can bring together experts and students, meaningful and productive mentor–protege relationships will develop only when that match has been appropriate and when the two individuals have felt that spark of intellectual and creative compatibility from which rich experiences develop.

REFERENCES

Atwood, A. (1979, November). The mentor in clinical practice. *Nursing Outlook, 714–717.*

Barr, M. J., & Keating, L. A. (1979). No program is an island. *New Directions for Student Services, 7,* 13–28.

Bolton, E. B. (1986). A study of the advantages, disadvantages and outcomes to the recipients of helping relationships. In W. A. Gray & M. M. Gray (Eds.), *Mentoring: Aid to excellence in career development, business and the professions. Proceedings of the First International Conference on Mentoring. Vol. II* (pp. 185–196). Vancouver, BC: International Association for Mentoring.

Borman, C., Nash, W. R., & Colson, S. (1978). *Career education for gifted and talented students: A triadic experiment in education.* College Station: Texas A&M University, College of Education.

Boston, B. O. (1976). *The sorcerer's apprentice: A case study in the role of the mentor.* Reston, VA: The Council for Exceptional Children.

Cameron, R. K. (1982). Wanted: Mentor relationships within nursing administration. *Nursing Leadership, 5*(1), 18–22.

Collins, E. G. C., & Scott, P. (Eds.). (1978). *Harvard Business Review, 56*(4), 89–101.

Colson, S. (1980). The evaluation of a community-based career education program for gifted and talented students as an administration model for an alternative program. *Gifted Child Quarterly, 24*(3), 101–106.

Colson, S., Borman, C., & Nash, W. (1978). A unique learning opportunity for talented high school seniors. *Phi Delta Kappan, 59,* 542–543.

Edlind, E. P., & Haensly, P. A. (1985). Gifts of mentorships. *Gifted Child Quarterly, 29,* 55–60.

Edlin, E. P., Haensly, P. A., Nash, W. R., & Proudfoot, S. (1983). A symposium on the mentor relationship [Abstract]. *Proceedings of the 30th Annual Convention of the National Association for Gifted Children,* p. 6.

Eng, S. P. (1986). Mentoring in principalship education. In M. M. Gray & W. A. Gray (Eds.), *Proceedings of the First International Conference on Mentoring, Vol. I* (pp. 124–131). Vancouver, BC: International Association for Mentoring.

Faddis, B. (1986). Linking career role models with minority young women. In M. M. Gray & W. A. Gray (Eds.), *Proceedings of the First International Conference on Mentoring, Vol. I* (pp.45–46). Vancouver, BC: International Association for Mentoring.

Fagan, M. (1985). How police officers perceive their field training officer. *Journal of Police Science and Administration, 13*(2), 138–152.

Fagan, M. (1986). Do formal mentoring programs really mentor? In M. M. Gray & W. A. Gray (Eds.), *Proceedings of the First International Conference on Mentoring, Vol. II* (pp. 23–42). Vancouver, BC: International Association for Mentoring.

Fagan, M., & Ayers, K. (1985). Professors of the street: Police mentors. *FBI Law Enforcement Bulletin, 54*(1), 8–13.

Fagan, M. M., & Fagan, P. D. (1983). Mentoring among nurses. *Nursing and Health Care, 4*(2), 77–82.

Fulbright, M. (1981). *Mentor's handbook, student's handbook.* Weslaco Independent School District, Weslaco, TX.

Fulbright, M., & McLaughlin, P. (1985). *Mentor's guide.* Spring ISD Pyramid Program, Houston, TX.

George, M. (1986). Teachers meeting needs of colleagues: Kern High School District's Mentor Teacher Program. In M. M. Gray & W. A. Gray (Eds.), *Proceedings of the First International Conference on Mentoring, Vol. I* (pp. 93–100). Vancouver, BC: International Association for Mentoring.

Gifted Children's Task Force. (1985). *A meeting of the minds: The mentor programs.* Education Department, State of Victoria, Australia.

Goertzel, M., Goertzel, V., & Goertzel, T. (1978). *300 eminent personalities.* San Francisco: Jossey-Bass.

Goodlad, J. (1984). *A place called school.* New York: McGraw-Hill.

Gray, M. M., & Gray, W. A. (1986). Mentor-assisted enrichment projects: A proven way of carrying out Type III triad projects and of promoting higher-level thinking in GTC student–proteges. In M. M. Gray & W. A. Gray (Eds.), *Proceedings of the First International Conference on Mentoring, Vol. I* (pp. 179–189). Vancouver, BC: International Association for Mentoring.

Haensly, P. A. & Edlind, E. P. (1986). A search for ideal types in mentorship. In W. A. Gray & M. M. Gray (Eds.), *Mentoring: Aid to excellence. Proceedings of the First International Mentoring Conference. Vol I* (pp. 1–8). Vancouver, BC: International Association for Mentoring.

Haensly, P., & Nash, W. R. (1983). *Mountains to climb: A handbook of resources for the gifted and talented.* St. Paul, MN: National Association for Gifted Children.

Herrington, C., & Harney, L. (1986). British Columbia Mentorship Program Pilot Project: Model for a province-wide program. In M. M. Gray & W. A. Gray (Eds.), *Proceedings of the First International Conference on Mentoring, Vol. I* (pp. 25–32). Vancouver, BC: International Association for Mentoring.

Hess, B. (1986). The role of mentors in the professional development of nurses: A comparative study. In M. M. Gray & W. A. Gray (Eds.), *Proceedings of the First International Conference on Mentoring, Vol. II* (pp. 161–168). Vancouver, BC: International Association for Mentoring.

Jackson, L. A. (1981). Enrich your writing programs with mentors. *Language Arts, 58,* 837–839.

Johnson, M. C. (1980). Mentors—The key to development and growth. *Training and Development Journal, 34*(7), 55–57.

Kanter, R. M. (1977). *Men and women of the corporation.* New York: Basic Books.

Kaufmann, F., Harrel, G., Milam, C., Woolverton, N., & Miller, J. (1986). The nature, role and influence of mentors in the lives of gifted adults. *Journal of Counseling and Development, 64,* 576–578.

Kelly, L. Y. (1978). Power guide: The mentor relationship. *Mentoring Outlook, 26,* 339.

Kennedy, M. (1985). Corporate politics 101. *Canadian Business, 158*(8), 57–63.

Lanier, P. A. (1986). A mentoring experience in the south Bronx: A successful strategy for conducting an inner-city mentoring program. In M. M. Gray & W. A. Gray (Eds.),

Proceedings of the First International Conference on Mentoring, Vol. I (pp. 20–24). Vancouver, BC: International Association for Mentoring.

Larke, P., & Wiseman, D. (1987, November). *Minority mentorship project.* Paper presented at the IRL Seminar, Texas A&M University, College Station, TX.

Levinson, D. J. (1978). *The seasons of a man's life.* New York: Knopf.

Moore, B. (1978). *Career education for gifted disadvantaged high school students.* Paper presented at the Annual Conference of the National Association for Gifted Children, Houston.

Moore, K. M. (1982). The role of mentors in developing leaders for academe. *Educational Record, 63*(1), 23–28.

Nash, W. R., Borman, C., & Colson, S. (1980). Career education for gifted and talented students: A senior high school model. *Exceptional Children, 46,* 404–405.

Nash, W. R., & Fulbright, M. S. (1984). *Establishing mentorship and internship programs for gifted and talented high school students.* Workshop presented at the 31st Annual Convention of the National Association for Gifted Children, St. Louis.

Phillips, L. L. (1978). Mentors and proteges: A study of the career development of women managers and executives in business and industry. *Dissertation Abstracts International, 38*(11-A), 6414–6415.

Phillips-Jones. L. (1982). *Mentors and proteges.* New York: Arbor House.

Reddick, D. C. (1979). *Wholeness and renewal in education.* Austin College, Sherman, TX: The Center for Program and Institutional Renewal.

Renzulli, J. S. (1977). *The enrichment triad model: A guide for developing defensible programs for the gifted and talented.* Wethersfield, CT: Creative Learning Press.

Richardson, H. B. (1986). Student mentoring: A collaborative approach to the school dropout problem. In M. M. Gray & W. A. Gray (Eds.), *Proceedings of the First International Conference on Mentoring, Vol. I* (pp.38–44). Vancouver, BC: International Association for Mentoring.

Roche, G. R. (1979). Much ado about mentors. *Harvard Business Review, 57*(1), 14–28.

Runions, T. (1980). The mentor academy program: Educating the gifted/talented for the 80's. *Gifted Child Quarterly, 24,* 152–157.

Runions, T. (1982). *Stewardship: Training the gifted as community mentors.* ERIC Clearinghouse on Handicapped and Gifted Children.

Sacks, S. R., & Wilcox, K. K. (1986). From master teacher to mentor: Mentor/new teacher project. In M. M. Gray & W. A. Gray (Eds.), *Proceedings of the First International Conference on Mentoring, Vol. I* (pp. 116–123). Vancouver, BC: International Association for Mentoring.

Schatz, E. (1986). Case stories in mentoring. In M. M. Gray & W. A. Gray (Eds.), *Proceedings of the First International Conference on Mentoring, Vol. I* (pp. 139–145). Vancouver, BC: International Association for Mentoring.

Schein, E. (1978). *Greater dynamics: Matching individual and organizational needs.* Reading, MA: Addison-Wesley.

Scobee, J. (1986). Your child's first mentor is you. *Gifted Child Monthly, 7*(8), 1–3.

Shaughnessy, M. (1983). The core of creativity. *Creative Child and Adult Quarterly, 8*(1), 19–23.

Silrum, L., & Pullen, J. (1986). Mentor connection: An advanced course offering for high school students. In M. M. Gray & W. A. Gray (Eds.), *Proceedings of the First International Conference on Mentoring, Vol. I* (pp. 159–160). Vancouver, BC: International Association for Mentoring.

Silverstein, N. A. (1986). Establishing a mentoring dialog with a campus school. In M. M. Gray & W. A. Gray (Eds.), *Proceedings of the First International Conference on Mentoring, Vol. I* (pp. 33–37). Vancouver, BC: International Association for Mentoring.

Stanley, J. C. (1979). How to use a fast-pacing math mentor. *Intellectually Talented Youth Bulletin, 5*(6), 1–2.

Stuart, J. (1949). *The thread that runs so true.* New York: Charles Scribner's Sons.

Taylor, S. (1986). Mentor teachers in selected districts in northern California: Profile, selection, and responsibilities. In M. M. Gray & W. A. Gray (Eds.), *Proceedings of the First International Conference on Mentoring, Vol. I* (pp. 109–115). Vancouver, BC: International Association for Mentoring.

Torrance, E. P. (1984). *Mentoring relationships: How they aid creative achievement, endure, change, and die.* Buffalo, NY: Bearly Limited.

Wenn, R. (1986). Starting from scratch: The Victorian (Australia) mentoring experience. In M. M. Gray & W. A. Gray (Eds.), *Proceedings of the First International Conference on Mentoring, Vol. I* (pp. 146–151). Vancouver, BC: International Association for Mentoring.

Wiseman, D., Larke, P. J., & Bradley, C. (1989). The Minority Mentorship Project: Educating teachers for a diverse society. *Mentoring International, 3*(3), 37–40.

Zey, M. (1984). *The mentor connection.* Homewood, IL: Dow Jones–Irwin.

Zey, M. G. (1986). Only the beginning: Five major trends that signal the growth of corporate formal mentor programs. In W. A. Gray & M. M. Gray (Eds.), *Mentoring: Aid to excellence in career development, business and the professions. Proceedings of the First International Conference on Mentoring. Vol. II* (pp. 153–160). Vancouver, BC: International Association for Mentoring.

24

Response to "Mentoring: Extending Learning for Gifted Students"

Jody Batten
Jan Rogers

In this chapter, we support the work of Nash, Haensly, Scobee Rogers, and Wright; expand upon several key points in their chapter; and provide examples of promising practices involving mentorships in a K through 12 public school setting.

Generally, educators of gifted students agree that mentorships are a viable, if not preferred, source of appropriate educational experiences for many gifted students. The importance of the relationship between a well-matched mentor and a student cannot be described in programmatic terms alone, for the relationship involves a fine interweaving of intellect and emotion, and is, therefore, synergistic in nature. Participants in mentorships often speak of the personal benefits each has received from the relationship before they speak of the educational benefits. Parents of gifted students typically describe a mentor in terms of the mentor's personal relationship with their child before speaking of the intellectual activities pursued in the mentorship. Because both intellectual and personal growth occur in such relationships, mentorships are examples of what Nash and his colleagues call "good teaching."

RATIONALE

The demands of contemporary living limit the opportunities of gifted children to have extended periods of time with individual adults. Working parents talk of spending "quality time" with their children, but often this interaction amounts to reading a bedtime story, playing a game, watching television, or engaging in a recreational activity with the child, rather than discussing issues or building a common philosophical base about a discipline of study. Educators talk of "individualizing" for students with special needs, but this provision often is made on a short-term special assignment basis with little personal interaction between student and adult. In settings such as these, outstanding talent often is not recognized, and, if recognized, given little opportunity to be developed. The establishment of a mentorship for a gifted child who has not had a large amount of adult attention gives the student the following immediate messages: (a) that the student does possess unusual talents, and (b) that these talents are to be developed. This acknowledgment is an important step in the process of educational maturation and can be considered by the student as a rite of passage in the pursuit of personal excellence.

The mentorship relationship is not to be taken lightly by mentors, students, or teachers. This relationship is important, if not vital, to the gifted child. Nash et al. are very clear on the point that students often will not—and cannot—reach high levels of proficiency in a field of endeavor if individual, expert attention is not given to their development. One can "march to a different drummer" alone for only so long without someone or something—usually lack of support—stopping the march. That the emotional burdens associated with the march toward developing a great talent are better carried by an adult and child than by the child alone is clear. The mentor's role as protector or guard gives the child the psychological safety needed to take necessary intellectual risks.

MENTORS

A successful mentor–student relationship begins with locating an appropriate mentor. If this person is to act as teacher, guardian, wise guide, and advocate for the student, possession of the following characteristics is imperative:

- *High academic qualifications*—To be paired with a student in Lincoln Public Schools (Lincoln, Nebraska), a mentor who is a college graduate must have majored in a field of study related to the student's area of interest. If the mentor is a college student majoring in the field, he or she must have an overall grade point average (GPA) of 3.0 and a 3.5 GPA in the major field. Other mentors are selected based on professional recognition of their work in the field.

- *Excitement about the area of study*—Haensly and Edlind (1986) wrote of the need for "mutual excitement by mentor and protege about the field, and the commonality of working and learning styles" (p. 6). A mentor also needs to be excited about learning in general and to be sensitive to the special learning needs of gifted students, including fast-paced, in-depth study.

- *Ability to relate personally to a gifted student without feeling threatened*— The mentor needs to feel that the relationship with the student is significant. One mentor noted the importance of the relationship: "You are different to the child. They have no other relationship like this one. It is a wonderful responsibility" (Lincoln Data Collection, 1988). One protege said to her mentor, "It doesn't bother me that you're smart. Does it bother you that I'm smart?"

"Of course it doesn't," explained the mentor, "It's why I'm here" (Lincoln Data Collection, 1988).

- *Ability to communicate well on a one-to-one basis*—Some potential mentors may have outstanding academic qualifications but may not have the ability to talk comfortably and successfully with children. "Some adults are good and smart people," said one mentor, "but it takes more to work with children" (Lincoln Data Collection, 1988). Bloom (1985) described a mentor as an "outstanding teacher" who "placed greater demands on practice time" (p. 517). In addition, the mentor's role requires recognizing the sensitivity of the child and consideration of personal issues when scheduling the student's responsibilities and experiences. For example, the mentor and the student should plan their work so that the greatest demands will not come when the protege is deeply involved in sports and other activities. The following quote from one mentor indicates a perceived relationship between open communication and a student's work: "You just couldn't plan like this for a roomful of kids. I'm sure [the student] works much harder for me at those times just because I am willing to communicate with him about his total set of responsibilities" (Lincoln Data Collection, 1988).

- *Willingness and ability to act as an advocate for the student under adverse academic and/or emotional situations*—One mentor, who has had the same proteges for several years, said, "I feel that they are my children at school. I'm there for them in that setting and I must help them if they need it. I realize that the parents are the primary teachers of these children, but at school, I understand some situations that the parents cannot [because they are not there] and I intervene" (Lincoln Data Collection, 1988).

  An outstanding science project was developed by a very young student and his mentor. When the project was placed in the school science fair, other teachers from the building doubted that the child had done the work. At this time, the mentor became an advocate for the child and instructed the staff in the techniques and environmental modifications that had led to the development of the highly unique project.

  Other examples of advocacy revolve around academic issues. Mentors provide the atmosphere the student must have to operate at a higher cognitive level. Edlind and Haensly (1985) quoted one student as saying, "This is something I could never have extracted from a textbook or a month of lectures. . . . This alone makes the mentorship a worthwhile endeavor for me" (p. 56).

- *Belief that the primary purpose for education is the "transformation of a human life"* (Boston, 1976, p. 19) *and commitment to this task*—One mentor noted that students often are "mentor dependent" when they begin the mentorship and need the mentor to encourage self-reliance "so that they'll feel good" (Lincoln Data Collection, 1988). She also stated, "You shape personality along the way," as you deal with issues such as "Is it cheating if we do this work together?" and "You tell me if that's a good plan for the project."

Bloom (1985) described the relationship with a master teacher as one ''in which the individual can reach the highest level of competence possible in the field and can successfully compete with its top leaders'' (p. 536). Although not all students participating in mentorships can reach this level of expertise, the ultimate goal of most mentorship programs is to develop the students' capabilities to such a level that they can become leaders in their fields of interest.

A K THROUGH 12 MENTORSHIP PROGRAM IN A PUBLIC SCHOOL SETTING: ONE EXAMPLE

In Lincoln Public Schools, a mentorship program is provided for those students of outstanding abilities who need an individualized environment not available in either the regular program or the program for the gifted. After an assessment of each student's needs, he or she may be placed with a mentor and also may be placed in courses that are differentiated for gifted students.

Mentors are contracted to work for up to 5 hours a week with gifted students requiring individual instruction. Each mentor works with a student in the student's area of competence, providing acceleration (typically completing the equivalent of 2 years of course content in 1 year), as well as in-depth exploration of content. The mentors meet with the students in the public school building at the time the subjects of interest to the students are being taught. For example, a mentor works with a student on a science project at the time science is being taught in the regular classroom.

When the students progress 4 years beyond grade-level expectation, determination is made as to whether they are to continue working with their mentors or to attend university courses in the area of competence. Students may take up to 6 hours of college credit each semester as an alternative to district courses, with the district providing tuition and basic texts and the parents or guardians providing transportation.

Different mentorship program models are designed to meet special academic or emotional needs of gifted students. For example, some gifted students are placed with mentors to bring up their academic skills to appropriate levels. This service is provided to students who are educationally disadvantaged in some manner until the desired level of proficiency is attained. Other gifted students receive a team mentorship, with experts in behavioral or psychological services working with the mentors and classroom teachers to help these students solve problems that impair their academic progress.

The Student

What does the student need to bring into the mentorship? Generally, interest and task commitment appear to be the most common traits of the successful protege. These and other important traits are listed below.

- *The student must be interested in and excited about the subject to be studied.* Bloom (1985) called this trait "strong interest and emotional commitment" (p. 544). One parent in Lincoln asked the district to provide a mentor for her second-grade son who was demonstrating a strong interest in biochemistry. His interest became increasingly apparent as she took him on regular visits to the public library and he asked her to help him locate materials on the subject. The student was able to pursue this interest throughout his school career with a series of mentors in the field of science.

- *The student "must be ready for the next stage of instruction"* (Boston, 1976, p. 14). Bloom (1985) agreed:

  > Most of our talented individuals had very good experiences with their initial teacher(s), and many of them had developed a very comfortable relationship with them. However, after a number of years during which they had made relatively good progress in the talent field, someone—a parent, a friend of the family, an expert in the field, or the teacher—thought that the child could make even greater progress if a new and more expert teacher was chosen. (p. 519)

Thus, a mentor sometimes is assigned to bring the child to one level of expertise, and then to provide higher levels of service.

- *The student must be willing to learn skills and constantly "recapitulate . . . experiences . . . to separate wheat from chaff"* (Boston, 1976, pp. 15–16). One elementary student spent several years working on an in-depth study of the events and issues surrounding the Watergate scandal. As information was gathered, the mentor asked for constant filtering of fact and opinion, underlying causes and primary causes of actions, and so forth. As a result, the student operated in what Boston (1976) called an "experiential learning" setting, with the technical skills being learned as an integral part of the activity.

- *The student must have a "desire to reach a high level of attainment in the talent field"* (Bloom, 1985, p. 544). A high school student told the accompanist in the music department that he "heard melodies in his head." When the boy was questioned further, he confided an interest in learning how to compose a piece of music using the criteria established within the discipline. After identification procedures and mutual agreement between the student's parents and the school, the accompanist became the student's mentor. The student's attainment of the skills of composition led to his desire to compose a piece that could be performed by other talented students for an audience. When this step was accomplished, the mentor felt that the student needed the services of a more skilled instructor to continue his study. The student then continued to progress under the mentorship of a college professor.

- *The student must have "willingness to put in the great amounts of time and effort needed to reach very high levels of achievement in the talent field"* (Bloom, 1985, p. 544). The student who pursued the study of the Watergate affair began the study in second grade. During the next several years, he engaged the help of his parents and the mentor and interviewed each principal character in the scandal either in person, by telephone, or by letter. He and his mentor met with the school district's social studies consultant several times over a 2-year period while putting together a slide–tape presentation of the material. Together, they developed a format and production that met district criteria for classroom materials. By fifth grade, the student was presenting the slide–tape production and an oral interpretation of the information to classes within the district and to other audiences such as adults and college students at a Nebraska Wesleyan University convocation. Today, the slide–tape is used by classes throughout the district and is housed in the central media center for distribution.

Matching the Mentor and Protege

After the student has been approved for a mentorship, either the school or the parent may initiate the search for the mentor. Mentors may be selected by the parents, subject to the approval of the program coordinator. In all instances, the parents and student must approve the mentor. The mentor pool consists of candidates who have applied to the Human Resources personnel for this position and people selected from university and community sources based on demonstrated expertise.

Planning the Mentorship

Within 3 weeks of acceptance into the mentorship program, students are matched with a mentor and participate in a planning conference. Attempts are made to carefully match the adult and child using the criteria mentioned earlier.

Typical planning conferences include a building administrator or program facilitator, a psychologist (when requested), parent(s), mentor, and student. Plans for the mentorship include the areas to be studied, anticipated levels of proficiency, evaluative procedures, and reporting systems. Some mentorships at the elementary level involve a period for exploration of many topics, which is then replaced by selection of topics for in-depth pursuit. Mentorships in the middle and upper grades typically center around study of a subject area, with acceleration in district work and enrichment through individualized projects. Mentorships for gifted students with special psychological needs or skill deficits are designed to last for the duration of the situation, then are modified to resemble the typical plan for achieving students.

Functions

The mentorship is one of the most powerful teaching situations schools can offer students. Little doubt exists about the amount of impact a one-to-one learning relationship brings. A Lincoln student who is now a sophomore at Harvard University looked back at his mentorship:

> In all my years in the classroom, I never took a course that was challenging to me. I never took a course at my ability level or beyond. I had to get challenges from [the mentor]. . . . There is no replacement for that experience. (Lincoln Data Collection, 1988)

Nash and his colleagues suggest four functions of the mentorship: enhancing creativity, shaping careers, role modeling, and shaping personal growth. In addition, consideration needs to be given to reciprocity.

Enhancing Creativity

The mentor is responsible for enhancing creativity by creating a learning environment in which the student can produce work exceeding the expectations of the normal school setting. One can imagine quite easily the kind of product the gifted student interested in the Watergate scandal would have produced without the mentorship experience. Chances are the report would have been created in the school library and handed to the teacher as an extra-credit assignment. The child may have continued with the interest as an avocation, but probably not as the multifaceted experience that it became.

A national magazine was started in the Lincoln Public Schools as a result of a mentorship. After a student had produced several poems and other examples of creative writing, her parents financed the production of a magazine to serve as an outlet for this work. Thus, a "young authors' magazine" was born, and other young writers were invited to submit their work. The student developed criteria and standards for judging the submissions and printed these standards so that other writers learned to evaluate their own work before sending it to the magazine.

One mentor invites many gifted students to her home to participate in informal sharing sessions and to write letters to gifted pen pals in Ohio schools through her computer modem. "I try to provide a safe place for gifted kids to hang out," she said. "You'd be amazed at the ideas these kids generate just by talking to one another" (Lincoln Data Collection, 1988).

Thus, the mentor's task is to establish an environment that fosters creativity and a free flow of ideas, and to defend the student's right to function within that and similar environments. Nash and his colleagues state that "Mentors provide a protected relationship within which the protege can take risks without fear of ridicule and rejection." This protected environment allows the student to take what one protege calls, "the intellectual voyage into the unknown" (Lincoln Data Collection, 1988).

Shaping Careers

When students participating in mentorships engage in career exploration, they typically focus on the three components listed by Nash et al.: career identification, development, and advancement. Although the career focus of the mentor program at Lincoln Public Schools includes these components at the secondary level, the major function at the elementary and middle school level is on the development of a future vision, including the creation of an integrated lifestyle in which the student sees possibilities for incorporating many avocations and a major vocational area into a whole life picture. Mentors and instructors involved in special classes for middle school gifted students help with this process, which includes interviews with a variety of adults and the formation of the future vision based upon interests, abilities, and preferences.

Mentors and district personnel together can recommend that a student participate in the offerings of the University of Nebraska–Lincoln Gifted Guidance Lab. (This program was initiated by Barbara Kerr, professor and author of *Smart Girls, Gifted Women,* during her stay at the university, and serves as a practicum experience for graduate students interested in gifted children.) A student's typical visit to the guidance lab includes participating in a series of small group sessions in which avocations, personal preferences, beliefs, and abilities are discussed. Each student then is given a battery of career-related tests and a tour of the campus. After students eat lunch in a group setting, results of the tests are presented in individual conferences with students, and counselors help each student identify areas of competence, institutions of higher learning that offer training in the competencies, and ways in which selection processes can be used to make career decisions.

In addition, students have participated in "shadow experiences" (visits and interviews with people working in an area of student interest), and have found after-school and summer work that relates directly to their areas of expertise. For example, one student works in the biochemistry laboratory at the University of Nebraska–Lincoln during the summer; another works at the Lincoln Children's Zoo.

Mentors can play critical roles in helping students cope with career-related pressure from parents or other teachers. One mentor listened to a protege bemoan the fact that her parents expected her to become a doctor even though she was not interested in doing so. The mentor located and gave the girl a series of self-scoring evaluation instruments concerning career plans, personality profiles, and interests. When the evaluation was completed, the mentor contacted the parents, explained the apparent results of the evaluation, and helped the family to make the decision to remove the pressure from their daughter.

Role Modeling

Role modeling is a key function of the mentorship relationship. In a mentorship, according to one mentor, "Everything is focused on the person you are" (Lincoln Data Collection, 1988). The mentor is a role model, both in the personal sense and in the professional or traditional sense. Nash et al. state that "A mentor's function as role model has been conceived as particularly important in school-related programs" (p. 319).

The position of a role model is a delicate one. Entering into the mentor relationship with the sole purpose of moving a child through instructional material demonstrates a limited perspective of the mentor's function. The mentor must not enter the relationship to "save the child" from the schools, parents, or other forces, or to impose personal views on the child. The mentor should provide instruction in (a) the use of specialized tools associated with the discipline being studied and (b) how to act as a professional in that field. As Bloom (1985) states, "No one reached the limits of learning in a talent field on his or her own" (p. 509).

One graduate student, who had worked in the university science laboratories with his young protege, received a doctorate in biochemistry. The protege then visited his former mentor in medical school, and now is preparing to become a physician also, starting with an undergraduate degree in biochemistry. The student believes that the mentor made his college laboratory courses easy for him, because he had become thoroughly familiar with established protocols long before entering college (Lincoln Data Collection, 1988).

Shaping Personal Growth

Nash and his colleagues state that "the effect on the individual's self-worth and self-directedness is intertwined with creativity nurturance, realization of the potency of particular abilities and skills, and the appropriate placement of those abilities in life plans and careers." Bloom (1985) agrees, placing the task on the shoulders of the mentor and protege: "The role of the teacher is to find flaws in their [work] and to help them overcome them. They [teacher and student] also are learning the history of their field and to search for their own personal style and work" (pp. 536–537). One mentor stated,

> My role is to provide consistent emotional support and to let them do things on their own. They must develop an open mind in order to express themselves. Their work must be their work—new and different. And they must be able to feel the satisfaction that can be theirs when they do things on their own. (Lincoln Data Collection, 1988)

Boston (1976) commented that the mentor takes the student to a high level of experience and competence. The student then is ready to "take on" the world on his or her own terms rather than imitating the mentor.

Because of the intensely personal relationship developed between many mentors and proteges, personal growth is supported and nurtured long after the formal mentorship ends. "It is difficult not to become involved in the family life of the child when you see her every day," stated a mentor. "You become a friend; you have to." This mentor also found that becoming friends with her proteges and linking them together socially by inviting them to her home has helped them establish other meaningful friendships. "They need that in order to grow in other areas," she said (Lincoln Data Collection, 1988).

Although reciprocity may not be a primary reason for establishing a mentorship, it certainly is a viable by-product of the relationship. This function involves the mutual growth of both mentor and student while engaging in the mentorship. It also involves the assumption of mentoring roles by the protege or former protege.

Mentors consistently note that they feel they "can never do enough" to help the students. One mentor finished her college degree because she felt she needed to act as a positive role model for the child; she also is working hard to perfect her own artistic talent "so that my kids will be able to say, 'Look what my mentor can do besides just teaching me'" (Lincoln Data Collection, 1988). Another example is the mentor who first earned a Ph.D. and then an M.D. with the encouragement of the protege's family. The mentoring relationship with a gifted student is motivating for the mentor as well as the protege.

Several students from the program in Lincoln also have become volunteer tutors and mentors themselves, either while still in the mentorship program or after leaving public school. One boy, who became the mentor for his younger sister, said, "Who else could understand what she was going through as well as I could?" (Lincoln Data Collection, 1988).

CONCLUSION

The examples provided in this chapter illustrate that successful mentorships can be provided in the public school setting. They also can be designed to accommodate gifted students' individual needs: acceleration, enrichment, and short-term remediation.

Mentorships in the public school setting are of the types described as exploratory in nature, "initially viewed . . . as play and recreational" sessions for the young child. "This is followed by a long sequence of learning activities that involve high standards, much time, and a great deal of hard work" (Bloom, 1985, p. 508). These experiences keep the exceptionally talented child challenged and motivated until a master teacher can be provided by the family or until the student enters college or other professional training.

The adult–protege relationship is important, whether the role of mentor is assumed by a parent, a neighbor, or an assignee of the school. If we truly believe in the worth of the gifted individual, we must provide such individual experiences to help them become contributing members in our society.

REFERENCES

Bloom, B. S. (Ed.). (1985). *Developing talent in young children*. New York: Ballantine.
Boston, B. O. (1976). *The sorcerer's apprentice: A case study in the role of the mentor*. Reston, VA: The Council for Exceptional Children.
Edlind, E. P., & Haensly, P. A. (1985). Gifts of mentorships. *Gifted Child Quarterly, 29*, 55–60.

Haensly, P. A., & Edlind, E. P. (1986). A search for ideal types of mentorship. In M. M. Gray & W. A. Gray (Eds.), *Proceedings of the First International Conference on Mentoring, Vol. I* (pp. 1–8). Vancouver, BC: International Association of Mentoring.

Kerr, B. A. (1985). *Smart girls, gifted women.* Columbus: Ohio Publishing.

Lincoln Public School Data Collection. (1988, Spring). Department of Gifted Education, Lincoln Public Schools, Lincoln, NE.

25

High School
Internship Program

Jeannette A. Bodnar

The Career Exploration Mentorship/Internship Program originated as a pilot program at a high school in Albuquerque, New Mexico, in 1980–1981, and now is implemented throughout the district. The Career Exploration Program (CEP) offers an expansion and enrichment of the learning environment far beyond the high school campus through an extensive program of school–community cooperation. The CEP, with its flexible options, is well suited to a wide spectrum of gifted youth, ranging from students who have outstanding academic records to those who frequently fail to perform successfully in a traditional classroom environment. However, in New Mexico, programs for gifted students are considered special educational services; therefore, students must meet two criteria to be eligible for this program: They must score (a) two standard deviations above the mean on an individual IQ test and (b) within the top 2% in achievement, critical thinking, or creativity.

Albuquerque has 11 high schools with about 18,000 students. The regular education high school curriculum includes advanced placement courses, enrichment classes, and additional advanced courses at a district magnet school. Most of the general academic needs of gifted high school students can be met through this curriculum or through concurrent enrollment at the University of New Mexico.

A district needs assessment conducted in 1979 revealed educational gaps in the curriculum for gifted students. These gaps included (a) limited opportunities for students to apply classroom learning to real problems, (b) no significant career exploration activities, and (c) no programs for special populations of gifted high school students. These special populations include gifted students with learning disabilities who are having problems with the regular curriculum, and creatively gifted students who are not performing according to expectancy in academic classes. The CEP originally was designed to fill these identified gaps in the curriculum.

Through the use of a wide spectrum of community expertise and resources, the program is a complement to the regular curriculum and an expansion of the students' learning environment. By their senior year, many gifted students have taken most or all of the challenging and appropriate courses offered. The CEP offers curriculum choices that provide the opportunity for an in-depth look at possible career choices, including actual work experience in a career field. Individuals in the community have shown a great willingness to commit resources and personnel to the program. More than 250 local mentors (representing a broad range of careers) are available for 100 to 140 students per semester. At a time when school budgets are declining and math and science teachers are in short supply, this program augments the high school curriculum for many gifted students.

OVERVIEW

The CEP faculty recognizes the wide range of interests, abilities, motivations, and ambitions of gifted students, and seeks to provide each student with a mentorship or internship experience that best fits his or her individual needs. Each mentorship or internship site, each mentor–student relationship, and each on-site experience is unique for each student. The CEP is structured to ensure that students are provided with learning experiences that are both consistent with and solidly linked to their goals for academic, career, and personal growth.

Two for-credit course offerings are included within the CEP structure: mentorship and internship. The mentorship course provides an introduction to a career. It requires a minimum of 5 hours of student involvement per week and represents the equivalent of one high school course. The focus usually is specific to a particular mentor's work. Students (a) complete application procedures; (b) conduct research and interviews regarding selected career choices; (c) interview with prospective mentors prior to placement; (d) meet with the high school teacher of the gifted on a regular basis; (e) maintain written logs of activities, data collected, feelings, thoughts and reactions during the mentorship; and (f) spend a minimum of 5 hours per week for 12 weeks working one-to-one with a professional.

The internship course involves an in-depth examination of a career field. It requires 15 to 20 hours per week for 17 weeks, depending upon the number of credits desired, and represents the equivalent of three high school courses. In the internship, the student is required to examine in detail his or her internship activities, look at the nature of the profession in general, identify salient features of his or her site, and be cognizant of the knowledge and skills required to be successful in this profession.

Each internship student (a) completes application procedures; (b) attends weekly seminars with the internship instructor, which focus on the internship experience and provide for ongoing evaluation; (c) writes a weekly essay focused by questions about various aspects of the profession, work environment, student's activities, and student's reactions; (d) plans and conducts one on-site seminar; (e) demonstrates increased career awareness, self-direction, independence, and competence in both written work and oral presentations; (f) communicates (through individual conferences, seminars, journals, and the synopsis) insights gained on the nature of the profession and the associated work environment; and (g) participates with the internship teacher and mentor in program evaluation. All these activities are described in the 20-page intern's manual (Bodnar, 1980) that each student receives upon entering the program.

Each community mentor receives a program brochure and manual (Bodnar, 1980) that contain an outline of the program; stated objectives; and the responsibilities of the student, mentor, and district coordinator. During the mentorship, high school teachers are provided with a manual (Bodnar, 1980) containing suggestions of ways to establish and monitor mentorships. Mentorships are part of the home high school curriculum, whereas internships are conducted on a districtwide basis. Because a limited number of students may participate in the internship course, the course is offered at the district's magnet school. All internship students must spend a minimum of 15 to 20 hours per week on-site. In addition, the interns attend a weekly 2-hour seminar in which they discuss and describe their internship experiences. The seminar teacher provides ongoing evaluation of the student's placement, a framework for sharing information about careers, and an opportunity for students to learn from the experiences of other interns. Because the internship is a more comprehensive course, it is the main focus of this chapter.

Throughout the application process, interviews, placement procedures, seminars, and actual internship work, students are engaged in activities that help them identify their strengths and weaknesses within the framework of a career choice. Students must evaluate how well they fit the requirements of specific careers and the associated work environments. Students learn to identify reasons for making certain career choices. The internship also is a learning experience in which students are engaged in productive work, making them assets to the organizations in which they are apprentices. They also are exposed to the field experiences and career interests of other students in the program as a result of the interaction that occurs in weekly seminars and on-site presentations.

The process of analyzing particular careers and professions enables students to answer questions about (a) entry-level requirements for a given career, (b) characteristics of the work and environment, (c) personal characteristics that seem essential to success, (d) responsibilities that accompany the work, (e) procedures for performance evaluation, (f) job outlook for the future, and (g) various work environment options. The program also fosters the development and refinement of personal skills and sensitivities necessary to function effectively in both college and the world of work. The educational objectives listed in Figure 25.1 provide the framework for the internship.

PROGRAM STRUCTURE

The following program materials were developed during the pilot phase of the CEP, but have undergone modification over the years and are updated on a regular basis:

Program Brochure
Mentorship Manual: "How To for Teachers"
Application Packets for Students

The learner-centered educational objectives that guide the interaction of mentor, internship teacher, and intern follow:

The student will:

1. Gain a realistic picture of a particular profession and associated work environment.
2. Identify career entry-level competencies, opportunities for lateral moves and promotions, intrinsic and monetary rewards, in-house educational programs for employees, and funds available for employees to earn advanced degrees or additional training.
3. Contemplate future trends in the profession, including employment opportunities for new persons entering the field, technological changes that are impacting on the career, and future demand for the services or products offered.
4. Interact with fellow students to discuss and relate perceptions about professional behaviors, career options, characteristics of various work environments, opportunities within professions, and patterns of interaction among coworkers.
5. Describe the mentor's work, organization position, status, and educational and experiential background. The student will gain information on the factors that influenced the mentor's career choice, the mentor's views about the advantages and disadvantages of his or her present and/or past career, and the mentor's future professional goals.
6. Participate actively in the learning process by questioning, and reflecting upon and relating observations, information, and experiences.
7. Establish and maintain a working relationship with the mentor. The student will be able to express interests, reactions, goals, and feelings about the internship. The student will negotiate with the mentor to develop a learning experience that is mutually beneficial and rewarding.
8. Increase confidence, independence, and the ability to initiate, plan, and follow through on tasks.
9. Develop increased sensitivity in personal relationships, and refine communication, coping, and negotiation skills.
10. Acquire insight into his or her own strengths, abilities, and interests, in order to discover if current ambitions are compatible with the requirements of the profession.
11. Obtain a more realistic appraisal of the need for credentials in securing professional-level employment. The student will have a heightened sense of the intrinsic value of education and the continual need to learn new skills, advanced technology, and up-to-the-minute information.

The internship educational objectives are defined in terms of long-range goals and corresponding specific objectives in the Individualized Educational Plan. The educational plan reflects the content of the internship agreement and is developed by the teacher in conference with the student and parents.

Figure 25.1 Educational Objectives.

Mentor Contact Forms
Master List of Community Mentors
Mentorship/Internship Contracts
Mentor's Manual for Internships
Intern's Manual for Internship Students
Student Performance Evaluation Forms
Program Evaluation Forms

TEACHERS

Each of the 11 high schools in Albuquerque has at least one special education teacher of the gifted. In addition, the district has one program coordinator. The high school teachers of the gifted are facilitators and are responsible for the following program components:

- Contacting new community mentors
- Assisting students in identifying appropriate mentorship sites
- Screening, placement, supervision, and evaluation of mentorship students

The district coordinator's responsibilities include the following:

- Coordinating the contact, allocation, and use of community mentors
- Reviewing all CEP applications and assigning potential mentors
- Screening, placement, supervision, and evaluation of internship students
- Evaluating CEP program components
- Providing inservice training of teachers

Specific responsibilities of the coordinator involving the supervision of students are the following:

- Monitoring the internship experience to assure that the program objectives are met
- Making at least two on-site visits per semester to evaluate student performance, reinforce both mentor and student, listen to suggestions, and make necessary changes
- Meeting with the intern on an individual basis at least twice a semester
- Conducting weekly seminars with interns that focus on various topics directly related to careers
- Evaluating student performance

A major concern of the Albuquerque CEP personnel is that high school teachers serving gifted students are often classroom teachers with limited training in specialized instruction and curriculum development. These teachers often have no background in counseling, career education, public relations, and/or on-site performance evaluation. In addition, these teachers have other instructional assignments at their high schools. Inservice training, considered a key factor in preparing teachers to provide students with appropriate mentorship experiences, is provided in the areas of mentorship implementation, identification of student strengths and weaknesses, mentorship procedures and requirements, instructional strategies, evaluation of student performance, and program evaluation.

COMMUNITY MENTORS

Mentors are members of the community who agree to sponsor a mentorship or internship student. The mentor may be (a) the person who always directs the activities of the student or (b) a member of the agency sponsoring the student, who asks others to work directly with the student. In many cases, the student may consider more than one person a mentor. The mentor agrees to provide the student with assistance, a variety of educational experiences, and meaningful activities while on-site. In return, the mentor receives the personal satisfaction of guiding and supporting a student. The mentor–student relationships allow the students to interact with adult role models, to test themselves in a work environment, and to develop a sense of career direction. A significant number of mentor–student relationships continue far beyond the high school experience. Many mentors continue to support and encourage their former interns through ongoing friendships and employment.

Special qualities are needed by mentors. They need to

1. Demonstrate a commitment to the education of the student, which involves a willingness to spend time personally with the intern and additional time ensuring that the intern is engaged in appropriate activities.
2. Serve as a role model of the profession.
3. Encourage the intern's talents, abilities, and skills by providing opportunities for the student to participate in actual work situations.
4. Share themselves, their skills, and talents with a young person who aspires to join the profession.

New mentors can be added to the master list through teacher contacts, student referrals, or volunteers. After a community mentor is contacted and interviewed, a mentor interview sheet (Figure 25.2) is submitted to the district coordinator. The mentor then is placed on a master list. A sample page from the master list is provided in Figure 25.3. Each semester, student application packets (see Appendix 25.A) are submitted to the coordinator from teachers at the 11 high schools. A selection committee matches each student with a potential community mentor. Matches are based on the information provided in the application packet. Information provided on resumes often becomes a key factor in placement of students. In large districts, a coordinator for the use of community mentors is essential.

Currently, over 200 community sites provide sponsorship for students, representing a wide range of career interests (see Appendix 25.B). At some sites on the master list, mentors are provided for several students. For example, Philips Laboratory provides mentors for 15 to 20 students.

The addition of mentors or sponsoring agencies generally takes hours of public relations work that includes (a) written correspondence, (b) explanations of the program, (c) meetings with interested parties, (d) descriptions of what will be available to students, and (e) clarification of responsibilities. Once the student is placed, the coordinator is responsible for ongoing evaluations of student performance, addressing any concerns of mentor or student, evaluating the program, and writing thank

New Mentor Contact Interview Form

The following form is to be completed by the teacher on **each "new" community mentor** you contact. Please submit this form, **"typed,"** to the coordinator at the Career Enrichment Center at the beginning of each new semester.

Interview Information

Teacher conducting interview: _____   Date: _____

Mentor's Name: _____   Phone #: _____

Title: _____

Organization/Business: _____

Address: _____   Zip: _____

Field of Expertise: _____

Times available for students: Hours: _____   Days of Week: _____

Clearly specify what student will be doing and learning during the semester:

_____

_____

_____

State the mentor's requirements of the student, such as math background, computer languages, writing ability, and grade level.

_____

_____

_____

Indicate the number of students the mentor will take per semester: _____

Additional Comments:

Figure 25.2 Mentor Interview Form.

FIELD: Engineering/Software and Hardware for Aviation
MENTOR: TITLE: Artificial Intelligence Analyst
SITE: Honeywell Defense Systems
ADDRESS:
PHONE: HOURS: 7:45–4:20
DESCRIPTION & REQUIREMENTS: Student will learn about computer programming as well as research and assimilation in artificial intelligence. A knowledge of Pascal is useful. Student must be neatly dressed. INTERNSHIP ONLY.

FIELD: Engineering/Most Areas
MENTOR: TITLE:
SITE: Sandia National Laboratories
ADDRESS:
PHONE: HOURS:
DESCRIPTION & REQUIREMENTS: Sandia Labs offers 35 positions in all fields of engineering. INTERNSHIPS ONLY. Student must be a senior and apply in September of his or her junior year because students must be processed for a security clearance. Students must have physics and be enrolled in calculus their senior year.

FIELD: Engineering/All Fields
MENTOR: TITLE: Chief Scientist
SITE: Philips Laboratory
ADDRESS:
PHONE: HOURS: 8–4:30
DESCRIPTION & REQUIREMENTS: Placement at Philips is made based on the information provided by the student in his or her application packet. Priority is given to seniors and early applicants. The placements include research and development of weapons, all types of engineering, computer work, and laser technology. Twenty positions are available.

FIELD: Engineering/Research/Prototype Design
MENTOR: TITLE: Liaison for Mentors
SITE: BDM Corporation
ADDRESS:
PHONE: HOURS: 8–4:30
DESCRIPTION & REQUIREMENTS: Activities will vary according to student's interests. Company is similar to Sandia Labs, but smaller. It does prototype development in aerospace, weapons, solar research, etc. Student should have strong math and science backgrounds, with an interest in computers.

FIELD: Engineering/Computers
MENTOR: TITLE: Engineer
SITE: Signetics
ADDRESS:
PHONE: HOURS: 8–4:30
DESCRIPTION & REQUIREMENTS: Student must have sound programming skills, strong math background, and interest in computer programming. He or she will be engaged in writing programs to explain the process of making computer chips.

Figure 25.3 Sample Page from Master List of Mentors.

you letters. Form thank you letters should *not* be used; each letter must be individualized and specific to the students who benefited from the experience.

Sandia National Laboratories (SNL) is a major engineering firm in Albuquerque. SNL's participation in the program began as a 6-week program conducted in cooperation with two other engineering firms. Students were rotated from one firm to another during the semester. Student hands-on participation was very limited. Over a 6-year period, this program evolved into a 20-hour per week full-year placement for 35 students. SNL processes these students for security clearances and includes them as productive members of the staff, earning $6.06 per hour. The evolution of this internship took 6 years. During this period, the mentor–student interaction was excellent, extensive program evaluation was conducted, discussions about program modifications took place, and proposals for changes were written and implemented. The success of a program such as this requires the support of a key person in the organization. In addition, that individual's supervisor and the organization's president must be kept informed about the program's progress and success. Once a successful internship program is developed at a key organization or with a respected member of the community in a particular career field, that information may be used when recruiting additional mentors.

The development of successful mentorship/internship relationships within the community requires a considerable amount of time. The initial steps in program development must be taken slowly because community and school support must be built. In addition, the success of mentorships/internships requires that the teacher help the student to identify his or her interests, abilities, expectations, and limitations prior to the actual placement. Teachers must develop the ability to recognize and nurture the delicate match between mentor and student.

Mentorships that are not successful are generally the result of teacher errors, such as their failure to screen students carefully for maturity, self-discipline, and independence, or teachers' inability to identify the students' strengths and weaknesses. Often teachers fail to consider prerequisites for success in a career field, such as strong math skills for engineering, knowledge of anatomy for medicine, and programming skills for computer work. *The mentor's role is not to teach basic skills or replace classroom instruction.* A mentor's role is to enrich and expand the basic curriculum and to offer expertise, equipment, and projects that are not available at the high school. Often teachers fail to teach students how to write resumes with clear statements of their talents and abilities, or to develop portfolios that demonstrate special abilities or talents. For example, a student with As in honors English may still be a poor candidate for a mentorship in science fiction writing. The student should, in this case, prepare a portfolio of writings to be reviewed by the mentor.

Some community mentors are willing to work with students who have limited ability or experience; however, others are not, and some do not possess the skills to do so. In addition, both mentor and student expectations and limitations must be considered when developing a mentorship/internship placement. The mentor should be assigned a student who (a) has a sincere interest in, and a basic awareness of, the field; (b) is motivated; and (c) has demonstrated a willingness to compromise. Too often, not enough time is spent preparing a student for a mentorship. The necessity of waiting a semester or a year for a mentorship or internship may allow students time to acquire additional knowledge, specialized skills, maturity, and career awareness that will enable them to benefit far more from the experience than they would benefit without the extra wait time.

PLACEMENT PROCEDURES

Participation in the Career Exploration Program is limited to students who are eligible for inclusion in the Albuquerque Public Schools' program for gifted students. No specific course prerequisite exists for either the mentorship or the internship. However, student participants must be mature and responsible. The application process and screening procedures are designed to identify students who will be successful in the program. The placement process begins the semester prior to actual placement. Students apply for a mentorship or internship through a formal process in which they must demonstrate a real commitment to and interest in the program.

The students must complete an application form, write a resume, secure recommendations, and complete the *Strong–Campbell Interest Inventory, John Holland's Self-Directed Search,* or the guidance information system available at their high school.[1] Information gleaned from these instruments provides the framework for the initial interview in which the teacher, student, and parents begin to design an appropriate career exploration placement for the student.

Students are matched with community mentors on the basis of their previous educational performance, transcript, resume, teacher recommendations, and interviews. During the application process, the career interests and preferences of the student are identified. A list of community mentors and sites is available through the high school instructor to help the student discuss and select a possible mentorship or internship.

Before actual placement at a career site, the student and teacher meet with the student's prospective mentor to discuss the possibility of a placement, to clarify the expectations of both mentor and student, and to specify the responsibilities of the mentor, student, and teacher. If the placement appears appropriate, parents, mentor, teacher, and student sign a program contract (Figure 25.4).

EVALUATION

Although the mentorship manual includes district guidelines for student evaluation and grading, the teacher may modify these guidelines. Thus, student performance in this program is evaluated according to specific criteria established by the high school teachers of the gifted. Teachers notify students in advance regarding course requirements and the evaluation process.

Assignments, journals, seminars or weekly meetings with teachers, presentations, and mentor evaluations are used to document and evaluate each student's learn-

---

[1]Strong–Campbell's and Holland's instruments are available from Consulting Psychologist Press, 577 College Ave., Palo Alto, CA 94306.

Albuquerque Public Schools
Special Education Department
Career Exploration Internship Program

Agreement

I. Student Section

I _____ will be responsible to/for:
(student's name)

1. Spend a minimum of 12–15 hours per week on-site and 5 additional hours per week in activities directly related to the internship.

   Time on-site _____
   (changes require notification of parent, mentor, and teacher)
2. Report promptly, dress appropriately, and follow instructions carefully.
3. Demonstrate responsibility in task or activity completion.
4. Write and submit a weekly study journal to the internship teacher.
5. Plan and conduct one on-site seminar.
6. Attend and participate at weekly seminars.
7. Write and submit an end-of-term synopsis.
8. Participate with internship teacher and mentor in program evaluation.

Complete descriptions of program requirements are found in the *Intern's Manual.*

I understand I am responsible for my own transportation to and from my internship site.

Student's Signature _____ Date _____

Address _____ Phone _____

High School _____ Grade Level _____

II. Parent Section

We, the parents of the above student, give permission for him/her to participate in the Internship Program coordinated by the district Internship teacher. We understand that the student and his/her parents are responsible for transportation to and from the internship site.

1. Please list any health problems that may affect his/her attendance and/or performance in the program.

   _____
   _____
2. APS carries medical excess plan. The family carries a primary health insurance plan.

   Yes _____ No _____ Please state firm _____
3. In case of emergency please contact the following:

   Parent _____ Home phone _____

   Work phone _____

I certify that my son/daughter has my permission to participate in the Internship Program. I have read the description of this program and fully understand the objectives, obligations, and requirements of the program.

Parent's Signature _____ Date _____

(Continued)

Figure 25.4 Program Contract.

Agreement

III. Mentor Section

The community mentor agrees to the following:

1. To spend time with the intern to ensure that he/she is engaged in educational activities.
2. To provide the student with a wide range of activities that allow the student to observe and participate in the actual work associated with the profession.
3. To develop with the student a mutual understanding about his/or responsibilities, assignments, and role as an intern.
4. To meet with the intern on a regular basis to discuss his/her performance, answer questions, make suggestions, and assign additional responsibilities.
5. To provide the student with instruction and supervision.
6. To make time available to meet with the internship teacher for ongoing and end-of-term assessment of the student's performance and evaluation of program effectiveness.

Mentor's Signature _____ Date _____

Site _____ Phone _____

Address _____

IV. Internship Teacher Section

The internship teacher agrees to the following:

1. To work with both the mentor and student to ensure a clear understanding of the procedures, objectives, and requirements of the program.
2. To monitor the internship experience through regular contact with mentor and intern.
3. To conduct weekly seminars with the interns.
4. To assist the student in the preparation of an on-site seminar.
5. To review on a regular basis the student's study journal.
6. To conduct both formative and end-of-term evaluation of the student's performance.
7. To assess the intern's overall performance and award academic credit for successful completion of all internship requirements.

Teacher's Signature _____ Date _____

Address _____ Phone _____

Figure 25.4 *(Continued).*

ing. From 40% to 50% of the CEP grade is determined by the community mentor, who completes a mid-term and final intern evaluation form (see Figure 25.5). The remaining part of the grade is determined by the student's performance in teacher-led activities. In the internship course, considerable emphasis is placed on student-to-student interaction during weekly seminars, and on the student-delivered on-site seminar at the end of the semester. The intern's manual contains clearly outlined program requirements, lists of specific questions for weekly essays, and guidelines for on-site presentations and final synopsis writing.

Internship Evaluation Form
Career Exploration Program

Intern: _____   Grading Period: 9/16 to 10/16

Mentor: _____   Phone #: _____

Please use the following scale to evaluate the intern's performance during the given grading period.

1—Below average (D)   2—Average (C)   3—Above average (B)   4—Excellent (A)

Student . . .

Has good attendance on-site	1	2	3	4
Demonstrates an interest in obtaining information and acquiring skills	1	2	3	4
Carries out work in an efficient and timely manner	1	2	3	4
Undertakes a variety of tasks and assignments	1	2	3	4
Asks meaningful questions	1	2	3	4
Demonstrates initiative and self-direction by assuming an active role in activities	1	2	3	4
Learns quickly and is able to work without constant supervision	1	2	3	4
Listens to ideas, implements suggestions, and follows directions	1	2	3	4
Accepts constructive criticism, works to resolve conflicts, and modifies behavior when necessary	1	2	3	4
Is self-confident, mature in attitude, and positive about the internship experience	1	2	3	4
Is productive and industrious in overall performance	1	2	3	4
Communicates effectively with other individuals	1	2	3	4
Reports ideas, issues, or problems clearly and concisely	1	2	3	4
Exercises good judgment, and demonstrates an awareness of abilities and limitations	1	2	3	4

(Continued)

Figure 25.5 Intern Performance Evaluation Form.

Specify areas where you would like to see improvement in the intern's performance:

Consider the individual's performance on assignments, knowledge of field, interpersonal skills, and creativity as measured by original contributions. Mention specific contributions, achievements, and capabilities:

Additional comments and/or concerns:

Your evaluation is a significant factor in determining the student's grade. Please assign a letter grade for the intern, sign, and date below:

Please indicate the actual number of hours per week the intern student works on-site ____.

Letter Grade: _____ Signature: _____ Date: _____

Figure 25.5 *(Continued).*

At the end of the semester, mentors, students, and parents also complete questionnaires regarding program effectiveness (Figures 25.6 and 25.7). Districtwide results indicate that program participants feel strongly that the program includes meaningful educational activities that extend and enrich the scope of the traditional high school. The continuing and significant annual increase in the number of community mentors and students who participate in the program reflects clearly the merit and educational value of the program.

The internship course has a component in which students receive guidance in selecting a college, as well as applying for scholarships and financial aid. The internship experience itself provides many students with an advantage in applying to out-of-state institutions. A student's experience in internships and mentorships looks extremely impressive to college admission personnel. Participation in this type of program indicates motivation, initiative, and something unique about the student during the high school years. These experiences "open doors" for employment opportunities because students have acquired marketable skills, work competencies, and meaningful references.

A majority of the students who participate in the program enter college. At least 85% of the interns are offered summer employment from their mentors. Many return to their internship sites every summer for employment while in college. This summer employment opportunity enables students to gain even more experience in their areas of career interest.

CONCLUSION

In this chapter, a basic framework is provided from which a career exploration program can be developed for gifted high school students. Clearly, the program could not survive without extensive community support, which takes years to establish. To build school and community support, program developers must define objectives clearly, establish guidelines, and employ evaluation procedures to ensure that meaningful educational experiences are provided and learning is documented. In addition, special inservice training for instructors is essential to maintain a quality program. The program is best suited for gifted students who are risk takers, independent, and able to assume the responsibility for their own learning. A preliminary follow-up study of CEP graduates indicates that the program had a significant impact on the students' career decisions.

Evaluation
Career Exploration Program
Special Education/Gifted
Albuquerque Public Schools

Mentor's Name _____ Phone # _____

Student's Name _____

Please check: Mentorship _____ or Internship _____

The purpose of this evaluation is to gather data which will help assess the effectiveness and value of the mentorship and internship components of the Career Exploration Program. Please indicate the extent to which you agree or disagree with the following statements.

Key: 1 = strongly disagree   2 = disagree   3 = undecided
4 = agree   5 = strongly agree

1. I am satisfied with the Career Exploration Program.   1   2   3   4   5

2. I feel that the program is a meaningful educational experience for a high school gifted student.   1   2   3   4   5

3. I feel that the student was well suited in interest and abilities for this placement.   1   2   3   4   5

4. My interaction with the student resulted in a more positive
   attitude toward high school students.   1   2   3   4   5

5. The program is an excellent means to expand the existing
   curriculum for gifted students.   1   2   3   4   5

6. I wish I had been able to participate in a program like this
   while in high school.   1   2   3   4   5

7. I feel that the student made meaningful contributions in
   various situations and/or to the work during the semester.   1   2   3   4   5

8. The program enables students to expand and enrich their
   classroom knowledge through direct application.   1   2   3   4   5

9. The program requires students to engage in constant
   evaluation of their abilities and knowledge during interactions with others and/or problem solving.   1   2   3   4   5

10. The program requires students to engage in the exchange
    of information, ideas, and concerns through both oral and
    written communications.   1   2   3   4   5

11. I benefited from my interaction with the student.   1   2   3   4   5

(Continued)

Figure 25.6 Program Evaluation Form.

12. I am willing to recommend the student for college or
    employment.   1   2   3   4   5

13. I feel that the student learned a great deal about human
    relations as a direct result of this experience.   1   2   3   4   5

14. I feel that the student learned a great deal about the
    profession and associated work environment as a direct
    result of this program.   1   2   3   4   5

15. I feel that this program is a valuable addition to the high
    school curriculum for gifted students.   1   2   3   4   5

16. I am willing to serve as a mentor again.   yes   no

Additional Comments:

Figure 25.6 *(Continued).*

Student Questionnaire
Career Exploration Program
Special Education/Gifted

Student's Name: _____ Phone #: _____

Address: _____ Zip: _____

High School: _____ Teacher: _____

The purpose of this questionnaire is to gather information to assess the effectiveness and value
of the mentorship and internship components of the Career Exploration Program. Please indicate the extent to which you agree or disagree with the following statements.

Key: 1 = strongly disagree   2 = disagree   3 = undecided
        4 = agree   5 = strongly agree

1. I was very satisfied with my mentorship/internship experience.   1   2   3   4   5

2. I feel that the experience offered me a variety of
   challenges and assignments very different from those in
   the classroom.   1   2   3   4   5

3. I felt that my placement was well suited to both my abilities and interests.   1   2   3   4   5

(Continued)

Figure 25.7 Student Form to Evaluate Program.

4. I enjoyed being able to work at my own pace and being required to assume responsibility for my own learning and behavior.　　1　2　3　4　5

5. I feel that being able to apply my skills and knowledge through a mentorship/internship was an incredible opportunity.　　1　2　3　4　5

6. I feel that the program required that I be able to communicate effectively with people.　　1　2　3　4　5

7. I feel that this program helped me to clarify, modify, and extend my understanding of my career choice.　　1　2　3　4　5

8. Without this program, I would have had little real knowledge and insight into the requirements and real nature of the work in my field of interest.　　1　2　3　4　5

9. The first-hand observation and participation required makes the mentorship/internship an extremely valuable learning experience.　　1　2　3　4　5

10. On a scale of 1 to 10, I would rate the program as a 10 with regard to the amount of knowledge gained in other high school classes.　　1　2　3　4　5

11. I feel that this program provided me with many opportunities to recognize and work with both my strengths and weaknesses in academic fields.　　1　2　3　4　5

12. I feel that the program provided me with insight into both my strengths and weaknesses in interpersonal skills.　　1　2　3　4　5

13. The program definitely had an impact upon my career direction/choice.　　1　2　3　4　5

14. I would highly recommend the program to other students.　　1　2　3　4　5

Please write a few additional comments about the program.

Figure 25.7 *(Continued).*

Appendix 25.A

Application Packet

INTERNSHIP APPLICATION INSTRUCTIONS
1991–1992

Read the following instructions carefully before filling out the enclosed application form.

The application packet should be an accurate account and expression of your personal achievements, interests, and goals.

Both the application form and resume must be typed.

It should contain no errors in content, grammar, or spelling.

It represents you! It immediately indicates a great deal about you to the reader, including the pride you have in yourself; the importance you place on quality work; and the ability you have to write in a concise and informative manner.

Resume

A resume must be included with your application. You may use the two sample resumes as guides for preparing your own.

1. Your resume should be brief, concise, and well written.
2. This is your personal ad. You should promote yourself.
3. Begin the resume with your name, age, complete address, and phone number.
4. Organization is important. The categories are up to you, but it is always better to have the information under special headings. Possible headings include education, academic skills, extra curricular activities, awards, and work experience.
5. Add a personal touch. Be creative. Use special words and sentences that make you unique.
6. Include specific information on the type of work that interests you. Explain what you like to do and describe the conditions under which you work best.
7. The resume should clearly reflect pride in your abilities, and accomplishments.

Your complete application should be submitted to the Career Enrichment Center, 807 Mountain Road N.E., Albuquerque, NM 87102. The application must include the application form, resume, two recommendations, and a copy of your transcript. Completed application forms with resumes are dated, and assignments to mentors are made on the basis of early application. This is a district program, and you will compete with students from all of Albuquerque's 11 high schools for internship sites.

If you have questions about the application process, internship sites, or the Internship Program in general, please contact Jan Bodnar at 292-0101.

Appendix 25.A (Continued)

Internship Application
Career Enrichment Center
807 Mountain Road NE
Albuquerque, New Mexico 87102

Student: _____ Date: _____

Address: _____ Zip: _____ Home Phone: _____

School: _____ Current Grade Level: _____ ID#: _____

Age: ____ Birthdate: ____ Sex: ____ Ethnic Background: (Optional) _____

Father's Name: _____ Work Phone: _____

Occupation: _____ Work Site: _____

Mother's Name: _____ Work Phone: _____

Occupation: _____ Work Site: _____

List three choices of possible internship from current list. (List available from teacher)

Site/Field

1. _____

2. _____

3. _____

Describe two specific career interests and explain what you would like to be doing in each area during your internship.

1. _____

_____

2. _____

_____

List the time of day you are available for an internship. (Note: Students are responsible for their own transportation to and from the site.) _____

List any health problems which may affect your participation in the program.

_____

I have read the internship course description and fully understand the requirements I must meet to receive credit.

Signature of Student: _____ Date: _____

Guardian Consent: I certify that my son/daughter has my permission to participate in the Internship Program.

Signature of Guardian: _____ Date: _____

Please return your application, transcript, two recommendations, and resume to the Career Enrichment Center.

Appendix 25.A (Continued)

Recommendation Form
Internship Program
Career Enrichment Center

Student: _____ High School: _____ Date: _____

The student is applying for the Internship Program offered by gifted education. The internship is an off-campus program where the student works directly with professionals in the community. In order to maintain the support of our community mentors, we select students who demonstrate independence, self-direction, good communication skills, and a strong sense of commitment to learning. We need an accurate appraisal of their abilities and potential. Please take a moment to fill out this form.

Use the following code: (Circle)

1-Below average   2-Average   3-Above average   4-Excellent

Student is willing to accept responsibility	1	2	3	4
Student completes assigned tasks	1	2	3	4
Student communicates well verbally	1	2	3	4
Student has sound writing skills	1	2	3	4
Student is able to work independently	1	2	3	4
Student demonstrates a mature attitude and interest in learning	1	2	3	4
Student often asks meaningful questions	1	2	3	4
Student responds well to instruction and constructive criticism	1	2	3	4
Student has a high level of interest in your subject area	1	2	3	4
Student is sensitive to situations and the feelings of others	1	2	3	4

Describe two of the student's strongest personality traits and/or abilities.

How long have you known this student? _____

Do you feel that this student would benefit from an in-depth and hands-on work experience in a specific career field? Yes _____ No _____ Undecided _____

Please explain:

Teacher: _____ Class: _____
           Signature

This recommendation should be returned to Jan Bodnar at the APS Career Enrichment Center. If you have additional comments or concerns, please contact Jan at 247-3658.

Appendix 25.A (Continued)

RESUME

Name
9105 Sonya Avenue SW
Albuquerque, NM 87105
Phone #

EDUCATION: West Mesa High School, Albuquerque, New Mexico
Date of Graduation to be May 1987
Grade Point Average: 4.39
Now enrolled in Honors Math Seminar (Calculus II)

Activities: MESA member, 1984–1987
MESA President, 1987
MESA Citywide Leadership Group, 1986–1987
MESA Vice President, 1985–1986
National Honor Society member, 1985–1987
National Honor Society Vice President, 1987
West Mesa Staters Historian, 1987
New Mexico Boys State, 1986
Academic Decathlon, 1986–1987
Contemporary Issues in Science Forum, 1984

Honors: National Merit Semifinalist, 1987
First Honors Academic Certificates, 1984–1987
New Mexico State University Honor Scholar, 1987
Who's Who Among American High School Students, 1987
MESA Outstanding Junior, 1986
APS Computer Problem Solving Contest, 2nd Place, 1986
New Mexico History Day, 1st Place Paper, 1986
APS Academic Decathlon, 1st Place Essay, 3rd Place
Mathematics, 1986
MESA Outstanding Student, 1985
ACTM Mathematics Contest, 3rd Place Computer, 1985
MESA Outstanding Freshman, 1984
ACTM Mathematics Contest, 4th Place Geometry, 1984
National Science Award, 1984
United States National Mathematics Award, 1984

EXTRACURRICULAR ACTIVITIES:
              Marching Band, 1984–1987
                   Clarinet Section Leader, 1986–1987
              Wind Ensemble, 1984–1987
              Basketball Pep Band, 1985–1987
              Chess Club, 1984–1987
              P.A.C.K. (Program for Academically Capable Kids), 1984–1987

WORK EXPERIENCE:
1986–1987   Career Exploration Trainee, Sandia Laboratories,
School Year Albuquerque, New Mexico
             Pulsed Power Research Center
             Working on drawings, construction, inspection of Saturn and
             Troll simulation facilities, SF Recovery System

WORK EXPERIENCE, CONT.:
5/85 to 9/85 Engineering Aide, Mechanical Engineering, UNM,
              Albuquerque, New Mexico
              Produced engineering drawing on CADAM and AutoCAD
              computer systems

1984–1985   Tutor, MESA Program, West Mesa High School,
School Year   Albuquerque, New Mexico
              Tutored up to tenth-grade honors level courses

5/85 to 9/85 Engineering Aide, Mechanical Engineering, UNM,
              Albuquerque, New Mexico
              Produced engineering drawing on CADAM and AutoCAD
              computer systems

1984–1985   Tutor, MESA Program, West Mesa High School,
School Year   Albuquerque, New Mexico
              Tutored up to tenth-grade honors level courses

SPECIAL SKILLS:
Use of AutoCAD
BASIC Programming
Basic Fortran Programming
Typing
Mathematics Skills

Appendix 25.A (Continued)

RESUME

NAME AND ADDRESS: *DATE OF BIRTH:* 4-3-68

Name   *HEALTH:* Good
12605 Loyola, NE
Albuquerque, New Mexico 87112
Phone #

EDUCATION:

Kennedy Middle School	Albuquerque, New Mexico	grades 6–8
Manzano High School	Albuquerque, New Mexico	grades 9–present
Gifted Program grades 3–6		

Cumulative High School G.P.A.: 4.4 (as of 3rd 9wks Junior Year)
Class Ranking: 1st out of 575
Academic Interests: Math and Science oriented classes

EXTRACURRICULAR ACTIVITIES	*GRADE*
Boys' Track Team Manager	9
Student Council Member	9, 10
French Club Member	10, 11
Honor Society Member	11
French Honor Society Member	11
Junior Advisory Member	11
Homecoming Committee	11
Part-time Employment as a Medical Bookkeeper	11
20 hours per week	

SPECIAL HONORS:

Honor Roll, Grades 9, 10, 11
University of New Mexico French Alliance Award, Grade 10
Recipient of United States Business Education Award, Grade 10
Recipient of the National Technical Association Award, Grade 10
1st Place Award in the 1982 Regional Science Fair in the Category of Physics,
    Grade 8

STATEMENT OF INTEREST IN THE INTERNSHIP PROGRAM:

I have been interested in engineering since age seven and I would like to have the opportunity to learn about it first-hand. I feel learning by doing is as important as the more familiar classroom method and often more beneficial to the student. The best education I can achieve is a well-rounded one that provides a variety of experiences, and I would like the Internship Program to be among my high school learning experiences.

Appendix 25.B

Master List of Possible Career Fields

CAREER EXPLORATION INTERNSHIP

Receive 1 1/2 academic credits
for an internship with work experience in your chosen field.

Applications for fall semester 1984 are now being accepted. Contact your High School Gifted Teacher.

SOME INTERNSHIPS AVAILABLE:

- Anthropology
- Architecture
- Ballet
- Biology
- Business Management
- Chemistry
- Computer Programming

- Fashion
- Forestry
- Graphic Arts
- Herpetology
- Investment Management
- Law—civil, criminal, corporate

- Medicine
- Music
- Politics
- Pottery
- Theatre Management
- Veterinary Medicine
- Writing

- Engineering—electrical, mechanical, civil, nuclear, aerospace

Placement contacts are made during the summer - therefore your application must be submitted as soon as possible. Placement priority is given to early applicants.

CURRENT SPONSORS

BDM Corporation
Intelligent Computer Systems
KAFB Weapons Lab.
KOAT Channel 7
Lovelace Medical Center
Molzen-Corbin & Associates
Naval Weapons Evaluation Facility
Presbyterian Hospital
Plaza III
Public Service Company
Sandia National Labs
Sandia Heights Pharmacy
Shma Tays Fashions
University of New Mexico
University of New Mexico Hospital

For information and details on specific fields, contact Jan Bodnar, 292-0101

Appendix 25.B (Continued)

CAREER EXPLORATION CAREER FIELDS

FIELD
Accounting
Advertising
Anthropology
Anthropology/Forensic
Archaeology
Architecture
Architecture/Architectural Engineering
Architecture/Interior Design
Art/Painting
Art/Advertising
Art/Boomerangs
Arts/Graphic Arts & Design
Arts/Ballet
Arts/Cartooning and Commercial
Arts/Graphic Arts
Arts/Graphics
Arts/Lithography
Arts/Medical Illustrations
Arts/Political Cartooning
Arts/Pottery
Arts/Wood Sculpture
Astronomy
Athletic Trainer
Aviation/Sales
Aviation/Weather and Traffic Control

Band Instrument Repair
Banking
Banking and Financial Planning
Biomedical Engineering
Biology
Business
Business/Educational Toys
Business/Exotic Birds
Business/Games
Business/Insurance
Business/Office Furniture

Business/Restaurant Management
Business/Retirement Home
Business/Travel Agency

Chemistry/Biochemistry
Chemistry/Soil and Water Analysis
Computers
Computers/Applications
Computers/Business
Computers/Business Programming
Computers/Business Programming/Marketing
Computers/Design
Computers/Education
Computers/Engineering Applications
Computers/Programming/Electrical Engineering

Dance/Ballet & Jazz
Dentistry
Drama

Ecology/Natural Resources
Education
Education/Elementary
Education/Child Care
Education/Deaf Education
Education/Elementary
Education/Elementary Gifted
Education/Reading
Education/Special Education
Electronics
Electronics/Repair
Engineering
Engineering/Civil
Engineering/All Fields
Engineering/Biomedical
Engineering/Chemical/Laser
Engineering/Civil
Engineering/Civil/Mechanical
Engineering/Computers
Engineering/Conservation
Engineering/Electrical
Engineering/Electrical Power
Engineering/Most Areas
Engineering/Most Fields
Engineering/Nuclear

Engineering/Research/Prototype Design
Engineering/Software and Hardware for Aviation
Engineering/Solar
Engineering/Weapons Research

Fashion Merchandising
Fashion/Modeling
Fashion/Retail Business
Forestry
Forestry/Timber

Genetic Counseling
Geology

Herpetology

Interior Design

Journalism

Law
Law/Antitrust
Law/Civil
Law/Contracts
Law/Corporate
Law/Criminal
Law/General
Law/Judge
Law/Medical Legal
Law/State Bar Association
Library Science

Machine Repair
Medical Research
Medical Research/Most Areas
Medical Research/Pharmacology
Medical Technology
Medicine
Medicine/Family Practice
Medicine/Ophthalmology
Medicine/Physician's Assistant
Medicine/Aviation
Medicine/Cardiology
Medicine/Emergency
Medicine/Family Practice

Medicine/Hospital Rotation
Medicine/Most Areas
Medicine/Neurology
Medicine/Nursing
Medicine/Paramedics
Medicine/Pathology
Medicine/Pediatrics
Medicine/Urgent Care Center
Meteorology
Museum/Art
Museum Work
Music
Music/Business
Music/Electronic
Music/Music Education
Music/Recording Studio

Photography
Photography/Portrait
Physical Therapy
Physical Therapy/Sports Rehabilitation
Physics
Politics/U.S. Senator
Psychology
Psychology/Peer Mentoring
Psychology/Administration
Psychology/Child Life Specialist
Psychology/Counseling
Psychology/Group
Psychology/Use of Animals in Psychology
Public Relations

Radio
Radio/Broadcasting
Radio/Operations
Radio/Production

Social Work
Sports
Sports/Albuquerque Parks and Recreation
Sports/Bowling
Sports/Horse Training
Sports/Tennis
Stocks and Investments

Television
Television/Community Cable Channel
Television/News Department
Television/Production
Television/Production/Videotaping
Theater

Veterinary Medicine
Veterinary/Ophthalmology
Videotaping

Writing
Writing/Creative
Writing/Creative and Technical
Writing/Free Lance
Writing/Magazine
Writing/Science Fiction

Zoology/Animal Research/Ecology
Zoology/Graphic Arts
Zoology/Horticulture

REFERENCES

Bodnar, J. (1980). *Mentorship manual, Mentor's manual,* and *Intern's manual.* Available from the author, Career Enrichment Center, 807 Mountain Rd., NE, Albuquerque, NM 87102.

26

An Expanded View of Internships

JoAnn B. Seghini

The Career Exploration Mentorship/Internship Program (CEP) described by Bodnar is designed to help gifted students make career choices through exploration of real-world situations. This application approach to career education can have a significant impact upon youngsters who have academic abilities but often fail to see the application of such abilities to the work world. The program also could be helpful in providing a transition from an academic setting to the work world, which is rapidly changing in response to technological and informational advances.

I am concerned, however, that such a program, available only at the end of a high school year, may be too little, too late, and may not attract students who have poor study habits or who lack motivation. Serving these students is identified as a major goal of the program. I also am concerned about a program that comes after students have made academic choices that may exclude them from a variety of career choices or post–high school training programs.

An internship experience, when combined with other intervention strategies, will provide opportunities for students to remediate academic behaviors and to make appropriate choices and plans for course taking. It could act as a bridge to post–high school training. The intervention examples included in this discussion include (a) a comprehensive high school counseling program, (b) implementation of the Renzulli Enrichment Triad/Revolving Door Model (Renzulli, 1986), (c) Wright, Jackson, and Mamales's (1989–1990) Business–Industry–Community–Education Partnership (BICEP), and (d) implementation of the Autonomous Learning Program (Betts, 1985). The Renzulli Enrichment Triad and Betts Autonomous Learning models are described in depth in Chapter 27. The focus of the discussion in this chapter is on how these models can be used to supplement an internship program and prepare students to be successful in it. All of these programs allow for career education, preparation, and planning as a part of the student's K–12 educational program.

This kind of comprehensive effort will help to ensure a successful internship and the selection of a greater number of qualifying students.

COUNSELING

A major problem faced by many gifted students involves predicting educational needs and planning for the options they may wish to have upon finishing high school. While many do not know what they want to become, or even in which area they may wish to specialize, they frequently plan to go to college. Such students may wait until their junior or senior year to really look at courses required by universities. This is much too late in the game for them to be competitive or selective. Exploration of careers and counseling programs that help students understand prerequisites and admission requirements of universities must begin at ninth grade or even earlier. This exploration should be combined with a comprehensive counseling program for pregraduation course taking that involves students and parents in the planning process. Students and parents need to be aware that choices made throughout high school can result in options available or options closed as they consider post–high school programs (Jordan School District, 1990–1991). The Jordan School District high school counseling program develops a financial aid and application handbook that is presented to students and parents as early as 10th grade. Such a publication, combined with counseling of students, is proactive and developmental.

Additional counseling with trained counseling staff should be an integral part of the program as early as possible. Counseling assistance can be given by counselors, teachers who have been trained, and community mentors, and should address a variety of issues related to planning and decision making. Students, for example, should be helped to understand that some careers, such as medicine and law, take a great deal of time and training. They then can analyze and compare salaries with less demanding specialties.

Counseling also should address gender equity and questions that might arise concerning the combination of careers with family priorities. The balance of career and family has been an issue for women, but is becoming increasingly important for greater numbers of men. Students need to understand that education and career training need not conflict with values related to family and parenting. Planning is important, however, so that careers support the priorities and time requirements of family plans (Bingham & Stryker, 1987).

Throughout the Albuquerque program, the responsibility for counseling rests only with the classroom teacher and the mentor and seems to occur mostly during the internship. Such an omission throughout the school program ignores the value of the counseling staff and does not prepare students to make critical decisions early. Use of counselors and counseling at earlier grades helps to prepare students for successful programs in community settings and in post–high school settings. Planned counseling also includes regular education resources in support of programs to meet the needs of gifted students. Counseling, whether part of a special program or part of a regular education program, represents a critical part of the student's preparation.

THE ENRICHMENT TRIAD/REVOLVING DOOR MODEL

Other programs should involve students in career education as an integral part of the K–12 curriculum. This would better prepare students to consider future internship choices. Such programs should be part of the regular education curriculum and can appropriately be part of the Enrichment Triad/Revolving Door Model. This model, which includes five service delivery components, is a natural for career exploration and for relating school experiences to the world of work (Renzulli, 1986).

Assessment of student strengths at early ages can help schools to identify strengths and weaknesses and to modify curricular experiences appropriately while exposing students to careers and real-world situations that might be of interest. Curriculum compacting then can be used to provide time and opportunities for students to explore.

School speakers and presentations planned around study units and using community resources are a natural for enrichment. These are considered general exploratory activities for all students (Type I activities in Renzulli's model). Exposure to people who are involved in a variety of careers helps students to explore work opportunities, consider their own strengths and abilities, and relate school activities to potential future choices.

Group training enrichment (Type II activities in Renzulli's model) can focus appropriately on cognitive and affective skills and a wide variety of topics related to work and careers in conjunction with the general exploratory experiences provided for all children. Individual and small group investigations of real problems involving specific in-depth investigations (Type III activities in the model) can be provided for students who express a high degree of interest in a specific area.

Renzulli's model can be expanded greatly when career exploration is combined with interests, abilities, and investigations. The Renzulli model has another advantage: It includes all populations at one time or another. Such an approach helps all students to explore, and it gains general community support for quality educational programs rather than limited support for activities that may be seen to be an elitist program if limited to special teachers, special students, and special programs.

BUSINESS–INDUSTRY–COMMUNITY–EDUCATION PARTNERSHIP

Another approach, which combines well with the Renzulli model, is a community-based career exploration program. Although several programs have been developed across the country, one model is BICEP (Wright et al., 1989–1990), in which a wide variety of services are provided to schools and students in the Salt Lake City, Utah, area (see overview in Figure 26.1). BICEP has an extensive file of resources for school use. Teachers can request classroom career speakers and on-site tours for students in Grades K through 12. In Grades 7 through 12, students can arrange for an on-site discussion in which they meet and talk with a worker and see the workplace. In Grades 11 and 12, students can arrange for a shadowing experience in which they talk with and observe a worker in the workplace for 2 to 4 hours.

BICEP
(Business–Industry–Community–Education Partnership)
3700 South 2860 East, Salt Lake City, UT 84109

INTRODUCTION
The majority of workers end up in their occupation more by default than through informed, systematic planning.

BICEP is a career education program with the mission of assisting students in career awareness and exploration.

The major service provided by BICEP is to arrange for community workers to come into the classroom to talk with students about their career. More than 1,300 companies in the Salt Lake Valley have agreed to assist students through BICEP.

MAJOR BICEP ACTIVITIES
- *Classroom Speakers*—Provide students with an awareness of occupations related to a subject or curriculum unit (K–12).

- *Vehicle Day*—Approximately 6 vehicles (fire trucks, army trucks, etc.) park in school parking lot where groups of students visit the trucks and listen to the drivers (K–6).

- *Career Day*—All students (in the school or a grade) have the opportunity of listening to two or three career speakers (K–12).

- *On-site Tour/Seminar*—Students go to a business or industry to see and talk with workers (K–12).

- *On-site Career Discussion/Shadowing*—Individual or small groups of students talk with and observe a worker (9–12).

- *Work/Service Internships*—Students spend ongoing time in a business or industry to gain work experience (unpaid).

BICEP VIDEOTAPES
BICEP has produced 25 videotaped interviews in which people talk about their occupations. Videotapes are less than 30 minutes and can be obtained from District Media Centers. Videotapes are interviews with a diesel mechanic, graphic artist, data processor, auto mechanic, clothing manufacturer, electronic technician, drafter, electrician, plumber, and carpenter.

OCCUBRIEFS
To help make teachers and students aware of related occupations, BICEP produced and distributed a set of Occubriefs for each elementary school. Occupations are described for each school subject (covering a total of 1,370 occupations).

PROFILES OF ACHIEVERS
One packet has been produced for each major subject area. Each packet contains dozens of brief stories of high achievers related to a particular subject. The stories are informative and inspirational and written in a role-play format.

Figure 26.1 Overview of BICEP Program.

Other activities include career days for a schoolwide experience related to several careers, vehicle days when five to eight vehicles and their drivers visit an elementary school, and on-site seminars focusing on one career or area of specialty. Career days typically fit into secondary programs, but have been used successfully at elementary levels. Vehicle days allow students to explore professions that involve specialty equipment and range from construction to public safety to truck driving. On-site seminars can be designed to meet specific needs and relate to specific courses. These seminars can be developed cooperatively with the community resource and the teacher, or the resource person and a sponsoring student or student group.

BICEP also has developed a set of videotapes showing interviews with 25 community workers and a set of Occubriefs of 1,370 written interviews related to specific careers. Also produced are profiles of achievers. These profiles are put together in subject-area packets that can be used to help students to relate school subjects and individual skills and interest to careers.

The approach taken in the BICEP program shows recognition of the need to expose students to a variety of careers throughout their school experience. Teachers in the program for the gifted can assess the students' interest and enthusiasm for specific careers that might be selected for the internship program.

The BICEP program is funded by several districts and operates to provide career education experiences for all participating districts. Such an approach reduces the cost to one district, reduces pressure on businesses and organizations, and provides for a wide range of experiences in both professional and trade occupations.

Although much of the career exploration discussed above can be used as part of the regular educational program, specific activities in which students are placed in nonschool settings must have a comprehensive evaluation process. The mentorship manual used in the Albuquerque program described by Bodnar stresses evaluation as a mandatory component. This evaluation component, in conjunction with a student portfolio, helps to give direction to teachers, community participants, students, and parents.

THE AUTONOMOUS LEARNER MODEL

The Albuquerque program has been designed to meet the needs of special populations, which include gifted students with learning disabilities and creatively gifted students who may not be performing well in academic classes. Bodnar's discussion, however, indicates that a majority of the graduates who participate in the program have received advanced placement status in one or more subjects upon college entry. Many special population students do not involve themselves in advanced placement programs. This being the case, the target population may not be served as well as the program developers would wish.

Students who desire certain educational opportunities must begin planning courses at the ninth-grade level. Some students choose the ''sure way'' to gain high grade point averages by taking minimum-level classes. They also may avoid rigorous programs so that they have time for employment.

A program that recognizes the need for earlier intervention on social, emotional, and academic levels is the Autonomous Learner Model (Betts, 1985). This model

> was developed to meet the diversified cognitive, emotional, and social needs of gifted
> and talented students. As the needs of the gifted are being met, they will develop into
> autonomous learners with abilities to be responsible for the development, implementa-
> tion, and evaluation of their own learning. (Betts, 1985, p. 1)

In this program, with its focus on individual development, educators begin to address problems that may characterize populations of gifted students that are frequently underrepresented in programs for the gifted. The individual development dimension, one of five dimensions in the model, is focused on the development of skills that prepare students for independent projects and activities. This dimension can be designed to focus on areas of greatest need in a given student group and can be adjusted as groups change. Suggested areas of study include career involvement, interpersonal skills, learning skills, and personal understanding.

In the area of personal understanding, students can look at activities that help them to understand and accept themselves, develop a positive self-concept, analyze appropriate behavior and characteristics of personal responsibility, and develop creativity. They also can study and apply principles relating to the psychology of healthy personalities. This particular component is extremely important to students who may be avoiding challenging programs.

The learning skills area can be designed to help students develop skills that can be used in a variety of self-directed activities. Students can learn goal setting, organization, journal writing, portfolio development, photography, planning, decision making, writing, and other skills that may be appropriate to independent learning. The interpersonal skills area can focus on communication, interviewing, discussions, leadership, group processing, and coping abilities, all of which are important career-related skills.

The career involvement area can be designed to help the student prepare for a future internship by being involved in career exploration, developing an understanding of careers in areas of interest, planning for career choices, and career participation. If this were the only dimension used, it would help underrepresented target populations to be prepared to participate successfully in an internship program.

Other dimensions of Betts's model include an orientation dimension, a seminar study dimension, and an in-depth study dimension.

The value of the autonomous learner program is that the developmental nature of independence and autonomy is recognized. The program originally was seen as a 3-year high school program, but has been expanded to elementary and junior high school levels. Again, educators recognize that the ability to be independent should be part of an educational program that is integrated into and becomes part of the student's total educational experience. Such a planned approach would increase the number of students who could benefit from internship and would help to address the need for attracting student groups who may not have been represented in the past.

CONCLUSION

The advantage of Renzulli's model, BICEP, and Betts's Autonomous Learner Model is that the need to begin career exploration and the development of study skills at an early age is recognized so that the student is able to select and perform in an internship program successfully. Teachers can provide for exploration and enrichment at every grade level while recognizing the specific goal and emotional needs of the gifted students to be served. These three programs can be meshed well with a comprehensive counseling component.

Internship programs are extremely valuable. They help students to begin to understand career choices and opportunities and related educational plans. Educators must, however, consider the development of student skills to ensure representation of a wider population than students who already are successful and who have made appropriate course-taking choices.

Early intervention programs such as the examples described in this chapter also can function within a setting in which specific funding for programs for the gifted is not available. Although many states include the gifted student as part of the special education population, many other states do not. This being the case, many needs must be met through grouping within the regular education setting, in partnerships between school districts, or between school districts and interested community participants.

REFERENCES

Betts, G. (1985). *Autonomous learning model for gifted and talented.* Greeley, CO: ALPS.

Bingham, M., & Stryker, S. (1987). *More choices: A strategy planning guide for mixing career and family.* Santa Barbara, CA: Advocacy Press.

Jordan School District. (1990–1991). *Financial aid and scholarship opportunities.* Sandy, UT: Jordan School District.

Renzulli, J. (Ed.). (1986). The enrichment triad/revolving door model: A schoolwide plan for the development of creative productivity. In *Systems and models for developing programs for the gifted and talented* (pp. 216–266). Mansfield Center, CT: Creative Learning Press.

Wright, D., Jackson, D., & Mamales, S. (1989–1990). *BICEP: Business–Industry–Community–Education Partnership, Annual Report 1989–90.* Salt Lake City, UT: BICEP.

27

Independent Study:
Panacea or Palliative?

Frances D. Burns

Independent study is a process designed to provide each student with an opportunity to select a content or topic to be studied in a personalized environment. Frequently, the study is formalized by the completion of a final "product" (Davis & Rimm, 1985; Renzulli, 1977). In some educational models, this final product must be created according to Bruner's structure of the discipline, the methodology and "thought systems" of the discipline within which the study topic logically belongs (cited in Maker, 1982a, p. 25).

Independent study can provide boundless opportunity for the student to go beyond the confines of the classroom and invade the world of work, while remaining protected and guided by a nurturing adult whose primary responsibility and motivation are to facilitate the student's learning experience. Ideally, both the school and the community provide optimal resources and access to persons and facilities that cultivate success for the student. Unfortunately, independent study in various guises is frequently misused, misdirected, and misadministered as a palliative for qualitatively differentiated education masquerading as a panacea (Betts & Neihart, 1986).

In this chapter, I (a) review the foundations and assumptions underlying independent study as a means of extending learning for gifted students beyond the regular classroom, (b) examine current models for implementing independent study, (c) discuss essential instructional components and teacher behaviors of successful independent study, (d) provide an overview of inherent pitfalls encountered and benefits engendered when integrating independent study as a curriculum approach into the regular classroom, and (e) conclude with a generalized summary.

FOUNDATIONS AND ASSUMPTIONS

The dictionary definitions of *independent* and *study* construct an image of persons engaged in "the act or process of applying the mind in order to acquire knowledge'' that is ''not subject to the control, influence, or determination of another'' (Webster, 1983). Pedagogy based on such a concept requires only that the student be permitted to seek his or her own way among myriad resources to eventual acquisition of learning.

This concept of education was popular during the 1960s and 1970s when teachers were directed to individualize instruction to meet individual needs and interests of students (Betts & Neihart, 1986). According to McNeil (1981), instructional individualization was expected to foster intrinsic learning motivation (i.e., a love of learning with an internal locus of control). Independent study as an instructional methodology appeared to fit this concept.

With the increased emphasis on meeting individual needs of students, education specifically designed for the gifted became a national focus (Marland, 1972). Curricula designed for the gifted during this period generally included independent study as a major component. The terms *individualized* and *independent* became analogous; other synonyms that appeared in the literature include *autonomous learning, self-teaching, self-directed learning, in-depth study,* and *personalized learning* (Betts & Neihart, 1986; Johnsen & Johnson, 1986).

Understanding independent study to be a means of individualizing and extending learning in the regular classroom requires a knowledge of the common instructional management system found in regular classrooms. Educators also must understand the relationship of independent study to the learning environment recommended for gifted learners and the learning characteristics upon which these recommendations for the gifted often are based.

Research indicates that delivery of curricula to a classroom of students seated in well-formed rows continues to be a time-tested, efficient method of teaching (McNeil, 1981). This method is commonly referred to in the literature as ''directed teaching,'' or ''whole group teaching.'' Students of average or above-average intelligence taught by this directed method are expected to learn the required syllabus in the allotted time. Teaching in this style in the public school generally aims for the student of average intelligence level, as measured by accepted intelligence tests. Because the majority of students within an average classroom fall within an average intelligence range, most do, in fact, reach mastery of delivered learning. Such mastery is assumed to be the optimal product, representing the capability limits of the average student who theoretically has been provided ample opportunity for cognitive development.

The learning environment most often recommended for gifted learners is far less structured than that described above. Although some directed teaching often is employed in the classroom for gifted students to promote the quick acquisition and understanding of fundamental concepts, a majority of class time should be planned to allow the student to extend or advance this understanding beyond the textbook, and beyond the limits of the instructor. Emphasis in this type of classroom is placed on inquiry and discovery. Activities that foster higher level thinking, as defined by Bloom (1956), could be expected to occur (e.g., open-ended tasks, in-depth learning of a self-selected topic within an area of study, integration of multidisciplinary basic skills and higher level thinking skills into the curriculum and the opportunity for development of individual learning "products" that are both creative and worthwhile) (Clark, 1979; Khatena, 1982; Maker, 1982a). Some pedagogy would require that these products be created according to Bruner's structure of the discipline, previously defined, and that these products be shared in some manner with adults working actively in the particular field of study (Renzulli, 1977).

The learning characteristics upon which the above-described learning environment generally is predicated include (Seagoe, 1974, pp. 20–21) persistent goal-directed behavior such as Renzulli's (1977) task commitment, power of critical thinking, power of concentration, liking for structure and order, high energy, independence, creativity, versatility, and retentiveness. These characteristics, admittedly generalized, are found in many gifted students, especially those who are highly successful in academic performance.

Comparing, then, the two teaching situations (regular classroom and special class for the gifted), we find the emphasis in the regular classroom is placed on the acquisition and understanding of a common pool of knowledge and the ability to put such learning to appropriate use (McNeil, 1981). The emphasis in the classroom for the gifted is on using a quickly acquired basic pool of learning similar to that offered in the regular classroom to progress to a differentiated curriculum in which unique, divergent learning opportunities for individual students are emphasized (Maker, 1982a). Curriculum in the regular classroom is focused on content delivered through convergent teaching that results in a storehouse of usable information (memory) as the product (Travers, 1982). This information then is available for retrieval from memory in an appropriately structured environment. Curriculum in the classroom for gifted students is focused on content acquired through divergent exploration that results in a storehouse of usable information coupled with experience in using the thinking processes associated with the discipline. These understandings and experiences are assumed to be available for retrieval under diversified conditions.

CURRENT MODELS

Three major models for integrating independent study into the classroom currently exist: Renzulli's Enrichment Triad (1977), Betts's Autonomous Learner (1985), and Treffinger's Self-Directed Learning (Maker, 1982b). In addition, many kits, resource books, and training manuals are available to guide the teacher and the student in organizing a generic independent study component within the curriculum (e.g., Johnsen & Johnson, 1986).

Each model is discussed below, from the perspective of use during a school year that starts in the early fall (August or September) and finishes in late spring (May or June) during which students receive instruction in many subjects. Each of these models, however, also would be very appropriate as a single instructional delivery system beyond the regular classroom for a special summer program.

Renzulli's Enrichment Triad

Renzulli's Enrichment Triad is divided into three types of activities; however, only Type III, individual and small group investigations of real problems, requires independent study. The three parts are interrelated and their inherent flexibility permits the teacher to move among the three primary components. Understanding of the model requires a knowledge of each of the parts.

Type I, general exploratory, activities are designed to introduce students to potential areas of interest through interest centers, field trips, special programs, speakers, and other activities. In Type II, group training activities, the student is introduced to training in a variety of processes designed to develop higher level abilities. Type III is the independent study component of the model. In this phase, students investigate a self-selected or identified real problem, emulating the professional. The stated purpose for the independent study is to produce new knowledge that must be communicated in a meaningful way to an interested professional audience rather than only for the teacher. Teacher involvement at this level is minimal, often described as that of a facilitator or guide at the side.

A modification of the model that I have observed in individual classrooms has recently evolved. Many teachers, recognizing a need for supervised experience in independent study methods, have developed an unofficial "Type II½" for Renzulli's model. This variation is similar to, and will be discussed in greater detail as, the generalized model in a subsequent section of this chapter.

The Enrichment Triad was conceived as a model for a resource program functioning during regular school hours and beyond. A special teacher arranges or assists regular classroom teachers in arranging for the exploratory activities of Type I, provides or assists in providing the small group training activities of Type II, and provides the management system for Type III, in addition to assisting students actively engaged in Type III investigations. Regular classroom teachers remain responsible for delivery of core curriculum, often at an accelerated or "compacted" rate, which then creates time within the school day for Type III investigations. Regular classroom teachers also are responsible for referral of students for the individualized Type III services.

The Enrichment Triad is included in this discussion because I frequently have observed attempts by regular classroom teachers to integrate a similar program into the regular curriculum without the assistance of additional resources or personnel. The model appears deceptively simple and relatively inexpensive, and therefore is attractive to regular classroom teachers and school systems operating with limited resources that seek to provide differentiated curriculum for gifted students (e.g., Carney, 1981; Clifford, Runions, & Smith, 1984). Such attempts are discussed in a later section of this chapter.

Betts's Autonomous Learner Model

Betts's (1985) Autonomous Learner Model for the Gifted and Talented comprises five dimensions: orientation, individual development, enrichment activities, seminars, and in-depth study. An autonomous learner is defined as "one who solves problems or develops new ideas through a combination of divergent and convergent thinking and functions with minimal external guidance in all areas of endeavor" (Betts & Knapp, 1987, p. 1). Inter- and intrapersonal understanding of self and others, as well as career development, are important concerns of this model. The major opportunity for independent study within this model is found in Dimension V, in-depth study.

In Dimension I, orientation, goals are to build self-understanding, establish group relationships, foster understanding of giftedness and generally introduce the student to the program. This component of the model includes a direct response to affective needs of gifted students.

Dimension II, individual development, has as its goal to add learning skills, personal understanding, interpersonal skills, and career involvement to the learning arena. The student becomes familiar with resources and methodology appropriate for in-depth study. In addition, the strong emphasis on affective development continues.

Dimension III contains enrichment activities, which include community explorations and investigations, cultural activities, service projects, and adventure trips. During this phase, increasing responsibility is placed on the students as learners rather than as recipients of learning delivered by an instructor.

Dimension IV, seminars, has the objective of stimulating involvement in topics that are futuristic, controversial, problematic, or that relate to general interest or advanced knowledge. Seminar topics are designed to promote discussion and activity, ultimately leading to identification of a topic for Dimension V, in-depth study.

In-depth study may be accomplished individually or in small groups, and may involve a mentor. The learner is expected to spend the majority of his or her time in this dimension investigating topics of personal interest. A "presentation" is expected from the student upon completion of the in-depth study. A final product is implied in the model, but no specific guidelines for design of this product are presented; only the required presentation is mentioned specifically in the literature. Although teacher support is available during this phase, learners are expected to function independently no less than 90% of the time.

This model can be implemented as a before- or after-school program or integrated into the regular school day, similar to Renzulli's Enrichment Triad. Initially conceived as a resource-type program, this program also requires the services of a specially trained teacher to provide instruction and direct supervision for the first four dimensions and to provide guidance and assistance during participation in Dimension V. Regular classroom teachers would be responsible only for referral of students to the program. The suggested time line indicates a 3-year period for complete implementation of all five dimensions of the model.

As with Renzulli's Enrichment Triad, the Autonomous Learner Model is more complex than it would at first appear. Because of its strong affective component and the suggested 3-year time line, this model probably could not be assimilated easily into a regular classroom setting. The need for student privacy and psychological safety, especially in Dimensions I and II, would preclude regular classroom accommodation during a regular school day; however, an after-school program for only gifted students could provide the necessary psychologically safe environment.

Treffinger's Self-Directed Learning

Treffinger (1981) defined *self-directed learning* as responsible autonomy, concerned with helping students learn how to make effective decisions about their own learning. Four basic factors or instructional areas are identified by the model: (a) identification of goals and objectives, (b) assessment of entering behavior, (c) identification and implementation of instructional procedures, and (d) assessment of performance. Within each area, four levels of teacher or student self-direction are identified: (a) teacher controls, (b) some student choice/option is available, (c) student assists teacher in creating options, and (d) learner controls choices while teacher functions as facilitator.

Treffinger's model, as conceived originally, is somewhat tenuous and provides the teacher with little structure for implementation in the classroom. Treffinger and Barton (1979, cited in Maker, 1982b, p. 352) subsequently identified and described five instructional styles that could be used in implementing the model: (a) command style, (b) task style, (c) peer–partner style, (d) pupil–teacher contract style, and (e) self-directed style.

Total teacher control is manifested in the command style; students are expected to follow teacher directions exclusively. Some choice is provided in the task style, where students interact with learning centers, discovery centers, and work stations. Students are paired with a partner chosen by the teacher for skill learning for the peer–partner style. Partners may be changed by the teacher based on the skill to be learned. The idea is to pair one student who is weak and one who is strong in a specific skill. Individual learning contracts are negotiated by the student and the teacher in the pupil–teacher contract style. Finally, in the self-directed style, students are expected to complete their learning with little or no assistance from the teacher.

A unique component of Treffinger's model is the requirement that teachers assess their own teaching behaviors in terms of their ability to facilitate students' development as independent learners. Subsequent changes in teaching behaviors to meet students' changing needs appear to be assumed. In addition, although the idea of assessing students' entry behavior and initiating instruction that proceeds from what is known to what is not known is not unique for delivery of content, frequently it is overlooked in the teaching of process skills such as those required for successful independent study. The inclusion of this assessment in the model is noteworthy.

Treffinger's model lacks structure, lacks the specific detailed instructional components found in Renzulli's and Betts's models, and would be incomplete as a model for implementation in the classroom. Nevertheless, it is included in this review of identified models related to independent study because it highlights (a) the need for preassessment of prerequisite skills for both student and teacher and (b) the need for skills instruction often lacking in independent study curriculum planning. Although the importance of these steps is acknowledged by Renzulli and Betts, the emphasis found in Treffinger's model is not apparent in the other models.

A Generalized Model

In response to the needs of teachers in programs for gifted students as well as in regular classrooms, many materials for teaching independent study skills and for guiding students through independent study have been developed (e.g., Doherty & Evans, 1981; Johnsen & Johnson, 1986; Kaplan, Madsen, & Gould, 1976; Karnes & Collins, 1984; Wilsey & Norberg, 1982). Some of these materials are linked directly to specific models identified previously (Betts, 1985; Renzulli, 1977). Others are generic handbooks and student guides, which allow teachers to create their own independent study programs. These materials, as formalized by the authors, often form the foundation for a generalized model of independent study. The common components of such a model include (a) use of commercially available instructional and management forms, (b) supervised instruction in skills needed to gather and compile information from many sources, (c) teacher supervision of students' topic selections, and (d) the requirement for a product at the completion of the study.

Commercially available materials often are integrated into the regular classroom setting within which the teacher has grouped the students by ability. Frequently, materials designed for a specific model are adapted to this generic model. An excellent example of this adaptation is found in resources designed by Renzulli (1977) for the Enrichment Triad. A major strength of the Enrichment Triad is the availability of numerous management forms and handbooks to assist students, teachers in both regular classrooms and special classrooms for the gifted, and administrative personnel in organizing a program at every stage in the program's development. These handbooks and forms generally are clear and well written. Many of these procedures and forms lend themselves to use on a more limited basis. For example, the Interest-A-Lyzer is valuable for helping all students and teachers to identify areas of interest for possible independent study, and the Management Plan is helpful in the planning and organization of an independent study regardless of topic or grade level (Renzulli & Reis, 1985). As teachers have attempted to integrate independent study into the curriculum, many of these materials have been adopted and have become part of a generalized model for implementing independent study into the regular curriculum.

Within the regular classroom, independent study is frequently a part of the language arts curriculum and is limited to students in the high reading group. Students in this reading group often advance through the standard basal text at a rate that, without the addition of supplemental activities, would allow them to finish the text long before the end of the school year. Students in this group are, therefore, offered independent study time each week to enhance the regular curriculum. In many school districts, students are not permitted to progress beyond the prescribed basal text in any one school year. When properly used, independent study can provide worthwhile learning for the student without violating district policies.

Many of the independent study skills discussed herein are considered library skills or language arts skills that historically have been incorporated into the reading curriculum—a practice that continues today. Consequently, this use of independent study for students in an advanced reading group appears reasonable to all concerned. The use of independent study resources beyond the school library frequently is perceived as an extension of the language arts curriculum.

Specific skills taught in this general model often mirror those specifically identified in Renzulli's and Betts's models (e.g., use of periodicals by young students, and interviewing an expert in the field of inquiry) (see, e.g., Johnsen & Johnson, 1986).

Rules governing topic selection appear to vary with the student's experience, the student's age, and the teacher's teaching style. Generally, students are directed initially to choose from a teacher-provided list of topics for which resources are readily available, and which is associated with a required major unit of study within the basic curriculum. For example, a science unit related to the study of oceanography may provide the foundation for individual study of kelp farming.

Restricting the individual study topics to those relating to a mandated area of study can benefit both the teacher and the students being introduced to independent study as a learning experience. The teacher can (a) assess, teach, and monitor student acquisition of prerequisite independent study skills; (b) gain expertise in the topic, expertise often lacking when students self-select topics, and then can assist the student more readily in finding necessary resources; (c) monitor the accuracy, relevance, and timeliness of data reported by the student; (d) assist in identifying an appropriate outcome or product and an interested audience with which the student can communicate new knowledge; (e) justify the expenditure of time and money for classroom instructional materials and resources; and (f) adapt the implementation of independent study to fit his or her teaching style. The student can (a) master prerequisite independent study skills in a practical and efficient manner under the direct guidance of a trained and knowledgeable instructor; (b) learn the special skills required for successful independent study such as product planning, time management, and audience finding, again, under the direct guidance of a trained and knowledgeable instructor; and (c) gain expertise in meeting established criteria for product evaluation and practice self-evaluation.

Students beginning their first independent study often perceive an encyclopedia as *the* primary source of information. Weaning students from this perception can be difficult and frustrating for the teacher. By limiting topic selection, the teacher can identify, in advance, more appropriate resources, such as local experts willing to be interviewed, articles in current periodicals, and businesses in the area that are engaged actively in the area of study.

Students beginning their first independent study often lack many basic skills needed for successful research. Teachers generally must teach skills such as note taking, outlining, time management, interviewing, letter writing for information, use of the printed reference guides such as *Children's Magazine Guide* or *Reader's*

Guide to Periodical Literature or equivalent computer data bases, and structuring higher level research questions. Often library skills such as the use of a card catalog need to be reinforced. By narrowing the range of topics, the teacher can then instruct students in the necessary basic skills using a common pool of resources. Teacher-made assessment instruments based on this common instruction also can be developed; however, the student's use of the skills during independent study is the best determiner of learning. Directed teaching to an entire class and peer grouping for instruction and research can be effected more easily when all students are engaged in researching closely related topics. Directed teaching generally is accepted as the most efficient method yet devised for delivery of instruction, and is considered appropriate for transmitting basic information to students at all ability levels, including gifted students. I believe strongly that basic skills in any discipline should never be taught in isolation, but should be related to content. Restricting the topic when teaching the prerequisite skills of successful independent study satisfies my concern.

In most cases, students are required to produce a product as a direct result of independent study. This product may be predetermined by the teacher; selected from a list of acceptable products, as determined by the teacher; or selected completely at the discretion of the student. Again, much depends on the student's grade level and expertise *and* the teacher's instructional style (Slocumb, 1984).

As with research skills, basic competencies needed for successful completion of a product often are nonexistent for the first-time student. Many educators, myself included, have generalized the definition of a product, based on Bruner's concepts (i.e., structure of the discipline), as the end result of an independent study that serves as a means of communicating new knowledge with an interested professional audience. By providing a list of suggested products, the teacher can structure and provide opportunities for the student, frequently working with other students, to learn the prerequisite skills. These skills include (a) selection of an achievable product, (b) establishing a workable time frame, and (c) creating a list of criteria for product evaluation.

Product selection by students new to independent study sometimes is unrealistic. Grandiose ideas far beyond the talent and time available to the student are not uncommon. By providing the beginning student with a list of acceptable products, the tendency to ''bite off more than one can chew'' is avoided. Conversely, for the student whose fear of failure hinders risk taking, the provision of a teacher-approved list provides some measure of security lacking when a product idea must come totally from the student.

Establishing a reasonable time line for product completion is complex. Projected dates often must be changed because of unforeseen difficulties. Planning together as a class or small group under a teacher's guidance allows students to practice the skill without having to pay the penalty of failure for lack of experience. I have, without exception, adjusted the required due dates for completion of various steps in product generation for every independent study initiated as a teacher instructing a class in independent study skills. This modeling of the need to reanalyze and realistically restructure planning in this way is a part of the teaching process, and is not a reflection of a lack of planning expertise.

I also have found a valuable practice creating product evaluation checklists for beginning student products such as learning centers, library displays, lectures, topical lessons for other classes, and computer programs. These checklists serve as guidelines for the student during product planning and creation and as the grading sheet for both teacher evaluation and student self-evaluation upon completion of the product.

Because communication of new knowledge resulting from the study with an appropriate audience is a required component of independent study, the teacher should be able to assist the student in identifying such an audience. With thorough grounding in the topic, an appropriate audience can be identified and suggested to the student. Gifted learners, allowed to self-select, often delight in selecting very esoteric topics for research. Locating an appropriate audience then may prove difficult. By limiting the topic, this problem is controlled until the student has gained the expertise to identify the audience on his or her own.

Limited funds in public schools often preclude the purchase of commercial materials for extras, that is, any materials for content beyond that prescribed by a state or local governing agency. By marrying independent study topics to a required content area, this stumbling block to the acquisition of resources might be overcome. Administrative approval for purchase often is given when a relationship to required content is established. Many educators within the field of education for the gifted suggest that curriculum content for the gifted be an extension or enrichment of such core curriculum; therefore, this marriage of core curriculum and curriculum for the gifted satisfies several levels of concern.

In some schools, the principal, the librarian, and interested parents may assist in the purchase of special materials, in the location of community resources, and in the solicitation of local experts as speakers or interviewees. When an independent study program is successful, the sharing of student products with interested professionals within the community often generates great community awareness and support. After a time, a successful independent study program becomes almost self-perpetuating as administrators and local businesses offer services and resources without being asked.

Finally, the structured independent study described herein provides a measure of security for the traditional teacher who feels lost without a teacher's guide and specific content to be covered. Teacher training, historically, has focused on directed teaching to a single class, or at most, to ability grouping of five or more students following a prescribed text. To expect teachers trained in this manner to suddenly turn loose and allow each student to do his or her own thing is unrealistic.

The failure of many early programs incorporating independent study can be traced to two primary causes: (a) the conflict between a traditional teacher-controlled and directed environment and the student-centered instructional methodology required for a true independent study—a study chosen, directed, and controlled by the student, and (b) the previously noted general lack of necessary skills by the student.

The introduction of an independent study program following this generic model teaches the teacher as well as the student. Teachers will progress and gain expertise as students acquire the necessary expertise. Hopefully, those teachers who risk using this model will find, as I have, that students who have received necessary training, can, in fact, be unbelievably successful in selecting a topic, researching it, and developing a suitable product. Examples of products that students in my classes have created include videotape instruction in preparing a chocolate mousse (an imitation of Julia Child); a videotape of the history of juvenile fashion; a simulated video interview of Margaret Mitchell, Vivian Leigh, and the fashion designer for *Gone with the Wind* done in the "Hedda Hopper" style; computerized instruction in oceanography complete with computerized classical music; a computer survey of potato chip preferences with statistical analysis; student learning centers that were purchased by an educational publishing company; board games; and slide programs with accompanying narration and music.

Many regular classroom teachers include the structured type of independent study, described above, as a regular part of the curriculum. As students gain expertise, teachers in upper grades may provide greater flexibility in topic and product selection, allowing the student increasing independence as proficiency grows. Although administrative support for alternative teaching strategies, such as independent study, is increasing as educators learn that higher level thinking skills (a current emphasis in education) are inherent to independent study, the teacher will find he or she is basically on his or her own when establishing such a program in a single classroom.

Teachers interested in starting a generic program of independent study would be well advised to purchase a commercial program such as that of Johnsen and Johnson (1986). Johnsen and Johnson's materials provide an excellent teaching guide for the teacher, student workbooks for both primary and upper grade students, and approximately 100 resource cards to which students may refer for additional guidance and examples. A resource list of these and other commercially available materials that I have found most useful for organization and management of an independent study program is provided in Appendix 27.A.

In many ways, the model described herein appears to follow Treffinger's self-directed learning model; however, a major difference lies in the absence in the generalized model of curriculum planning for the progressive skill development as outlined in Treffinger's model. Some teachers may limit student choice to the particular instructional style with which they are most comfortable, never allowing the student to gain true independence. Continuity across and between grades also is lacking in the generalized model. Processes taught in one classroom may differ from processes taught in another classroom in the same school and at the same grade level.

Although each model discussed in this section contains flaws, and school use and/or student progress may be hindered, each also contains strengths, students may be assisted by users of the models in becoming productive contributors to the Western world. A comprehensive discussion of the relative merits and disadvantages of each model is included in subsequent sections of this chapter.

ESSENTIAL INSTRUCTIONAL COMPONENTS

Few would argue that an ideal independent learner is a highly self-motivated paragon of erudition simply awaiting the removal of restraints to learning to forge ahead to astounding accomplishments. For such an individual, our dictionary defi-nition of *independent study* would require no alteration; a teacher would need only to get out of the way.

However, a learner such as this rarely is found within a formal public edu-cational system; therefore, based on the assumption that the majority of students (a) will have had little or no opportunity to learn the processes of independent study and (b) will have been schooled thoroughly in academic behaviors appropriate for group learning, in this section, components necessary for a successful independent study program in an average U.S. school will be reviewed.

Essential instructional components for a successful independent study include (a) sequential development of independent study skills as delineated in the preced-ing discussion of a generalized model; (b) training in the identification of resources and sources of information; (c) self-selection of study topic; (d) self-selection of final product; and (e) assistance of a trained facilitator, especially in the early stages of an initial study (Maker, 1982a, 1982b).

Skills Training

The need for sequential development of individual learning skills is an assump-tion of the major models discussed previously. Educators who attempted to imple-ment an independent study program without this training and guided practice for students testify to the necessity for inclusion of such training (Maker, 1982b). Many programs failed because students were not taught these prerequisite skills. The inability of individual students to complete an independent study successfully is, in my experience, most often the result of a student's (a) failure to use necessary research skills, (b) inappropriate product selection, and/or (c) inability to plan realistically and execute a plan (i.e., time management skill).

Sequential development of independent study skills also requires articulation between grade levels (Daniels, Affholder, & Sims, 1986). As students become familiar with elementary resources, they should be introduced to increasingly complex processes and procedures for acquisition of learning, ultimately becoming skillful in securing information from both primary and secondary sources. Increas-ingly sophisticated products would be a logical outgrowth of such developmental progress.

Another important consideration in skill training should be the development of greater understanding of self and others as identified by Betts (1985). Psychological factors, such as fear of success and paralyzing perfectionism, can impede success-ful completion of any study (Kerr, 1985; Webb, Meckstroth, & Tolan, 1982). In some instances, teachers may need to give specific permission, in the psychological sense, for students to diverge from common patterns of knowledge acquisition. Increased understanding of others often facilitates communication between individ-uals, which can be an important research skill. However, only those with appropri-ate training should attempt to address this concern.

Information Sources and Resources

Assistance and/or training in the identification of sources and resources also is implied in each of the specific models discussed previously and, as discussed, is a required component of the generalized model. Introduction to periodicals, media, personal interviews, and other sophisticated resources as sources of information is mandatory. Instruction in the use of and experience with the many indices that make locating information more efficient should be a part of this component. Introduction to computer data bases now available at many libraries and universities is most desirable.

Self-Selection of Topic and Product

Self-selection of topic and final product, as early as possible, is essential. The opportunity to investigate a passion (Betts & Knapp, 1987) and to communicate this passion with others through a sharing of learning is an unparalleled motivator. This freedom of selection is the heart and soul of independent study. Without this freedom, *independent study* becomes a misnomer and a contradiction of the concept. This freedom, however, must be given freely by the teacher and allowed to operate within a psychologically safe environment; the teacher must function as a facilitator for the student.

Facilitators

The final component essential for successful independent study is the assistance to the student of a trained facilitator (Renzulli & Reis, 1985). A *facilitator* is defined as one who is familiar with many resources and methods of finding information, who can guide the student in making decisions without making those decisions for him or her, who will permit the student to make mistakes without recrimination, and who can accept and encourage divergent thinking.

Facilitator training, as such, does not exist. Instructional programs in which teachers are trained specifically to work with gifted learners do, however, emphasize the characteristics described previously as important for working with gifted students. Teachers interested in becoming facilitators will find, as I have, that most librarians and other experts are delighted to share their knowledge with interested individuals. The many resources available for training students also are valuable for assisting the teacher. A teacher who models a willingness to explore and learn, and who is willing to work along with students, is perhaps the greatest facilitator of all.

PITFALLS

The difficulties and benefits of implementing each of the models discussed previously are compared in this and the next sections. Readers should keep in mind that some of the difficulties cited are generic and applicable to most models. Conclusions are based on my personal observations and experiences as a regular classroom teacher, as a resource teacher in several programs for gifted students (Grades 1 through 8), and as a coordinator of programs for the gifted (Grades K through 12).

Renzulli's Enrichment Triad Model

The Enrichment Triad, as designed by Renzulli and colleagues (Renzulli, 1977; Renzulli & Reis, 1985), appears to be an ideal program for fostering independent study. This model is extensive, well formulated, and supported by numerous handbooks, guidebooks, student materials, management forms, and teacher/administrator training workshops and materials. Using these resources, program implementation should be organized, orderly, and successful. Difficulties arise, however, when local school districts or individual classroom teachers attempt to modify the model to fit local or personal philosophies and constraints.

Most frequently these constraints relate to funding of materials, resources, and personnel. Although the costs involved may not be extensive, any additional expense when budgets are limited will be scrutinized closely. Time required for training, the cost of this training, and the cost of the materials also are important factors to consider.

As noted previously, the program appears deceptively simple to implement. Because of the wealth of support materials available, educators may be encouraged to initiate a program based on the naive perception that the materials by themselves are sufficient. Unfortunately, the practitioner soon discovers that the organization and management of such a program is complex and not achieved easily. Lack of administrative support often complicates efforts.

Resource teachers are needed to relieve regular classroom staff of the additional responsibilities required by the program. The assignment of special resource teachers, whose responsibilities lie only within the program for the gifted, permits the resource staff to focus only on program needs; however, funding for resource teacher salaries and instructional materials may be limited. With limited funds available, too few resource teachers may be employed, which then results in heavy student loads, insufficient planning time for the resource teacher, and ultimately teacher burnout with consequent high teacher turnover.

Individual teachers attempting to introduce the program into a single classroom, where the entire classroom might constitute the "talent pool," often find that the teaching of prerequisite skills and the management of numerous independent studies are more time-consuming than anticipated. Arranging for speakers and creating discovery centers also entail more time than might be expected. However, once the organizational problems have been mastered, many teachers endorse the program enthusiastically and believe that the advantages far outweigh the disadvantages.

A major difficulty for program application is encountered when the gifted population is defined as a percentage of the total student body. Frequently, this percentage is based on the bell curve approximation of 3% to 5%, far short of Renzulli's suggested 15% to 20%. Because state funding often is predicated on a relatively static identified group of students, district administrators may be reluctant to serve a greater number than that counted by the state.

In small communities, the lack of resources can be another inhibiting factor. Communities located near a large metropolitan area and/or near a major college or university will have an easier time supporting the interests of individual students. Although interlibrary loan and personal correspondence with experts can be invaluable, the importance of experts within easy driving distance cannot be underestimated. Most successful independent study programs appear to be in schools located in close proximity to high-level information resources, and appear to function best when located near a university. The availability of university staff and college students willing to work with young gifted students is beyond price.

Betts's Autonomous Learner Model

The Autonomous Learner Model also appears to be an excellent program for fostering independent study. Like Renzulli's model, Betts's is extensive and well formulated. A handbook, management forms, and training workshops are available. However, these support materials, while adequate for implementation of the model, are not as extensive as those available for Renzulli's model. Attempts to modify the program based on local philosophies and constraints, including budgetary constraints, time constraints, and limited community resources, would create difficulties similar to those outlined for Renzulli's model. The program requires specially trained resource teachers, again similar to those required for Renzulli's model. An additional requirement for these teachers would be training in the affective components of this model. A foundation in general counseling theory and some instruction in the psychology of the gifted also would seem to be desirable. An advantage of this model over Renzulli's model is that it does not advocate the creation of a talent pool of 15% to 20% of the total body of students, and consequently could be structured to coincide with state identification and funding limitations. Individual teachers attempting to introduce the program into a regular classroom would encounter problems similar to those outlined for Renzulli's model, as well as the limitations of trying to address affective or psychological concerns of the gifted in a heterogeneous classroom—an environment that would not be conducive to open discussion.

Treffinger's Self-Directed Learning Model

The relative simplicity of this model precludes many of the problems delineated for Renzulli's and Betts's models; however, this simplicity also creates differing problems for implementation. Specific handbooks, management forms, and other support materials are not available for this model. Specific student identification procedures or teacher training requirements have not been identified. Instead, this model highlights the previously noted important considerations for successful independent study and provides a broad framework for implementation. The local school district and/or classroom teacher is allowed great freedom and flexibility; however, freedom and flexibility also create great opportunities for failure. Attempts to implement this model without support materials may have been responsible, in part, for the evolution of the generalized model. Creative teachers would, in time, develop similar general materials necessary for success.

A Generalized Model

Regular classroom teachers and teachers of the gifted attempting to initiate an independent study program or curriculum component in the absence of a district-wide single model for education of gifted students, probably would find this generalized model the most practical. This model allows the teacher to use whatever commercial materials appear to be most suitable to his or her current needs. Care is needed to select materials that are compatible with each other; some customizing may be needed.

Teachers could take advantage of traveling experts who provide inservice training in specific models and in general curriculum methods for working with gifted populations. University classes have become increasingly available. These classes seldom are geared to only one model, but instead introduce the teacher to many approaches and teaching models appropriate for gifted students. Teachers may then choose segments that best fit their needs and the needs of their students.

Budgetary constraints, time constraints, and limited community resources again would create difficulties for this model, as for previous models. These considerations are inherent in any special programming, regardless of the population being served.

Student identification for this model would follow local and state mandates. In the absence of mandates, teachers in the regular classroom would be free to make this opportunity available to the total class or to selected groups of students within the class. Educators in some individual schools have elected to institute generic independent study programs by grade levels within specific content areas.

The major drawbacks to this model, previously discussed, warrant repetition: concerted efforts should be made to move the students to *total* independence as quickly as possible, and articulation across and between grades should be instituted. Teachers will need to agree on skills to be taught at each grade level, mutually acceptable formats, and other program guidelines.

BENEFITS

A review of typical characteristics of gifted learners underscores their need for independence in learning. Their intellectual curiosity about a far-ranging panoply of topics surpasses the knowledge and understanding of any one individual and demands access to many sources for satisfaction (Clark, 1979; Gallagher, 1985;

Khatena, 1982; Maker, 1982a, 1982b; Perrone & Male, 1981; Seagoe, 1974). The appropriateness of independent study to fill these needs cannot be denied.

Opportunities for discovery, use of higher level thinking, extension of textbook learning, increased motivation for learning, fostering of independence, and development of a life-long love of learning are only a few of the recognized benefits of successful independent study. Independent study allows students to develop, experience, and internalize processes and skills that form a foundation for future excellence. The critical thinking components of this experience diverge along a continuum from simple knowledge acquisition to complex decision making and problem solving. Student creativity is limited only by the skill, erudition, and ability of the student.

CONCLUSION

Three published models and a generalized model for independent study have been reviewed in this chapter. Major benefits and negative concerns have been shared; however, the most important ingredient for success is the teacher. Materials, models, and methods are only a Band-Aid™, a palliative, in the hands of an instructor who cannot or will not provide the critical environment. Only in the hands of an instruction who *does* supply the critical environment—the freedom of choice, the facilitating, and the support, seeking to assist only where and when needed—does independent study become a panacea.

Appendix 27.A

Suggested Resources for Independent Study Instructional Materials

Betts, G. T. (1985). *Autonomous learner model for the gifted and talented.* Greeley, CO: Autonomous Learning Publications and Specialists.

Doherty, E. J. S., & Evans, L. C. (1980). *Self starter kit for independent study.* Special Education Associates, P.O. Box 9497, Austin, TX 78700.

Johnsen, S. K., & Johnson, K. (1986). *Independent study program.* Old Wagon Learning Associates, 1404 Old Wagon Rd., Austin, TX 78746.

Kaplan, S., Madsen, S., & Gould, B. (1976). *Big book of independent study.* Santa Monica, CA: Goodyear.

Renzulli, J. S., & Reis, S. M. (1985). *The schoolwide enrichment model: A comprehensive plan for educational excellence.* Mansfield Center, CT: Creative Learning Press.

Weber, P. (undated). *Promote.* Buffalo, NY: DOK Publishers.

Weber, P. (undated). *Question quest.* Buffalo, NY: DOK Publishers.

REFERENCES

Betts, G. T. (1985). *Autonomous learner model for the gifted and talented.* Greeley, CO: Autonomous Learning Publications and Specialists.

Betts, G., & Knapp, J. (1987). *The autonomous learner model for the gifted and talented.* Handout from Texas Association for Gifted and Talented Annual Conference, Dallas, TX.

Betts, G. T., & Neihart, M. (1986). Implementing self-directed learning models for the gifted and talented. *Gifted Child Quarterly, 3*(4), 174–177.

Bloom, B. (1956). *Taxonomy of educational objectives. Handbook I: Cognitive domain.* New York: David McKay.

Carney, F. M. (1981, March/April). Another look at triad: Practical considerations in implementing the model. *G/C/T,* pp. 40–43.

Clark, B. (1979). *Growing up gifted.* Columbus, OH: Merrill.

Clifford, J. A., Runions, T., & Smith, E. (1984, April). The learning enrichment service (LES): A multi-optioned approach to programming for gifted secondary school students. *Roeper Review, 6*(4), 226–229.

Daniels, R. R., Affholder, L. P., & Sims, S. B. (1986). *Selected basic competencies for education of the gifted.* Available from Arkansas State University, State University.

Davis, G. A., & Rimm, S. B. (1985). *Education of the gifted and talented.* Englewood Cliffs, NJ: Prentice Hall.

Doherty, E. J. S., & Evans, L. (1981, January/February). HELP! Need direction in independent study? *G/C/T,* pp. 43–46.

Gallagher, J. J. (1985). *Teaching the gifted child* (3rd ed.). Boston: Allyn & Bacon.

Johnsen, S. K., & Johnson, K. (1986). *Independent study program.* Austin, TX: Old Wagon Learning Associates.

Kaplan, S., Madsen, S., & Gould, B. (1976). *The big book of independent study.* Santa Monica, CA: Goodyear.

Karnes, F. A., & Collins, E. C. (1984). *Handbook of instructional resources and references for teaching the gifted.* Boston: Allyn & Bacon.

Kerr, B. A. (1985). *Smart girls, gifted women.* Columbus, OH: Ohio Psychology Publishing.

Khatena, J. (1982). *Educational psychology of the gifted.* New York: Wiley.

Maker, C. J. (1982a). *Curriculum development for the gifted.* Austin, TX: PRO-ED.

Maker, C. J. (1982b). *Teaching models in education of the gifted.* Austin, TX: PRO-ED.

Marland, S., Jr. (1972). *Education of the gifted and talented.* Report to the Congress of the United States by the U.S. Commissioner of Education. Washington, DC: U.S. Government Printing Office.

McNeil, J. D. (1981). *Curriculum—A comprehensive introduction* (2nd ed.). Boston: Little, Brown.

Perrone, P. A., & Male, R. A. (1981). *The developmental education and guidance of talented learners.* Rockville, MD: Aspen Systems.

Renzulli, J. S. (1977). *The enrichment triad model: A guide for developing defensible programs for the gifted and talented.* Mansfield Center, CT: Creative Learning Press.

Renzulli, J. S., & Reis, S. M. (1985). *The schoolwide enrichment model: A comprehensive plan for educational excellence.* Mansfield Center, CT: Creative Learning Press.

Seagoe, M. (1974). Some learning characteristics of gifted children. In R. Martinson, *The identification of the gifted and talented.* Ventura, CA: Office of Ventura County Superintendent of Schools.

Slocumb, P. (1984). *Research and process skills, Scope and sequence, Bank of objectives.* Workshop handout available from Dickinson ISD, TX.

Travers, R. M. (1982). *Essentials of learning* (5th ed.). New York: MacMillan.

Treffinger, D. J. (1981). Guidelines for encouraging independence and self-directed learning among gifted students. In W. B. Barbe & J. S. Renzulli (Eds.), *Psychology and education of the gifted* (3rd ed., pp. 232–238). New York: Irvington Publishers.

Webb, J. T., Meckstroth, E. A., & Tolan, S. S. (1982). *Guiding the gifted child.* Columbus: Ohio Psychology Publishing.

Webster's deluxe unabridged dictionary (2nd ed.). (1983). New York: New World Dictionaries/Simon & Schuster.

Wilsey, C., & Norberg, C. M. (1982, January/February). The isle of independent study. *G/C/T*, pp. 17–20.

28

Reaction
to "Independent
Study"

Reva C. (Jenkins) Friedman
Tom J. Gallagher

It is impossible for us, in these times of very rapid social and technological change, to teach children everything they will need to know for their futures. Instead, we hope that children will learn things that will be valuable and useful when we are no longer present to guide or direct them. (Treffinger, 1980, p. 9)

Teaching students how to work independently is a key goal shared by teachers in general education as well as those in special programs for gifted and talented students. Independent study can be an avenue to reaching this important outcome. Consequently, we frame our reactions to the previous chapter by Burns from the perspective of a general model of school learning. In applying this model to teaching gifted and talented students through independent study in general education classrooms, we discuss what is needed to make independent study a viable and effective instructional alternative.

A GENERAL MODEL OF SCHOOL LEARNING

How does learning take place in school situations? What are its key attributes? What are the implications for educating bright students? Examining a generalized model of school learning (see Bloom, 1976; Treffinger, 1975; Treffinger, Hohn, & Feldhusen, 1979) seems to be a most appropriate starting point in attempting to answer these questions. The key components of the model are shown in Figure 28.1 and are discussed in the following sections.

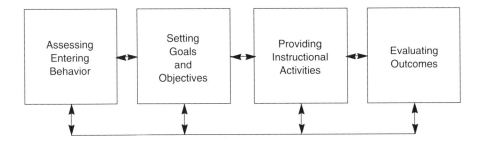

Figure 28.1 A Generalized Learning Model.

Assessing Entering Behavior

Description

The first component of the model is determining what students know so that an appropriate place to begin instruction can be chosen. The assumption is made that effective instruction is not preset. Rather, instruction is adapted to students' previous experiences, knowledge, and abilities. Recommended assessment procedures range from objective psychometric instruments, such as published criterion-referenced tests, standardized pretests, and general achievement measures, to subjective indicators, such as analyses of student products, self-ratings, and interviews.

Assessment of entering behavior is crucial for working productively with gifted and talented students in general education classrooms. Many bright learners are likely to have mastered basic and/or introductory material prior to grade-level instruction. Assessing what students know can make teaching and learning more efficient, in that students would not repeat previously mastered content simply for the sake of demonstration. Implementing this step of the model presupposes some degree of accommodation to individual differences (i.e., all students would not necessarily be learning the same material at the same time, because they might be entering an instructional process with different levels of expertise).

Assessing gifted and talented students' entry level supports a key belief of the field of gifted child education: that the learning environment should be accommodated to characteristics of bright students. Relevant qualities would include advanced knowledge level and a broad storehouse of information (Renzulli, Smith, White, Callahan, & Hartman, 1976). Furthermore, assessment implies that a procedure is needed whereby teachers can determine and document prior knowledge so that learners do not repeat content simply for the sake of demonstration.

Reaction

Of the four models presented by Burns, none seems to be directed specifically to accomplishing this task. However, considering the models presented in their entirety yields a different image. For example, both Renzulli's (1977) Enrichment Triad and Treffinger's (1986) Self-Directed Learning models are part of systematic approaches based on blending general education and specialized programming for gifted children (i.e., Schoolwide Enrichment Model and Individualized Programming Planning Model, respectively).

Two features of the Schoolwide Enrichment Model (Renzulli & Reis, 1985) are germane to this aspect of learning: assessment of student strengths and curriculum compacting. Assessment of student strengths includes analyzing cognitive strengths, interests, and learning or instructional style preferences. Curriculum compacting is designed to adapt the general education curriculum to meet the needs of bright learners through either eliminating the reteaching of work mastered previously or streamlining and pacing content to fit relevant characteristics of gifted students (i.e., rapidly mastering "basic" information with little drill or practice) (Renzulli & Reis, 1986).

Three aspects of the Individualized Programming Planning Model (Treffinger, 1986), a system developed from Treffinger's work in learner-controlled instruction, are relevant to assessing student entry level: identification, individualizing basic instruction, and effective acceleration. According to Treffinger, the identification process should reflect an analysis of student needs rather than a designation based on generalized characteristics. Individualizing basic instruction includes recognizing and responding to learning styles and interests, then adjusting the content, rate, and pace of instruction according to each student's needs. Treffinger defined effective acceleration in terms of compacting classroom curriculum, which he advocated as a means to provide additional time for advanced learning opportunities.

Neither Betts's Autonomous Learner Model nor Burns's generalized model deals specifically with this aspect of learning. Assessing entering knowledge is not as relevant to the Autonomous Learner Model as it is to the two models discussed above, because Betts's model focuses on out-of-classroom, enrichment experiences. In addition, the model's strong affective orientation allows it to accommodate to students at various stages of personal growth.

Burns mentions the need for gifted students to develop skills in conducting independent studies in their general education classrooms. However, she does not specifically address assessing learner entry levels of the skills she names: selecting an achievable product, establishing a workable time frame, and creating criteria for product evaluation.

Setting Goals and Objectives

Description

The fact that this is the second component of the learning model reflects the model's orientation to learner- rather than curriculum-centered instruction. In developing goals and objectives, educators need to deal with (at least) the following questions: In what ways should the learning experience affect students? What should they know, understand, apply, create, and judge as a result of the proposed instruction? How will students be taught about thinking?

Of course, learning goals and enabling objectives could be taken from the school district's curriculum handbook; however, they should be modified after assessment of what learners know *prior* to beginning instruction.

Setting goals and objectives for bright students to meet within the general classroom curriculum is an important and often neglected component of their education. For example, in states in which services to identified students are determined through the Individualized Education Program, often no goals are established for the general education program. This lack contributes to an unfortunate discontinuity of services (Treffinger, 1986). Since the current practice is for gifted students to spend the bulk of their educational careers in general education classrooms, increased support should be provided for classroom teachers to modify curriculum goals and objectives to nurture the cognitive growth of bright learners.

Some general goals for gifted students participating in independent study are contained in the models reviewed in Burns's chapter. In framing our comments, we analyze the goals on which the four models rest.

Enrichment Triad Model

Three sets of goals define the Enrichment Triad Model (Renzulli, 1977). Type I—enrichment, general exploratory—activities are designed to accomplish the following three purposes:

> to bring the learner in touch with the kinds of topics or areas of study in which he or she may have a sincere interest . . . to give both students and teachers some hints about what might be a *bona fide* Type III Enrichment activity . . . [and] to assist teachers in making decisions about the kinds of Type II Enrichment activities that should be selected for particular groups of students. (p. 17)

Type II—enrichment, group training—activities are aimed toward the learner developing "the processes or operations (the 'powers of mind') that enable him or her to deal more effectively with content" (p. 25). Type III—enrichment, individual and small group investigations of real problems—has as its purpose the learner becoming "an actual *investigator* of a real problem or topic by using appropriate *methods of inquiry*" (p. 29).

Autonomous Learner Model

The general focus of this five-dimension model is on promoting gifted students' abilities "to be responsible for the development, implementation and evaluation of their own learning" (Betts, 1986, p. 29). Betts identified eight general program goals:

> (1) developing more positive self-concepts, (2) comprehending their own giftedness in relation to self and society, (3) developing the skills to interact effectively with peers,

siblings, parents and other adults, (4) increasing their knowledge in a variety of subject areas, (5) developing their thinking, decision making and problem solving skills, (6) participating in activities selected to facilitate and integrate the cognitive, emotional and social development of the individual, (7) demonstrating responsibility for their own learning in and out of the school setting and (8) becoming responsible, creative, independent learners. (p. 32)

Self-Directed Learning Model

In his discussion of issues in implementing this model, Treffinger (1978) listed five goals developed by Barton (1976): (a) effective functioning in one's environments with peers, teachers, parents, and other adults; (b) making choices based on realistic self-analysis of needs and interests; (c) assuming responsibility for choices and decisions by completing all activities at a satisfactory level of achievement and in an acceptable time frame; (d) defining problems and determining a course for their solution; and (e) evaluating one's work.

Generalized Model

Burns enumerates three student goals:

(a) master prerequisite independent study skills in a practical and efficient manner under the direct guidance of a trained and knowledgeable instructor; (b) learn the special skills required for successful independent study such as product planning, time management, and audience finding, again, under the direct guidance of a trained and knowledgeable instructor; and (c) gain expertise in meeting established criteria for product evaluation and practice self-evaluation. (p. 388)

Reactions

From the perspective of building goals based on students' entering behavior, certainly nothing is objectionable in any of the models described above. Their goals are sufficiently open to permit determining an entry point into the particular model's processes for bright students, although at first blush the goals of the Enrichment Triad and the generalized models seem to be translated more easily into specific enabling objectives than do the Autonomous Learner or Self-Directed Learning models.

Our next criterion, defensibility of program goals and objectives for gifted students, further differentiates the models. Of the four models profiled in the chapter, only the Enrichment Triad is built on a unique theory of giftedness (see Renzulli, 1978). This theory allows Renzulli to address the following differentiation–defensibility concerns in the context of his model: "What is (or should be) different about the types of learning experiences that are advocated for gifted students?" and "Isn't what you're doing for the gifted also good for nearly all youngsters?" (Renzulli, 1977, p. 1). In implementing Renzulli's model, goals for gifted students are coordinated with classroom program services, especially in the areas of interest development and process activities for students in the "talent pool" (for a more complete explanation, see Renzulli & Reis, 1985, 1986).

The Autonomous Learner Model draws from a humanistic education perspective. Its goal of self-actualization is highly appropriate for all learners. Its defensibility lies in applying its "context-free" activities to concerns of bright students and in addressing these concerns in a differentiated setting—a resource room program or specialized course for gifted students. (Although Betts mentions adapting the model in general secondary language arts or social studies classes, that is not the model's prime environment.)

Self-Directed Learning is a general education model emanating from the field of learner-controlled instruction (Treffinger & Johnsen, 1973), with this adaptation based on the work of Muska Mosston (1972). Although Treffinger (1975, 1978) argued persuasively that the model fits an important subset of characteristics and needs of bright students, its key field testing was conducted in general education elementary classrooms (Barton, 1976). However, as described previously, Treffinger has since elaborated on the model and incorporated its tenets into a comprehensive approach for working with gifted students. In his description of the elaborated model, Treffinger emphasized the *process* of adopting a *defensible* definition of giftedness, rather than a *particular* definition, as the foundation for all programming activities. He singled out Renzulli's "three-ring conception" for its articulation with the model's independent learning goals. Regarding the differentiation issue, Treffinger (1986) affirmed the importance of coordinating student goals with general classroom services: "How should the regular program be modified to be more effective and challenging? What services outside or beyond the regular program seem important to provide, and how might these be accomplished?" (p. 445). From the perspective of the Self-Directed Learning Model, Treffinger would add a dimension of increasing learner determination of individual goals and objectives, based on a realistic self-analysis of strengths and needs.

Burns's generalized model neither espouses a particular conception of giftedness, nor deals overtly with the ever-present concern of providing experiences that are suited uniquely for bright students. Burns mentions the Enrichment Triad Model several times in presenting her model, which hints at an acceptance of the model's key features; however, this is an unsubstantiated speculation on our part.

Providing Instructional Activities

Description

This component of the learning process is based on the assumption that instruction reflects an analysis of student knowledge and subsequent modification of curriculum goals and objectives. In their monograph on planning instruction, Treffinger et al. (1979) emphasized the importance of instruction reflecting individual differences and needs. They recommended that teachers provide several instructional alternatives for accomplishing related goals. Given the many variations in configurations of abilities within the gifted population, as well as between bright students and their chronological peers, this approach is eminently sensible.

Reactions

This philosophy is applied most clearly in the Enrichment Triad and Self-Directed Learning models. Renzulli urged teachers to encourage students to explore the ways in which they prefer to pursue their interests, as well as to identify particular interests. Learning styles analysis is designed to help teachers develop a smorgasbord of alternatives for interest development and process-oriented activities. In her field studies of the Self-Directed Learning Model, Barton (1976) identified a carefully orchestrated sequence of learning alternatives, cross-referenced by the model's goals and companion teaching styles. These learning alternatives are adapted easily to any content area, particularly on the elementary and middle school levels, and shape increased independent learning for teachers and students.

Authors of the Autonomous Learner Model and the generalized model do not specifically advocate varying learning activities based on students' learning styles, interests, abilities, and needs. Inclusion of this dimension is not precluded in these models; however, at least some elaboration would be required to enhance adaptability to general education settings.

Evaluating Student Outcomes

Description

The final component of the learning process, evaluation, creates a bridge between learning cycles. Evaluation is an opportunity to assess the appropriateness of teachers' instructional choices throughout the learning process, as well as to ascertain learner growth. Learner evaluation criteria include speed, accuracy, and quality; however, Treffinger et al. (1979) made the point that teachers using more individualized approaches often find that traditional evaluation criteria and procedures are not valid indicators of student learning. They pointed out that assessment of the correctness of the content of a student's project could be difficult if the teacher has not read the same material. As one solution, they suggested that teachers provide opportunities for students to become involved in evaluating their own work.

We believe that the importance of learning to set and apply meaningful evaluation criteria cannot be overstated. Bright students, whose work so often outshines that of their peers, may complete their public school education without learning this important aspect of the learning process. They often are devastated when, upon entering higher education, their work receives any less than thunderous applause. Consequently, they find that setting realistic standards is difficult. Students then may become hypercritical, which leads to other adjustment problems beyond the scope of this discussion.

Reaction

The philosophy outlined above is particularly fitting for gifted students. Evaluating the fruits of independent investigations is an integral aspect of all four models. The Enrichment Triad's emphasis leads to employing real-world criteria for judging work (i.e., reactions from knowledgeable peers, such as publishers, panels of judges, and the consuming public). The Self-Directed Learning Model supports peer evaluation as well as self-evaluation at the "pivotal" peer–partner stage of the model. The generalized model emphasizes including students in establishing evaluation criteria, and the Autonomous Learner Model shapes self-evaluation through involvement in a mentorship experience.

MAKING INDEPENDENT STUDY WORK IN GENERAL EDUCATION CLASSROOMS

Three categories of issues—related to students, teachers, and systems—determine the degree to which independent study is a useful option for gifted and talented students in general education settings. We highlight our key concerns and make related recommendations.

Students

To imagine that all gifted and talented students qualify automatically as candidates for independent study is absurd. Even more absurd is to imagine that, by their nature, gifted learners are prepared for the rigors of independent study. However, those students who are prepared, able, willing, motivated, and facilitated adequately are likely to benefit from an in-depth independent study project. In planning to implement an independent study strategy, the teacher must decide whether independent study is the best method to achieve a specific educational goal for bright students (e.g., independent learning) or whether independent study is itself the goal. The difference between the objectives is enormous.

When the above considerations are not taken into account, an educational model such as the Enrichment Triad is likely to be implemented mechanistically into a curriculum. Thus, the model simply would be superimposed over the existing structure with no adaptive changes made to the structure. This is akin to putting a Cadillac body on a Model-T frame: It may look nice, but it will collapse before going very far.

A great deal of planning and preparation is needed to avoid mechanistic errors. Individual differences need to be taken into consideration; the needs, abilities, maturity levels, and educational objectives for each student must be accounted for. We must emphasize that the group of learners referred to as "the gifted and talented" is heterogeneous. Like any other collection of learners, a group of gifted students will exhibit a full range of learning styles, interests, world views, patterns of abilities, degrees of motivation, and levels of maturity. Each student needs individualized goals and objectives.

Instructional plans that are effective for a particular gifted student in a given situation may well fail for another gifted student in the same situation. Furthermore, the same plan that is effective for a student this month should be reviewed for needed modifications next month. Gifted and talented students do possess some collective and even quantifiable abilities and characteristics that tend to become the criterial attributes of the group; however, stereotyping gifted youngsters is unjust. Moreover, an old but egregious error is to operate educational programs on the basis of a one-dimensional conception of such a multifaceted group.

Teacher

Ideally, every teacher would follow this instructional plan for each learner: (a) reflect on what is in the best interest of the learner; (b) conduct a content analysis of the material, including a task analysis for specific intermediate objectives; and (c) choose the instructional methodologies to accomplish those objectives in the best way. In the case of independent study, we want to reemphasize that *if independent learning is the objective, it should not be treated as the process.*

Self-selection is at the heart of independent study, but the teacher/facilitator needs to help focus the student's selection. For example, a student's stated interest in robotics is only a rough start, not an end. How can a general interest be narrowed to a specific inquiry? What can be studied and how might that study best be conducted? Should or could a project or product result from the inquiry? What is a reasonable way to begin? (Many ideas for focusing are contained in Chapter 13.)

At best, facilitating is an instructional methodology fraught with subtlety and complexity. Teachers who function as independent study facilitators are much more than resource directors or permission granters, just as in discovery learning, teachers are more than chaperones. To maximize discovery time, teachers must be guides who help students focus on underlying principles and concepts and sift through the debris of irrelevant information. Analogously, independent study facilitators must ceaselessly yet unobtrusively monitor the educational process as students develop executive planning strategies.

Unfortunately, a high probability exists that the teachers themselves have limited personal experience with independent learning. The ensuing lack of confidence can lead to a severe mismatch between learner capabilities and teacher expectations. Teachers should no more expect their bright students to learn independently than they should expect a newborn thrown into a lake to start swimming. The sad truth is that both tend to drown. Whatever their abilities as instructors, teachers need to learn how to manage independent study.

The senior author has explored ways to prepare teachers to act in a facilitating capacity by restructuring two graduate courses in her university's gifted and talented child education certificate program, using an adapted version of the Self-Directed Learning Model (Jenkins-Friedman, 1982). She found that teachers express and demonstrate a much clearer understanding of the qualities necessary to guide independent study successfully once *they* have experienced the process from a student's perspective.

The System

By their very nature, systems are self-serving, operating first of all to assure survival. Accomplishing growth-oriented goals is a distant second priority. Three clusters of related forces determine whether independent study will be workable in a school or school district: uniformity, efficiency, and status.

Uniformity

Individualization requires that instruction accommodates to learner strengths, prior knowledge, and needs in a meaningful way. Requiring all students of a particular age to master the same goals at the same time and in the same manner makes uniformity a choke collar around independent study's neck. For instance, consider the following situation: When school boundaries changed, a gifted fourth grader was required to attend a different neighborhood school. In his new school, grade skipping was an unacceptable alternative for working with bright students. Because the student completed the fourth-grade reading series the previous year, his teachers were at a loss for an appropriate plan for this youngster. Their solution was to let the child read ''ahead'' in the fifth-grade series with the lowest ability group in the fifth-grade class. Thus, he was occupied constructively for the year and would advance to the next grade with his same-age peer group.

Uniformity also can affect how resources are deployed in school systems. In one district, the superintendent pressured a middle school teacher into dropping her popular, challenging, and innovative integrated humanities course. His argument was based on the fact that the course was not available at the other middle schools. ''Equal opportunity means the same opportunity for everyone,'' he asserted to the frustrated teacher, angry parents, and disappointed students.

A successful independent study program requires flexibility. Students will progress through required material at individual rates. They will study different topics, depending on their interests. Students will not be doing the same learning activities at the same time. Educators, as a part of a school system, need to encourage and reward flexibility and individual differences, rather than uniformity, for independent study to benefit rather than punish bright students and their teachers.

Efficiency

Undue devotion to the harsh taskmaster of efficiency has been named as the prime cause for the increase in student social promotion and the accompanying drop in standardized achievement test scores. The push for ever-greater efficiency can be seen in the almost religious adherence to the local curriculum guidebook objectives that must be covered for every grade level each year (every district has one).

Some state departments of education and local districts even specify the number of minutes per week to be spent covering objective-related material. Not to lose sight of the importance of teaching students rather than curriculum is difficult.

The most important discoveries were not accomplished in 45-minute intervals allotted for work. Independent study can be an option for general education teachers only when they have the authority and support to choose curriculum goals, determine courses of instruction, and set or modify as needed the time frames for accomplishing goals.

Status

We were taken aback to read in our local paper last month that many school districts around the country were using outdated editions of standardized tests so they could "truthfully" report that their students performed above the national average. Perhaps the trend stems from the accountability movement gone haywire, or simply an inappropriate application of the business productivity model to educational outcomes. In any event, the practice is damaging to students and their schools.

Unfortunately, no evidence exists to support that independent study will boost test scores. A school system, under pressure from its consumer public, will have difficulty maintaining its image without those above-average test scores. Independent study projects might result in a few newspaper stories—the children who win the state history day competition, the teens who place in the regional science fair—but they lack the punch of national percentiles.

Successfully implementing independent study techniques requires that teachers and administrators espouse a different kind of perspective on the learning process. "Shhh—minds at work" is a slogan that might fit. Resisting the pressure to push for assessing student performance through applications of number-oriented evaluation models as well as reeducating the general public about important outcomes of instruction are key elements to creating a new mind set—one that allows learners to become all they can be instead of operantly conditioned puppets.

CONCLUSION

War stories abound. A "good" student is turned loose on an independent study project and fails to complete it. Honors students are found using their independent study time to hang around the computer room and play games or to go to the gym and shoot baskets. High achievers profess an interest in a topic but will not (or cannot) focus on a project. A teacher agrees to let a student complete a partially mastered unit through independent study and never receives a project. The stories exist, as do the realities behind them; the realities have causes that we have linked to student, teacher, and/or institutional issues.

Burns states that "an ideal independent learner is a highly self-motivated paragon of erudition simply awaiting the removal of restraints to learning to forge ahead . . ." (pp. 391–392), but the ideal learner would never wait for the restraints to be removed.

History demonstrates repeatedly that these learners work around restraints or quit school (literally or figuratively) because it interferes with education.

In addition, Burns's contention regarding "essential instructional components" (p. 392) is cogent, but inadequately developed. She points out that "many programs failed because students were not taught these prerequisite skills" (p. 392). We believe that the real issue should be that many *students* failed because they were not taught necessary skills. The issue is *not* programs. The issue *is* helping gifted students learn and gain a positive, energizing self-image as learners. If a surgeon's knife fails and the patient dies, we mourn the loss of the patient; we do not waste our remorse on the instrument.

The teacher functioning as facilitator may well be the key to most of the issues involved in independent study. Good facilitators need substantive preparation—no model or system is more effective than its implementer. Likewise, the success of particular approaches is dependent on administrative support, as well as the teacher's ability and energy. Without needed support systems, teachers are forced to over-compromise, and the predictable result is failure.

All the models mentioned in Burns's chapter potentially are manageable; however, none are "turn-key" operations. Time, education, resources, and incentives and rewards for students and their teachers are imperatives for the success of this "panacea."

REFERENCES

Barton, B. (1976). *Toward the development of a self directed learner.* Unpublished master's thesis, University of Kansas, Lawrence.

Betts, G. T. (1986). The autonomous learner model for the gifted and talented. In J. S. Renzulli (Ed.), *Systems and models for developing programs for the gifted and talented* (pp. 29–56). Mansfield Center, CT: Creative Learning Press.

Bloom, B. S. (1976). *Human characteristics in school learning.* New York: McGraw-Hill.

Jenkins-Friedman, R. (1982). Self-directed learning for educators of gifted and talented students: Teachers need it, too! *Journal for the Education of the Gifted, 5*(2), 104–119.

Mosston, M. (1972). *Teaching: From command to discovery.* Belmont, CA: Wadsworth.

Renzulli, J. S. (1977). *The enrichment triad model.* Mansfield Center, CT: Creative Learning Press.

Renzulli, J. S. (1978). What makes giftedness? Reexamining a definition. *Phi Delta Kappan, 60,* pp. 180–184.

Renzulli, J. S., & Reis, S. M. (1985). *The schoolwide enrichment model: A comprehensive plan for educational excellence.* Mansfield Center, CT: Creative Learning Press.

Renzulli, J. S., & Reis, S. M. (1986). The Enrichment Triad/Revolving Door Model: A schoolwide plan for the development of creative productivity. In J. S. Renzulli (Ed.), *Systems and models for developing programs for the gifted and talented* (pp. 218–266). Mansfield Center, CT: Creative Learning Press.

Renzulli, J. S., Smith, L. H., White, A. J., Callahan, C. M., & Hartman, R. (1976). *Scales for rating behavioral characteristics of superior students.* Mansfield Center, CT: Creative Learning Press.

Treffinger, D. J. (1975). Teaching for self-directed learning: A priority for the gifted and talented. *Gifted Child Quarterly, 19*(1), 46–59.

Treffinger, D. J. (1978). Guidelines for encouraging independence and self-direction among gifted students. *Journal of Creative Behavior, 12,* 14–20.

Treffinger, D. J. (1980). *Encouraging creative learning for the gifted and talented.* Ventura, CA: National/State Leadership Training Institute on the Gifted and the Talented.

Treffinger, D. J. (1986). Fostering effective, independent learning through individualized programming. In J. S. Renzulli (Ed.), *Systems and models for developing programs for the gifted and talented* (pp. 429–460). Mansfield Center, CT: Creative Learning Press.

Treffinger, D. J., Hohn, R. L., & Feldhusen, J. F. (1979). *Reach each you teach.* Buffalo, NY: DOK Press.

Treffinger, D. J., & Johnsen, E. P. (1973). On self directed learning: When you say hello, do they write it in their notebooks? *Liberal Education, 59,* 471–479.

PART VI

VOLUME CONCLUSION

Gifted Students in the Regular Classroom: What Practices Are Defensible and Feasible?

C. June Maker

In this final part, I present an analysis of the many ideas and solutions proposed in the volume. Many answers were given to the question presented as the title of this part, and readers are encouraged to examine those answers thoroughly. My purpose in writing this section is not to repeat those ideas or be exhaustive in reviewing their merit. Rather, I wish to highlight some suggestions that seem particularly relevant as answers to the key and guiding questions for this part, and to identify underlying connections among the many solutions presented whenever possible. The guiding questions for this section are addressed first; then the key question is answered as a summary and conclusion to the volume.

How can regular classroom teachers challenge gifted students appropriately while also being fair to a classroom of children with a wide range of abilities?

This question expresses the essence of the regular classroom teacher's dilemma and the decision making that must occur all day, every day, and during the planning of instruction. Schiever (Chapter 15) suggests that providing an appropriate learning environment for gifted students in the regular classroom requires the equivalent of a juggling act. She gives teachers many practical ideas for becoming better jugglers. Lopez and MacKenzie (Chapter 21) believe that teachers must provide differentiation in "depth, scope, pace, and self-directedness of expectations" to meet the needs of gifted students. Most authors in the volume seem to agree with this state-

413

ment, although they may use different words for the concepts. Following are some ways to provide this appropriate differentiation and remain "fair" to everyone.

1. *Provide stimulating and challenging educational experiences for everyone.* Schiever (Chapter 15) presents this idea in her chapter on environments. Many programs for the gifted have been criticized because the gifted students go on field trips, have continual access to the library, listen to exciting speakers, and participate in simulations and other exciting hands-on experiences. Both unidentified students and teachers develop resentment because they know all can benefit from these exciting learning experiences and—I agree—all students deserve to be challenged and excited about learning. Nothing, however, prevents the teacher in a regular classroom setting from designing experiences and opportunities to challenge gifted students and then encouraging and allowing any others who are interested to participate. In some cases, teachers may need to limit participation to those who have progressed to a certain level of skill development or those who have completed certain assignments. These kinds of limitations are not unfair; they are necessary to the success of the students.

Orzechowski-Harland (Chapter 12) recommends that teachers examine their unit and lesson plan goals, assessing the ratio of open-ended to closed questions and the ratio of multilevel to one-level activities, and Schiever (Chapter 15) and Sisk (Chapter 16) present a set of principles to guide the questioning process and provide challenges for all. Questions, according to Schiever, should (a) be focused to give direction, (b) be open-ended, (c) require the use or processing of information, and (d) require that students explain and support their conclusions and opinions. In discussions, wait time must be allowed, questioning must be paced appropriately, student responses must be accepted without comment by the teacher, student responses should not be repeated by the teacher, the teacher should seek a variety of ideas, and the teacher should seek to develop higher levels of thinking through questions for clarification and extension. Sisk recommends that teachers go beyond the basic skills of observation, correspondence, classification, and seriation to integrated thinking skills, such as logical multiplication, compensatory thinking, proportional thinking, probabilistic thinking, and correlational thinking.

The multileveled learning center activities recommended and described by Feldhusen (Chapter 19), Lopez and MacKenzie (Chapter 21), and Follis (Chapter 22) are examples of exciting learning experiences provided for everyone. Learning centers contain materials and activities for developing basic skills as well as for extending learning to higher levels. A variety of challenging tasks can be provided, and students encouraged to try as many of them as possible. Independent study, mentorships, internships, special projects, field trips, and other exciting and interesting options need to be made available to all students.

Kitano (Chapter 20) presents a list of questions teachers can ask themselves about every activity developed:

1. Do the activities include provisions for several ability levels?
2. Do the activities include ways to accommodate a variety of interest areas?
3. Does the design of activities encourage development of sophisticated products?

4. Do the activities provide for the integration of thinking processes with concept development?
5. Are the concepts consistent with the comprehensive plan?

Finally, Rice (Chapter 7) and Szabos (Chapter 8), in their discussions of the demonstration teaching model, emphasize that many aspects of teaching recommended for the gifted are effective for all students. The teaching model they advocate has been successful in raising the level of instruction for all students. My way of thinking about this idea in the past is that in programs for the gifted, the teacher is attempting to establish a *floor,* but not a *ceiling* for learning. We do want a foundation so that learning can occur, and so that later learning is built on a solid foundation, but we do not want to place limits on what students can learn when they have the desire and the ability (Maker, 1986b). When teachers provide instruction for all children that meets these same conditions, they have been both challenging and fair.

2. *Teach and encourage all students to establish their own learning goals, and plan activities to meet their goals.*

All students are better learners when they are highly involved in their own learning. When discussing classroom management, both Conroy (Chapter 17) and Vuke (Chapter 18) make comparisons between schools and businesses, recommending a team effort among all those present. Vuke believes that *learning,* rather than *students who have learned,* should be viewed as the "products" of school. In this view, students are equal partners with teachers, administrators, volunteers, and even parents. Students, then, are expected to assume responsibility for their own learning. Frequently, students are held responsible for decisions about learning experiences (e.g., they are allowed to choose which learning centers in which to work, what topics to study, or what activities offered in a particular learning center they wish to complete). Seldom, however, are they asked to participate in assessing their strengths and weaknesses, setting their own goals, and assessing the outcomes of instruction. (Readers are referred to Friedman and Gallagher, Chapter 28, for an explanation of this generalized model of instruction.) If students are to be and become responsible for their own learning, they must participate in *all* phases of instruction. Most importantly, they must establish their own goals and be assisted in reaching these goals and/or reevaluating the appropriateness of such aspirations.

Goal setting needs to be viewed as a skill to be developed and exercised, not as an ability possessed by some (those who are gifted) and not others (those who are not gifted), or as an ability that develops automatically at a certain age. I was quite surprised one day as I observed a class of gifted 3-year-olds. The teacher was having individual conferences with children, and they were evaluating the extent to which they had achieved certain previously established learning goals by giving themselves gold, silver, or red stars. She assisted them in this process by asking questions, helping them remember classroom situations and events, and listening carefully to their perceptions of what they had learned.

All children, regardless of their age or learning ability, can be asked what they want to learn and what they believe they need to learn. As they become more familiar with setting goals and more convinced that the teacher will respect and honor their choices, students will become better at the process of goal setting. In her chapter on individualizing instruction, Feldhusen (Chapter 19) explains how her second-grade students plan, schedule, and record their activities. They begin by planning only a morning at a time, and by spring, they plan for a week at a time. Lopez and Mac-Kenzie (Chapter 21) also recommend that students establish their own goals, and that these goals guide the selection of centers and center activities. In all of the chapters (Section V) describing program models for extending learning beyond the classroom, authors recommend extensive involvement of students in the learning process, especially in determining the goals for these experiences, and in assessing their progress toward reaching these goals.

Learning contracts are described by many authors as methods that can be used to assist in individualization of goals, experiences, and assessment. Contracts can be formal, and signed by student, mentor, teacher, and parents, as described by Bodnar in Chapter 25 on internships. Because an internship is an intensive, 20-week experience, and many individuals, agencies, and organizations are involved, the agreements must be formalized. Goals and procedures are agreed upon by a committee of individuals, including the student and parent. Batten and Rogers (Chapter 24) describe a similar procedure, although the formal signing of an agreement is not emphasized. Contracts also can be informal, and take the form of a ''management plan'' (Reis & Schack, Chapter 13) or a plan of action agreed upon verbally by a teacher and student. Contracts in some form are mentioned or described by the following authors: Rosselli (Chapter 11), Reis and Schack (Chapter 13), Lethem (Chapter 14), Schiever (Chapter 15), Conroy (Chapter 17), Feldhusen (Chapter 19), Lopez and MacKenzie (Chapter 21), Follis (Chapter 22), Nash et al. (Chapter 23), Batten and Rogers (Chapter 24), Bodnar (Chapter 25), and Burns (Chapter 27).

To help students develop goals, identify needs, and focus interests, teachers can employ a variety of methods. Often teachers must begin by presenting students with a list of options from which they can choose. Students can be invited to add options to the list, and must be assisted in making their choices. Remember, however, that choices are not real unless students truly believe they are free to select an activity or a goal not recommended by the teacher. Reis and Schack (Chapter 13) describe an interview process to help students identify and focus, and Lethem (Chapter 14) agrees, but recommends keeping a file of topics and projects from former students to provide information about the range of possibilities. Individual conferences are mentioned most frequently as a vehicle for individual goal setting, and most authors recommend that students keep a folder, log, or journal in which they record their activities and progress.

Finally, the process of helping students establish appropriate goals and plan their own learning experiences must be a part of instruction for all students if we are to realize an important goal of regular education and education of the gifted: the development of self-directed, independent, autonomous learners. Friedman and Gallagher note, in the beginning of Chapter 28 on independent study, that teaching students to learn independently is a goal shared by most educators. I would add, however, that many educators say this is a goal, but practice teaching methods that accomplish the opposite: development of learners dependent on the teacher to tell them what to do, how to do it, and whether they have been successful. Three teaching–learning models with the goal of development of independent learners have been introduced in several chapters: Renzulli's Enrichment Triad Model, Betts's Autonomous Learner Model, and Treffinger's Self-Directed Learning Model. I would recommend that readers consult Chapters 11, 13, 26, 27, and 28, and the references cited in these chapters if they wish to work toward this stated goal of developing autonomous learners who are capable of establishing and reaching appropriate personal goals. Not all aspects of all models are compatible with each teacher's style and situation, but all teachers can incorporate some aspects of these models.

3. *Provide a variety of print and nonprint resources, and help students create and locate additional ones.*

The contrasts between regular classrooms and classrooms for the gifted often are startling when one begins to examine the learning resources available. This should not be true; nor should the resources be removed from classrooms for the gifted and placed in other classrooms. Resources can be books, maps, slides, videotapes, microscopes, newspapers, slide projectors, timers, tapes, pictures, toys, construction materials (both ''junk'' and commercially produced materials such as Erector sets), people, markers, chart paper, dictionaries, atlases, computers and computer programs, typewriters, synonym finders, plants, animals, how-to books, rocks, crystals, cooking utensils, boxes, baskets, and so on; the list is endless. Resources can (and should) be those needed in all phases of learning—including exploring, gathering information, and creating products.

An incredible array of free and inexpensive materials can be located and made available in the classroom. Used book stores, yard sales, recycling centers, and various community agencies are sources of inexpensive materials, equipment, and other resources. Out-of-date college textbooks can be made available in high school classrooms, and out-of-date high school textbooks can be made available in elementary and middle school classrooms at little or no cost. The fact that books are out-of-date or that free materials have a bias due to their source (e.g., their underlying purpose is to sell a certain product) should not be reasons for eliminating them from classroom use. Such materials can be used as teaching tools because of these characteristics, as Lopez and MacKenzie note in Chapter 21 on learning centers.

In short, teachers who wish to provide a rich array of learning resources can do so regardless of the money available. Volunteers always are willing to talk to students or share their knowledge and experience in some way. Retired and elderly people enjoy the contact with youngsters, and youngsters benefit from their wisdom and years of living. Students themselves can create learning materials and activities for their own and other classrooms, and can become resource persons who make presentations to their own and other classrooms. The age and maturity of students or the sophistication of their products should not be factors in deciding for or against their being made available as resources in a classroom. Students can assist teachers and teachers can assist students in locating, securing, and evaluating resources. Several authors discuss teacher and student roles in the provision of multiple resources: Hooker (Chapter 5), Reis and Schack (Chapter 13), Lethem (Chapter 14), Schiever

(Chapter 15), Feldhusen (Chapter 19), Lopez and MacKenzie (Chapter 21), Follis (Chapter 22), Batten and Rogers (Chapter 24), and Burns (Chapter 27).

4. *Use teaching–learning models or theories as curricular frameworks that provide for recognition and development of multiple types of giftedness.*

If teachers develop a one-dimensional or narrow view of giftedness as a quality existing only in those students identified or served in a special program, or as a quality of those students who are good lesson learners, they will be unfair to some students and will not provide appropriate challenges for the gifted students in their classes. Most authors recommend that teachers assess a variety of student strengths and weaknesses, and caution teachers against assuming that gifted students constitute a homogeneous group. Vuke (Chapter 18) is the first author to recommend specific approaches. She mentions Taylor's Multiple Talent Approach and Williams's Strategies for Thinking and Feeling. Lopez and MacKenzie (Chapter 21) advocate the use of Gardner's model. These and other models are discussed by Rosselli (Chapter 11) in the context of the development of thinking processes.

In Taylor's (1986) model, different types of talents are identified: academic, planning, forecasting, decision making, productive thinking, communication, implementing, discerning opportunities, and human relations. Gardner (1983) identified seven areas and called them ''intelligences'' rather than talents: linguistic, logical–mathematical, spatial, musical, bodily–kinesthetic, interpersonal, and intrapersonal. Both Taylor and Gardner believe that all individuals possess abilities and the potential to develop abilities in all areas unless disabled by brain damage or other such conditions. All individuals, however, do not possess the same levels or the same capacities in all intelligence or talent areas. These and other such models offer the teacher a way to organize learning activities and a way to make the development of a wide range of abilities operational in the classroom. They are different in their categorization of abilities, the level and type of research on which they are based, and the resources available for implementation. More curricular resources are available based on Taylor's model because it was developed for use in the classroom. Gardner's is a theory of intelligence with implications for classroom and school use. More resources are becoming available as educators apply the theory in the classroom.

Regardless of the categories one uses to describe giftedness or talent, implementation in the regular classroom can make learning positive, exciting, and challenging for everyone, including the teacher. When the focus is on what students *can* do and on finding and developing these talents rather than on what students *cannot* do (and bringing everyone up to some minimum standard), all students benefit. Use of a multiple talent model in a regular classroom setting also can provide a way of organizing instruction to accommodate students' varied interests and learning styles. If, for example, learning centers contain activities to develop each of the seven intelligences identified by Gardner, as Lopez and MacKenzie (Chapter 21) recommend, students can be encouraged to choose activities in the area(s) they are most interested in developing.

Based on my reading and study related to both Gardner's and Taylor's models, and others similar to them, I recommend that teachers employ them in three basic ways. One, as described above, is to provide options from which students can choose.

Another is to provide variety in the learning experiences in which students are required to participate, thereby encouraging students to explore and develop new or previously unknown abilities. A third, related way in which such models can be applied, is to provide options for the types of products developed as a result of a learning experience. For instance, instead of requiring that students produce a written report on a book (linguistic intelligence according to Gardner), teachers could suggest or even require other choices, such as a mime based on the book (bodily–kinesthetic intelligence); a musical composition to accompany the reading of some part(s) of the book (musical intelligence); a word-free flow chart or diagram of the major plots (logical–mathematical, spatial); a logical analysis of the plots and their relationship(s) (logical–mathematical, linguistic); an illustration or series of illustrations of the book (spatial); an analysis of ways the main character is like and unlike the student (intrapersonal); and an analysis of the motivations and other traits of the characters in the book (interpersonal).

Finally, the use of a multiple talent or multiple intelligence model can provide a focus and organizational scheme for integrating all the teaching principles described herein. If giftedness is viewed as multifaceted and broad, teachers must provide a variety of stimulating and exciting learning experiences. They must design open-ended questions and multileveled activities in each area. Students can be encouraged to assess their own strengths and weaknesses in each ability area, and to set individual goals for developing both strong and weak intelligence or talent areas and specific strengths and weaknesses within selected intelligence or talent areas. Choices among alternatives are then guided by a broad view of their personal development and potential rather than a limited one. A multiple talent or multiple intelligence model can help the teacher organize, select, and assure variety in the resources made available to students. Students focusing on development of spatial abilities, for example, will need a variety of nonprint media, such as construction materials, slides, and pictures, whereas those focusing on interpersonal and intrapersonal areas will need access to people and social situations.

Summary

In this volume, many practical solutions and ideas are provided to help regular classroom teachers who wish to provide a challenging curriculum to meet the needs of gifted students while being fair to students with a wide range of abilities. In this section, only a few of those solutions are highlighted, and four underlying ideas or types of solutions are identified. I encourage you to read and examine the chapters in this volume, and to develop even more of your own personal strategies.

How can gifted students be motivated to go beyond what other students are expected to do in a regular classroom situation?

After challenging options have been identified, teachers usually ask the "motivation" question: What do I do about those students who do not want to do these wonderful, exciting activities I have provided? Very few of the authors in this book gave direct answers to this question, but several provided examples and advice I believe will be helpful.

First, the activities themselves can be highly motivating, and the fact that students can choose among several options as well as determine goals and objectives gives them a sense of control that is motivating to many gifted students. Second, involvement in designing learning experiences, choosing resources, and evaluating learning outcomes is important in increasing the desire to learn.

Whenever I think of motivating gifted students in the regular classroom, I am reminded of my nephew, Glenn, a highly creative, gifted boy. As a young child, he was interested in everything. He had collections and books, and his questions were penetrating. During the first 3 years of school, Glenn was a model student. He loved to learn, he finished all his assignments, and he made the highest grades. In fourth grade, however, things changed. Whenever Glenn finished an assignment early, the teacher gave him more of the same work to do. Glenn learned quickly, so he stopped finishing early; and when the teacher pushed him to stop "dilly-dallying" and do his work quickly the way she knew he could, he stopped working entirely! He refused to finish any of his work. He was very good in math, and liked doing it, so he would do the problems in his head and record only the answers on paper. This frustrated the teacher immensely, and I can remember my sister's equal frustration after her conferences with her son's teacher. At one of these meetings, the teacher told her that Glenn always got the answers to his math problems correct, including long division, but she could not give him a good grade because he would not show his work.

Glenn had a very difficult year, and he has continued to have problems in school. His achievement test scores were very high, mostly in the 90th percentile and above, but his grades ranged from A's in subjects he liked or with teachers he liked to D's and F's in subjects he did not like or with teachers he did not like. Glenn also was not considered eligible for special programs for gifted students because of his low grades, low motivation, and low score on an IQ test given during the fourth grade. Educators ignored his higher IQ scores from other years, as well as the fact that his lack of motivation could have been due to the need for the more challenging, interesting learning experiences provided in a special program. Glenn's story leads me to the statement of the first important answer to the guiding question in this section:

1. *Do not assign or expect gifted students to produce a greater volume of work.*

More work does not constitute appropriate differentiation for gifted students, and it destroys their intrinsic motivation to learn. Always remember that the purpose of, for instance, drill and practice exercises or worksheets is *to learn a concept or skill.* If the student has already learned the concept or skill, he or she has no need to complete a worksheet—and certainly does not need to complete two worksheets.

2. *A positive, supportive psychological climate must be provided in all classrooms.*

Glenn's story also illustrates the critical role of the learning atmosphere in the learning process. Schiever (Chapter 15) states that all children need an environment in which their psychological, emotional, and physical safety is assured. In such an environment, the teacher respects all students and encourages them to respect each other, establishes consistent discipline policies (providing freedom within clear limits), avoids intentional and unintentional ''putdowns,'' and teaches children how to handle conflicts. Schiever also recommends that the teacher incorporate student centered-ness, independence, openness, complexity, mobility, and acceptance, dimensions I outlined (Maker, 1982) as important aspects of an environment for gifted students. Schiever explains how these dimensions can be incorporated in a regular classroom setting. Sisk (Chapter 16) agrees with Schiever, and adds the dimensions of inter-dependence and encouraging creativity.

In her critique of Schiever's chapter, Sisk also reminds teachers to develop in all students excitement about learning by giving them opportunities to question; free-dom to experiment; freedom to reflect; encouragement to develop complex and intense thinking; supportive experts, peers, and professionals; and opportunities to identify real problems and find solutions, and to experience complex feelings. Maslow's hier-archy of needs is a helpful tool for teachers to use when considering the issue of motivation, and Sisk provides examples of the needs gifted students have in each of the categories identified by Maslow. In essence, Maslow reminds everyone that certain psychological needs, such as physical, security, and belonging, must be met before people have a desire or the capability to meet higher level needs.

3. *Counseling needs to be made available to all students.*

Some psychological needs of students cannot be met in the classroom or without intensive outside intervention. As Seghini (Chapter 26) points out in her review of Bodnar's chapter on internships, counseling is needed by many students to take care of problems that may interfere with their ability to take advantage of challenging learning opportunities. Seghini notes that some gifted students make decisions about classes that severely limit their ability to participate in internships in areas of interest to them. They also make decisions that limit their career options. Counseling at an early age, as well as knowledge of the consequences of course selection, is impor-tant to help students who may have or develop low motivation.

Vuke (Chapter 18) recommends special attention to underachievers, and sug-gests that classroom teachers may need assistance in understanding these sometimes difficult students. She recommends special support services for teachers.

4. *Clustering and other grouping arrangements in which gifted students work together can be motivating.*

Several authors—Hooker (Chapter 5), Conroy (Chapter 17), and Vuke (Chap-ter 18)—recommend grouping students according to their interests and abilities. Others—Hooker (Chapter 5), Sisk (Chapter 16), and Conroy (Chapter 17)—recommend the use of cooperative learning. Cluster grouping of gifted students usually is thought of as a classroom management strategy, and certainly it is. It pro-vides a structure for the teacher to work with students who learn at a similar rate, and provides a structure for students to interact with their intellectual peers. The value of interacting with a stimulating, challenging group of peers cannot be over-looked as a motivating tool.

Grouping does not need to be (and should not be) static. Students should be grouped by ability in each subject area, as Vuke (Chapter 18) recommends, and groupings should be reevaluated throughout the school year. Students also should be grouped by interests, regardless of ability, for certain kinds of activities. Special interest groups can meet on a regular basis with mentors, volunteers, the teacher, or by themselves. Older students also can be invited to work with interest groups. In one school in which I worked, every Friday afternoon was spent in special 2- to 3-week mini-courses offered by teachers, administrators, parents, retired people, students, and a variety of individuals from the community. These courses were in-depth studies or introductions to topics that were not part of the regular curriculum. Courses could be added at any time at the request of anyone or whenever someone offered to teach a new topic. Friday afternoons became exciting and motivating rather than a time to be endured before the weekend began.

Cooperative learning is another powerful motivating and teaching tool when used appropriately. It can be effective as a response to student needs for belonging, power, freedom, and fun—some of the needs found in Maslow's hierarchy. However, Conroy (Chapter 17) reminds educators that gifted students need to be grouped with other gifted students for some cooperative learning tasks. If gifted students always must assume the role of teacher or must "pull along" the slower students, they will begin to resent the other students, the teacher, the task, and the idea of working in groups. As adults, we belong to many different groups. Some of these contain individuals with widely divergent abilities and points of view, whereas others comprise those with abilities and interests similar to our own. If the cooperative learning technique is to be a method for preparing students for working cooperatively as adults, they must experience a wide variety of groupings to serve different purposes.

5. *Mentors and other adults are motivators.*

Another type of interaction educators must not overlook is the interaction of a gifted student with a special adult—often gifted also. Role models are crucial for gifted students. Mentors have been cited in all studies of talent development as critical elements. Nash and his colleagues (Chapter 23) note that gifted students may fail to reach their potential without a mentor because unusual talent needs intensive personal attention for development. Two of the important functions of mentorships are role modeling and shaping personal growth. Nash et al. give examples and data to show the value of a mentor's involvement in the motivational process. Batten and Rogers (Chapter 24) agree with these four functions of mentors, although they recommend motivation and excitement about learning as prerequisites to student involvement in a mentorship experience.

As all authors writing on this topic recommend, students need opportunities to seek out their own mentors. If a student perceived as having low motivation finds a mentor and experiences a spark of intellectual and creative compatibility, this relationship needs to have a high priority. The teacher should encourage the student and mentor to work together and assist them in any way possible. This experience may change the student's life in a very positive way.

Summary

In summary, the issue of motivation is a complex one, and needs to be addressed by all teachers. The most important advice I can give, however, is to capitalize on the intrinsic motivation of gifted students by providing a variety of challenging, exciting opportunities. Next, give *true* freedom to set personal goals, choose activities and experiences, and assess progress. Avoid giving more work and excessive reviews of material already learned. Provide opportunities to interact with stimulating peers and adults. Do not expect all gifted students to have the same level of motivation in all subject areas or in the same subject area at all times. Finally, give gifted students the freedom to choose *not* to participate and not to work hard. They are children, too, and need time to play, relax, and daydream just like everyone else.

How can administrators be certain that regular classroom teachers are meeting the needs of gifted students?

I now turn the focus of this chapter to the need to view services for gifted students from a wider perspective than one teacher's classroom. Perhaps the biggest problem faced by program developers attempting to provide services to gifted students in a regular classroom setting is the variability across teachers and classrooms. Let me hasten to add that I am not suggesting that every classroom teacher must provide the *same* kinds of experiences or the same level of instruction in all areas. I am suggesting that learning experiences need to be placed in a developmental perspective so that the student's needs across his or her 12 or so years of school experiences fit together. I also am persuaded that to meet the requirement of educational equity, we cannot continue to provide for the needs of gifted students in some regular classrooms and not in others, and expect parents and students to be quiet about the problem.

1. *A comprehensive plan for curriculum and services to gifted students must be developed and used.*

Three authors discuss the need for a comprehensive curriculum plan in a direct way, and others make suggestions that imply that such a plan needs to be available. In her critique of the advocate liaison program described by Hooker (Chapter 5), VanTassel-Baska (Chapter 6) recommends the development of a framework in which the following goals, or needed outcomes, are defined: cognitive products, cognitive processes, affective products, affective processes, and instructional processes. Product goals, in this schema, are outcomes gifted students should achieve, and process goals are representative processes teachers should or must employ in the teaching of gifted students. A framework such as that described can provide a way to examine programs for gifted students across grade levels and content disciplines. The "outcome statements" are linked to curriculum differentiation models and strategies.

In her chapter describing the demonstration teaching model, Rice (Chapter 7) lists as the first necessary element the existence of an effective curriculum—one built around content generalizations and key concepts within and across the academic areas, in which open-endedness and higher levels of thinking are developed. Integration of content and processes is emphasized. Demonstration teaching then is used to help teachers learn how to implement this ''effective curriculum'' in a regular classroom setting. Szabos, in her critique of Rice's chapter, emphasizes the need to recognize the connection of demonstration teaching with the goals for the program for the gifted *and* with the general requirements for effective schools: experimentation, collegiality, tangible support, honest communication, and reaching out to the knowledge bases about teaching.

Kitano (Chapter 20), in her critique of Feldhusen's chapter on individualization, states emphatically that comprehensive, long-term planning of educational experiences for the gifted is essential. The main content or subject matter for the gifted should be outlined over a number of years, and should consist of a flexible core with the goal of having students become content experts. She states that an additional consideration should be to extend advanced/enriched learning to all children. She then describes two general approaches to curriculum. The first is one in which a special curriculum is designed for gifted students. It might contain content areas or concepts different from those required in the regular curriculum. In the second approach, the regular curriculum and concepts are used as a framework, and differentiation is provided through activities presented and children's responses.

As these and other authors state, the existence of a comprehensive plan has numerous advantages, the most important of which is that, if the plan is followed, the result is a connectedness in services and curricula to meet the varied and changing needs of gifted students. The advantage for teachers is that they know what is expected of their teaching, as well as how the program in their classroom is expected to fit into the overall plan for a child's education. If the plan is a good one, it will be a framework from which a myriad of appropriate learning activities can be generated. For the administrator, a comprehensive curricular framework is the tool needed to help facilitate the training, management, and monitoring functions necessary to assure that the needs of gifted students are being met.

2. *Administrators must foster an attitude of cooperation, mutual goal setting, and problem solving.*

Conroy (Chapter 17) and Vuke (Chapter 18) discuss the important role of administrators in school and classroom management, comparing schools to businesses. In a well-run business, for instance, employees with outstanding skills are recognized, are asked to provide training for their colleagues, and are rewarded with benefits. At evaluation conferences, employees are asked to identify career goals, and often a career development plan is devised, including special training as well as practical experiences. In Szabos's (Chapter 8) examination of the effective schools literature, she states that collegiality, tangible support, and honest communication are elements needed in a ''business'' whose product is learning. Perhaps schools can be made more effective through the application of principles derived from the study of successful businesses. In the introduction to Part II, I review the school-wide management models presented and show how the effective schools norms are incorporated into each model. Readers are referred to that material for additional analysis of management issues.

Many of the models discussed in Part II, Schoolwide Management and Programs, have as a key element an atmosphere of cooperation, mutual goal setting, and problem solving. Chalfant and Van Dusen Pysh's (Chapter 3) teacher assistance teams (TATs) are problem-solving teams in which teachers provide assistance to other teachers. The atmosphere is one of cooperation and concern for the learning of all students, but is focused on one student at a time. Advocate liaisons, as described by Hooker (Chapter 5), are teachers who volunteer their time to provide special assistance to regular classroom teachers in making provisions for the gifted students they serve. Use of the demonstration teaching model, as described by Rice (Chapter 7) and Szabos (Chapter 8), is one way for teachers to provide training for each other.

In all the Part V chapters describing models for extending learning beyond the classroom, cooperation, mutual goal setting, and problem solving are emphasized. A committee consisting of teachers, parents, the student, mentor(s), psychologist, and administrator establishes goals for each student. These goals, however, are expected to fit within the overall plan for the program, as recommended in the previous section of this chapter.

The administrator's role is crucial in all of these programs, and no program would succeed without the extensive involvement of administrators in the planning, development, implementation, and monitoring phases of programming. In the following section, some recommendations are made for monitoring programs (based on the existence of a comprehensive plan) to assure that all teachers are making appropriate provisions for the gifted students in their classrooms.

3. *Continuous monitoring must be done at the classroom level.*

One of the most effective management strategies administrators can employ seems so simple it requires very little explanation. However, because it is seldom incorporated into a school setting, it needs attention. The technique is simple: management by walking around (Peters, 1987). Often, administrators are so busy attending to paperwork, going to meetings, and responding to emergencies that they do not get out of their offices or out of meeting rooms enough to know what is going on in schools or classrooms. A principal should not be a stranger to a teacher or the students, and should not appear only when conducting a required formal evaluation of a teacher's performance. Conroy (Chapter 17) recommends management by walking around, but does not make specific suggestions for implementation. VanTassel-Baska (Chapter 6) states that monitoring must be done at the classroom level, and that teacher performance is compared with the standards outlined in the comprehensive plan. The districtwide plan can provide the administrator with the well-defined, differentiated teaching expectations Conroy believes are needed by administrators if they are to be effective managers.

Hooker (Chapter 5) suggests that teachers keep monthly logs of activities that can be examined by administrators or other teachers to determine the kinds of experiences provided for students. Examination of logs, however, should not substitute for actual observation and visits to classrooms and events. Continuous monitoring can and should lead to the next phase, which is evaluation and modification.

4. *Programs must be evaluated through comparisons of experiences provided in classrooms with the comprehensive plan, and the plan itself must be assessed and modified.*

Many of the authors in this book discuss the need for program and student assess-ment, and most provide data from evaluations to show that the programs they recom-mend have been successful. However, only one author, Bodnar (Chapter 25), describes an extensive program evaluation, and only one, Orzechowski-Harland (Chapter 12), recommends an examination of the districtwide goals for all students.

Orzechowski-Harland's suggestion is that teachers examine districtwide goals for all students, and assess the degree to which they include the development of skills identified by Rosselli in Chapter 11 on differentiation of processes. Orzechowski-Harland's recommendation calls to mind the need to make certain that all students are challenged and motivated. If districtwide goals are limited, for instance, to the development of knowledge-level skills, they cannot be considered appropriate for all children, and should be modified.

Bodnar (Chapter 25) presents a clear, comprehensive evaluation procedure for the internship program she describes. Actual forms used in the evaluation are included, and the process used for assigning student grades is outlined. Because so few authors addressed the evaluation issue, and a comprehensive treatment of it is beyond the scope of this chapter, the reader is referred to Appendix VI.A for a list of applicable publications.

5. *Administrators must choose teachers carefully.*

Every author in this book discussed the key role of the teacher in providing an appropriate program for gifted students. Regardless of the type of program, the teacher is the most important ingredient in its success. Certainly, administrators can provide inservice education, support, and a variety of services to classroom teachers that will increase their skill and ability to provide for the gifted students they teach. However, I do not believe that every teacher can become, or even has a desire to become, an excellent teacher of the gifted. Thus, I believe that administrators who are concerned about the quality of teaching gifted students receive in the regular classroom must select their teachers carefully.

The question of whom to select has been addressed in other contexts, the most frequent being discussions of how to select specialists in education of the gifted. Although such discussions and lists of characteristics may be helpful to examine, the duties of a regular classroom teacher go far beyond providing for the needs of gifted students, and the role of these teachers includes serving gifted students in a different context from a specialized program.

None of the authors in this volume were asked to address the question of teacher selection or skills. However, a review of the various chapters has revealed that many authors considered the issue. I have compiled the information into two tables. Table VI.1 contains a list of traits that are personal, and that seem to be present in indi-viduals regardless of their skills and prior training. Table VI.2 contains a list of skills teachers need to develop to enable them to increase their effectiveness in teach-ing gifted students in a regular classroom setting.

Perhaps the most important of all these traits are the teacher's genuine desire to become a more effective teacher of gifted students and his or her willingness to develop new skills through attendance at workshops, visitations to other classrooms, self-study, and college coursework. Administrators need to keep the above lists of

Table VI.1 Some Teacher Characteristics and Attitudes Important in Teaching
Gifted Students

Rosselli (Chapter 11)
• Commitment
• Belief that people learn differently
• Belief that characteristics of gifted students should influence how they are taught

Orzechowski-Harland (Chapter 12)
• Understanding of one's own thinking style processes and preferences, and of how these impact curriculum development (teachers teach best the skills they perform best, understand, and enjoy)
• Willingness or openness to recognizing that some gifted students may know all or more about a subject than the teacher intends to teach—*before* it is taught

Schiever (Chapter 15)
• Ability to juggle

Sisk (Chapter 16)
• High expectations
• Frequent monitoring of progress
• Businesslike
• Achievement oriented

Conroy (Chapter 17)
• Organized
• Effective
• Consistent
• Enthusiastic
• Demanding

Vuke (Chapter 18)
• Willingness to talk less, and listen more

Lopez and MacKenzie (Chapter 21)
• Facilitative
• Creative
• Understanding of different types of thinking required for different tasks

traits in mind as they choose and provide support for regular classroom teachers in their efforts toward teaching gifted students.

*What training does the regular classroom teacher need
to meet the needs of gifted students?*

Almost all authors address the need for inservice education by everyone involved in providing for gifted students. This perception seems to come from a recognition that a teacher very seldom possesses all the skills necessary for providing for a spe-

---

Table VI.2 Some Teacher Skills that Need to Be Present or Developed to Teach Gifted Students Effectively in the Regular Classroom

---

Vuke (Chapter 18)
• Behavior management (a variety of techniques)
• Time management
• Strategies for teaching children time and behavior management
• Varied strategies for student assessment in many areas

Lopez and MacKenzie (Chapter 21)
• Strategies for helping children understand the thinking required in different tasks
• Observation
• Keeping of anecdotal records
• Strategies for helping students reflect on and evaluate their own performance

---

cial group of students. When designing inservice education, teachers need both a general orientation to giftedness and specific training in skills and strategies needed to implement a particular type of program. For instance, Moller (Chapter 4), Hooker (Chapter 5), Rice (Chapter 7), Szabos (Chapter 8), and Conroy (Chapter 17) all recommend inservice for teachers to enable them to understand and recognize characteristics of giftedness. Chalfant and Van Dusen Pysh (Chapter 3) recommend inservice in problem-solving strategies, skills integral to the implementation of teacher assistance teams (TATs); Szabos (Chapter 8) advocates training in how to observe, a skill important in the demonstration teaching model she describes; Vuke (Chapter 18) notes that teachers need to be taught varied methods for assessing independent learning skills; and Conroy (Chapter 17) recommends that both teachers and administrators participate in inservice on general classroom management and specific management skills related to teaching gifted students.

Both Moller (Chapter 4) and Szabos (Chapter 8) advocate inservice education based on teacher-identified and administrator-identified needs. Many administrators have a tendency to plan inservice for a year based entirely on their perceptions of the needs of their faculty, and to neglect or ignore faculty input. Teachers, on the other hand, may not realize the importance of certain needs identified by administrators because the teachers often are limited to the experience of their classroom and the classrooms nearby.

Orzechowski-Harland (Chapter 12) recommends inservice to enable teachers to understand their own thinking styles and preferences because she believes teacher style and preference have a tremendous and quite subtle influence on curriculum development. Teachers must become aware that they have a tendency to neglect the teaching of processes they do not value personally and to avoid or teach poorly those processes they perceive as personal weaknesses. Certainly, teachers will continue to teach best the processes they value and are good at performing. However, inservice can be designed to minimize the negative impact of preferences and styles on instruction. Orzechowski-Harland also recommends inservice education designed to increase teacher skills in self-assessment and to increase knowledge and understanding related to a variety of program and teaching–learning models.

Anyone who has participated in ineffective inservice knows how frustrating poor workshops can be. Several authors have addressed the "how" as well as the "what" of inservice education. Rice (Chapter 7), Szabos (Chapter 8), Conroy (Chapter 17), and Vuke (Chapter 18) emphasize the importance of observing master teachers, and Chalfant and Van Dusen Pysh (Chapter 3) add the general strategy of having inservice education done by other classroom teachers. Inservice education needs to consist of relevant, hands-on experience, according to Chalfant and Van Dusen Pysh. Their TAT model, as well as the demonstration teaching model advocated by Rice and Szabos, provide this relevant experience. Rice and Szabos, however, remind educators that modeling and observation are not substitutes for direct teaching, and that direct teaching is needed as a supplement to the demonstration teaching model.

Finally, Orzechowski-Harland (Chapter 12) cautions educators against assuming that one short (or long) inservice session on a particular topic will result in desired changes in teacher behavior. She cites Joyce, an expert on teacher change, as concluding that teachers need to practice a new strategy 30 times before it is internalized. Practice must include receiving feedback on use of the new strategy. My own experience shows that teachers not only need to practice a strategy and receive feedback from others on its use, but also must develop methods for self-observation and self-assessment. Teachers who believe in and practice continuous self-monitoring and self-assessment will never stop growing and learning. The same is true of administrators.

What support services could be made available to assist the regular classroom teacher in meeting the needs of gifted students?

The major focus of the chapters in Part II is schoolwide management and providing a network of support for regular classroom teachers. In those chapters, three models are presented and described (teacher assistance teams, advocate liaisons, demonstration teaching). A review of these models and their associated support services would be repetitions of those chapters and of the introduction to the part. To avoid such repetition, I focus the present review on techniques and needs identified by authors in other parts of the volume, and simply recommend that readers add to their reading of this section a brief review of at least the introduction to Part II.

In addition to the many support services described in Part II (see especially Chapters 3, 4, 5, 7, and 8) and inservice education needs outlined in the answer to the previous question, three major needs are identified by authors in this volume:

1. *Teachers need support for their efforts to provide learning beyond the classroom.*

If the models described in Part V (internships, mentorships, independent study) are to be implemented, teachers cannot do it alone. Administrators need to facilitate, and to remove obstacles and barriers rather than placing them in the way. Students need to be given permission to meet with mentors during the school day, and to miss classes to do so. They need to be allowed to go off campus or remain at the school, depending on the experiences planned and/or the mentor's availability. Legal issues must be resolved, transportation arranged, and out-of-school contacts made. Teachers who have no free time, or very little free time, during the working day, and no telephone available for making and receiving telephone calls, cannot be expected to make arrangements for out-of-school learning experiences. One way to provide such support is to make available the services of a resource person who can organize and supervise out-of-school experiences for students from several classrooms. Another way to provide support is to arrange planning periods and access to telephones in or near classrooms.

2. *Teachers need released time and substitute teachers.*

This support would allow them to observe other teachers, provide peer counseling or tutoring, and attend inservice education sessions both on and off campus. Teachers also need released time on a regular basis for planning with special resource teachers. Teachers who have no free time during the school day cannot be expected to make observations or to discuss ways to coordinate a variety of services and curricula designed to meet the needs of a gifted student. Flexible scheduling and use of volunteers can be helpful in solving this problem on a daily or weekly basis, and requesting funds for substitute teachers can be an important long-term solution to the problem. A number of schools with which I am familiar have developed creative schedules and use of volunteers to free small and large groups of teachers from their teaching responsibilities while providing exciting, challenging learning opportunities for children. For instance, creative drama, movement, and music can be done in large, mixed-age or same-age groups if one experienced teacher or community member is paired with several volunteers. Such experiences can be provided in a gym, cafeteria, or recreation room, and teachers can meet to develop or coordinate their programs.

3. *Administrators can provide for or allow experienced observers to spend time in classrooms to assist teachers.*

Chalfant and Van Dusen Pysh (Chapter 3) discuss the need for teachers, as members of a TAT, to observe the student(s) being discussed. Szabos (Chapter 8) also recommends that other experienced observers be invited into the classroom to assist teachers in recognizing and meeting the needs of gifted students. Based on my personal experience, this suggestion is a valuable one that is often not recognized. Someone knowledgeable about and experienced in recognizing traits of gifted students can be very helpful in identifying student strengths. Sometimes teachers are so involved in management of behavior problems, in planning and implementation of teaching activities, and in attending to problems, that they miss subtle cues or subtle behaviors. Highly verbal children may be noticed and recognized as gifted, for instance, whereas quiet children or children whose abilities are in the spatial or intrapersonal areas may go unrecognized. Often, children who are perceived as behavior problems or unmotivated are viewed from a negative perspective; teachers, who are only human, may miss or overlook the talents or strengths of these children. An observer without previous long-term contact with a child can view him or her from a fresh perspective and provide information helpful to the teacher. Administrators can establish a nonthreatening atmosphere to facilitate cooperative efforts between observers and classroom teachers.

Finally, I recommend that all administrators concerned about providing support for classroom teachers in their efforts to serve gifted students remember (on an hourly and daily basis!) that teachers need a facilitator—more than they need an "obstacle generator." Certainly, legal issues and responsibilities must be kept in mind, but the purpose of most laws and regulations is to protect students and teachers, not to restrict them unnecessarily. Effective administrators are managers, and they also are guides and facilitators. In these roles, their relationship to teachers needs to be similar to the relationship expected between teachers and gifted students. I offer again for your consideration a list of synonyms for the three roles I see as important in this context: manager, guide, facilitator (verbs are used for the last two) (Rodale, 1978).

Manager	*Guide*	*Facilitate*
helmsman	steer toward	ease
pilot	direct	smooth
leader	show the way	simplify
organizer	accompany	uncomplicate
adviser	attend	alleviate
proctor	map out the route	assist
foreman	escort	aid
skipper	drive	befriend
straw boss	navigate	promote
steward	head toward	encourage
(p. 702)	(p. 390)	(p. 477)

How can the necessary elements of a defensible program be addressed by and incorporated into a regular classroom delivery system?

To answer this last question, I would like to return to eight key concepts that were derived from the writing of authors of the first volume of this series: *Defensible Programs for Gifted Students* (Maker, 1986a). Those eight key concepts are important indicators of quality, and are needed elements in a defensible program for the gifted. The same key concepts also emerged from an examination of the writings of authors in Volume II of this series: *Defensible Programs for Cultural and Ethnic Minorities* (Maker & Schiever, 1989).

Each of the concepts is listed below, and a definition is provided. Following that definition is an explanation of how that key concept applies to the education of gifted students in the regular classroom setting.

Appropriate

The services provided to gifted students must be appropriate—to their ages, intellectual abilities, types of giftedness, learning styles, levels of independence or self-directedness, motivation, and prior experiences. Learning experiences appropriate at one time and in one setting may not be appropriate at another time or in another setting. The content taught, the thinking processes emphasized, the products expected, and the environment (both physical and psychological) provided must be appropriate for the students individually and as members of a larger community. Student and teacher assessment must be appropriate for the goals and growth being evaluated and the setting in which that evaluation occurs.

Articulated

Articulated services are those in which students' needs are considered at some point in time as well as in the context of their long-term development. Students need a program in which their learning experiences in the regular classroom are coordinated with their learning experiences in all programs in which they are involved, including those outside the school setting. Gifted students also need to participate in experiences that are designed to build upon each other from year to year. If no schoolwide or districtwide comprehensive plan for curriculum or service delivery for gifted students exists, or if the existing plan is not followed by all teachers, needed long-term, developmental articulation is missing. Individual teachers have a responsibility to provide experiences outlined for their grade level or type of classroom, whereas administrators must assume the responsibility for monitoring such experiences across programs and classrooms as well as from one school year to the next.

Clear

Clarity is important at all levels and in all aspects of a program designed to serve gifted students. Policies regarding identification, goals of instruction, teaching strategies, out-of-school experiences, teacher roles, student assessment, parent involvement, and relationships among program elements should be defined clearly and carefully. At the building level, administrators must communicate these policies clearly to teachers, students, parents, counselors, and community members. Within classrooms, expectations for student behavior must be stated clearly and communicated to students. This clarity must be present when communicating with students as a group or individually. Individual goals for mentorships, internships, and independent study need to be communicated clearly, regardless of whether developed by students, teachers, parents, mentors, or a committee consisting of several of these individuals.

Consistent

Programs for gifted students must be based on and consistent with an underlying philosophy of learning and education, and all components of the program must be consistent with each other. The teaching methods of various teachers, although different due to different strengths and interests, need to be consistent with the goals of the program, and with the individualized goals for particular students. The goal of self-directedness, for instance, cannot be achieved if students never are allowed to establish their own goals for learning, to choose their own learning experiences, and to evaluate their own performance or growth toward established goals. Management policies must be applied consistently across grade levels and across teachers, and, in the same vein, teachers' behavior management techniques must be applied consistently across students and across situations. Expectations and consequences of behavior are especially important areas in which classroom teachers need to be consistent.

Comprehensive

A comprehensive program for gifted students includes provisions for development of strengths within the regular classroom settings, as well as special provisions for services outside the regular classroom setting. Very seldom can all the needs of gifted students be met within the regular classroom setting. One important area is the need for interaction with intellectual peers. Gifted students need to interact with and be challenged by others who have similar levels and types of giftedness. This need presents a problem if the major or only delivery system is based in the regular classroom. An even greater problem exists when a student's abilities are unusually advanced for his or her age (i.e., the student is highly gifted) or if the student's abilities are in unusual areas or areas not ordinarily included in the school curriculum. Mentorships and independent studies, however, can be employed to supplement the program for highly gifted students, and a variety of acceleration and special grouping arrangements are useful for meeting students' needs for interaction and challenge. Comprehensive services also include provisions for meeting the affective and emotional needs of gifted students, as well as their cognitive and academic needs.

Responsive

A program that is responsive is designed to fit a particular community, as well as to fit individuals within that community who come from varying backgrounds and have differing needs. A responsive program also includes provisions for continuous adaptation as new needs arise. Teachers in a regular classroom setting need to be responsive to a wide range of interests, needs, abilities, styles, and types of giftedness of students in their classrooms. A responsive teacher includes students in setting goals for themselves, creating and choosing learning experiences, developing criteria for assessment of their processes and products, and evaluating the effectiveness of the climate for learning. Parents and students need to be allowed and encouraged to locate mentors and to participate in decisions regarding all phases of these learning experiences. Programs and students must be evaluated on an ongoing basis, and these evaluation results must be used to make changes in programs and teaching strategies. Administrators must be responsive to the inservice and support needs of teachers, and teachers must respond to the needs of administrators as well as the needs of other teachers (especially those who are providing services to the gifted students in their classrooms).

Unique

The uniqueness of each child must be the major consideration in programs designed to meet the needs of gifted students. Each child has a particular combination of strengths, weaknesses, talents, interests, learning styles and preferences, and experiences. Each child needs a program that is unique and fitted to his or her goals. Often, consistency implies sameness. This should not be true. An educator who consistently meets needs of unique individuals will not treat each child the same. Parents, school boards, and funding agencies need to be told how a child's educational program is tailored to his or her needs, and provisions need to be indentifiably different. This statement does not mean that every student is doing something different from other students at all times during the day, but that the *combination* of things each child will do over the course of days, weeks, or a year will be unique and dependent on that child's individual traits.

Valid

The educational program must be valid. The use of instructional strategies, models, and techniques that have been tested and evaluated is one way to achieve validity. Another is to continually test and collect evaluative data on the procedures used in the program. I have noticed, however, a disturbing tendency of educators in public school settings to try new or different procedures for one year, and if the evaluations do not show what they expected, to return to an old program or begin a new one. To establish validity or to evaluate the success of new methods, one must use them long enough to assess their long-term results, and must judge relative effectiveness by making comparisons to previous or other current programs. In addition, changes need to be made *after* evaluation results are compiled, not before!

Appendix VI.A

Evaluation References

Archambault, F. X. (1984). Measurement and evaluation concerns in evaluating programs for the gifted. *Journal for the Education of the Gifted, 7,* 12–25.

Baron, J. B. (1987). Evaluating thinking skills in the classroom. In R. J. Sternberg & J. B. Baron (Eds.), *Teaching thinking skills: Theory and practice* (pp. 221–247). New York: Friedman.

Buchanan, N. K., & Feldhusen, J. F. (Eds.). (1991). *Conducting research and evaluation in gifted education: A handbook of methods and applications.* New York: Teachers College Press.

Callahan, C. M. (1983). Issues in evaluating programs for the gifted. *Gifted Child Quarterly, 27,* 33–37.

Callahan, C. M., & Caldwell, M. S. (1986). Defensible evaluations of programs for the gifted and talented. In C. J. Maker (Ed.), *Critical issues in gifted education: Vol. I. Defensible programs for the gifted* (pp. 277–296). Austin, TX: PRO-ED.

Carter, K. R. (1986). A cognitive outcomes study to evaluate curriculum for the gifted. *Journal for the Education of the Gifted, 10,* 41–55.

Dinham, S. M., & Udall, A. J. (1986). Evaluation for gifted education: Synthesis and discussion. In C. J. Maker (Ed.), *Critical issues in gifted education: Vol. I. Defensible programs for the gifted* (pp. 297–316). Austin, TX: PRO-ED.

Nasca, D. (1983). *Evaluating gifted programs: Formative evaluation.* East Aurora, NY: DOK Publishers.

Peters, T. (1987). *Thriving on chaos: Handbook for a management revolution.* New York: Knopf.

Renzulli, J. S. (1975). *A guidebook for evaluating programs for the gifted and talented.* Ventura, CA: National/State Leadership Training Institute.

Seeley, K. R. (1986). Evaluation for defensible programs for the gifted. In C. J. Maker (Ed.), *Critical issues in gifted education: Vol. I. Defensible programs for the gifted* (pp. 265–276). Austin, TX: PRO-ED.

Van Tassel, J. (1980). Evaluation of gifted programs. In J. B. Jordan & J. A. Grossi (Eds.), *An administrator's handbook on designing programs for the gifted and talented* (pp. 110–128). Reston, VA: ERIC Clearinghouse on Handicapped and Gifted Children.

REFERENCES

Gardner, H. (1983). *Frames of mind: The theory of multiple intelligences.* New York: Basic Books.

Maker, C. J. (1982). *Curriculum development for the gifted.* Austin, TX: PRO-ED.

Maker, C. J. (1986a). *Critical issues in gifted education: Vol. I. Defensible programs for the gifted.* Austin, TX: PRO-ED.

Maker, C. J. (1986b). Curricula for gifted preschool students. *Topics in Early Childhood Education, 6*(1), 62–73.

Maker, C. J., & Schiever, S. W. (1989). *Critical issues in gifted education: Vol. II. Defensible programs for cultural and ethnic minorities.* Austin, TX: PRO-ED.

Rodale, J. I. (Ed.). (1978). *The synonym finder.* Emmaus, PA: Rodale Press.

Taylor, C. (1986). Knowledge and brainpower talents: Two radically different types of human resources. *Illinois Council for the Gifted Journal, 5*(2), 6–11.

INDEX

THE EDITOR
AND CONTRIBUTORS

C. June Maker, Ph.D.

Dr. Maker is associate professor of special education at The University of Arizona in Tucson. She coordinates graduate degree concentrations in education of the gifted at the master's, specialist, and doctoral levels. She has been active in both the National Association for Gifted Children (NAGC) and The Association for the Gifted (TAG), serving on the board of directors of NAGC for 19 years, and as officer and chair of various committees for both organizations.

Her publications are related to the topic areas of gifted handicapped, teacher training, development of talents in exceptional children, teaching learning disabled students, curriculum development for the gifted, and teaching models in education of the gifted. She serves on editorial boards for journals in education of the gifted and special education, and is series editor for *Critical Issues in Gifted Education.*

In the past, she has been a teacher, a regional supervisor for a state department of education, an administrative intern in the federal office for the gifted, and an assistant professor at the University of New Mexico. She has consulted with numerous local school districts, state departments of education, and other public and private agencies, both in the United States and in other countries. Her educational background consists of degrees in education of the gifted and related areas from the University of Virginia (Ph.D.), Southern Illinois University (M.S.), and Western Kentucky University (B.S.).

Jody Batten, M.Ed.

For the past 21 years, Ms. Batten has been the administrator of the program for the gifted in the Lincoln Public Schools, Lincoln, Nebraska. She had her first experience teaching gifted students in the Palo Alto Unified School District, Palo Alto, California.

Jeannette A. Bodnar, M.A.

Ms. Bodnar has had over 21 years experience teaching high school regular and special education classes, counseling, and coordinating programs for the gifted, and has taught several university level classes. She has served as the chair of the New Mexico Legislative Ad Hoc Subcommittee on Gifted Education. Also, she has served as a consultant to several districts on curriculum for the gifted, counseling under-achieving gifted students, and promoting family involvement. She recently received the Pi Lambda Theta Innovative Teacher award in recognition of her designing the major components of the high school gifted program and for her extensive work in the community developing mentorships and internships for gifted students.

Frances D. Burns, Ph.D.

Dr. Burns currently is an instructor/lecturer at the Center for Professional Teacher Education at the University of Texas at Arlington. In addition to her work at the University, Dr. Burns coordinates programs for gifted students in Allen, Texas, and is the Assistant Principal for Instruction at Rountree Elementary School. She also is a book and curriculum reviewer for *Gifted Child Today.*

James C. Chalfant, Ed.D.

Dr. Chalfant is a professor in the Division of Special Education and Rehabilita-tion at The University of Arizona. He was trained and has published in every area of exceptionality, but is noted primarily for his work in learning disabilities and school-based teams. Dr. Chalfant has served as chair and principal writer of three federal task force reports: Educating Students with Learning Problems: A Shared Responsibility (1985); Identifying Learning Disabled Students: Guidelines for Decision Making (1984); and Central Processing Dysfunctions in Children (1969). Dr. Chalfant is an internationally recognized speaker, serves as consultant to school agencies and state departments of education, and has implemented teacher assistance teams in over 40 states and six provinces in Canada.

Janet Conroy, M.A., M.Ed.

Ms. Conroy currently is employed as a counselor in a large high school in Mesa, Arizona, and teaches evening graduate classes in education for Northern Arizona University. She holds an M.A. in English, an M.Ed. in counseling, and Arizona endorsements in gifted education, counseling, and administration. Her varied back-ground includes teaching, counseling, and career guidance. She has worked as a resource specialist of the gifted using the consultative model in elementary, middle, and high school settings. From 1986 to 1989, Ms. Conroy held the position of specialist in education of the gifted with the Arizona Department of Education in Phoenix, where she worked to improve legislation, funding, and services for gifted students statewide.

Hazel J. Feldhusen, M.S.

Ms. Feldhusen taught second grade at Cumberland School, West Lafayette, Indiana. She has published a number of articles and a book, *Individualized Teach-*

ing of Gifted Children in Regular Classrooms (DOK Publishers). She has done workshops and presentations on teaching the gifted in the regular classroom throughout the United States and in a number of other countries.

Helen D. Follis, M.S.

Ms. Follis has taught in programs for gifted students and in regular classrooms in Grades 2 through 9. She first used learning centers in a classroom dominated by bright students in the mid-1970s. She continues to use centers in her current teaching position as a teacher of heterogeneously grouped fifth-grade students. Ms. Follis is also an adjunct faculty member of NOVA University, where she teaches a class on creativity in the elementary schools for teachers pursuing graduate degrees.

Reva C. (Jenkins) Friedman, Ph.D.

Dr. Friedman is a former classroom teacher and teacher in a program for the gifted, and is currently an associate professor in the Educational Psychology and Research Department at the University of Kansas. She is responsible for degree and graduate certificate programs in gifted child education. She serves on the board of the National Association for Gifted Children, and has served on the board of The Association for the Gifted. Her recent activities include director of the American Psychological Foundation's Esther Katz Rosen Symposium on the Psychological Development of Gifted Children, and work on three projects funded by the Jacob K. Javits Gifted and Talented Children's Education Act. She has made over 85 presentations at international, national, regional, state, and local meetings of professional associations, including invited, refereed papers, and keynote addresses. Dr. Friedman's current research interests center on family systems and psychological dimensions of giftedness. Her two most recent publications are the chapter "Families of Gifted Children and Youth" in M. J. Fine and C. I. Carlsen's *A Handbook of Family, School Problems and Interventions: A Systems Perspective,* and the chapter "The Family with a Gifted Child" (with Tom Gallagher) in M. J. Fine's *Collaborative Involvement with Parents of Gifted Children.*

James J. Gallagher, Ph.D.

Dr. Gallagher is a Kenan Professor of Education and Director of the Carolina Policy Studies Program at the Frank Porter Graham Child Development Center at the University of North Carolina at Chapel Hill. He has been active in special education for over a quarter of a century. In addition to over 100 published articles, chapters and reviews, Dr. Gallagher is author of *Teaching the Gifted Child* and coauthor or editor of seven books. Dr. Gallagher is an active lecturer and presenter. In addition to lecturing in the United States, he has lectured in Russia, Finland, Sweden, Australia, Taiwan, and other countries. He also serves on numerous advisory boards. He currently is First Vice President of the National Association for Gifted Children. He also is editor for the *Journal for the Education of the Gifted.*

Tom J. Gallagher, Ph.D.

Dr. Gallagher is a writer, consultant, lecturer, and educational psychologist who specializes in the cognitive and affective behaviors and learning styles of gifted children. He has been a teacher of English, journalism, and education of the gifted for over 20 years in middle schools, high schools, and universities throughout the United States. For the past 2 years, Dr. Gallagher has resided in Asuncion, Paraguay, where he is a lecturer at the National University of Paraguay. In addition, he does private lecturing and educational consulting throughout the southern cone of South America. His most recent publication is ''Families of Gifted Children and Youth'' (with Reva C. Friedman) in M. J. Fine and C. I. Carlsen's *A handbook of Family, School Problems and Interventions: A Systems Perspective.*

Gloria Grotjan, Ph.D.

Dr. Grotjan is a professor of education at Lincoln University in Jefferson City, Missouri. She was a classroom teacher prior to spending the past 20 years as a teacher educator. She has developed courses in education of the gifted at Lincoln University and has directed a summer enrichment program on that campus since 1983. Learning Unlimited, the summer program, was cited as one of the major reasons for her selection as 1990 Missouri Gifted Educator.

Patricia A. Haensly, Ph.D.

Dr. Haensly is an assistant professor in the educational psychology department at Texas A&M University, where she also is associate director of programs for the Institute for the Gifted & Talented, and director of a summer program for gifted preschoolers and teacher training. As an educational consultant, she has presented inservices and workshops on education of the gifted to teachers and parents throughout Texas, and presented at numerous state, national, and world conferences. Dr. Haensly has been involved in mentoring through coordination of high school programs for the gifted, publishing articles in *Gifted Child Quarterly* and other sources, and serving as a charter member and currently senior reviewer of the editorial board of *Mentoring International.*

Sharon K. Hooker, Ph.D.

Dr. Hooker currently is working as a coordinator and teacher for the Gifted and Talented Program in Sunnyside Unified School District in Tucson, Arizona. Her doctorate is in special education from The University of Arizona.

Margie K. Kitano, Ph.D.

Dr. Kitano serves as Associate Dean for Faculty Development and Research in the College of Education at San Diego State University. She also directs the college's Multicultural Infusion Initiative, which has as its purpose to integrate multicultural content and strategies into the college curricula. She has directed a preschool for gifted children and publishes extensively on academic and affective needs of gifted children in regular and special classrooms. Current projects focus on the socio-emotional needs of gifted individuals and life-span development of culturally diverse gifted women.

Sandy Lethem, M.A.

Ms. Lethem has been a teacher of the gifted for more than two decades, with the majority of that time spent with upper elementary gifted students in a self-contained classroom. Curriculum development for the gifted has been her major focus for many years, particularly in the areas of futures studies, composition, and mathematics. Ms. Lethem is a member of the Futures Division, Creativity Division, and Global Awareness Division of the National Association for Gifted Children and the TAG Division of the Council for Exceptional Children. Currently, she teaches a self-contained class for the highly gifted at Zuni Magnet School for Computers and Communication in Albuquerque, New Mexico.

Roseanne Lopez, M.Ed.

Ms. Lopez is a teacher of the gifted in Amphitheater Public Schools in Tucson, Arizona. For the past 2 years, she has served as a peer evaluator for the district's career ladder program. She is a member of the board of directors for the Arizona Association for Gifted and Talented, and has served as an officer in various state and local organizations. Ms. Lopez has used the learning center approach for 7 years, combined with large group investigations in a resource room for gifted students in Grades 4 through 6.

Joy MacKenzie, M.A.

Ms. MacKenzie develops curriculum for teachers. During 1990, she and Imojene Forte co-authored six books for Incentive Publications. The topics of these books included cooperative learning activities, composition and creative writing, and ideas for teachers in the middle grades. She also has worked recently as a consultant to teachers of gifted students through the State Department of Education in Tennessee.

Thomas R. McDaniel, Ph.D.

Dr. McDaniel is a professor of education, Vice President for Academic Affairs, and Dean of the College of Arts and Sciences at Converse College in Spartanburg, South Carolina. Among his over 100 publications are five books and 15 textbook chapters.

Barbara W. Moller, Ed.D.

Dr. Moller currently is a supervisor in the Gifted and Allied Programs for Dade County Public Schools in Miami, Florida. She previously was a teacher, curriculum writer, and assistant principal. Dr. Moller has published articles in such subjects as teaching enrichment activities for minorities, programs for the gifted, developing leadership in gifted students, and teaching gifted learning disabled students.

William R. Nash, Ed.D.

Dr. Nash is a professor of educational psychology and director of the Institute for the Gifted & Talented at Texas A&M University. He is a past president of the National Association for Gifted Children and served as Chair of the Charter Board of Directors of the American Creativity Association. His previous work on mentoring includes a federally funded project to develop a mentorship/internship model program for gifted high school students.

Diane Orzechowski-Harland, B.A.

Ms. Harland is the president of Friends of the Gifted, Inc. (a not-for-profit corporation DBA SATORI Schools), the goals of which are to meet the needs of young gifted children and their families. She teaches education courses for Pima Community College, and provides direct service to primary grade–level teachers and students at Amphitheater Public Schools in Tucson, Arizona. An adjunct faculty member of Lincoln University in Jefferson City, Missouri, Ms. Harland teaches a variety of courses for students majoring in early childhood education and special education. She also is the staff development specialist for Learning Unlimited, a summer enrichment program sponsored by the university.

Sally M. Reis, Ph.D.

Dr. Reis is an assistant professor of educational psychology at The University of Connecticut, where she also serves as a principal investigator of the National Research Center on the Gifted and Talented. She was a teacher for 15 years, 11 of which were spent as a resource specialist/coordinator of a program for the gifted and talented. She is a board member of the National Association for Gifted Students and is the chair of the Research and Evaluation Review Panel for *Gifted Child Quarterly*. She has published widely and most frequently is known for her work on *The Schoolwide Enrichment Triad Model* and on gifted females.

Marilyn A. Rice, Ph.D.

Dr. Rice was coordinator of a program for the gifted in a magnet school before piloting one of the first programs for the gifted in Texas in the late 1970s. She now works as a resource teacher for students in Grades 4 through 6 in Richardson, Texas. Although developed independently, the "High-Tech Thinking Model" which is used by her program, is an application of a consensus model similar to one advocated in Art Costa. Currently, she is working as an educational consultant on a video series to teach children the principles of magic in a way that enhances learning and thinking skills. She also is serving as an educational consultant in the development of an 8-hour video program on a laser disk designed to educate children on the Superconducting Super Collider that is being built by the federal government in Waxahatchie, Texas.

Jan Rogers, M.A., M.Ed.

Ms. Rogers is the social studies consultant for the Lincoln Public Schools. She is the former project director of two Title IV-C programs involving gifted students in rural settings and served as president of the Nebraska Association for Gifted. Ms. Rogers currently is a doctoral student in administration, curriculum and instruction at the University of Nebraska–Lincoln.

Hilda Rosselli, Ph.D.

Dr. Rosselli began developing curriculum and training teachers while teaching in a middle school program for the gifted. She currently coordinates the graduate program in education of the gifted at the University of South Florida. She also serves as co-chair of the Futures Studies Division of the National Association for Gifted Children and is on the board of many state and local groups related to education of the gifted. She is coauthor of *Leadership: Making Things Happen* with Dorothy Sisk, and has a new book in press, *Gifted Education and The Middle School Movement*.

Gina D. Schack, Ph.D.

Dr. Schack is in the Department of Early and Middle Childhood Education at the University of Louisville, where she works in the areas of education of the gifted and teacher education. Her current interests include increasing the sophistication of student's work through the teaching of original research, as well as her ongoing search for "how-to" books that teach the methodologies of practicing professionals.

Shirley W. Schiever, Ph.D.

Currently, Dr. Schiever is a curriculum specialist at a fine arts magnet middle school in the Tucson Unified School District (TUSD). She is a member of the TUSD Staff Development Teacher Cadre, and involved in several curriculum and staff development projects. Her primary interests include developing students' critical thinking skills, meeting the needs of ethnically different students, and developing multicultural, interdisciplinary curriculum. She has been a regular classroom teacher at many levels, a teacher of the gifted, and a coordinator of a program for gifted students. Additionally, she authored a book on teaching thinking within a comprehensive curriculum.

V. June Scobee Rodgers, Ph.D.

Dr. Scobee Rodgers has been an active and prominent leader in education throughout her professional life. Currently, she is serving as a member of the President's National Advisory Council on Education Research and Improvement, a national advisory team. She was nominated to the position in late 1990 by President Bush, and confirmed by the U.S. Senate shortly thereafter. Prior to her service with the council, Dr. Scobee Rodgers gained international recognition as board director and founding chair of the Challenger Center for Space Science Education, positions she still holds. Challenger Learning Centers are located nationwide and in Canada at science museums, science centers, and school districts. As an educator, consultant, and author, Dr. Scobee Rodgers developed special programs for both gifted and disadvantaged children, and taught all grade levels from kindergarten to graduate school. She has provided workshops on mentoring and written articles on the topic of parents as mentors.

JoAnn B. Seghini, Ph.D.

Dr. Seghini is currently the director of curriculum and staff development in Jordan School District in Sandy, Utah. She has been involved in education of the gifted since the early 1970s when she worked with the development teams to develop curriculum and to train teachers to use Calvin W. Taylor's multiple-talent training model. She has written several curriculum packets and books that help parents and teachers to develop the higher level thinking skills of students as a critical part of differentiated curricular planning. Dr. Seghini works as adjunct faculty at the University of Utah and at Brigham Young University in support of training programs for teachers of the gifted.

Roger Shanley, M.Ed.

Mr. Shanley is a teacher of gifted and talented students at Rincon High School in Tucson, Arizona. During his 13 years of teaching gifted and talented students, Mr. Shanley has completed sabbatical research to determine the effects of strategies for gifted students on the composition process of student writing. He currently is working on a project to align advanced placement requirements with strategies used in the education of the gifted. Also, he is coauthoring a book with Shirley Schiever titled *Life Organizational Guide*, a text emphasizing organizational, study, and thinking skills for all students as well as coauthoring a chapter in a book about writing across the curriculum, edited by Anne Ruggles-Gere.

Dorothy A. Sisk, Ed.D.

Dr. Sisk, world renowned for her leadership in education of the gifted over the past 20 years, currently is holding the C. W. and Dorothy Ann Conn Chair in gifted education at Lamar University, Beaumont, Texas. Dr. Sisk also coordinates teacher training in education of the gifted and directs the Gifted Children Center and The Centre for Creativity, Innovation, and Leadership. Dr. Sisk has served as the director of the U.S. Office of the Gifted and Talented. Editor of *Gifted International* and a member of the advisory boards of *Gifted Children Monthly* and *International Journal for Gifted*, Dr. Sisk is the current executive administrator of the World Council for Gifted and Talented Children, president of the American Association for Creativity, a member of the National Association for Gifted Children executive board, and past president of The Association for the Gifted. She also has authored or coauthored numerous articles and papers, and has coauthored two recent textbooks in education.

Janice R. Szabos, M.Ed.

Ms. Szabos recently has taken the position as principal of Haycock Elementary School, which houses a full-time center program for 250 highly gifted students. She previously was the coordinator of programs for gifted and talented students in the Fairfax County Public Schools, Fairfax, Virginia. She also works as an adjunct instructor for George Mason University and the University of Virginia, and is a former regular classroom teacher and teacher of highly gifted students. She serves as a consultant in curriculum for gifted students and currently is chair of a district committee on the identification of highly gifted students.

Margaret Van Dusen Pysh, Ph.D.

Dr. Pysh has administered programs in the public schools in all areas of special education for the handicapped. She recently has joined the faculty of The University of Arizona where she is adjunct associate professor in the Department of Special Education and Rehabilitation. She was project director for federal grants, studying teacher assistance teams with mainstreamed learning disabled students and learned helplessness in visually impaired students. She currently is project manager for the special education supervision and administration program. Dr. Pysh is the author of numerous articles and multimedia programs on teacher assistance teams, parent conferencing, and IEP development. She is an internationally recognized speaker and consultant to school agencies and state departments of education on learned helplessness and has implemented teacher assistance teams in over 40 states and six provinces in Canada.

Joyce VanTassel-Baska, Ed.D.

Dr. VanTassel-Baska is The Jody and Layton Smith Professor of Education at the College of William and Mary in Virginia, where she has developed a graduate program and a research and development center in education of the gifted. Formerly, she created and directed the Center for Talent Development at Northwestern University. She also has served as the state director of programs for the gifted for Illinois, as a regional director of a service center for the gifted in the Chicago area, as coordinator of programs for the gifted for the Toledo, Ohio, public school system, and as a teacher of gifted high school students in English and Latin. She has worked as a consultant on education of the gifted in over 40 states and for key national groups, including the U.S. Department of Education, National Association of Secondary School Principals, and American Association of School Administrators. She currently serves on the editorial board for *The Journal for the Education of the Gifted* and *Gifted Child Quarterly* and is past president of The Association for the Gifted of the Council for Exceptional Children. Dr. VanTassel-Baska has published widely, including three recent books: *Comprehensive Curriculum for Gifted Learners* (with John Feldhusen et al.); *Patterns of Influence: The Home, The Self, and The School* (ed.); and *Excellence in Educating the Gifted* (with John Feldhusen and Ken Seeley). She also has published several monographs, 22 book chapters, and over 50 articles in journals. Her major research interests are on the disadvantaged gifted as a special population and effective curricular interventions with the gifted.

Mary Vuke, M.A.

Ms. Vuke comes from a background in special education. She has been teaching gifted students in rural areas since 1979. Currently, she holds the position of coordinator of programs for gifted students in Santa Cruz Valley, Arizona. Ms. Vuke's experiences with gifted children include working with them as a regular classroom teacher, in a resource room program model, and as the mother of her own gifted children.

Nilah L. Wright, M.A.

Ms. Wright has been a public school administrator since 1985. She currently is an assistant principal at Knox Junior High School in The Woodlands, Texas. She presently is completing a Ph.D. program in educational psychology at Texas A&M University with an emphasis in education of the gifted and talented.